# THE SOUND OF DETECTION:

# ELLERY QUEEN'S ADVENTURES IN RADIO

### Francis M. Nevins
### & Martin Grams, Jr.

OTR PUBLISHING
2002

# DEDICATION

For Doug Greene and Bill Nadel,
our "shadow" collaborators,
and for Maye Emily-Lee Sohboff,
born January 25, 2002,
Manny Lee's newest great-grandchild and
(dare we hope?) the youngest living Ellery Queen fan.

# TABLE OF CONTENTS

# A FEW WORDS IN REMEMBRANCE
## By Larry Dobkin

My time with Ellery came shortly after WWII. (I was one of almost a dozen different actors who played him on radio.)

Ellery Queen was the property of a pair of cousins who had created the books as well as the radio show. (Television was on the verge of taking over. We were quoting Fred Allen's line about Television, 'If you don't look at it, it'll go away.') And we were still doing a 'live repeat' some three hours later for the East Coast. The network was avoiding recording the show for reasons of their own. That is, they were avoiding 'playing' the recording. I learned that when I slept through the repeat time and phoned the station in a panic, only to be told that they 'played the recording.'

Radio was still top of the entertainment heap. The actors 'dressed' for the big audience shows. The 'guest' in the radio studio who was invited to match wits with 'Ellery Queen' a few minutes before the end of the show – 'Now you and the audience have heard everything I have heard, who do you think is the criminal?' – was given publicity as well as champagne and fruit. And we actors were haunted by autograph seekers, fans plucking at our clothes, begging for our used scripts.

Many a time, after TV came in, have we said to each other, we didn't know how good we had it, not having to memorize, to walk and talk at the same time.

We listened. Audience and players alike, how we listened. And how imagination paid us back.

If I could find a way to return to those days, would I hesitate?

The answer – in a moment.

Larry Dobkin

# PREFACE

I discovered Ellery Queen in my early teens, those formative years when the heroes a person adopts can last a lifetime. I can still see myself sitting in a creaky old rocking chair in front of my grandmother's house during the heat of the 1957 summer, lost in ecstasy as I wandered with Ellery through the labyrinths of *The Greek Coffin Mystery*. Through my high school and college years I found and devoured in haphazard order all the other Queen classics: *The Egyptian Cross Mystery, The Tragedy of X, The Tragedy of Y, Calamity Town, Cat of Many Tails*. It was many years after my introduction to the Queen novels that I learned about the Queen radio programs, which had come on the air several years before I was born and had gone off when I was five. Eventually I became interested in that aspect of the Queen saga too, and a chapter on the program – a chapter all too sketchy and inadequate – were included in my 1974 book *Royal Bloodline: Ellery Queen, Author and Detective*. But the full story of that program remained untold until 1983 when *The Sound of Detection* was first published.

A book of this sort can't be written without a great deal of help, and while I was writing the first edition, large amounts of generous assistance were given to me by Professor Richard Arnold (Department of Theatre Arts, Northern Illinois University), Jon L. Breen, Douglas and Richard Dannay, Rose (Mrs. Frederic) Dannay, David L. Godwin, Douglas G. Greene, the late William Hennessey, Arlene Osborne, the late Catherine (Mrs. Manfred B.) Lee, John J. Newton, Ester (Mrs. Sydney) Smith, the late Sydney Smith, Saundra Taylor (Curator of Manuscripts, Lilly Library, Indiana University), Katherine Thorp, Roi A. Uselton, and the late Phyllis White (Mrs. Anthony Boucher). The deepest debt of all, however, I owed to the late Ray Stanich, whose bulging research files provided most of the basic data that went into the week-by-week episode log. Since his death I have reworked the format of the log and, with help from Martin Grams, Jr., Terry Salomonson, Dave Siegel, Karl Schadow, Douglas G. Greene and William Nadel, added a great deal of newly discovered information. Amanda Osborne who worked out the index for the book. This book owes much of whatever value it may have to the contributions of these people, the living and the dead.

Francis M. Nevins
St. Louis, Missouri
February 28, 2002

**THE ELLERY OF THE AIRWAVES**
**Francis M. Nevins**

# CHAPTER ONE
## The Brooklyn Cousins Mystery

One noon during the late spring or early summer of 1928, two young cousins met for lunch at an Italian restaurant in midtown Manhattan. Over a spicy antipasto one of them – later neither could remember which – mentioned that he'd seen an announcement in the morning *Times* about a $7500 mystery novel writing contest sponsored jointly by *McClure's Magazine* and the publishing firm of Frederick A. Stokes. By the time they'd set down their last cups of coffee, the cousins had not only decided to enter the competition but had devised the nucleus of a plot. "It was a lark," Frederic Dannay recalled fifty-one years later. "We had no intention in the world of doing more than one book." Lark it may have been but they took it dead seriously, working frantically on evenings and weekends and holidays over the next several months, writing in the one cousin's office or the other's or wherever they could get together for a few hours, pushing themselves to complete the manuscript before the contest deadline of December 31, 1928. "I remember Manny Lee had to go to a wedding in Philadelphia during the time we were writing it," Fred Dannay told a *Playboy* interviewer in 1979. "And I had to go with him, to the wedding of a complete stranger, just so we wouldn't lose the time it took to get there and back on the train." At times they were tempted to scrap the project but by then, as Dannay put it during a visit to the San Diego campus of the University of California in 1977, they had "reached a point of no return where if we stopped all the work would be wasted, and it seemed that it would be reasonable to go on and finish it." They completed the manuscript on December 30, 1928, turned it in on the following day – the last day entries could be submitted – and, as Fred said at the University of California, "sat back with a sigh of relief to await the outcome." Thus Ellery Queen was born, both as the detective (and detective-story writer) within the novel and as the joint pseudonym of the authors.

The young men who called themselves Frederic Dannay and Manfred B. Lee were born nine months and five blocks apart, in Brooklyn's teeming Brownsville district. Lee, the older cousin, was born Manford Lepofsky on January 11, 1905. His parents were Benjamin and Rebecca (Wallerstein) Lepofsky. The name Manford came from a character in a magazine love story which Mrs. Lepofsky had been reading just before the delivery. Her doctor took it upon himself to register the boy's birth certificate under the name Emanuel Lepofsky. Rebecca and her sister Dora were the daughters of Russian Jewish immigrants named Leopold and Rachel Wallerstein, and Dora had married Meyer H. Nathan, a liquor salesman. On October 20, 1905, a little more than nine months after the birth of the Lepofsky child, the Nathans had a son whom they named Daniel. However, Mrs. Nathan was using the same doctor who had attended her sister, and the Kildare of the Brownsville tenements seems to have disliked the name Daniel no less than that of Manford, for he registered this child's birth certificate under the name of David Nathan. Eventually both cousins opted for names of their own choosing. Manford or Emanuel Lepofsky truncated and de-ethnicized his last name to Lee and altered his first name to Manfred, which means man of peace and was probably also intended as homage to the hero of Lord Byron's romantic poem. Daniel or David Nathan decided to take the name of Frederic Dannay, the first name in honor of the composer Chopin and the last a combination of the first syllables of Daniel and Nathan. As adults they called each other Manny and Danny.

"My family moved to the small upstate town of Elmira, New York, when I was a baby," Dannay recalled in his seventies, "and the twelve years I spent there were a great gift. Elmira was bisected by the Chemung River, and I lived a Tom Sawyer boyhood in one of Mark Twain's hometowns. My cousin stayed in Brooklyn and became street-wise, while I was sort of a country bumpkin." In a 1944 reminiscence he described vividly what that boyhood was like:

"When I was a child my family lived in a small town in western New York. I didn't realize it then, but I was given a colossal gift early in life – a Huckleberry Finn-Tom Sawyer boyhood spent, by a strange coincidence, in the very town in which Mark Twain lived shortly before I was born.

Does any man with a spark of boyhood still in his heart ever forget his home town? No–it's an unconquerable memory. Most of us never return, but none of us forgets.

I remember we had a river at our back door--the gentle Chemung. I remember how, in the cycle of years, the spring torrents came down from the hills; how they overflowed our peaceful valley – yes, over the massive concrete dikes that towered with grim Egyptian austerity above the shallow bed of the Chemung. I remember how old man river burst through our back door, flooding our kitchen and parlor, driving us – temporary refugees – to our top floor. Happy days for a wide-eyed boy, proud in his hip boots and man's sou'wester, with the prospect of daily trips by rowboat – voyages of high adventure – to the nearest grocer!

I remember the unpaved streets – the heavily rutted road that slept in the sun before our house. I have a queer memory about those ruts. Every 4th of July we boys would plant our firecrackers deep in the soft earth of those ruts. Then we'd touch our smoking punks to the row of seedling fuses, run for cover, and watch the "thunderbolts" (that's what they were called in those days) explode with a muffled roar and send heavenward – at least three feet! – a shower of dirt and stones. It wasn't so long after the Spanish-American War that we couldn't pretend we were blowing up the *Maine* – in some strangely perverted terrestrial fashion only small boys can invent.

I remember the long walks to and from public school – three miles each way, in summer mud and winter drifts; the cherry trees and apple trees and chicken coops and dogs – the long succession of dogs ending with that fine hunter that was killed by a queer-looking machine called an 'automobile.' I remember the all-day trips to the brown October hills, gathering nuts; the wood fires and the popping corn; the swimming hole that no one knew about but ourselves; the boyhood secret society and its meeting place in the shed behind my best friend's house."

His best friend in Elmira was named Ellery.

Such was the childhood of Daniel Nathan, who roamed the woods and fields, took part in elaborate business adventures with his playmates (like exhibiting the ghost of Long John Silver for a two-cent admission fee), and, as the son of the town liquor dealer, enjoyed the prestige of being the only boy in the community who was allowed into saloons.

Meanwhile the Lepofskys remained in Brooklyn, raising their son in what he later called "a typical *Sidewalks of New York* atmosphere." But the allusion to the old ballad is misleading. The Brownsville section of Brooklyn was a rough environment, and early in life the boy performed an inner emigration. "I knew I was going to be a writer from the time I was eight years old," he said in 1969. "I think boys of American Jewish background can't take the brutality of the streets and turn for refuge to books." During the summer he went upstate to Elmira to visit his cousin – usually for a week, but in 1914 for the entire vacation – and the boys would spend their time competing against each other in games of one-upmanship which they would continue playing, in altered forms, during their more than forty years of collaboration as writers.

In 1917 the Nathan family moved back to Brooklyn and into the house of Danny's maternal grandparents, the Wallersteins, which was in a neighborhood several steps up from Brownsville. That winter, while 12-year-old Danny was in bed suffering from an abscess of the left ear that periodically afflicted him, one of his aunts walked into his cubbyhole sickroom and handed him a book which she'd borrowed from the neighborhood public library. It was Conan Doyle's *Adventures of Sherlock Holmes*, and it changed his life. Young Danny had been a voracious reader – of Dumas' *The Three Musketeers* and the books of Horatio Alger, Jules Verne, and James Fenimore Cooper, of Viking legends and the adventures of Tom Swift and the Rover Boys, Frank Merriwell and Baseball Joe, Tarzan and Peck's Bad Boy, of the multi-colored Andrew Lang fairy tale collections and the Oz stories of L. Frank Baum – but until that winter day his only exposure to crime fiction had been in the form of silent cliffhanger serials like *The Exploits of Elaine* (1915). Reading those fabulous adventures of Sherlock Holmes, which he devoured in one gulp, so fired the boy's imagination that the next morning he slipped out of the house and down to the library, where he wangled a card and stripped the shelves of all the Holmes books he could lay his little hands on. A year or so later, while exploring the bookcases in the house of one of his uncles, he stumbled upon *Mastertales of Mystery*, a three-volume anthology of short stories bound in rich blue cloth, which introduced him to Anna Katharine Green and Baroness Orczy's tales of the Old Man in the Corner and Arthur B. Reeve's scientific detective Craig Kennedy and Jacques Futrelle's Thinking Machine. The Elmira bumpkin quickly became an unquenchable fan of the genre that was to shape his life.

With the return of the Nathans to Brooklyn there developed a powerful friendship between Danny and Manny. "We were cousins," Fred Dannay said more than sixty years later, "but we were closer than brothers." Besides mutual interests in such typical teen-age concerns as baseball, the boys also shared a passion for detective fiction. Both of them attended Boys' High, and as early as 1920, Dannay remembered, while "walking together to and from high school, and while sitting together on streetcars in bad weather," he and his cousin began "to experiment with ideas, to play with the strings of plot." They planned to write a tale of murder in the public library but changed their minds. "A public library was dear to our hearts, it was our treasure-house, our fountain of life. It was too sacred a place to be defiled by crime, and murder in a public library was unthinkable." They changed the crime scene to a museum and imagined a locked-room situation, "a room in the museum, with all doors and windows locked on the inside, and a body found dead behind a desk." The solution? The murderer had hidden inside a suit of armor all day, stepped out of the armor that night, killed the victim, stepped back into the armor, slipped through a convenient hole in the floor to the room below, and somehow or other escaped from the museum. "I can recall, almost as if it were last week," Dannay wrote in 1979, "the two of us strolling home, discussing heatedly, sparking ideas, laughing at the patently ridiculous suggestions, and finally coming up with" their masterstrokes.

Manny Lee graduated from Boys' High and went on to New York University, working as a Western Union messenger for pocket money, eventually leading a five-piece jazz band, but still convinced as he had been since high school that he "was going to be the Shakespeare of the twentieth century." Fred Dannay had his own after-school job – as a soda fountain clerk – and his own youthful literary ambitions, specifically to be a poet (he'd written verse since his early teens); but the coming of Prohibition put his father out of the liquor business and forced him to quit Boys' High before graduation. "At the end of my third year in high school my family was in financial straits so desperate that I had to help out. In 1921 jobs were easy [to find], even if you were sixteen years old." Dannay's first full-time position was as a bookkeeper, and over the next seven years he hopped from job to job like a kangaroo. In time family finances improved to the point where he received his high school diploma and then enrolled in a few courses at the Art Students' League. That experience, he said in 1979, convinced him that "I could not be happy if I wasn't a first class painter, but I could be a second class writer and be happy."

In 1926 Dannay married Mary Beck, the first of his three wives, and by 1928 he was working as a copywriter and art director for a New York advertising agency. Lee had graduated from NYU in 1926 and then entered the business world, although his mother had wanted him to go on to law school. In 1928, Lee was married to his first wife, Betty Miller, and making his living writing publicity releases for the Manhattan-based Pathé movie studio. His office and Dannay's were only a few blocks apart, and the cousins met for lunch almost every day. In the late 1920s the foremost detective novels in the United States were the best-selling Philo Vance books, written by art critic Willard Huntington Wright (1888-1939) under the pseudonym of S.S. Van Dine, and among the subjects Dannay and Lee discussed over their meals was the possibility of collaborating on a detective novel of their own, this time not a teen-age fantasy but a serious book in the Van Dine manner, complete with super-intellectual sleuth and reams of erudite deduction. But it was the announcement of the $7500 prize contest that catalyzed them into serious action. And so Ellery Queen, author and detective, was born.

With their backgrounds in advertising and publicity, the cousins decided to take great pains over the name of their protagonist. "What we wanted," Dannay said on television's *Dick Cavett Show* in 1978, "was a name which, once heard, read, or seen in print, would have a mnemonic value and remain in the person's memory." It had to be slightly unusual, easy to remember and rhythmic in sound, and after a few false starts like James Griffen and Wilbur See, they had it. Ellery had been the name of Dannay's best friend in Elmira, and he admired both the magazine editor Ellery Sedgwick and the poet William Ellery Leonard. Queen apparently was chosen purely for the way the sound of it meshed with the sound of Ellery. As the cousins reiterated again and again in later interviews, in their youthful innocence they had no idea that the word was a derogatory synonym for homosexual.

The $7500 prize consisted of $5000 which *McClure's Magazine* was offering for serial rights to the winning manuscript plus $2500 which Stokes was putting up for hard-cover rights. The contest was open to all comers, established professionals as well as beginners, but in order to make sure that all entries would receive equal consideration, the sponsors had adopted a rule that each entry had to be submitted under a pseudonym. "We

4

both had our personal ambitions," Dannay said in 1979, referring to his own desire to be recognized as a poet and Lee's to be the Shakespeare of his time, "so we were perfectly content not to make known who we were." But instead of picking a pseudonym out of a hat, the cousins hit upon the brilliant idea of using Ellery Queen as their own joint byline as well as the name of their detective. As fans of the genre they knew that readers of detective fiction tended to remember Sherlock Holmes and Philo Vance, not Sir Arthur Conan Doyle and S.S. Van Dine. But, they reasoned, people *couldn't* forget their pseudonym if they used the same name for themselves *and* their character. The only precedent for this device was the ever-popular Nick Carter pulp stories which had been turned out by a variety of hands for Street & Smith Publications under the Nicholas Carter house name since the 1880s. No individual mystery writer had done it before, and it must have contributed hugely to the cousins' success.

After submitting the manuscript of *The Roman Hat Mystery*, they continued in the routine of their jobs in advertising and publicity and waited for word of the contest results – and heard nothing. In his 1977 University of California interview, Dannay described what happened next.

"We sat back and waited and actually forgot about the contest. And about three months later – this would be somewhere around March 1929 – we had our usual lunch, and one of us – I don't remember again which one – said: 'Say, what ever happened to that contest that we went into and submitted a manuscript to?' And whoever asked that, I said: 'You know, I think I'll go out and call the agent who was in charge.'

All the manuscripts had been given to the Curtis Brown literary agency, which represented both the publisher Stokes and *McClure's*. So I went out to the lobby of the restaurant, to a public phone, and called up the agent, a man named Mr. Rich whom I had never seen. And I said to him: 'We submitted a manuscript to the contest and we haven't heard a word in three months.' He said: 'Under what name did you submit it?' I said: 'Ellery Queen.' And there was a pause, an ominous pause on the phone. And he said: 'Can you come over right away?' I said: 'We sure can.' So I went back and told Manny that we were supposed to see Mr. Rich.

We finally got there. Mr. Rich's office was Old Curiosity Shop on a small scale, absolutely cluttered, mostly with manuscripts stacked more than waist-high everywhere on the floor. We met Mr. Rich, who had a long full Dickensian beard, and he said to us: 'Now this is not for public report, but confidentially, you have won the contest, and it will be publicly reported in a few days, and I congratulate you.'

So Manny and I walked out on Cloud Nine. And we said to ourselves: 'We have to commemorate this event.' So we went into Dunhill's [the famous New York tobacconist shop] and bought each other a pipe and had the initials EQ put on the stem of each pipe. Manny had his till the day he died. I either lost mine or had it stolen from me . . .

In any event, we waited a couple of days for the public announcement, and it never came. So we called up Mr. Rich again, and he said: 'Can you come over right away?' And we said: 'We sure can.' We went over to see Mr. Rich, and he said: 'Since I last talked to you something terrible has happened. *McClure's* has gone bankrupt'."

The magazine's assets had been taken over by another magazine, *Smart Set*, whose editors had decided to award the prize to another manuscript more suited to that periodical's female readership. That was the bad news. The good news was that the Stokes editors liked the Queen novel enough to publish it anyway, provided the cousins would accept a whopping advance of $200 apiece. "We with great dignity said that if they wanted to publish the manuscript the least they could do for us was to publish it ahead of the prize winner, which they agreed to do."

Dannay in his seventies was philosophical about having won the contest only to lose it. As he said on *The Dick Cavett Show*:

"We thought at the time that it was a terrible blow from fate . . . Seventy-five hundred dollars, to us at least, was a considerable amount of money. What we had planned to do was to pack up our families, give up our jobs, go to the south of France, where at that time there were many American expatriate writers, and write in the south of France. And of course when we lost the contest and lost the first prize we had to stay with our jobs. And that actually was the best thing that ever happened to us. Because I think if we had gone to the south of France we'd have frittered the money away, produced no work, whereas the way it happened, we buckled down and started a career."

True to its word, *Stokes* published *The Roman Hat Mystery* on August 15, 1929, a few months before it issued *Murder Yet to Come* by Isabel Briggs Myers (1897-1980), the winner of the $7500 price. I happen to own a copy of Myers' book. It's a creaky old-dark-house melodrama featuring a ruby stolen from a Hindu temple, an enigmatic turbaned butler, a lot of hypnotized characters making idiots of themselves, and an excruciatingly obvious Least Likely Suspect whose guilt is exposed by Peter Jerningham, witty playwright and amateur sleuth. Myers favored an overwrought silent-movie kind of prose, redeemed only by one unforgettable sentence: "For a moment he gave all his attention to passing a milk truck that was bottling up traffic on our side of the pike." After a second Jerningham exploit, *Give Me Death* (Stokes, 1934), Myers vanished from the genre, although years later she became famous in her own right as the originator (with her mother Katharine Cook Briggs) of the highly respected and widely used Myers-Briggs Type Indicator personality inventory.

Although superior to them in plotting, characterization and style, the early Queen novels were heavily influenced in all sorts of ways by S.S. Van Dine's Philo Vance best-sellers. The strict Queen title-pattern, **The** Adjective-of-Nationality Noun **Mystery**, is clearly derived from Van Dine's **The** Six-Letter-Word **Murder Case** pattern. Each of the principal characters surrounding Vance has a close analogue in the Queen novels: District Attorney Markham and Inspector Queen; block-headed Sergeant Heath and concrete-brained Sergeant Velie; Dr. Doremus and Doc Prouty for the examination of corpses at the most awkward times; Currie the Vance butler and Djuna (named, Dannay told me, for the avant-garde novelist Djuna Barnes) the Queen houseboy.

But the most important element young Dannay and Lee borrowed from Van Dine was his concept of the detective as a towering intellectual, full of scholarly quotations, interested not in people but only in abstract problems. Here is Ellery walking on stage in *The Roman Hat Mystery*:

"There was a square cut to his shoulders and an agreeable swing to his body as he walked. He was dressed in oxford grey and carried a light stick. On his nose perched what seemed an incongruous note in so athletic a man – a pince-nez. But the brow above, the long delicate lines of the face, the bright eyes were those of a man of thought rather than action."

His father, Inspector Richard Queen of the NYPD, is described in the same scene as "a small, withered, rather mild-appearing old gentleman" who walks "with a little stoop and an air of deliberation that somehow accorded perfectly with his thick grey hair and mustaches, veiled grey eyes and slender hands . . . " Ellery usually calls him "pater" or "Inspector darling."

In their last active years as mystery writers the cousins developed a marked antipathy to the Harvard-educated dilettante bibliophile who might be called Ellery I. Dannay described him to an interviewer from *MD* as "really a most unpleasant character," and Lee ridiculed him as "the biggest prig that ever came down the pike." But those novels of Queen's first period are among the most richly plotted specimens of the Golden Age deductive puzzle at its zenith, bursting with bizarre circumstances, conflicting testimony, enigmatic clues, alternative solutions, fireworks displays of virtuoso reasoning, and a constant crackle of intellectual excitement. Most of the distinctive Queen story motifs – the negative clue, the dying message, the murderer as Iago-like manipulator, the patterned series of clues deliberately left at crime scenes, the false answer followed by the true and devastating solution – originated and were given classic treatment in these books of the first period. But if one element more than any other made the Ellery Queen novels stand out from the rest of the detective fiction of the Golden Age between the world wars, it was the cousins' insistence on playing fair with the reader. "We stressed fairness to the reader," Dannay said in 1979, "in the sense that in the Golden Age type of detective story, the reader had to know everything that the detective knew, and therefore had an even chance of beating the detective before the solution was given at the end of the book." And they did play the game with scrupulous fairness, not only presenting all the facts honestly (albeit with a great deal of trickiness on occasion) but stopping most of the novels at a certain point to issue a formal "Challenge to the Reader" to solve the puzzle ahead of Ellery. The odds of course were stacked in favor of the house, and when Fred Dannay once boasted to a *Look Magazine* interviewer that Queen was always "completely fair to the reader," Manny Lee rightly interjected: "We are fair to the reader only if he is a genius."

*The Roman Hat Mystery*, the first Ellery Queen "problem in deduction," had to do with the murder of a shady lawyer in a theater during the performance of a hit play, and to make the scheme work the cousins (and their villain) needed a poison that would kill with split-second accuracy under precisely specified circumstances. Having no medical expertise themselves, they consulted Professor Alexander Goettler, the chief toxicologist for the City of New York, who advised them to use tetra ethyl lead, a component of gasoline whose exact chemical workings were still something of a mystery to scientists. The authors not only followed Goettler's suggestion but gratefully dedicated their book to him.

*Roman Hat* was a relatively minor title on Stokes' 1929 list and received little promotion or advertising from the publisher. But the publicity-conscious cousins hyped the book on their own by writing pseudonymous letters to newspapers, accusing "Queen" of disclosing dangerous information about tetra ethyl lead to potential murderers in real life.  Many years later they learned that the controversy had prompted secret conferences among oil company executives on how to deal with this problem.  The book wound up selling about 8,000 copies in its original edition.  "In a word," Dannay said in 1943, "that was sensational."  "It was a minor miracle," Lee chimed in modestly.

The cousins weren't so imprudent as to abandon their secure jobs and become full-time writers on the strength of one fairly successful novel.  "We buckled down and did more work," Dannay said, "producing a second and third book by working nights and weekends."  *The French Powder Mystery* (1930), which begins with the discovery of a corpse in a pull-down bed in a department store window, was inspired when one of the cousins passed the display window of such an establishment and stopped to look at an exhibit of contemporary apartment furnishings which included a Murphy bed.  And *The Dutch Shoe Mystery* (1931) opens with a woman murdered in the anteroom of a hospital's operating theatre just before she is to undergo surgery.  Although this novel was dedicated to a physician who apparently gave them technical advice, after its publication they received a ten-page letter from a Chicago doctor, Maurice B. Wolff, disputing their notions of what was possible in a hospital setting.  Dannay and Lee didn't agree with all of Dr. Wolff's points but they answered his letter courteously, and from that time until Wolff's death years later he was their expert on all medical aspects of the Ellery Queen series.

It was in 1931, after the release of *Dutch Shoe* and in the pit of the Great Depression, that, as Dannay told a *Playboy* interviewer, "our agent said to us, in more earthy language than I will give to you now, fish or cut bait."  The agent's words as Dannay gave them to me were: "Shit or get off the pot."  And so they decided to make it as professionals or go broke.  With no other jobs to occupy them they discovered that they could turn out a 90,000-word detective novel every three months.  Between 1932 and 1935 they wrote six more Ellery Queen novels, including those early masterpieces *The Greek Coffin Mystery* (1932) and *The Egyptian Cross Mystery* (1932); four novels under the byline of Barnaby Ross and centering around actor-detective Drury Lane, whose best cases are *The Tragedy of X* (1932) and *The Tragedy of Y* (1932); and eleven short stories which were collected as *The Adventures of Ellery Queen* (1934).  As if all that weren't enough, the cousins were also responsible for editing four huge 150,000-word issues of the ambitious but short-lived magazine *Mystery League*.

By 1932 "Ellery Queen" had attained such eminence in the genre that Columbia University's School of Journalism invited "him" to deliver a lecture on mystery writing.  Neither Dannay nor Lee particularly wanted to go that day, so they flipped a coin to see who would do the honors.  Lee lost the toss and went up to Morningside Heights to give the lecture as Queen, wearing a black mask for the occasion.  During the next year or so he wore the mask several more times as he sat at tables in various department stores, autographing Ellery Queen novels.  Not to be outdone, Dannay bought his own mask and started to go around telling people he was Barnaby Ross.

Lee's appearance at Columbia came to the attention of W. Colston Leigh, proprietor of a well-known lecture bureau, who put the cousins under contract and, over the next two years, sent them out together on several cross-country speaking tours, with Dannay posing as Ross and Lee still playing Queen, both men sporting what Dannay described as "domino masks with little ruffles at the bottom so that no part of our faces, except the glasses over the masks, could be seen."  They would appear on the lecture platform as rival mystery writers and challenge each other's skill as detectives, with Ross tossing off clues in a complex murder case and defying Queen to solve it on the spot.  "It

8

was really a vaudeville act," Dannay remarked in 1970, and the whole performance was intensively rehearsed before the cousins hit the road. Soon they had developed a knack for reacting spontaneously to each other's verbal cues during interviews, so that one reporter in the late 1930s wrote:

> "[They share an] intellectual Siamese twinship that binds them together . . . Their minds blend so easily and naturally that a third person, talking to them, gets the slightly uneasy impression that he is conversing with one man. Never prompting each other by as much as a glance (in one hour-long interview neither ever once addressed the other), one would begin a sentence, in the middle of which the other would hook on a subjunctive clause, with the first reappearing in the caboose of the train of their thought."

Their lecture tours as Queen and Ross were so convincing to audiences that they often posed a credibility problem which the cousins once described for the press in a series of those alternating segments.

Dannay: "Almost everywhere we went as Ellery Queen and Barnaby Ross we were asked to work on some local mystery."

Lee: "But we remembered Van Dine's experience when he undertook to solve a murder mystery out in Jersey."

Dannay: "He worked long and hard at it and was getting nowhere..."

Lee: ". . . when along came a flatfoot who didn't know the difference between analytical deduction and postular acne..."

Dannay: "...and solved it in two hours."

Whenever they were asked to play real-life detective, their invariable response was to extemporize some fast double talk and then politely inquire the way to the nearest exit.

In time these little games focused a good deal of attention on the masked authors. As veterans of the advertising business, Dannay said in 1979, he and Lee "were advertising-minded, and while we didn't intend our hiding behind a mask or hiding behind a pseudonym to create publicity, whether we intended it or not it did create publicity, and the more publicity it created the more successful we were." Soon rumors began to appear in print that Ellery Queen was none other than S.S. Van Dine and that lurking behind the mask of Barnaby Ross was the celebrated raconteur Alexander Woollcott. A brief paragraph in *Publishers' Weekly* for October 10, 1936, finally revealed the true identities of both Ross and Queen. But by that time the cousins had gone through their first period as mystery writers and were in the initial stages of their second.

By the mid-1930s Van Dine had lost much of his appeal not only for whodunit readers in general but for Dannay and Lee as well. As Dannay put it, "He influenced us because he made so much money; and then, the kind of thing he did appealed to us in those days. It was complex, logical, deductive, almost completely intellectual." During the years from 1936 through 1939 that are bracketed together as Queen's second period, what radically reshaped the cousins' fiction was not the example of any other writer but the requirements of two extremely well-paying media to which they'd begun to sell very late in Period One: the slick-paper magazines like *Redbook* and *Cosmopolitan*, and the movies. (Donald Cook played Ellery in a low-budget 1935 quickie entitled and distantly based on *The Spanish Cape Mystery*, and in the following year wiry vaudeville hoofer Eddie Quillan proved that his only qualifications for the role were his initials when he stared in *The Mandarin Mystery*, a feeble adaptation of the 1934 Queen novel *The Chinese Orange Mystery*.) Their fiction output during Period Two consisted of a paltry five novels; the stage play *Danger, Men Working* (1937) which they wrote in collaboration with Lowell Brentano for producer Jed Harris and which closed after a few nights in Baltimore and Philadelphia; and a handful of short stories collected in 1940 (along with the last short exploits of Period One) as *The New Adventures of Ellery Queen*.

In 1979 Dannay described his and Lee's second-period strategy as follows: "We loosened the construction . . .; we put more emphasis on character development and background; we put more emphasis on human-interest situations. And what we were doing, frankly, was to aim at getting magazine serialization, which paid very good money in those days, and to sell to the movies, which was the only other means of getting extra money. We turned to commercialism because we frankly wanted to make more money."  Compared with the great detective novels of Period One, most of what the cousins wrote in the later 1930s suffers from intellectual thinness, an overabundance of so-called love interest (meaning a tedious boy-meets-girl counterplot), and characters all too obviously tailored to please story editors in the slick magazine suites and the studios.  But in the longer view they succeeded at least partially in opening up the formal deductive puzzle and making room within its cerebral rigor for more of the virtues of mainstream storytelling.  And Ellery II was no longer a priggish Philo Vance derivative like Ellery I but had taken several steps along the road to recognizable humanity.

One reason for the relative scarcity of Queen novels during these years was that Dannay and Lee were invited to Hollywood for three stints as screenwriters, a term apiece at Columbia, Paramount and M-G-M.  In an interview with the press after returning from one of these excursions they described their impressions in their own brand of crosstalk.

Dannay: "There's enough material in Hollywood for a thousand books."

Lee: "Don't let anyone tell you that fantastic stories of Hollywood are exaggerated."

Dannay: "They don't tell the half of it.  Our first assignment was to do a racing story."

Lee: "Neither of us had ever seen a horse race and we haven't yet."

Dannay: "But we found a man who knew racing from the ground up, lived with him for three days and nights, and wrote the picture."

Lee: "Which delighted the producer."

10

In their novels *The Devil to Pay* (1938) and *The Four of Hearts* (1938) the cousins made use of their wildest Hollywood experiences by transplanting Ellery to the film capital, making him a frustrated screenplay scribe, gifting him with a girlfriend in the person of reclusive gossip columnist Paula Paris, and modeling the wacky head of the studio on Irving Thalberg. And in the 1939 story "Long Shot" (collected in *The New Adventures of Ellery Queen*, 1940) Ellery is himself assigned to write a horse-race script despite never having seen a track. In real life the cousins' racing screenplay was shelved and they received not a single screen credit for their contributions to the movies of the late thirties. "The place was filled with crazy people," Dannay said in 1979. "I told Manny even if I had to dig ditches for the rest of my life, I wasn't coming back."

They had tried the stage and accomplished little, tried the movies and accomplished less. Perhaps it was time to look around for another medium in which to write detective stories. Fortunately for Dannay and Lee, that medium existed and was on the brink of its own Golden Age--and it was looking for them.

# CHAPTER TWO

# The Zachary Connection

In 1939 Fred and Mary Dannay and their children, six-year-old Douglas and newborn Richard, were living the suburban life in Great Neck, Long Island. Fred continued to collect stamps and write poetry in odd moments and was progressing toward his ultimate goal as a bibliophile, owing a copy of every book of detective-crime short stories ever published. By that time Manny Lee was divorced from his first wife and living in an apartment at 1050 Park Avenue. Between visits from his daughters Jacquelin and Patricia, he played the violin and added to his already sizable collection of classical record albums. But there wasn't much leisure for either cousin. They were putting in average twelve-hour workdays at home and meeting once a week to consolidate their material at one or another nondescript office – first at 545 Fifth Avenue, later in the Fisk Building near Columbus Circle – which was rented under the name of Ellery Queen. The atmosphere of the office tended to be thick with tobacco smoke (both men alternated between Pall Malls and pipes, with cigars thrown in for good measure), and its floor was home for a tattered brown envelope labeled "IDEAS."

How did they collaborate? Or, more precisely, what was each cousin's function in the Ellery Queen partnership? This is incontestably the question Dannay and Lee were asked by reporters most often, and their replies varied. Sometimes they'd toss back questions of their own.

Dannay to a *New Yorker* interviewer in 1940: "Did you ever ask Hecht and MacArthur how they collaborated?"

Lee: "Or Nordhoff and Hall?"

Sometimes they'd answer the second form of the question as if they'd been asked the first. Dannay to Dick Cavett in 1978:

"Our own method was to write a complete outline before the finished work was started, and the complete outline could easily have been 20,000 words, the outline covering not only the details and the sequence of events but broken down into scenes, with character sketches and dialogue and so on. That's the only way I know how to work."

Sometimes they'd drop a tantalizing clue and then throw dust in the interlocutor's eyes with one of their cross-talk acts. They told John Bainbridge, who was profiling them in 1943 for *Life*, that they'd begin with a "a 25,000 word outline, complete to a full description of the last false suspect," and then proceed to the full-length version of the novel, which usually ran about 100,000 words. But exactly who does what? Bainbridge asked.

Lee: "In its simple form our collaboration is like this: one of us does a plot and shoots it off to the other for writing."

Dannay: "Or one of us writes a plot and the two of us start writing."

Lee: "Sometimes one of us writes a plot and the two of us tear it to pieces."

Dannay: "Other times the two of us write a plot and one of us tears it to pieces."

The only conclusion a bewildered Bainbridge could reach was that "apparently one partner is strong on plots, the other on writing." On some occasions they'd reply in terms of their divergent personalities.

Lee to Israel Shenker of the *New York Times* in 1969: "[Fred's] a very clever, driving kind of individual and a perfectionist. I'm a perfectionist too, but I tend to be more of an extrovert. I've always thought I have a sense of humor. Whether he does he'll have to tell you."

Dannay to Graham Lord of the *London Sunday Express* in 1970: "We're two entirely different people, with different philosophies and make-ups. I'm quieter and more introverted while Manny is more impulsive and tends to speak a very earthy language. He's louder, more aggressive."

Dannay to Paul Bargren of the Waukesha (Wisconsin) *Freeman* in 1979, after Lee's death: "I am more of an indoors, introspective country person, and Mr. Lee was streetwise, citified, an outdoor person."

On other occasions their response would be framed purely in terms of logistics.

Dannay to Lord of the London *Sunday Express* in 1970: "We've used every collaboratory system invented by the mind of man. We've worked in the same room, at the same typewriter, and separately. We've worked in the same city and three thousand miles apart. The only difference then was that the telephone bills were bigger."

And once in a while their answer would evoke memories of the one-upmanship games they'd played as children during Manny's summer visits to Fred in Elmira. Witness this bit of cross-talk from an interview with *MD*, the medical magazine, in 1965.

Dannay: "The truth is, we are competitors and always have been. We are always trying to out-top each other."

Lee: "We fight each other. We've been fighting each other for thirty-nine years. We have basically different attitudes toward the detective story."

Dannay: "We have basically different attitudes toward everything."

And:

Dannay to Robert W. Wells of the *Milwaukee Journal* in 1979: "We collaborated for forty-three years, but we were as much competitors as collaborators. He brought a certain sharpness to our writing that otherwise wouldn't have been there.

Each of us was always trying to top the other, and I think it showed. We were always battling each other to do the best we could, and competition brings out more creative energy."

But the bottom line tended to be the same in every interview. "We will never reveal how we work," Dannay exulted to Israel Shenker of the *New York Times* in 1969, "at least [not] until we hang up our gloves." And he gave the British journalist Graham Lord a dose of the same medicine the following year: "I don't know why we don't answer it and I don't mean to be mysterious but we just don't. Perhaps it's psychological." More likely it stemmed from their backgrounds in advertising and publicity and their calculation that keeping a veil of secrecy drawn over their division of labor would keep their readers interested in their output. In any event Dannay carried on the policy after Lee's death, claiming it was what his cousin had wanted.

But the truth was deducible, at least in skeletal form, to anyone who read the author's remarks with the infinite care of a mystery fan determined to beat Ellery to the murderer's identity. Here are two clues from the last years of Manny Lee's life.

Lee to Shenker of the *Times*, 1969: "In the beginning we'd plot together and write together. But Fred and I never agreed on anything."

Dannay to Lord of the *Sunday Express*, 1970: "In time we've mellowed and our quarrels have got less frequent. But once we were almost as bad as Gilbert and Sullivan, who wouldn't even talk to each other and had to pass each other handwritten notes."

And Lee told Shenker that when he and Dannay were working at Paramount as screenwriters their office was directly underneath the studio's mimeograph department, which generated a permanent clatter from the scores of duplicating machines. "*They* complained about the noise *we* were making," Lee said.

The conclusion is inescapably indubitable – as Ellery I might have put it – that in their salad days Fred and Manny fought like a pair of wildcats. So why did they continue to collaborate at all? That's an easy one: they literally couldn't afford to stop.

Dannay to Wells of the *Milwaukee Journal*, 1979: "We had manufactured a benevolent Frankenstein's monster. If we ever considered a divorce--well, it would have been easier for a husband and wife to part than for us. We had a valuable property in Ellery Queen and we couldn't let go of it."

But why couldn't they let go of it? Why couldn't they have agreed that one of them would do this Ellery Queen novel from start to finish and the other the next? Since these were supremely rational men we must adopt the working hypothesis – again as Ellery I might have put it – that they had considered the possibility and rejected it. The question that logically follows this conclusion all but asks itself: on what grounds could they conceivably have rejected such an eminently sensible solution to their problem? And the answer virtually shouts back at us that they must have rejected it because it wouldn't have worked; in other words, because for reasons of talent, temperament, whim or whatever, *neither of them could complete a piece of fiction without the other*.

John Bainbridge of *Life* inadvertently hit the nail on the head in 1943: plotting was the strong suit of one cousin, prose the forte of the other. Which cousin performed which function? A year or two after Manny Lee's death Fred Dannay told me, and he approved of the way I explained it in *Royal Bloodline*:

> "As a general principle the conceptual work on a Queen novel – themes, plotting, basic characters, deductions, clues, etc. – is by and large the creation of Dannay, while the detailed execution, the fleshing out of character and incident and the precise choice of words, was by and large the creation of Lee."

It was Dannay who wrote the 25,000-word skeletons that John Bainbridge mentioned, and Lee who put the meat on the bones. In an article about Ellery Queen in *TV Guide* for October 11, 1975, Manny's son Rand Lee confirmed this account: "Cousin Fred plotted all the novels and short stories, creating the characters and providing Dad with detailed skeletons that Dad fleshed out. Their talents determined this arrangement. I'm sure Dad could never have come up with the sort of plots Fred did."

While Dannay and Lee were arguing with each other over the phone and in their $45-a-month office, a young executive in the program department of the Columbia Broadcasting System was toying with the concept of a new kind of radio drama. George Zachary (1911-1964) had been associated until then with CBS musical variety series like *99 Men and A Girl*, which featured the Raymond Paige orchestra and "the incomparable Hildegarde." What he really wanted was to produce and direct an hour-long detective series which would invite listeners to match wits with the principal character and – if they were very smart and very lucky – beat him to the solution of the week's mystery. To make this concept a reality was George Zachary's dream, but first he needed a writer who'd be at home with such a program and capable of turning out a 60-minute script each week. No one of that description was then working in dramatic radio. In 1939 the medium was still in its adolescence, and mystery series on the air were few and far between. The spooky anthology *Lights Out!* was doing well, as were the cop show *Gang Busters* and the news-hawk series *Big Town* and, of course, the weird weekly exploits of *The Shadow*, portrayed in 1937-1938 by a young genius named Orson Welles. But except for an occasional cycle of adventures of Sherlock Holmes, who was first heard over the airwaves in 1930, radio had no genuine "detective" programs at all.

If we are to believe the anonymous article in the March 1940 issue of *Radio Varieties*, Zachary spent night after night sitting up "until the early hours of the morning, reading mystery author after mystery author, looking for the one perfect writer who could turn out a complete detective story every week, make it puzzling enough to intrigue the radio audience, and yet fair enough so that they could solve it if they marshaled all the facts correctly." The clear implication of this article is that Zachary knew next to nothing about the detective fiction of his time and didn't have the sense to seek advice from fans of the genre, for according to *Radio Varieties* it was only "after reading some 200 odd stories" that he "stumbled upon the first of the mysteries connected with Ellery Queen." This tidbit smacks more of publicity hype than of truth, but in any event once Zachary had read a few Queen novels and realized that their "Challenge to the Reader" device was the exact literary equivalent of his own plan to enlist the radio audience as detectives, he got in touch with Dannay and Lee and made them an offer. What he proposed was that Ellery Queen should

15

become the star of his own weekly series on CBS.

At first the cousins were reluctant. They knew nothing about radio writing and were being offered a starting salary of $25 a week to learn the ropes. Then – and most of this reconstruction is informed guesswork – they must have thought long and hard about their economic situation and their literary goals. Between them they had a wife, an ex-wife and four children to support, and their most recent novel, *The Dragon's Teeth* (1939), had been the first in years which hadn't been bought by a major national magazine prior to hard-cover publication. Twenty-five dollars was only ten less than they'd received for the first Ellery Queen short story six years before, and currently the short adventures of their character were appearing in slicks like *Blue Book* that paid top prices. But the audience for a successful radio program could be counted in the millions, astronomically larger than the readership of the most profitable Queen novels. And the cousins had already proved their own and Ellery's ability to change with the times and the needs of different media when they'd converted him from the Philo Vance clone of the early books to the slick magazine and Hollywood sleuth of Period Two. So why not invest some time and energy and give this new form of storytelling a try?

First of course they had to learn the fundamentals of writing for radio. This they did by turning out a number of scripts, without credit and at minimal pay, for two existing crime series. One of these was *Alias Jimmy Valentine* (1/18/38 to 2/27/39), a program produced by soap-opera specialists Frank and Anne Hummert and very remotely based on the O. Henry short story "A Retrieved Reformation" which had earlier spawned a popular song, a stage play and three silent movies. Bert Lytell starred as a reformed safecracker who helped the police by not quite legal means. In his introduction to *Cops and Robbers* (1948), a paperback collection of O. Henry's crime stories that he had edited, Dannay claimed that he and Lee wrote "weekly scripts" for this series. The only episode they are known to have written is the one broadcast November 21, 1938. *Alias Jimmy Valentine* has long been forgotten but the other series on which the cousins honed their radio-writing skills was that audio immortal *The Shadow*. Unfortunately, how much they enhanced the saga of that mysterious character with the power to cloud men's minds will probably never be known for sure. When I asked Fred Dannay he couldn't remember any episode titles he and Manny Lee had written, nor even whether The Shadow was being played by Orson Welles or his successor Bill Johnstone when the cousins' scripts were aired. It now seems clear that they made their contributions to *The Shadow* during the first of Johnstone's five seasons as the character. In the Appendix that follows these chapters, radio scholar William Nadel pinpoints the episodes that were probably the cousins' work.

A little more than two months before the Ellery Queen series debuted, Dannay and Lee became involved in another radio venture which to the end of his life Fred Dannay believed to be one of the most fascinating experiments in the medium's history. *Author! Author!* was an impromptu melange of game and panel show which the cousins created and sold to the Mutual network. It debuted on April 7, 1939 under the sponsorship of the B.F. Goodrich Rubber Company and with Robert Lewis Shayon as director. The moderator for the series was humorist S.J. Perelman, although light-verse wizard Ogden Nash took Perelman's place for one broadcast. Dannay and Lee, billed respectively as "Mr. Ellery" and "Mr Queen," served as permanent panelists, and the guests each week were media figures like Dorothy Parker, Heywood Broun, Moss Hart and George S. Kaufman, Mark and Carl Van Doren, Fannie Hurst, Erskine Caldwell and Quentin Reynolds. The format of the program was described by the announcer as "a fiction funfest." Each week's show would begin with a dramatized version of some inexplicable event. Here's an example, employed on the first program (which has survived on tape) and summarized by Dannay exactly forty years later for David Behrens of *Newsday*:

"A young man arrives for the reading of his uncle's will. The only heir, he is desperately in need of money to cover gambling debts. The will gives him a choice: Accept $10,000 in cash or the contents of an envelope. He opens the envelope, which is empty, with no stamps or writing on it. 'I will take the envelope,' he says."

At this curtain line the sketch would end and the moderator would challenge each of the week's four panelists – Dannay, Lee, and two guests who varied from program to program – to devise on the spot a set of circumstances that would make sense of the scene. Dannay's explanation for his own example was as follows:

"The young man could not wait for his uncle to die. He killed him instead. The murder was committed with a slow-working poison placed on an envelope in his uncle's study. But the uncle realizes his nephew's evil deed and scrawls a revision in his will, to create a malicious dilemma. His nephew has to choose between $10,000 in cash or the chance to recover the only evidence of the murder – the uncle's final revenge."

After each panelist had offered an ad-lib rationale for the situation, everyone would proceed to attack the others' constructions and defend his or her own. At the end of the first broadcast the announcer invited listeners to send in their own impossible story situations, with B.F. Goodrich promising $25 for each one used on the air. The panel members seemed to have a marvelous time heckling each other, but the whole concept presupposed an absurdly mechanical approach to storytelling and offered little to the millions of listeners who had no desire to hear writers match wits. Surprisingly, *Author! Author!* survived for almost a year before vanishing into the ether.

During that program's first weeks on Mutual, George Zachary over at CBS was lining up the actors and support troops who would bring *The Adventures of Ellery Queen* to audible life. For the crucial role of Ellery he picked suave and slender Hugh Marlowe (1911-1982), who had played the dumb rich boy in Victor Schertzinger's Broadway musical comedy *Kiss the Boys Goodbye*. Inspector Richard Queen was portrayed by radio veteran Santos Ortega (1899-1976), the doughty Sergeant Velie by utility actor Howard Smith, and medical examiner Doc Prouty by Robert Strauss (1913-1975), whose best-known part was as a homesick GI in *Stalag 17* (1953). In order to provide the mandatory "love interest" that was supposed to attract the female audience, Dannay and Lee and Zachary added a new member to the Queen radio family: Ellery's pert secretary, Nikki Porter. Her role went to lovely Marian Shockley (1908-1981), who had been a 1932 Wampas baby star in Hollywood and had debuted on Broadway with George M. Cohan in *Dear Old Darling* (1936). She and Zachary were married in October 1939, and Zachary made sure that Nikki was written out of the scripts during the weeks the newlyweds were off on their honeymoon. The first announcer for the series was Ken Roberts (who also announced for *The Shadow*). During its initial ten weeks on the air, the orchestra that performed the background music for episodes was conducted by Bernard Herrmann (1911-1975), who accompanied Orson Welles to Hollywood a year later, wrote the score for

Welles' classic film *Citizen Kane* (1941), and went on to compose the music for such Alfred Hitchcock masterpieces as *Vertigo* (1958) and *Psycho* (1960).

Zachary's analogue to the Queen "Challenge to the Reader" device was to stop each week's drama at a certain point after all the clues had been set forth so that a panel of well-known guests who "represented" the home listening audience would engage in an unrehearsed debate as to whodunit. At first these guest sleuths were drawn from the ranks of New York media celebs – Princess Kropotkin, writer Gelett Burgess, music critic Deems Taylor, playwright Lillian Hellman, photographer Margaret Bourke-White – and were paid $25 to $50 apiece. Most of them turned out to be less than scintillating. One claimed that the murderer was his fellow guest detective, another spent five minutes arguing that the week's culprit must have been Ellery himself, and a third, whose regular job was as a producer for CBS, became so confused by the plot that all she could say was: "I'm an Ellery fan Queen." The most perceptive of the early guests was Lillian Hellman, who solved the case of "Napoleon's Razor" (aired July 9, 1939) in a nick. After a few months Zachary decided to replace the big-name armchair Sherlocks with ordinary men and women. But neither the members of the live studio audience at CBS nor the home listeners who were chosen on a write-in basis contributed satisfactorily, and soon Zachary returned to using celebs like playwright Harry Kurnitz, better known to whodunit fans under the pseudonym of Marco Page, who cracked "The March of Death" (October 15, 1939) mystery in jig time.

The special guests weren't the only people in the CBS building who were trying to solve each Sunday evening puzzle. Zachary had decided to withhold the last scenes of each script from the actors until the final moments of the dress rehearsal, so that the one playing the murderer wouldn't blow the show by trying too hard to act innocent. By late in the year the regular cast had organized a pool, with the proceeds going to whoever identified the murderer. The most frequent winner was Ted de Corsia (1904-1973), who had taken over the role of Sergeant Velie in November, and the runner-up was Robert Strauss.

**Tonight — GULF Presents**
**The Adventures of**

**ELLERY QUEEN**

*Are you a born detective?*
*Tune in and find out...*

**GULF 7:30 WABC**

**The photo on the left is one of many advertisements placed in newspapers and radio magazines across the country, inviting readers of the periodicals to join the millions of other radio listeners who tuned in each week, trying to solve the mystery themselves. This advertisement was printed during *Ellery Queen's* sponsorship by Gulf Oil. WABC is a New York radio station. 7:30 was Eastern Standard Time.**

Zachary must have been one of New York's busiest men that summer of 1939. Not only was he producing and directing a 60-minute drama each week, but whenever a Queen script ran short he and his assistant, Charles Jackson (1903-1968), who was to become famous a few years later for his novel about alcoholism *The Lost Weekend* (1944), had to insert additional dialogue as needed. On top of all these chores Zachary functioned as story editor, taking special care to make sure that the Queen plot premises were sound. The series' first episode, "The Adventure of the Gum-Chewing Millionaire," hinged on a scorecard from a baseball game supposedly played that very Sunday afternoon, June 18, 1939, between the Washington Senators and the St. Louis Cardinals. A few hours before air time, Zachary made a routine check and discovered to his horror that the game had been cancelled because of rain. But a frantic phone call to Washington satisfied him that the clue was still viable: several thousand fans had gone to the stadium before the game was called. The next week's episode, "The Adventure of the Last Man Club," (June 25, 1939) dealt with a favorite theme in the Queen novels and short stories, red-green color-blindness, and Zachary made it his business to find out whether someone with this handicap could tell the difference between crème de menthe and a cherry liqueur. For "The Adventure of the Bad Boy" (July 30, 1939) he had to research whether arsenic would kill a rabbit. So it went as week followed week and a new kind of radio drama was born.

**Photo above: Fred Dannay and Manny Lee look over an Ellery Queen script.**

# CHAPTER THREE

## Of Flying Needles And Scorpion Thumbs

During 1939 Fred and Manny must have spent almost every minute of their workdays writing for *The Adventures of Ellery Queen*, which required a 60-minute script week in and week out. Dannay spoke of those hectic days when he visited the University of California's San Diego campus in 1977.

> "Each week we received the magnificent sum of $25. Imagine doing a one-hour original drama each week for $25! And we didn't really keep the money, because at the end of each show we'd take the cast out for coffee and cake – that's all we could afford, coffee and danish pastry – and blew the $25 each week."

The cousins wrote and Zachary produced and directed a total of 34 hour-long radio dramas that CBS broadcast between June 1939 and February 1940. No recordings of the performances seem to have survived but we can gain some idea of what they were like because several of them were later translated into other forms.* Indeed the first two episodes of the series were recast by an anonymous hack into painfully infantile prose and published, in 1942 and 1940 respectively, as Whitman Better Little Books, with the story on the left-hand pages and line-drawing illustrations on the right. (Decades later the two were reprinted in one volume without illustrations as *The Last Man Club*, Pyramid pb #R1835, 1968.) I am lucky enough to own a copy of one of the Whitman minibooks, inscribed to me by Fred Dannay. With some knowledge of dramatic radio and a bit of imagination, one can read these awful prose versions ("Reaching the door, Ellery tried the handle. It gave! Opened! The door Peter Jordan always kept locked was – UNLOCKED!") and extrapolate backwards to the broadcast originals.

Frankly, the debut episode, "The Adventure of the Gum-Chewing Millionaire" (June 18, 1939; translated into story form as *The Murdered Millionaire*, Whitman, 1942), doesn't appear to have been one of the best. The kickoff is intriguing enough as Ellery receives a friendly letter from a complete stranger asking him to recommend a nurse. Soon he's trying to solve the bludgeon murder of a crippled, gum-loving, will-changing old tyrant. As in Queen's 1938 novel *The Four of Hearts*, no one seems to have had a motive for the crime. But this time Ellery handles the problem poorly, never considering the possibility, for example, that the killer might have been a person who mistakenly believed he'd benefit from the old man's will. And what turns out to be the real motive is lifted bodily and unconvincingly from Queen's then most recent novel, *The Dragon's Teeth* (1939). Ellery solves the case by determining that the murderer must have had a scorecard from the afternoon's Senators-Browns game and then deducing that only one person in the circle of suspects could have had that item; but since he forgot to establish that the killer must be among the people we've met in the story, his deduction proves nothing. The most

---

* The only existing recording from the hour-long radio dramas is that of a few minutes of "The Adventure of The Woman From Nowhere." Sadly, the sound quality is very poor and not one minute of the drama exists, merely the conversation with guest armchair detectives.

interesting part of the play is its casual reference to how Nikki Porter became a member of the Queen household: she was a professional typist to whom Ellery had been taking his near-illegible manuscripts until she decided to do both herself and Ellery a favor by asking for a full-time job as his secretary so that he could dictate to her instead of scribbling.

The next week's tale, "The Adventure of the Last Man Club" (June 25, 1939; translated into story form as *The Last Man Club*, Whitman, 1940), is a superior job on all counts – and the last one whose title I shall preface with that ridiculous obligatory "The Adventure of . . . " Ellery and Nikki witness a hit-and-run and are caught up by the victim's dying words into the affairs of a survivor-take-all group to which the dead man belonged. The clues are neat and subtle and Ellery's solution plays perfectly fair with the audience. Queen fans might have recalled certain elements of the denouement from the 1932 novel *The Greek Coffin Mystery* and the 1935 short story "The House of Darkness" but these elements were carefully reworked into the context of the radio play, which is the first Queen script but by no means the last to feature a misleading dying message and a death-plagued tontine.

The plot of Ellery's third radio adventure, "The Fallen Angel" (July 2, 1939), was reworked by Dannay and Lee several years later into a short story of the same name, first published in the July 1951 issue of *Ellery Queen's Mystery Magazine* and collected with eleven other transformed radio scripts in the 1952 volume *Calendar of Crime*. On a Fourth of July weekend Nikki pulls Ellery into the affairs of her girl friend, who recently married an aging laxatives tycoon and moved into the monstrous family mansion and apparently into an affair with her husband's artistic younger brother. Then murder enters the picture, along with a few plot elements from Queen's 1936 short story "The Hollow Dragon" (collected in *The New Adventures of Ellery Queen*, 1940). Ellery solves the crime by puncturing an incredibly chancy alibi gimmick (if he'd been even a few minutes late for his appointment, the scheme would literally have gone up in smoke) that could have worked only at that particular time of year. The apparent triangle consisting of old husband, young wife and young artist was revived many years later in Queen's superb 1948 novel *Ten Days' Wonder*.

In the fourth week's episode, "Napoleon's Razor" (July 9, 1939), Ellery and Nikki are returning from California on a transcontinental train when a French historian asks the gentleman sleuth to find out which of the other passengers – an alcoholic salesman, a pair of newlyweds, an aging movie star, three characters calling themselves Smith, Jones and Brown – stole one of his most prized possessions, a razor which had once been given to Napoleon by the Empress Josephine. One of the week's guest armchair detectives was playwright Lillian Hellman who, according to a write-up of the Queen series in the October 23, 1939 issue of *Time*, cracked the case instantly. Of course she had an edge over her fellow armchair guests in that she was the lover and protégée of Dashiell Hammett.

Ellery's fifth audio exploit, "The Impossible Crime" (July 16, 1939), deals with the stabbing of an escaped convict in the office of Nikki's doctor at a time when all the office doors were being watched. This was followed by "George Spelvin, Murderer" (July 23, 1939), in which Ellery and his entourage stop at a New England hotel where the cast members of a summer-stock theater are staying and quickly find themselves involved in the murder of a blackmailing actor. Learning that the weapon was a cane carried by a missing thespian named George Spelvin, Ellery warns his colleagues that "as ridiculous as it seems, everything is known about the murderer – and nothing!" The title hints at a connection

21

with Queen's 1953 novel *The Scarlet Letters*, in which the name George Spelvin (the traditional pseudonym adopted by an actor with both a bit part in a play and a featured role) crops up again, but nothing of the radio script seems to have been used in the book.

The next week's adventure, "The Bad Boy" (July 30, 1939), is the earliest Queen radio play to survive on tape, although not in its original form. On January 4, 1948, eight and a half years after its presentation on CBS, George Zachary reassembled the actors who'd been regulars on the Queen series for most of its first fifteen months on the air – Hugh Marlowe as Ellery, Santos Ortega as Inspector Queen, Ted de Corsia (who wasn't in the July 1939 cast) as Sergeant Velie – and restaged the episode for NBC's Sunday afternoon series *The Ford Theater*. Surviving tapes of this broadcast allow us to hear a 60-minute Queen radio play, but without the theorizing of the guest armchair Sherlocks and with substantial revision of the original script. In a December 1947 letter to mystery writer and critic Anthony Boucher, Manny Lee said that upon hearing of Zachary's plan to rebroadcast the play "I asked George to send me the script. It confirmed some of my worst fears, and I spent about 36 hours more or less consecutively rewriting it. Gad, some of the dialogue!" Apparently the plot remained unaltered. "The Bad Boy" is set in an old brownstone overlooking Washington Square and furnished with several elements from Queen's 1932 novel *The Tragedy of Y* including a secret room, a vicious old matriarch and a precocious little boy. The challenge for Ellery and the listener is to solve the murder of hateful Sarah Brink, who was poisoned by arsenic in a serving of rabbit stew and found dead in her bed with several dozen live bunnies loose in the room. Among the clues is a top hat more or less borrowed from Queen's 1929 debut novel, *The Roman Hat Mystery*, although this time its owner is a vaudeville magician. The plot is far from watertight: Ellery never explains how the one portion of stew could have been harmless and the other fatal, and a quick phone call to the police would have stopped the story in its tracks before the curtain ever rose. But Brad Barker gives a fine performance as the eight-year-old whose fantasies of intrigue and death suddenly become real.

The gimmick in "The Flying Needle" (August 6, 1939) seems to have involved blowing a poisoned needle through a soda straw, a feat to which George Zachary devoted several hours one afternoon before the air date to make sure it would work. "The Secret Partner" (August 27, 1939), which entangles Ellery and Nikki in a plot to smuggle diamonds from the Netherlands into the United States in shipments of tulip bulbs, was later adapted into a serialized comic book whose nine 4-page installments, given away at Gulf Oil stations on successive Sundays during May and June of 1940, are extremely rare and valuable today.

"The Three Rs" (September 10, 1939) is another of the dozen which Dannay and Lee later recycled as short stories (this one published in *EQMM*, September 1946) and as installments in *Calendar of Crime*. As a new academic year begins and students and teachers all over the United States return more or less voluntarily to their classrooms, the administration of Barlowe College hires Ellery to locate one of its faculty, a Poe scholar who vanished in the Ozarks during the summer. Ellery's investigation along the Missouri-Arkansas border turns up some intriguing clues like a detective-story manuscript and a skeleton with two missing fingers, but the solution sounds more like a Jon L. Breen parody than like genuine Queen, and the final plot twist turns the whole show into a farce. Just two weeks later came "The Lost Treasure" (September 24, 1939), in which a retired explorer is murdered after inviting Ellery to do some detective work on his private island, where Captain Kidd is rumored to have buried some of his loot centuries before. This episode was also adapted by Dannay and Lee into a short story ("The Needle's Eye," *EQMM*, August 1951) collected in *Calendar of Crime.*

In "The Mother Goose Murders" (October 8, 1939) Ellery visits an old hotel to investigate a series of killings with nursery-rhyme motifs. Robert Strauss, taking a week off from his Doc Prouty role to play the mild-mannered proprietor Mr. Wiggins, turned out to be the killer. But the major significance of this play is that it may inadvertently have saved the Queen series from early cancellation. The high executives of CBS, Dannay recalled at the University of California in 1977, "did not believe that mysteries [meaning fair-play detective stories] would serve as good materials for radio in those days." And to make matters worse, the series had so far failed to attract a commercial sponsor and was still running as a "sustainer." But that evening a water hose burst in the transmitter cooling system of WBBM, the CBS affiliate station in Chicago, and forced the episode off the air nine minutes before the end of the hour. The station was besieged by literally thousands of angry phone calls from listeners demanding to be told the murderer's identity. Ad agency veteran that he was, Fred Dannay believed at first that this widely reported incident was just a publicity stunt. He visited the CBS vice president who had insisted that mystery stories would never make it on radio and asked him point blank: "Did you plant that incident in Chicago? If so it's one of the most brilliant moves you've ever made!" But the executive swore that it had really happened and, as both he and Dannay saw at once, it was a demonstration more convincing than any poll that the Queen series was drawing a large and avid audience. The cousins' pay was raised to $350 a week and sponsors soon began to make offers, although it wasn't until late April 1940 that Gulf Oil picked up the series and commissioned the EQ comic books that the company's filling stations gave away during May and June.

In "The Haunted Cave" (October 22, 1939) Ellery is invited to a lodge in the Adirondacks where a serial strangler had operated a century earlier, but soon finds himself sleuthing a new strangulation murder when a psychic investigator is found dead inside a cavern that no one else could have entered. This episode was adapted (not by Dannay and Lee) into a sort of short story of the same name, published in *Radio & Television Mirror* for May 1940.

The Hallowe'en episode "The Dead Cat" (October 29, 1939) was later recast by Fred and Manny themselves into a real short story, first published in the October 1946 *EQMM* and later collected in *Calendar of Crime.* Almost immediately after the story version appeared in *EQMM* it was mentioned in mystery writer/critic Anthony Boucher's weekly column for the *San Francisco Chronicle* (September 29, 1946). Queen, Boucher said, "has transformed a good routine radio plot into a first-rate short by adding elements of ironic subjective commentary impossible to radio." Without the original script I can't judge the radio version but in story form this is a tightly plotted fair-play puzzle, in which Ellery and Nikki attend a Hallowe'en party in cat costumes and stay to find out who cut the throat of one of the guests in pitch darkness during a game of Murder. EQ fans might once again have been reminded of that oft-recycled 1935 short story "The House of Darkness," in which Ellery also had to figure out how a murder in a totally dark place was possible, but this time the problem is resolved in a substantially different way, although I'm still wondering how the killer could have anticipated that someone would suggest the murder game that was a precondition of the scheme's success.

The script of "The Cellini Cup" (November 12, 1939) has never been published, but a heavily condensed summary in a semi-story arrangement appeared in *Radio Guide* for January 26, 1940, as "Here Is a Mystery" under the byline of Ellery Queen. It's a minor exploit that begins with Ellery receiving a visit from an irate man who claims that an art-gallery proprietor cheated him out of a priceless cup from the hand of the great Benvenuto. The next day Ellery and Nikki attend the auction at which the cup is to be sold and encounter a variety of people with motives for wanting the item. That night the cup is stolen from the son of the art dealer, in total darkness and in the presence of Ellery and Nikki, but it takes Ellery no time at all to deduce who the thief was and how he vanished in the dark.

More interesting than the plot is an editorial sidebar accompanying the *Radio Guide* story, in which it was claimed that the Queen radio series had inspired regular Sunday evening whodunnit parties in living-rooms across the country, "where the armchair sleuths gather around the loudspeaker with loud shushes to hear the evidence and match wits with the personable and brilliant Ellery in reaching a solution to the mystery." George Zachary's dream of a detective series in which the listening audience would act as armchair sleuths had come true. Apparently this issue of *Radio Guide* came to the attention of Dannay and Lee, who had nothing to do with the prose version of the script and promptly let the editors know it, for the following week's issue contained an abject apology:

"In presenting this fictionization, our intent was to present an illustration of the program so that such of our readers as may not have heard this program would and could perceive the high interest it held out for listeners and would tune in. We indicated that this fictionization was written by Ellery Queen. It was not, and in fairness to the writers who are the real Ellery Queen, we want our readers to know this fact. In translating the drama of the broadcast into prose, our staff writer who did the fictionization undoubtedly lost some of the original qualities that have made the Ellery Queen novels the outstanding detective fiction of our day. For this, we are sorry, and we refer any reader who read that story to their many best-seller novels."

In November 1939 the Queen series experienced its first major cast change, with Howard Smith being replaced in the role of Sergeant Velie by Ted de Corsia, who was to keep the part for most of the program's long run. One of the first episodes featuring de Corsia was the Thanksgiving drama "The Telltale Bottle" (November 19, 1939), another of the dozen which Dannay and Lee later recast into a short story (this one published in *EQMM*, November 1946) whose ultimate home was the *Calendar of Crime* collection. At least in the prose version it's a dreadful effort, in which Ellery and Nikki go out delivering holiday food baskets to the poor, blunder into a cocaine-pushing operation and a murder, and resolve the mess through means both unworthy and incomprehensible.

The following week came "The Lost Child" (November 26, 1939), in which Ellery searches for a small boy who vanished shortly before the finalization of his parents' divorce. This script was the source of the later short story "Child Missing!" (*This Week*, July 8, 1951; collected in *Queen's Bureau of Investigation*, 1955). The following week's play, "The Man Who Wanted To Be Murdered" (December 3, 1939), was published eight months later as a rather creditable short story (*Radio and Television Mirror*, August 1940), without a byline but billed as "An Ellery Queen Mystery." A wheelchair-bound old gambler deliberately tempts his brother, nephew, niece and doctor into trying to murder him when he executes a will dividing most of his estate among them if he dies within one week but leaving everything to charity if he lives longer. Simultaneously the old man makes a $25,000 bet that Ellery can't solve his murder – which sure enough takes place on the last day of the specified week. Ellery connects a Caruso aria, a missing sock, and a solid glass ball that was replaced by a thin glass bubble and comes up with a neat solution.

The last play of the year was "The Scorpion's Thumb" (December 31, 1939), which was adapted into another story for *Radio and Television Mirror* (December 1940). At year's end Ellery is asked to look into an embezzlement from a Wall Street brokerage house but then a partner in the firm dies of a poisoned cocktail during a New Year's Day party. Ellery's solution is fair and satisfying even if a bit familiar to those who remember Queen's superb 1939 story "Man Bites Dog."

The first episode of 1940 was "The Dying Scarecrow" (January 7, 1940). Part one is set in July: Ellery, Nikki, the Inspector and Velie are driving through midwestern farm country when they stop to take home movies of a picturesque scarecrow and find a badly knifed man inside the scarecrow outfit. The victim pulls through but remains unidentified and vanishes from the local hospital soon afterwards. Six months later Ellery and his entourage return to the area during a blizzard and discover the same man once again, this time dead as a doornail and concealed inside a snowman in a farmyard. The solution rests on some neat deductions from the absence of the traditional pipe from the snowman's mouth.

By this time Fred and Manny were understandably beginning to feel the strain of coming up with a 60-minute radio script each week. The Queen series continued at hour length only for the first seven weeks of 1940, and two of those seven broadcasts were repeats. The final 60-minute episode, aired on February 18, was a repeat performance of "The Last Man Club." On February 25 the series was cut from sixty to thirty minutes and moved to the 8:00-8:30 p.m. (EST) time-slot on CBS's Sunday schedule. At around the same time an obscure actor named Arthur Allen took over the role of Doc Prouty from Robert Strauss. Of the first nine half-hour *Adventures of Ellery Queen* the only one that made it into published form is "The Emperor's Dice" (March 31, 1940), which Dannay and Lee later adapted into a short story (*EQMM*, April 1951; collected in *Calendar of Crime*, 1952). The characters and atmosphere are standard old-dark-house stuff and the puzzle revolves around the apparent ten-year-old murder of a millionaire collector of gambling implements. Ellery's elucidation of the "dying message" sounds like another Jon L. Breen parody, and the final twist, like that in the equally weak "The Three Rs," infuriates more than it surprises.

# CHAPTER FOUR

## Of Missing Magicians And Bleeding Mice

On April 28, 1940, *The Adventures of Ellery Queen* ceased being a "sustainer" and came under the sponsorship of the Gulf Oil Company. Its time-slot was moved back an hour to 7:30-8:00 p.m. and the character of Doc Prouty was dropped, but the rest of the continuing cast remained unchanged – Hugh Marlowe as Ellery, Santos Ortega as Inspector Queen, Ted de Corsia as Sergeant Velie, Marian Shockley as Nikki. Announcer Ken Roberts was replaced by a young man named Bert Parks, who is better remembered as host of the Miss America pageants than for his stint with the Queen show. In this format the series was broadcast over 66 CBS-affiliated stations for a total of 22 weeks. Fourteen of these episodes have been preserved: one on tape (albeit in a repeat performance of a few years later), two as unpublished scripts to which I've had access, and the rest as scripts printed in early issues of *EQMM* or elsewhere.

The first of these sponsored adventures was "The Double Triangle" (April 28, 1940), whose script was included in that hardest-to-come-by of all Queen story collections, *The Case Book of Ellery Queen* (Bestseller pb #B59, 1945). Although not a top-drawer play, it ties together so many strands from earlier exploits of Ellery that to the Queenphile it's a source of endless fascination. Ellery tries to locate the anonymous lover who's romancing the wife of a volatile young bookkeeper, but his efforts to keep the husband from murdering the lover culminate in his becoming a virtual eyewitness to the killing of the wife. The central clue depends on the ways in which a man puts away his clothes differently from a woman – the exact reverse of the situation in *The French Powder Mystery* (1930). The female who impersonates a male she wants to incriminate is derived from *The Dutch Shoe Mystery* (1931) and the triangular burn in the camel's-hair coat comes from the ripped coat in *The Devil to Pay* (1938). Fred and Manny were borrowing from themselves to the limits of their credit in this one!

Next week came "The Man Who Could Double the Size of Diamonds" (May 5, 1940; script printed in *EQMM*, May 1943), a most awkward title joined to a gorgeous plot. Ellery solves the murder of an eccentric scientist who claims to have discovered a chemical process for growing diamonds and simultaneously untangles the impossible theft of four such stones from a locked and heavily-guarded vault. The culprit "devised a theft of such colossal simplicity that I was nearly taken in by the complicated props," Ellery remarks at the summing-up – words that fit Queen's own best detective plots superbly.

The next few episodes were somewhat pedestrian but four out of five in a row survive in printed form. In "The Fire Bug" (May 12, 1940; script printed in *EQMM*, March 1943) Ellery investigates a series of suspicious blazes in his neighborhood, each of which destroyed a building owned by the same man. The fairness of his solution depends on how much high-school physics one remembers. In "The Honeymoon House" (May 19, 1940; script printed in *The Case Book of Ellery Queen*, 1945) love rivalries among the offspring of munitions manufacturers lead to a bride's murder on her wedding night and to a solution which Ellery admits is largely conjecture. In "The Mouse's Blood" (May 26, 1940; script printed in *EQMM*, September 1942, and in *The Fireside Mystery Book*, ed. Frank Owen, 1947) Ellery happens to be outside the house where a blackmailer is stabbed to death by one of the four athletes who were to have made payoffs to him that night, and he solves the murder by deducing which suspects are southpaws and which are right-handed. "The Good Samaritan" (June 9, 1940; script printed in *EQMM*, November 1942) poses an odd problem as Ellery hunts the elusive benefactor who's been sending stolen $100 bills to the needy tenants in a certain tenement. He finds his man by neat reasoning but never satisfactorily explains the mechanics of the elaborate cover-up that the fellow engineered for himself.

Ellery's job in "The Blind Bullet" (June 30, 1940; script printed in *EQMM*, September 1943) is to protect a ruthless tycoon from an anonymous enemy who has threatened to kill the magnate at a precise minute on a precise day. Sound familiar, Queen fans? It's the situation Dannay and Lee later made the springboard for that flawed but fascinating novel *The King is Dead* (1952). But in the radio play the threat is carried out in a pitch-black railroad tunnel under the noses of Ellery and his father, so that we're back to the murder-in-darkness gimmick that recurs so often in these adventures. Two weeks later Queen borrowed from himself once again in "The Frightened Star" (July 14, 1940; script printed in *EQMM*, Spring 1942), in which Ellery solves the locked-room death of a mysteriously "retired" Hollywood actress. The plot gimmick comes straight out of *The American Gun Mystery* (1934) and Ellery's main deduction presupposes listeners' familiarity with the workings of the Postal Savings System current in the early 1940s. Next came "The Treasure Hunt" (July 21, 1940), which I strongly suspect is an adaptation of Queen's 1935 short story of the same name (collected in *The New Adventures of Ellery Queen*, 1940), in which Ellery has to find a rope of pearls that one of a retired general's house guests stole from his daughter's bedroom and devises a treasure-hunting game as a psychological trap for the thief.

"The Black Sheep" (July 28, 1940) was never published per se but thanks to having a copy of the script I can describe it here. A masked thief steals a $15,000 payroll from the owner of a mill in the village of Fallboro and the victim's surly stepson is arrested for the crime on circumstantial evidence. The boy's distraught mother appeals to Ellery for help, and soon not only Ellery but the Inspector and Velie and Nikki are tramping through the quiet woods for clues. The play was repeated in 1944 as "The Robber of Fallboro" and recast several years later as a short story ("The Accused," *Today's Family*, February 1953; collected as "The Robber of Wrightsville" in *Queen's Bureau of Investigation*, 1955), in which a neater solution is grafted onto the identical plot.

I am lucky enough to have a copy also of the following week's script, "The Fatal Million" (August 4, 1940), in which Ellery hunts the impersonator who murdered the owner of a chain of roadside restaurants, posed as his victim during a secret sales transaction, and walked away with a suitcase containing a cool million in cash. The gimmick is rather routine and depends on the withholding from the listener of any information about the time the murder took place, but unless my memory is deceiving me this is one of the few Queen plays which Dannay and Lee neither based on a previously published plot idea nor utilized in a later novel or story. Another play of this sort was the next week's episode, "The Invisible Clock" (August 11, 1940; script printed in *The Case Book of Ellery Queen*, 1945), in which a priceless ruby disappears during a society ball Ellery and Nikki are attending. The clue is a clock that is heard ticking where no clock exists and the solution revolves around a device called a radio nurse which I gather was well known to the 1940 audience.

Fred and Manny were never terribly convincing when they introduced elements from the world of law and lawyers into the Queen novels, and they fared no better when they wrote a law-based Queen radio play. "The Meanest Man in the World" (August 18, 1940; script printed in *EQMM*, July 1942) opens with the kind of situation that makes so many mysteries laughable to lawyers: Ellery and Nikki are empaneled side by side as jurors in the same murder trial. The destitute defendant, Will Keeler, seems to be the only one who could have plunged the paperknife into the back of skinflint Sylvester Gaul's neck, but Ellery reads the evidence differently, jumps out of the jury box, cross-examines witnesses himself, and extracts a confession in open court from the real murderer. The plot itself is rather interesting, although a bit similar to the second murder in *The Dutch Shoe Mystery* (1931), but the courtroom behavior is strictly from *Alice in Wonderland.*

No crime at all is committed in "The Disappearing Magician" (September 15, 1940; the 1943 repeat performance under title of "The Vanishing Magician" is available on tape), but it's still one of the neatest episodes of the season. The scene is a two-story Chelsea brownstone owned in common by four decrepit ex-vaudevillians and threatened with mortgage foreclosure. Avanti the Magician tries to save the house for himself and his colleagues by issuing a challenge to Mr. Steele, a sharp businessman who has made a standing offer of $25,000 for any illusionist's trick he can't solve within 24 hours. Avanti claims that he can disappear from the brownstone after it has been minutely examined for secret compartments and while the place is surrounded by a small army of police. Inspector Queen generously supplies the bluecoat guards and the trick is miraculously pulled off. Ellery penetrates the gimmick but refuses to reveal his solution until the 24 hours are up.

The final episode of the Queen series broadcast on CBS and sponsored by Gulf, the last to star Hugh Marlowe as Ellery and to feature Bert Parks as the announcer, was "The Mark of Cain" (September 22, 1940; script printed in *The Pocket Mystery Reader*, ed. Lee Wright, Pocket Books pb #172, 1942). Ellery, Nikki, Sergeant Velie and Inspector Queen masquerade as servants in an attempt to prevent murder among the heirs of eccentric millionaire John Cain. After a full complement of clichés like the gloomy mansion with non-working lights and the enigmatic servant who prowls by night, a murder is indeed committed. It turns out that the killer knew four detectives were in the house, had no assurance that they wouldn't observe or interfere, yet went on to do in the victim for ridiculously weak motives. Ellery's solution rests on a creative variant of the ticket-book clue in *The Tragedy of X* (1932).

It had been a grueling fifteen months for everyone who had brought *The Adventures of Ellery Queen* to the air: Dannay and Lee, George Zachary, the regular cast of the show. To the end of his life Fred Dannay credited Hugh Marlowe, the first man to play Ellery on radio, with being the best interpreter of the role in that medium. In a letter of December 1947 to Anthony Boucher, Manny Lee registered a blistering dissent, describing Marlowe as "the greatest ham that ever strode the stage clad in imaginary buskins . . . The only thing the guy has is an organ-like voice which gives old ladies in Jersey City contractions of the uterus, what's left of it; but it's combined with a brain composed of murky and mysterious mud crawling with all sorts of algae, and the combination is frustrating." Certainly Manny wasn't pleased when George Zachary hired Marlowe to reprise the role of Ellery in *The Ford Theater* version of "The Bad Boy." "I wrote George to please, please try to take the stuffing out of Marlowe's shirt and make him sound – I know it can be done only approximately – like a human being." He must have been equally unhappy when Marlowe was chosen to play the role yet again in the filmed television series *The New Adventures of Ellery Queen* (1955-56).

If we are to believe an anecdote often told by Fred Dannay, Marlowe identified with Ellery so closely that at times during his tenure he lost track of the distinction between the character and himself. As Fred related (without mentioning Marlowe by name) in a

1947 reminiscence reprinted in *In the Queens' Parlor* (1957):

"One first-of-the-month [Manny and I] were shocked to receive a handful of statements from department stores and men's furnishing establishments for a large number of suits, shoes, and sundries, all charged to Ellery Queen. The curious fact was that we had never purchased any of the items listed. Naturally, we checked with the business firms in question, only to learn that a man calling himself Ellery Queen had opened the charge accounts and selected all the articles in person. Further investigation revealed that [Marlowe] had come to think of himself so realistically as Ellery Queen that he had stepped over the borderline of mere play acting and had become Ellery in the flesh . . . [He] had no intention whatever to defraud [and] paid all the bills out of his own pocket . . . But we have often wondered if the shirts he ordered were monogrammed and if the monogram was EQ."

Considering the breakneck conditions under which they had had to come up with scripts, Fred and Manny must have welcomed the end of the radio series as two men lost in the Sahara would welcome the sight of an oasis. The money had been satisfactory, the weekly exposure had been gratifying, but it was time to return to their other lines of work under the byline of Ellery Queen.

**Photo above: In 1941, Dannay (left) and Lee (center) celebrate the 100th anniversary of the publication of Edgar Allan Poe's *The Murders in the Rue Morgue* by visiting the Poe House in Philadelphia. The woman was the curator of the Poe House at the time.**

# CHAPTER FIVE

## The Time of the Talking Train

The fifteen months in which the Ellery Queen series was off radio were among the most fruitful in the creative lives of Fred Dannay and Manny Lee. It was during the hiatus that they wrote one of the finest Queen novels, *Calamity Town* (1942), which launched their third and richest period as mystery novelists. Dannay, the historian and bibliophile of the partnership, had substantially completed his collection of volumes of short stories of crime and detection, and he used this private library as the basis for editing *101 Years' Entertainment* (1941), the definitive anthology of short mystery fiction between Poe and Pearl Harbor. And when he found a huge number of first-rate stories left over after finishing that anthology, he persuaded publisher Lawrence E. Spivak to launch *Ellery Queen's Mystery Magazine*, which Dannay actively edited from its first issue (Fall 1941) until shortly before his death in 1982. Especially when one remembers that a near-fatal auto accident in 1940 had put him in the hospital for several weeks, workaholic seems much too mild a word for Dannay in his middle thirties. But as if all this effort weren't enough, late in 1941 the cousins decided to put their noses back against the radio grindstone and commit themselves once again to a script a week. Their highest priority became the return of Ellery Queen to the airwaves.

The reason why they felt they had to go back to radio was discussed most fully by Fred himself during his Carroll College appearance in 1979:

> "One day we wrote the best book that we thought we had written up to that time. It was a book called *Calamity Town*, and it was submitted in the usual way to a national magazine, and it was turned down. And we couldn't understand it. So we set up a three-party telephone conversation, a telephone conference with the editor and our agent and Manny and me. And I asked the editor certain questions like: 'Didn't you like the book?' And he said: 'Oh, I liked the book very much. In fact it's the best story you've sent to us.' So I said: 'Why didn't you publish it, why didn't you accept it?' And he said: 'I don't know.' So I said, 'May I probe?' And I said: 'Is it possible that our price has risen to the point where it's too high for your budget?' And he said: 'No.' And I said: 'Is it possible that you have too many stories in inventory and don't want to add to the inventory?' He said: 'No.' And I asked various other questions, and I finally wound up by saying: 'Why are you rejecting this manuscript?' And his answer was . . . 'I don't know.'
>
> So Manny and I walked out of our agent's office where the conference took place, and I think it was I who said to Manny: 'We'd better find another basket for our eggs, because we can't keep all our eggs in the basket we thought we could keep them in. If you can be turned down with no reason apparent on the best book you've ever written . . . then you've got to do something else'."

The two obvious contenders for the position of "something else" were the movies and radio. But their three stints as screenplay writers had been unsatisfactory, the pair of Ellery Queen movies in 1935-1936 had been wretched, and Columbia Pictures' then current EQ series, produced by Larry Darmour and starring Ralph Bellamy and later William

Gargan, wasn't much better. (In 1942, after seven pictures, Darmour died, and the series perished with him. In 1970 Dannay rightly described these pictures to British journalist Graham Lord as "each one more dreadful than the others.") Dannay and Lee had had to work a lot harder in radio, but they'd had far greater input into that medium and more luck with the results. So they asked their agent to find them a new network and a new sponsor.

*The Adventures of Ellery Queen* returned to the air in January 1942, one month after Pearl Harbor, on NBC's Red Network and under the sponsorship of the Emerson Drug Company, makers of Bromo-Seltzer. On the west coast it was heard Thursdays from 12:30 to 1:00 a.m. Eastern War Time (which translates to 9:30-10:00 p.m. conventional Pacific time), and on the east coast from 7:30 to 8:00 p.m. Saturdays. The role of Ellery was taken over by reliable utility actor Carleton Young (1907-1971). The new announcer for the series was Ernest Chappell and background music was supplied by organist Charles Paul. But Santos Ortega, Ted de Corsia and Marian Shockley were back as Inspector Queen, Sergeant Velie and Nikki Porter. George Zachary carried on as producer of the series, although others took over the director's chair. And of course Dannay and Lee were back with scripts that hewed to the same pattern as in 1939-1940. Indeed several episodes were simply tightened rewrites of 60-minute dramas from the program's earliest months on the air. "A new plot every week knocked me out," Dannay admitted in the late 1970s. It's no wonder that the cousins borrowed liberally from themselves, nor that some of their scripts were routine and mechanical in nature. What is astonishing is that so many Queen dramas were so good. In the memories of fans in the forties who became writers later, it was the best whodunit on the air.

One of those fans was Chris Steinbrunner (1933-1993), whose article "Challenges to the Listener" (*The Armchair Detective*, Summer 1979) conjures up the framework of the program.

"The audio memory machine clicks on. First the commercial, 'the one and only talking train' rolling you into the show, hoarse and chugging voice-box locomotives: 'Fiiight headache threeee ways! Bromo-Seltzer Bromo-Seltzer Bromo-Seltzer . . .' Then the smooth-voiced announcer (generally Ernest Chappell, who was also the velvet-mild spokesman for Pall Mall cigarettes, and whom Ellery with mischievous familiarity would always call 'Chappie') introduced you to the 'celebrated gentleman detective in person' – Ellery Queen. And Ellery 'invited you to match wits with him as he relates another story of a crime he alone unraveled.' Then, at the point where he is able to solve the mystery, he stops the play, [and] gives you a chance to solve the mystery."

That point was signaled by Ellery's announcement: "Now, Dad, I know who killed so-and-so." Then both he and Nikki would step out of their roles – a device which, according to Dannay many years later, "added distinction and suspense, and broke some radio rules" – and Nikki would introduce the evening's guest armchair detectives, who tended to be government bureaucrats, media personalities or people with special knowledge bearing on the plot. Ellery would ask each guest who he or she thought was guilty, the sleuths would propound and defend their solutions, then Ellery would step back into character and explain his own deductions to Nikki and his father and the perpetually dumbfounded Sergeant Velie and the audience. Finally the Maestro (as Velie called him) would step outside his role again, congratulate the rare armchair guest who had come up

31

with the right answer, and present all the guests with copies of the latest Queen novel or anthology plus a subscription to *EQMM*. Apparently they got a cash gift as well.

The first episode in the reconstituted Queen series was "The Song of Death" (January 8/10, 1942), in which Ellery visits a night club and becomes involved in the murder of a female FBI agent on the trail of counterfeiters. The following week's play, "The Invisible Clue" (January 15/17, 1942), has been preserved in the pages of a rare old anthology, *Adventures in Radio*, edited by Margaret Cuthbert (1945). A terrified man writes a letter asking Ellery to wake him up at seven o'clock the next morning. Thus the gentleman detective walks into the case of the unseen persecutor, which is reminiscent of G.K. Chesterton's famous Father Brown story "The Invisible Man" but without the overtones of GKC's religious philosophy. Ellery solves the puzzle appropriately enough through the invisible (i.e. negative) clue of the title, but I found it hard to believe that the victim wouldn't have thought of the answer himself while he was being exhaustively questioned.

The topical episode for the third week in February was "George Washington's Dollar" (February 19/21, 1942), which Queen later adapted as a short story, "The President's Half Disme" (*EQMM*, February 1947; collected in *Calendar of Crime*, 1952). Although the tale lacks any crime, it boasts an intellectual adversary fully worthy of Ellery's mettle, namely our first president. Ellery's challenge is to find a rare coin which Washington is believed to have buried on a remote Pennsylvania farm in 1791 and, though the answer is perhaps too obvious and the whole plot too dependent on multiple coincidence, the overall effect is delightful.

In the 1940s the income tax returns of all Americans had to be filed by March 15, so it was fitting that the Queen exploit broadcast closest to that date was "The Income Tax Robbery" (March 12/14, 1942), later revised as the short story "The Ides of Michael Magoon" (*EQMM*, March 1947; collected in *Calendar of Crime*, 1952.) Ellery's client this time is another detective – a middle-aged, overweight, asthmatic, nearsighted and mini-brained private eye who reports that someone stole all his income tax records from his briefcase 48 hours or so before the filing deadline. The oddball theft quickly balloons into a case of blackmail and murder which Ellery solves deftly, surprisingly and with full fairness to the reader. Although no tapes of this episode seem to be in circulation, a cassette is available for listening at the Library of Congress in Washington.

In "The Black Syndicate" (April 2/4, 1942) Ellery is called in when the head of an export firm disappears after his four partners, following his instructions, have liquidated the business and sent him all the proceeds. Manny Lee happened to visit the NBC studio during the rehearsal of this episode and met a young actress named Kaye Brinker who had a featured role. They began dating almost at once and were married three months later.

Next week came the disappointing "Ellery Queen, Swindler" (April 9/11, 1942; script printed in the Queen-edited anthology *Rogues' Gallery*, 1945). With no conceivable motivation except that he's German, a respectable jeweler named Adolf Humperdinck bamboozles one of his employees out of $4,000. Ellery enlists the equally unmotivated aid of a M. Jallet, who as a good Frenchman needs no reason for combating an Adolf, and works out a jewel-switching maneuver to get the young man's money back.

At the end of the month, in "The Millionaires' Club" (April 23/25, 1942), Ellery takes a hand when four members of a subgroup within a larger club of tycoons are threatened by a series of fatal "accidents." This episode was rerun at the end of 1944 as "The Inner Circle," the same title Fred and Manny used for their later adaptation of the script into a short story (*EQMM*, January 1947; collected in *Calendar of Crime*, 1952). In the story version, the plutocrats' club is transformed into the first graduating class of Eastern University, who call themselves the Januarians. One of that group's last living members visits Ellery shortly before the annual New Year's Day class reunion and tells of a survivor-take-all tontine among an "inner circle" of the class – and of the recent sudden deaths of three of the circle's members.

Listeners who were tuned in to the series during the last week in May heard the Memorial Day case of "The Old Men" (May 28/30, 1942), which Fred and Manny later adapted into the short story "The Gettysburg Bugle" (*EQMM*, May 1951, as "As Simple as ABC"; collected in *Calendar of Crime*, 1952). Ellery stumbles upon the hamlet of Jacksburg, Pennsylvania and into another case involving a tontine, whose last survivor is slated to enjoy a fabled Civil War treasure. The solution to the series of Memorial Day deaths among the town's Union Army veterans is neat and satisfying but takes a back seat to the depiction of patriotic solidarity in small-town America.

June being the traditional month for weddings, it was natural that Dannay and Lee would write a script entitled "The June Bride" (June 11/13, 1942) and equally natural that they'd later turn the script into a short story ("The Medical Finger," *EQMM*, June 1951) to represent that month in their 1952 collection *Calendar of Crime*. Ellery attends a wedding but has to put on his detective hat when the lovely and very wealthy young bride drops dead seven minutes after the ceremony. The chief but by no means sole suspect is a violent-tempered former boyfriend who had threatened to kill the woman rather than see her marry another man. Ellery has almost nothing to do with the solution and what deductions he does venture, at least in the short-story version, are illogical (neither eliminating the other suspects nor incriminating the guilty person conclusively) and come too late.

On July 4, 1942, Manny Lee married Kaye Brinker after a whirlwind three months' courtship. Not only was the ceremony unmarred by a murder but the marriage lasted until Lee's death almost twenty-nine years later. The wedding day was also the last day *The Adventures of Ellery Queen* was broadcast for the next three months, and the break gave Manny not only time for a honeymoon but afterwards the chance to work with Fred on the next Queen novel, *There Was an Old Woman* (1943), a labyrinth of plotting and deduction in a zany Lewis Carroll-like milieu. Reviewing the novel in the San Francisco *Chronicle* (March 28, 1943), Anthony Boucher said: "What it's most like is an E.Q. radio program in book length: the same freakish situation, grotesque characters, rapid movement, economical dialogue, low comedy relief. And the same consummate combination of devious trickery and absolute fairness that is the Queen trademark."

It was apparently during the three-month hiatus that the cousins had lunch with a visitor from Washington which led to radical alterations in the shape of some segments of the radio series. Fred Dannay recounted the incident while visiting the University of California in 1977:

"One day, and it happened to be me, I got a call from someone who said that he represented the head of OWI. And the head of OWI, which was the Office of War Information during World War II, was at that time Elmer Davis. He asked if he could meet the two of us for lunch in New York; he had something important to tell us. So of course we went down.

When we met him he said that they were having a problem with getting propaganda to the American people during wartime. There was a rule or a law at that time which said that if the United States government put on its own program it had to begin: 'The United States Government Presents . . .' And the moment you got to the word 'Presents' everybody turned the dial, because they didn't want to – they wanted entertainment, they didn't want this kind of open propaganda. So he said that they would like to crack this problem, and that they had thought and thought, and that the two of us, my partner and me, were the answer."

Earlier in 1942 George Zachary had left the Queen series to work for the OWI, and it's likely that he initiated the proposal made by the man from Washington – a proposal both breathtakingly simple and completely improper. Would Fred and Manny agree, without telling anyone at the network or the sponsor, to incorporate certain official propaganda motifs into some of their scripts so that "the message" would get across to unwary Americans in the guise of a detective story? They would retain complete control over their plots and the OWI would supply only the slogans. Fred and Manny said that they'd be happy to co-operate.

Fred first opened up this hidden page of history to me in 1972 or 1973, the time of the Viet Nam nightmare from which we still have not awakened, the time of Richard Nixon's assault on the traditions of freedom and integrity. Fred knew that I had been two years old at the war's end, that people of my generation could not feel in their blood the patriotic fervor that gripped the nation after Pearl Harbor any more than the people of the World War II generation could feel in their blood the intense revulsion at the government that was epidemic among the young of the late 1960s and early 1970s. He told me the OWI story with total frankness and let me deal with it in *Royal Bloodline* as I saw fit. If the parents of Viet Nam dissidents had been able to communicate with their children as Fred communicated with me, how much of the anguish of the Generation Gap might have been aborted!

# CHAPTER SIX

# Of Murdered Ships And One-Legged Men

In October the Queen program returned to NBC's Red Network with Carleton Young, Santos Ortega, Ted de Corsia and Marian Shockley all back in their respective roles as Ellery, Inspector Queen, Sergeant Velie and Nikki Porter. Ernest Chappell returned as the announcer, Bromo-Seltzer continued as sponsor, and the 39 episodes of the 1942-43 season were broadcast in the same east coast and west coast time-slots as before. The season's first drama, "The World Series Crime" (October 8/10, 1942), happens to survive on tape and provides a good example of how Dannay and Lee used a script as a vehicle for OWI propaganda. Three hours before the seventh game of the Series, the "Eagles" team hires Ellery to break the jinx on its powerhouse hitter, Sparky, by retrieving his lucky bat, Uncle Sam, which was stolen the morning after game three. Ellery succeeds just in time for Sparky's home run to lead the Eagles to victory and to demonstrate the OWI's slogan for the day: "You Can Always Trust Your Uncle Sam!" Ironically enough, in 1985 the Japanese publisher Gogaku Shunjusha printed the script as a booklet, with Japanese notes apparently aimed at helping youths in that country who were studying English.

Near the end of the year, in "The Yellow Ledger" (December 17/19, 1942), Ellery replaces a wounded FBI agent and deliberately walks into a trap while traveling to Washington with a ledger containing evidence against a Nazi spy ring. Long after the war Fred and Manny recast this play into a short story ("The Black Ledger," *This Week*, January 26, 1952; collected in *Queen's Bureau of Investigation*, 1955) with the Nazis replaced by a domestic crime syndicate.

In "The Singing Rat" (January 7/9, 1943; available on tape) Ellery investigates the disappearance from his father's office of a hollowed-out cigarette containing a document that incriminates four suspects. It's a glaringly artificial puzzle with a solution that could have occurred only to two men who had been chain smokers all their adult lives.

The next week's play was not only a distinct improvement but one of the finest in the entire eight years of the Queen series. "Mr. Short and Mr. Long" (January 14/16, 1943; script printed in *The Misadventures of Sherlock Holmes*, ed. Ellery Queen, 1944, as "The Disappearance of Mr. James Phillimore") is a superbly mounted specimen of the impossible problem, inspired by Dr. Watson's famous cryptic reference to the man who returned to his house for an umbrella and was never seen again. Confined to bed, Ellery functions as his own armchair detective, devising all sorts of wonderful suggestions as to how Phillimore could have vanished from a house surrounded by police, before finally topping even the best of them with a magnificent analysis of how the trick was really worked.

Two weeks later came one of the most unadulterated pieces of OWI propaganda that has survived from the Queen series, "Tom, Dick and Harry" (January 28/30, 1943; script printed in *EQMM*, July 1943, as "The Murdered Ship"). Ellery is summoned to Washington by "an extremely important official of the Government, who must remain anonymous." Whoever this bureaucrat is, he inspires in Ellery an all-but-religious awe. ("An urgent summons from such a distinguished Government official as yourself, Sir – I can't imagine why I should be so honored.") Nameless entrusts Ellery with a double mission: to find out how the slimy subs of the filthy Japs were able to ambush a heroic American convoy on the high seas, and why the captured enemy commander was carrying a note on him with the message "ELLERY Q." Accompanied by Nikki, Inspector Queen and Sergeant Velie, Ellery sets out on a cross-country journey to interview the families of every American killed in the ambush. After talking to literally thousands of people, he arbitrarily pieces together three little scraps of talk out of the millions of words he's heard, assumes that the countless Axis agents among us could do and had done likewise, and thereby demonstrates another OWI slogan: "The Slip of a Lip Can Sink a Ship." Literally!

OFFICIAL: Yes, if people would only remember not to talk about anything but what they hear over the radio or read in their newspapers!
INSPECTOR (quietly): We're all prone to be offenders once in a while, Sir. But we mustn't be – ever.
NIKKI: I'll make the resolution to keep my mouth shut – right now!
VELIE: That goes double.
ELLERY: Amen.
(The music comes up.)

A few years later, when this script was reprinted in Leslie Charteris's anthology *The Saint's Choice, Volume 7: Radio Thrillers* (1946), it was prefaced by a letter to Charteris from Manny Lee, explaining the genesis of this and similar Queen plays.

"This was a command performance, so to speak, by the OWI, with whom we co-operated in the "loose talk" campaign. As a special assignment from Washington, it represents – we think – something superior in radio propaganda, inasmuch as it doesn't bat its audience over the head, but approaches the lesson through entertainment.
This sort of program, serving a higher purpose than mere commercial entertainment, surely deserves being anthologized."

"All propaganda is lies," George Orwell wrote in his war diary, "even when one is telling the truth." If he had heard of these stern warnings to say nothing to anyone unless it's been released or approved by Big Brother, he might have thought that 1984 had come early.
In "The One-Legged Man" (February 25/27, 1943; script printed in *EQMM*, November 1943) Ellery visits a munitions plant on a mission for the nameless official of "Tom, Dick and Harry." The setting permits Dannay and Lee to push not one but two OWI slogans of the moment. One: War Is Good.

INSPECTOR QUEEN: See those cannon? Big babies!
NIKKI: Makes you feel all proud inside, Inspector.

Two: Keep Your Mouth Shut. Throughout most of the play's first half Ellery and his cohorts systematically humiliate any plant worker who tells them a blessed thing.

ELLERY: Miss Muller, do you know who I am? Any of us? . . . How do you know we can be trusted with this information? You haven't any idea how we got into the plant.
INSPECTOR: We might be carrying false credentials.

ELLERY: The fact is, you've told us a lot of things some Axis agent would give a great deal to learn!
MISS MULLER (nervously): I didn't say anything important. I'm just a secretary. . .
VELIE: It ain't your job to say what's important.
NIKKI (gently): You're working in a War plant, Miss Muller.

Ellery's assignment is to investigate some mysterious one-legged tracks in the snow within a sealed courtyard that forms part of the plant, but the case quickly becomes one of murder and sabotage when the head of the plant is incinerated to death by a booby-trapped pencil. Despite all the obtrusive propaganda, purely as a deductive puzzle this is one of the better entries in the series.

Four weeks later came "The Circus Train" (March 25/27, 1943; available on tape), in which Ellery, Nikki, the Inspector and Velie find that their return reservations on the train from Chicago to New York, have been commandeered by the Army. They manage to hitch rides in the passenger car of a circus train heading east, but while en route the show proprietor's skull is bashed in by the shoe of the circus giant and three $10,000 bills vanish from the speeding train. The denouement makes use of the two-solutions device so common in the Queen novels, but few will swallow the plot premise that the police would return the fatal shoe to its 8-foot-tall owner right after the murder.

In "Crime, Inc." (June 10/12, 1943; condensed version of script published as "The Crime Corporation" in *Story Digest*, November 1946), Ellery tries to deduce which of the surviving members of the so-called Secret Six who rule the city's organized criminals stabbed sextet kingpin Oscar Wunsch in the back shortly after Wunsch had framed another member of the group as a squealer and had him executed. The problem is that all four suspects seem to have unbreakable alibis. At least for longtime Queen readers, Ellery's solution would have been reminiscent of a device on which Fred and Manny had worked many a variation in their early novels.

This middle year of the war was the peak of success for the Queen series. In his profile of Dannay and Lee for the November 22, 1943 issue of *Life*, John Bainbridge reported the cousins' earnings as slightly more than $50,000 apiece per year. The vast bulk of that money came from the radio adventures, which were drawing more than fifteen million listeners every week. At the time Bainbridge interviewed them, Manny and Kaye Lee had moved into a charming old rented house at 5 Cannon St., Norwalk, Connecticut, where they lived with his two daughters by his first wife, Kaye's daughter by her first husband, and their own newborn daughter Christopher. (Motherhood didn't stop Mrs. Lee's continuing career as a radio actress under her professional name Kaye Brinker.) Fred and Mary Dannay and their sons were still living in Great Neck, although Mary was severely ill from cancer and virtually bedridden in the Dannay home.

Perhaps her absence as a force in Fred's life explains the bizarre outfit of loud sport blouse and bright corduroy trousers that he wore during the Bainbridge interview. He and Manny still met weekly at the 545 Fifth Avenue office, which they rented for $45 a month under their joint pseudonym. And, thanks largely to radio, that name had become so well known that whenever Fred dropped in the mail an empty envelope addressed to "Ellery Queen, N.Y." – and he did this as a sort of private Gallup poll every time he took a trip out of town – he invariably found the envelope waiting for him the next time he visited the EQ office. Indeed the Queen name was so prestigious that, shortly before the

Bainbridge interview, the New York *Journal-American* offered Dannay and Lee a fortune to go to the Bahamas and report on the sensational trial of Alfred de Marigny in the courts of Nassau for the murder of his wealthy American-born father-in-law Sir Harry Oakes. Their radio commitments and disinterest in true crime led them to turn down the paper's offer, which was then extended to and accepted by Erle Stanley Gardner, the creator of Perry Mason.

During the summer months of 1943 the Queen series aired thirteen reruns: a dozen from the 1940 season plus, during the appropriate week in late September, a rebroadcast of "The World Series Crime." Apparently Dannay and Lee used part of their free time to work on the next Ellery Queen novel, *The Murderer is a Fox* (1945).

That August, Carleton Young signed a Hollywood contract and left the series. He was replaced by Sydney Smith (1909-1978), a seasoned professional in both radio and the theatre who in the late 1930s had done live broadcasts of *Gang Busters*, literally on the same evenings he was playing Laertes on the stage opposite Maurice Evans as Hamlet. In a letter he wrote me in 1977, Smith described how he got the Ellery Queen job:

"I was well enough established as a radio actor that I knew when they had auditions I would be called. Since I had always been a mystery fan in general and Ellery in particular (and also because the salary budgeted for the part was generous) I decided to do some research so I perhaps might have an edge. I read and reread all the [Queen] novels in order to establish a distinctive approach. I decided the intent was to create an American [Sherlock] Holmes. I took the novels in chronological order and discovered a change in [Ellery's] outward characteristics . . . The later ones were not as fussy as the earlier. This gave [Ellery] more of a sophisticated manner than before. Keeping that in mind, I began to work on a characterization. As for the outward vocal characterization, I adopted a Ronald Colman approach but with no attempt to ape an English intonation or accent. I was pleased when Manny [Lee] said I was an American Sherlock."

Good as Smith was in the role of Ellery Queen – and he was good enough to keep the part for more than three years, longer than any other actor in any medium – one suspects that listeners noticed the differences in voices. But it's unlikely that anyone was aware of the next change in the regular cast. Near the end of the summer reruns, Marian Shockley, whose husband George Zachary had transferred from the OWI to the Navy and by then was stationed in the Pacific, took two months' leave from the role of Nikki on her doctor's orders. Her stand-in was Helen Lewis, who had been her roommate six years earlier at the Rehearsal Club, a residence hall for hopeful actresses. Lewis's specialty was voice impersonations, and on the *March of Time* program she had mimicked everyone from the Queen of England to Eleanor Roosevelt to Ginger Rogers. During her two months as Nikki she made it a point to sound as much as possible like Shockley.

It was with these changes in personnel – Sydney Smith as Ellery, Helen Lewis as Nikki, Santos Ortega and Ted de Corsia valiantly carrying on as Inspector Queen and Sergeant Velie – that the next cycle of EQ's audio exploits opened in October.

38

# CHAPTER SEVEN

# Of Dauphins' Dolls and Booby Traps

For the rest of 1943 and all of 1944 *The Adventures of Ellery Queen* was on the air every single week with no time off. Sydney Smith, Santos Ortega, Ted de Corsia and announcer Ernest Chappell continued in their accustomed parts every week through the long stretch, but Helen Lewis left the role of Nikki after the first episode of November 1943 and Marian Shockley returned to the part the following week.

If Fred Dannay and Manny Lee fell behind schedule or if Fred failed to come up with a new idea in a given week, the cousins had only two alternatives: either to condense a 60-minute drama from 1939-1940 into half-hour form, or to recycle one of the golden oldies from the first season of 30-minute plays. Research confirms that they exercised both options rather often. Taking instances of the first option first, "The Disaster Club" (January 6/8, 1944)is a condensed version of "The Last Man Club," second of the 60-minute episodes from 1939; "The Scarecrow and the Snowman" (January 20/22, 1944; available on tape) is a rewrite of "The Dying Scarecrow" from early 1940, and stacks up very well indeed against the first-run episodes of four years later. "Wanted: John Smith" (March 9/11, 1944) is based on "The Devil's Violin" from January 1940, and "The Glass Ball" (March 23/25, 1944) on "The Silver Ball" from March of that year. "Dead Man's Cavern" (April 13/15, 1944; available on tape) is derived from the October 1939 episode "The Haunted Cave" and "The Buried Treasure" (April 27/29, 1944) from the even earlier "The Lost Treasure". "The Thief in the Dark" (May 4/6, 1944) was originally the hour-long episode "The Cellini Cup" and in fact some of the scenes preserved on tape in the Armed Forces Radio Service "sneak preview" of this episode contain dialogue identical to lines of "Cellini" as they were printed without permission in *Radio Guide* back in 1940. "The Great Chewing Gum Mystery" (May 25/27, 1944) was a condensation of the first of all the Queen radio plays, "The Gum-Chewing Millionaire." "The Murder Game" (June 1/3, 1944) comes from "The Dead Cat"; "The Dark Secret" (June 8/10, 1944) from "The Black Secret"; "The Corpse in Lower Five" (June 22/24, 1944) from "Napoleon's Razor"; "The Egyptian Tomb" (July 6/8, 1944) from "The Pharaoh's Curse"; "The College Crime" (September 14/16, 1944) from "The Three Rs." Moving on to the second option, at least seven episodes from this period were first heard in the summer of 1940: "The Frightened Star" (October 21/23, 1943), "The Vanishing Magician" (November 4/6, 1943; originally titled "The Disappearing Magician"); "The Egyptian Tomb" (July 6/8, 1944; originally titled "The Pharaoh's Curse"); "The Man Who Wanted Cash" (August 17/19, 1944; originally titled "The Fatal Million"); "The Mayor and the Corpse" (August 24/26, 1944; originally titled "The Picnic Murder"); "The Robber of Fallboro" (September 21/23, 1944; originally titled "The Black Sheep"); and "The Invisible Clock" (September 28/30, 1944). An eighth episode, "The Inner Circle" (December 28/30, 1944), dates back to April 1942 when it was called "The Millionaires' Club." Overworked as they were during this period of intense pressure, Fred and Manny recycled as much of their earlier output as was humanly possible.

Of course there were also a respectable number of brand-new episodes that were heard during 1943-44. One of the best from that period was that audacious miracle problem "The Dauphin's Doll" (December 23/25, 1943), which was unique among the 355

39

episodes of the series in that it was written by Manny Lee alone, without any input from Fred Dannay. Ellery, his father and dozens of the Inspector's men join forces to protect the titular doll and its diamond crown from the legendary thief Comus, who announces that he'll make the figure vanish while it's on exhibition at a major department store on the day before Christmas. Despite a gauntlet of security arrangements Comus lives up to his boast, but Ellery's reasoning exposes the working of the miracle and nets both thief and loot as Christmas dawn floods the city. Manny later recast this script into the short story of the same name (*EQMM*, December 1948; collected in *Calendar of Crime*, 1952), which is equally dazzling.

On the other hand "The Mischief Maker" (January 13/15, 1944; available on tape) is a routine exercise with Ellery trying to find out who's writing poison-pen letters to the residents of a single apartment building – the exact obverse of the problem in "The Good Samaritan." The motivation for the letter-writing binge turns out to be ridiculous and Ellery's key deduction pedestrian.

In "The Dark Secret" (June 8/10, 1944), which as we've seen is a 30-minute version of the hour-long first-season episode "The Black Secret," the tyrannical owner of a rare-book emporium fires all his help after the theft of some valuable first editions, and Ellery and Nikki apply for clerks' jobs in order to find the missing volumes and save the innocent employees' positions. There's no way to judge how ingenious the solution was for, as with "The Thief in the Dark," all that exists of this episode are a few "sneak preview" scenes on tape from the Armed Forces Radio Service.

And speaking of the armed forces, what ever happened to the cousins' commitment to lace a certain number of Queen scripts with OWI material? No episodes heard on the regular series in 1944 have titles that clearly signal a propaganda blitz, but there is a 15-minute script that was broadcast as a "special" under the overt sponsorship of OWI and was published that summer in *EQMM*. Like "Tom, Dick, and Harry" from the previous year, "The Wounded Lieutenant" (available on tape; script published in *EQMM*, July 1944) is another diatribe against "loose talk." This time the military catastrophe takes place in the China-Burma-India theater and once again Ellery demonstrates that agents of the fiendishly clever enemy are ever waiting to overhear scraps of casual chatter and deduce from them the plans for D-Day or whatever.

"The Foul Tip" (July 13/15, 1944; available on tape) is free of Big Brother messages and full of Dannay and Lee's love for the great American game of baseball. For publicity reasons a New York press agent arranges a reserved box at a big-league game for cowboy movie star Chick Ames and several other people – such as Ames's nightclub-dancer wife and her oily Latin rumba partner – who would like to see Ames dead. In the box Ames agrees to sign some autographs for his pint-sized fans, but when, as is his habit, he moistens the tip of the pencil with his tongue, suddenly he's a corpse, for one of the pencils he's been handed was coated with poison. With great reluctance Ellery leaves his own box seat and solves the crime, which is a variant on the gimmick in Queen's great 1939 baseball-murder story "Man Bites Dog."

Only two episodes of the series survive from late 1944, and to hear one of them you must visit the Library of Congress where a cassette is preserved. In "The Booby Trap" (November 9/11, 1944) Ellery is dragooned into appearing as a guest on the radio quiz program "Life and Literature," whose host Sid Sherman is a wizard at identifying literary quotations and allusions. After the show Sherman is murdered by a bomb inserted into a hollowed-out copy of *Alice in Wonderland* and planted in his study. But just before dying

Only two episodes of the series survive from late 1944, and to hear one of them you must visit the Library of Congress where a cassette is preserved. In "The Booby Trap" (November 9/11, 1944) Ellery is dragooned into appearing as a guest on the radio quiz program "Life and Literature," whose host Sid Sherman is a wizard at identifying literary quotations and allusions. After the show Sherman is murdered by a bomb inserted into a hollowed-out copy of *Alice in Wonderland* and planted in his study. But just before dying he manages to pull down a few books from his shelves – one each by Shaw, Shakespeare, Walt Whitman and Ulysses S. Grant – and Ellery's challenge is to translate Sherman's last literary act into the name of his murderer. Many years later, in the short story "Enter Ellery Queen" (*Argosy*, June 1960; collected as "Mystery at the Library of Congress" in *Queen's Experiments in Detection*, 1968), Dannay and Lee recycled the same gimmick with a different plot.

Whether working with new scripts or with plays that originally had starred Hugh Marlowe or Carleton Young, Sydney Smith took to the part of Ellery like a cat to a mouse. Indeed, like Marlowe before him, he apparently convinced himself for a time that he was Ellery Queen in the flesh. As a publicity gimmick NBC was keeping the identity of the actor who played Ellery a secret, and in newspaper stories dealing with the series he was usually photographed with his back to the camera. The network even booked him in his EQ persona as a guest on various NBC talk shows and elsewhere. The character of Ellery made a guest appearance on *The Texaco Star Theater* starring Fred Allen, during the summer of 1944. Another was *The Colgate Sports Newsreel* starring Bill Stern, broadcast on September 1, 1944. Ellery was also a guest detective on the radio quiz program *Quick As A Flash* for at least two broadcasts. January 21, 1945 and October 21, 1945.

One of the non-broadcast appearances was at Carnegie Hall, where "Ellery" was scheduled to lecture to a large group of children on the subject "Crime Does Not Pay." Anya, Kaye Brinker Lee's 10-year-old daughter by her first marriage, happened to be taking ballet lessons at one of the Carnegie Hall studios, and she and her mother were more than mildly surprised to read the placards on the building walls announcing that Ellery Queen was to make a public appearance. Kaye checked with Manny, who in turn checked with Fred, and after Smith's lecture the cousins pointed out to him that he was not authorized to play Ellery anywhere but on the weekly radio program. As Fred described the incident in a 1947 memoir reprinted in *In The Queens' Parlor* (1957), Smith

". . . was both amazed and resentful. Why, he had done no harm--indeed, in his opinion he had done the real Ellery Queen a favor! Hadn't he been the instrument of considerable publicity? Hadn't he been photographed? How could the real Ellery Queen be offended? Why, we should actually be grateful! When we pointed out that there was one small error in his thinking – the small matter of the wrong person having been publicized and photographed – [Smith] woke with a start and half of the double image in his mind suddenly evaporated."

But the matter was no more than a tempest in a teapot, and Smith carried on as Ellery without further fuss. NBC continued to broadcast and Bromo-Seltzer to sponsor the series until the end of 1944. After the last episode of December, which as we've seen was a retitled retread from two-and-a-half years earlier, the Queen series left the air for almost a month.

# CHAPTER EIGHT

## New Blood on the Typewriter Keys

When *The Adventures of Ellery Queen* returned to the air, it had migrated from NBC back to the CBS network where it had been born and Anacin had taken over the sponsorship from Bromo-Seltzer. Its new time-slot was from 7:30 to 8:00 p.m. on Wednesday evening. Sydney Smith, Santos Ortega and Ted de Corsia still played Ellery, Inspector Queen and Sergeant Velie, but Marian Shockley had retired from the role of Nikki and been replaced by Barbara Terrell. Don Hancock took over the announcer's duties from Ernest Chappell, a new organist whose name is unknown sat down at the bench formerly occupied by Charles Paul, and new producers and directors were assigned to the show as well. With only two brief summer vacations the series remained on CBS from late January of 1945 until mid-April of 1947.

What was not known outside the inner circle of the production team was that Fred Dannay was no longer involved with the series, having found it impossible to go on dreaming up the plots for so many Queen scripts so quickly. His wife Mary was suffering from cancer and near death (which came to her later in 1945) and Fred knew he'd have to make arrangements for himself and his 12- and 6-year-old sons. In the time he had left for work he wanted to concentrate on the projects he found more congenial, like editing the monthly issues of *EQMM* and compiling hardcover anthologies of short mystery fiction and creating plots for new Ellery Queen novels. But he didn't want and, especially with two children to raise, couldn't afford to give up his share of the huge weekly checks that the radio series was generating.

To the creator of Ellery Queen the solution of the problem was simplicity itself. In the early years of the radio program Fred and Manny had authorized the publication of *Radio and Television Mirror* short stories and two Whitman Better Little Books, all based on Queen scripts but adapted into prose versions by uncredited authors and issued under the Ellery Queen byline. If prose adaptations could be successfully subcontracted, why couldn't the creation of the detailed plot outlines that were Fred's contributions to the radio show? As long as the writers who took over the Dannay function were chosen with sufficient care, the listening audience wouldn't be able to tell the difference.

The first person picked for the role of plot creator was Tom Everitt, a professional radio scripter about whom little is known except for the titles of the episodes on which he worked with Manny Lee. As chance would have it, a substantial excerpt from the first of these has been preserved on tape as another of those "sneak previews" from the Armed Forces Radio Service. "The Diamond Fence" (January 24, 1945) involves the murder of a middleman for stolen gems and the disappearance of five diamond rings from the scene of the crime under impossible circumstances. The scenes on tape make it sound like a puzzler of the first water.

For the next five-and-a-half months the vast majority of EQ episodes were written by Lee from plot synopses by Everitt. Then a new idea generator was brought in to provide plots for Ellery to unravel.

The man who took over this function and continued in it till the series went off the air was Anthony Boucher (1911-1968), the well-known mystery writer and reviewer of whodunits for the San Francisco *Chronicle* and later the New York *Times*. It was an ideal selection. Boucher had started writing detective novels out of admiration for fair-play masters like Queen, his character Fergus O'Breen had been conceived as a sort of West Coast Ellery Queen with an Irish brogue, and several Boucher short stories had already been published in *EQMM*. In addition, as shown by his comments in the San Francisco *Chronicle*, he was a fan of the radio series. Beginning with "The Corpse of Mr. Entwhistle" (June 13, 1945), about 70 of the *Adventures of Ellery Queen* scripts were the joint work of Boucher, who was never credited, and Manny Lee.

Both Boucher and Dannay were devotees and practitioners of the pure deductive problem that played eminently fair with the consumer, but their personalities were poles apart. Fred was an apolitical person, uninvolved in causes, at home in abstractions, a private man in almost every sense of the phrase. Boucher like Manny Lee was a public man, a political activist and a staunch liberal. Unlike either Fred or Manny, Boucher was deeply religious. When Fred was with the series, his specialty had been the kind of script in which Ellery would confront three or four suspects with diagrammatic names and purely functional characterizations – Mr. Anson the attorney, Mr. Benson the ballplayer and Mr. Charleson the cheesemaker – and would deduce that only one of them possessed a trait which the murderer must have had. Boucher could conjure up this kind of story-line as well as Dannay but his tended to be more rooted in the real world and he devoted more care to rounded characterizations. And during the years of the Boucher-Lee regime, Ellery was portrayed less as the Celebrated Gentleman Detective and more as the Socially Concerned Citizen.

Boucher's file copies of 77 synopses, each one banged out in minuscule type on six or eight sheets of yellow paper, are preserved at Indiana University's Lilly Library, along with copies of most of the final scripts as fleshed out by Lee and of the Boucher-Lee correspondence. Reading this material is a fascinating experience akin to traveling backward in time. Boucher's synopses are almost like friendly letters, full of little asides in which he explains to Manny where this or that plot notion came from or what movie actor Boucher had in mind in creating this or that suspect. Comparing any given synopsis with the final script reveals that Manny often made radical changes in Boucher's conceptions. Indeed several synopses (including the three printed in this book) were never used at all.

On the other hand, some of the broadcast scripts whose origins remain unknown to this day may have been based on Boucher synopses that for some reason were never deposited at the Lilly. Born list-maker that he was, Boucher numbered most of the synopses he sent Manny Lee. The highest number he used was 77. Does this mean he wrote exactly 77 synopses, no more and no less? Hardly! The Lilly archives contain two separate and distinct synopses numbered 14 and none at all with the numbers 18, 21, 24 or 28. Does this mean Boucher never used these numbers? Perhaps. But as Ellery Queen himself might have asked, why would a systematic person like Boucher have skipped them? Isn't it just as likely that the Lilly either never received or misfiled the synopses to which he assigned those numbers? Close examination of Boucher's correspondence with Manny Lee confirms that four scripts with previously unknown origins were indeed based on Boucher synopses that somehow never made it to the Lilly. Does this mean that we know for sure that Boucher wrote exactly 78 synopses, no more and no less? Hardly! The Lilly also has three synopses numbered 13a, 15a and 17a. To how many other synopses might Boucher have assigned a number with a letter after it? Any script that can't be traced to a source might possibly have been based on a lost Boucher synopsis. All we can say for sure is that Boucher prepared at least 81 synopses, 77 of which are at the Lilly. My own view is that there are no unknown others but I've been wrong before.

Of the last ten episodes from the series' fifth season, eight were demonstrably based on Boucher synopses. The only one known to survive on tape is "Nick the Knife" (August 1, 1945), which is not only immensely exciting in its own right but historically crucial as a forerunner of perhaps the finest Queen novel of all, *Cat of Many Tails* (1949). A madman has slashed the wrists and faces of more than thirty beautiful women on the night streets of Manhattan. Finally a woman is attacked inside an ornamental maze with only one exit, which is being watched by Ellery and several policemen. But later events seem to prove beyond a doubt that not one of the handful of suspects found in the maze could possibly be the slasher. Ellery resolves the dilemma magnificently, although most listeners probably fell into the trap for the overly clever that Boucher and Lee cunningly built into the story.

After Boucher and Lee's "The Time of Death" (August 15, 1945) the series took a brief vacation, coming back on the air three weeks later for a sixth season that lasted a full 52 weeks, with no changes in sponsorship, network or time-slot and only one newcomer in the regular cast, namely Gertrude Warner, who had replaced Barbara Terrell as Nikki four weeks before the end of the previous season. Boucher provided the plots for 36 of these episodes, Tom Everitt for four, newcomer Richard Manoff for two. At least five and possibly six new episodes were written by Lee based on synopses by Fred Dannay and held in reserve against emergencies after Fred left the series. The origins of three or perhaps four episodes remain unknown. One was a rerun from the war years.

How much Everitt and Manoff and the other synopsis writers (if any) were being paid remains unknown, but Boucher's compensation is clear from Manny Lee's letter of November 29, 1945: of the $2,000 being paid by the sponsor for each script, Manny was receiving roughly $1,000, Fred Dannay (who of course had dropped out of the series completely by this time) roughly $500, and Boucher roughly $500 for each of his synopses that Manny turned into a script. These are only approximations because Dannay and Lee were paying the agent commissions on Boucher's take out of their own shares.

The fourth episode of the season was "The Green House" (September 26, 1945). Both Lee's script and the untitled Boucher synopsis on which he based it are preserved at the Lilly. In both versions Ellery is kidnapped and taken to a mythical country to solve a crime for its dictator. Boucher in his synopsis points out to Lee that he named his imagined country San Pedro after the banana republic whose fugitive dictator figured in the Sherlock Holmes story "The Adventure of Wisteria Lodge" (1908). Lee kept Boucher's plot but changed the setting to a postage-stamp dictatorship in middle Europe that he called Serakia. The concept of Ellery being dragged off to solve a crime in an isolated fascist domain was recycled by Dannay and Lee a few years later in their novel *The King is Dead* (1952).

In "The Kid Glove Killer" (October 10, 1945) Ellery's quarry is a masked criminal who committed murder in order to steal a box of kid gloves from a men's store. Boucher's version is entitled "The Criminous Commando" and deals with a masked thief who wears an outfit resembling that of a World War II commando and who is described differently by everyone who sees him.

In "The Message in Red" (November 7, 1945) a public stenographer, a manuscript reader for a publishing house and a French maid are all shot to death on the same night with the same gun, and Ellery soon realizes that someone is out to drop a certain incriminating document down the memory hole by killing everybody who's seen it. The "dying message" solution is rather tame but, being based on the fact that people tend to think in their native language in times of crisis, it hints at the multi-lingual Boucher. And sure enough, a document in the Boucher-Lee correspondence files confirms that Lee's script was based on Boucher's synopsis "The Calloused Maid," which is missing from the Lilly. Luckily the episode survives on tape.

"The Ape's Boss" (November 21, 1945) finds Ellery trying to identify the secret mastermind who's giving orders to Ape Loogan, the moronic front man for a gang whose crimes are terrorizing the city. Boucher's more topical synopsis, "The Reluctant Restaurateur," had the proprietor of Ellery's favorite restaurant blown up by a time bomb after telling the sleuth he's being forced to buy meat from a black market ring led by a mystery man. In these months just after the war, Lee seemed to be trying to eliminate as much wartime ambiance as possible from Boucher's plots.

A sixth-season episode that is preserved not entire or on tape but condensed and in print hints at a Boucher connection just like "The Message in Red." In "The Curious Thefts" (December 19, 1945; condensation of script published in *Story Digest*, September 1946) a well-known novelist whose marriage is collapsing comes to Ellery for help when his household is plagued by a rash of bizarre pilferings culminating in murder. The solution presupposes a fairly intimate knowledge of the Bible like Boucher's own, but the title doesn't appear in the legal document I found at the Lilly, listing all of Boucher's contributions to the series through early 1946. My hunch is that this is yet another of those plays based on synopses by Fred Dannay that Manny had held back after Fred's departure in case there were a sudden need for a script. My reason? There are curious similarities between this episode and certain elements in Queen's powerful religious detective novel *Ten Days' Wonder* (1948). Perhaps someday we'll know for sure.

Three episodes from the early months of 1946 nicely illustrate how Lee's final drafts altered Boucher's originals. "The Green Eye" (January 16, 1946) pits Ellery against an international criminal who, doubtless inspired by the stick figures habitually left behind by Simon Templar the Saint, leaves an eye drawn in green ink at the scene of each of his jewel robberies. For the most part Lee followed Boucher's synopsis, "The Stormy Petrel," but in Boucher's version the criminal left bird drawings as his sign.

Much more radical changes can be seen in "Ellery Queen's Tragedy" (January 30, 1946). The Boucher synopsis at the root of this episode was entitled "Murder at EQMM" and had Ellery solve a murder in the offices of his own magazine, the victim being a Frenchman in New York to locate a fellow countryman who had stories published in *EQMM*. By the time Lee had rewritten the story, it became that of two men who show up in New York claiming to be the famous French mystery writer for whom a fortune in wartime U.S. royalties is waiting. *EQMM* is left completely out of Manny Lee's version. Manny goes on to have the impostor shoot Inspector Queen and leave him near death, apparently because Santos Ortega was taking a leave of absence from the part and somehow or other had to be written out of the series for a while.

Manny Lee was not the easiest of taskmasters, as we can see in a letter of January 30, 1946 where he criticizes "The Scarlet Ghosts," Boucher's latest synopsis. "When I actually got into it – in fact, the first draft was half-finished – I suddenly made the ghastly discovery that the 'solution' didn't solve a goddam thing. It had a hole big enough to take a nap in – and no way that I could see of stopping it up without chinks and crannies, although I spent two full days trying to do just that thing . . . Finally I saw the handwriting on the wall and gave up. Behind schedule, harassed and biting my nails – I threw the whole damn thing out and invented brand-new material which affected the entire second half of the show and, of course, gave you a new solution entirely." Lee's script based on this synopsis was "The Living Dead" (February 13, 1946).

"The Phantom Shadow" (March 6, 1946) was based on a Boucher synopsis called "The Shadow of Murder" in which a woman visits Ellery and claims that while working late at night, she witnessed a murder through the window of the lawyer's office across the street, although when the office was examined neither a corpse nor any signs of a struggle were found. Lee kept the basic plot, which is an obvious take-off on Cornell Woolrich's classic "Rear Window" (1942), but in his version the woman is Nikki, who witnesses the murder that wasn't while substituting on a night secretarial job for a girlfriend.

The only sixth-season episode known to be by Boucher and Lee and preserved on tape (in a repeat performance dating from two years later) is "The Armchair Detective" (March 27, 1946), a rare gem in which Ellery solves a poisoning that takes place on the Queen radio show itself. The idea obviously came to Boucher from Orson Welles' 1938 adaptation of *The War of the Worlds*, which convinced thousands of panicky listeners that Martians had invaded Earth. But the dying-message situation is a neat one indeed: first Ellery interprets the clue in the conventional way, then he gets fancy and works out a much more complex reading, whose possibility the killer has also seen and planted evidence to support.

"Mr. Warren's Profession" (June 5, 1946) is based on Boucher's synopsis "The Man Who Liked Bad Puns," in which Ellery probes the murder of a professional blackmailer who, just before dying, intoned "The safe...is safe" and shook a bell upside down. In Lee's script the blackmailer is addicted to making wordplays based on book titles and his dying message is wordless, consisting only of ringing a bell over and over in double peals.

In "Cokey and the Pizza" (June 19, 1946) Lee fairly closely follows Boucher's synopsis "The Perilous Pizza," in which Ellery tries to figure out how a fugitive gangster holed up in a room above an Italian restaurant is being supplied with cocaine. The titular dish was so unfamiliar to the 1946 radio audience that both the synopsis and the final script include a scene where Ellery explains to Nikki what pizza is while they watch one being made. In his synopsis Boucher even spells the word phonetically, peet-za, so that it won't be mispronounced over the airwaves!

The last of the scripts that Manny Lee had written from a Fred Dannay synopsis and was holding in reserve was "The Doomed Man" (August 28, 1946), in which Ellery uses a candlestick clue to clear a young man charged with the murder of his father. After that episode the series left the air for a vacation well-earned by everyone but perhaps most of all by Tony Boucher, whose radio commitments at their peak involved writing script synopses for the Queen program, the Basil Rathbone-Nigel Bruce *Sherlock Holmes* series, and *The Case Book of Gregory Hood*, a detective show in the Queen vein created by Boucher and Denis Green, who fleshed out each of Tony's *Holmes* and *Hood* synopses into a full script, just as Manny Lee was doing on the EQ program. Being one of those rare people who lives joyously at 78 r.p.m. while the rest of the world revolves lazily at 33, Boucher thrived on that kind of life.

On October 9 the Queen series returned to the air for a seventh season, this one lasting 27 weeks and with a much tighter budget. According to a letter from Manny Lee to Boucher dated September 12, the total script allocation had been cut by one-third so that Manny would now receive $600 per script, Fred Dannay $300, and Boucher $450. But by now Boucher was so deeply involved with *Holmes, Hood* and countless additional projects that he found time to contribute only ten new synopses for Manny Lee to expand into scripts. Tom Everitt provided eleven, Richard Manoff four, pulp veteran Ken Crossen one, and one episode was a retitled Dannay-Lee rerun from the war era. Since Gertrude Warner had recently married and retired from radio, the producers needed a new Nikki Porter for the seventh season and, after auditioning more than forty actresses, hired Charlotte Keane.

Six weeks into the season a format change that had been under discussion for some time was implemented. Beginning with Manoff and Lee's "The Prize Fighter's Birthday" (November 20, 1946) the guest armchair detectives in the studio were dropped and instead, at the point where Ellery issued his Challenge to the Listener, he placed a long-distance phone call to a pre-selected member of the home audience and invited him or her to deduce whodunit. The experiment was dropped after two and a half months and the series returned to celebrity armchair sleuths.

At some time late in 1946 or early in 1947, and perhaps simultaneous with the temporary abandonment of celebrity guests, the three longest-lived of the four regulars in the *Ellery Queen* cast were replaced: Ted Corsia as Sergeant Velie by Ed Latimer, Santos Ortega as Inspector Queen by Bill Smith, and Sydney Smith, who had played Ellery since the summer of 1943, by Richard Coogan (1914- ), the oldest person alive to have portrayed the master sleuth in any medium. After "The Hunted House" (February 5, 1947) Coogan in turn was replaced by Lawrence Dobkin (1919 - ), the second oldest person alive to have played Ellery and the author of this book's Introduction.

In "The Crooked Man" (March 12, 1947) Ellery frames himself for Nikki's murder in order to set a trap for a blackmailing private eye. The head of the blackmail ring eventually captures Ellery and taunts him with the clue that the key to the combination of the safe containing the crucial evidence may be found in the second verse of the nursery rhyme "Simple Simon." Lee changed the clue from the hint Ellery is given in Boucher's version – that the safe "is doubly guarded by magic numbers – the Bullet and the Beast" – because he thought it was both too difficult and likely to run into censorship problems. Why Manny thought so you will understand if you grasp Tony's clue.

# CHAPTER NINE

## Of Clubbs and Frogs And Social Ills

During the second half of April 1947 and all of May, the Queen series again left the air. On its return it was still sponsored by Anacin, but in virtually every other respect – network affiliation, time-slot, cast, geographic origin – the program underwent radical alterations. During the six-week break the Queen show, along with Manny and Kaye Lee and four of their children (three they had together and one by Kaye's first marriage) moved from the eastern seaboard to the Los Angeles area.

Fred Dannay wasn't even tempted to accompany the series and resume his function of supplying the weekly plot skeleton. After Mary's death Fred had sold the Great Neck home and bought a house in Brooklyn, on Carroll Street, a few blocks from Ebbets Field. A sister of Mary's and her husband had moved in to care for Fred's sons. Fred lived and worked furiously in one upstairs room, coming down only for meals. This hiatus in his life lasted about two years. In 1947 he married again, and he and his second wife – Hilda Wiesenthal, the widow of a doctor who had died in the war – bought an unpretentious new colonial house in Larchmont, a quiet New York suburb about forty minutes by train from Manhattan. The house was on Byron Lane, in a tree-lined area of Larchmont where every street was named for one of the world's great poets, and there Fred at age 41 moved himself and his family and started life over.

By this point in the radio series Ellery had morphed into a socially involved liberal very much like Tony Boucher and Manny Lee. At the start of each episode from the series' eighth and final season, Ellery would solemnly intone: "I dedicate this program to the fight against crime – not only crimes of violence and crimes of dishonesty, but also crimes of intolerance, discrimination and bad citizenship – crimes against America." And there was a similar speech at the end of each adventure. "This is Ellery Queen saying goodnight till next week, and enlisting all Americans every night, and every day, in the fight against bad citizenship, bigotry and discrimination – the crimes which are weakening America."

At a time when legally mandated segregation was still proudly being practiced in many states of the Union, and when the game of baseball that Fred and Manny so dearly loved was being torn apart over whether one black man should be allowed to play on a major league team, these were brave words indeed in a mass medium notorious for its timidity. But Lee's motivation for writing them was also rooted in survival instincts. The radio whodunit had come under attack from various self-anointed social critics who claimed the genre glorified crime, and several series had already been canceled. "I am trying to work out a new opening for Queen," Manny wrote Boucher on April 7, 1947, "and a new gimmick, which will attune E.Q. more closely to 'the forces of law and order.' (SHIT!) And of course I am going to try to make every possible Queen show on NBC this summer some sort of 'crusade,' or some damn thing, so that they won't have any possible kick coming about how we're an evil influence on the kiddies." Replying on April 26 to Boucher's question what the notoriously apolitical Dannay would think of the format change, Lee said: "I frankly haven't thought much about it."

With the episode broadcast June 1, 1947, the series returned to the NBC network where it had been a staple item from 1942 through 1944. Lawrence Dobkin, Bill Smith and Charlotte Keane contined respectively as Ellery, Inspector Queen and Nikki, but Ed Latimer as Sergeant Velie was replaced by George Matthews. Don Hancock kept his job as announcer. Musical duties were taken over by organist Chet Kingsbury. The series was heard from 6:30 to 7:00 p.m. on Sunday, the evening on which it had first been aired back in 1939. It lasted this way for exactly two performances, one a rerun, then left the air again, resurfacing in the same time-slot at the beginning of August but with Ed Latimer back in the regular cast as Sergeant Velie.

The new social conscience of the Queen program wasn't confined to the introductory and closing remarks but also permeated many of the scripts broadcast from the summer of 1947 until the series left the air for good. Manny Lee based the scripts for six of the first eight episodes on synopses by Tom Everitt and two on outlines by Boucher, but with either collaborator the liberal tone came forth loud and clear. In a letter to Boucher dated May 2, 1947, Manny reveals that his wife Kaye came up with the title for his latest script based on a Boucher synopsis and goes on: "I think I can say that it is the most important script I have done in eight years of this kind of labor." "Murder for Americans" (July 17, 1947) takes place in an upstate New York community that is being flooded by hate pamphlets attacking Jews, Catholics and blacks. While visiting the city Ellery is asked by a 10-year-old Jewish girl to find her vanished friend, the daughter of an Irish cop. The hate literature turns out to be the work of a white businessman, looking to buy up a certain neighborhood cheap by turning its people against each other, but the script is careful to give the villain a black accomplice so that Ellery can point out: "Virtue and vice co-exist in all races. No race has a monopoly on either."

Working with outlines by other writers had no effect on Lee's social conscience. In "Number 31" (September 7, 1947), which Manny wrote from a synopsis by Tom Everitt, Ellery tries to crack the secret of international mystery man George Arcaris's success at smuggling diamonds into the Port of New York and to comfort a wonderfully dignified black woman by solving the murder of her son, the servant for a wealthy man-about-town. The cases seem unconnected until Ellery discovers the number 31 popping up in both.

After Boucher and Lee's "The Man Who Squared the Circle" (September 21, 1947) the series once again went on hiatus, returning late in November as a "sustainer," the way it had been during its first months of life back in 1939-40. Most likely the liberal slant of the scripts had given the people at Anacin a headache. As if the loss of sponsor weren't enough to contend with, every regular performer in the series except for Larry Dobkin was fired and replaced during the hiatus. Herb Butterfield took over as Inspector Queen, Alan Reed as Sergeant Velie, and Virginia Gregg as Nikki. Paul Masterson became the announcer and Rex Koury played the organ. After a few months the role of Nikki was taken over by Kaye Brinker, who outside the studio was Mrs. Manfred B. Lee.

Manny of course continued to alter Boucher's plots as and when he pleased. "The Saga of Ruffy Rux" (November 27, 1947) pits Ellery against a gangster who talks like Elmer Fudd and has a habit of constantly jingling the two silver dollars he carries in his pocket for luck. The gangster in Boucher's synopsis had a different speech defect (as witness his title "Louie the Lisp") and the plot is infinitely wilder, with both Inspector Queen and Sergeant Velie getting seriously wounded and Ellery being kidnapped and replaced by a double.

One of the most unusual scripts from the eighth season was Boucher and Lee's

"The Private Eye" (January 22, 1948), a rather feeble parody-diatribe aimed at the hardboiled detective programs that by 1948 were saturating the airwaves. Ellery's nemesis in this episode is a meatheaded fascistic boor named Cam Clubb, who bullies Nikki into leaving Ellery and going to work for him.

> CLUBB (easily): Sure I'm tough, Nikki. It's a tough world. Take these chivalry boys, like your former boss.
> NIKKI (demurely): My *present* boss . . .
> CLUBB: He lives back in the time of King Arthur. Gentleman Detective! The Deductive Method! That's for old maids – of *both* sexes.
> NIKKI: And what's *your* method, Mr. Clubb? . . .
> CLUBB: My method? Get the jump. Blast first. Unfair play. If I have to kick a man's teeth in, I kick a man's teeth in. If I have to break a pig's nose, I break a pig's nose.
> NIKKI: Pig?
> CLUBB: Dame.

Remembering that Mickey Spillane's sadistic private eye had debuted only a few months earlier in *I, The Jury* (1947), one might conclude that Cam Clubb was intended as a lampoon of Mike Hammer – until one reads more of the script and learns that Boucher and Lee are attacking not just the sociopath excesses of Spillane but the legitimate hardboiled tradition typified by Dashiell Hammett's Sam Spade, whose radio exploits were on opposite Ellery's at this time.

> NIKKI: You know Cam Clubb's name as well as you know your own. After all, he's a competitor of yours.
> ELLERY: Clubb – a competitor? Don't be funny! Why, the fellow's no more than a paid thug.
> NIKKI: Ellery –
> ELLERY: Oh, don't feel bound by any loyalty to *me*, Nikki. If you want to live in a Dashiell Hammett novel . . .
> NIKKI: I've been seeing Cam because – well, he *is* a fascinating sort of monster.
> ELLERY: So was Hermann Goering!
> NIKKI: Enormous vitality – the kind of strength a woman can't help noticing –
> ELLERY: You can find the same thing at the gorilla's cage in the zoo.
> NIKKI: When I'm with him I – almost begin to feel he's right. We do live in a world where only toughness works.
> ELLERY: Then let's all go back to the jungle, shall we? Please, Nikki. I'll listen to your half-baked, second-hand Nietzscheisms some other time.

Eventually the outrage dissolves into a detective plot in which Ellery and Clubb apply their diverse methods of sleuthing to the murder of a statesman in exile from a mythical Balkan country. Both of them identify the right person as the killer but Boucher and Lee leave no doubt about who did it the right way. "He was guessing, Nikki," Ellery says. "I wasn't." Then he says to his rival: "The trouble with your method, Clubb, aside from the fact that it's inhuman and degrading, is that it doesn't prove anything. Also – it's...going to cost you your private detective's license."

After this episode a final wave of changes washed over the series. Its time-slot was moved to Thursday evenings, 8:30 to 9:00 p.m., and Howard Culver replaced Larry Dobkin as Ellery for the final 18 episodes, eight new scripts written by Lee from Boucher synopses and ten repeats.

"The Three Frogs" (April 29, 1948) is another tale of social concern, the subject this time being juvenile delinquency. Nikki finds an implausible young tough hiding out in her apartment and bravely sets out to reform him – a project that meshes with Ellery's hunt for a Faginesque hidden mastermind known as the Frog, who has organized a youth gang for criminal purposes. The crucial deductions presuppose that the listener is an expert on bubble-gum chewing procedure but take a back seat to a Boucher-Lee sermon against racial bigotry. Ellery and Sergeant Velie are trying to figure out which of their suspects is the Frog.

VELIE: Hey, wait a minute. Frog! The Frenchman! That's a slang word for Frenchman!
ELLERY: Yes, and as nasty a word, Sergeant, as kike, nigger, wop, Polack or any of the other insulting terms some people use to assert their purely imaginary superiority over their fellow citizens.
VELIE: Aww, I didn't mean it that way, Maestro.

But even at trail's end not every Queen episode was a vehicle for social messages, and indeed the next week's adventure, "One Diamond" (May 6, 1948), is a "pure" detective story by Boucher and Lee in which Ellery solves the murder-by-hanging of germophobe millionaire Mark Gallows and the puzzle of the killer who wasn't able to steal the fabulous Gallows Diamond because he couldn't read a simple map correctly. It's a rather clever tale, although not too hard for the listener to solve ahead of Ellery.

The last new episode of the series was Boucher and Lee's "Misery Mike" (May 20, 1948). The title character, who in the synopsis is called Miserere Mike, reflects both Boucher's function in the Queen series and his love of opera: Mike's nickname comes from his penchant for playing the Miserere from *Il Trovatore* on the accordion and he earns his living dreaming up new ideas for rackets as Boucher earned his conjuring up plot outlines. Listeners the following week were treated to yet another rerun, at the end of which *The Adventures of Ellery Queen* left network radio for good.

Manny Lee explained the axing of the series in a letter to Boucher dated May 5, 1948. "I have very few details. I was told (this happened very suddenly) that the reason is 'the time situation' – in other words, they have sold our time out from under us for a commercial [series], apparently, and have nowhere else to put us, commensurate with the cost of putting the show on. This is the second time this has happened; that we've built up a time spot for ABC and they've sold it – for some other show. Exactly what I was afraid of when the deal was first set up, exactly what happened . . . I am as thoroughly disgusted with the chicanery of mortal man as ever in my life and I could wish for a sign from heaven or anywhere else that man is not the lowest form of animation in the whole of creation."

Apparently all the Boucher-Lee episodes of the series survive on tape and may someday be released, and it's also possible that the small house of Crippen & Landru will publish a collection of the Boucher-Lee scripts – accompanied, let us hope, by Boucher's synopses for each and excerpts from the letters in which Tony and Manny discuss them. What likely will never be explored unless here and now is the question what Boucher's unused synopses were like. Thanks to the Lilly, that question can be answered in detail.

The earliest of the unused synopses is #12, "The Beethoven Manuscript," written in the summer of 1945. Fridolin Kleebauer, a German refugee who crossed into the U.S. from Mexico carrying a sheaf of music paper, comes to New York and gets in touch with wealthy choral conductor Hesketh Miller, claiming that the papers he smuggled out of Germany contain two-thirds of an unknown Beethoven symphony, for which his asking price is $100,000. Miller takes one sheet to Ellery and asks him to determine whether the manuscript is real or a fake. Soon after Ellery concludes that the document is genuine, Kleebauer is stabbed to death. Then Miller is stabbed in his home and the manuscript vanishes. The only clue to the perpetrator is that just before being attacked, Miller had mentioned on the phone that there was a tenor in the room with him. The suspects are three members of Miller's choral group: Hermann Stolz, a basso; Anthony Linton, a tenor; and Carol Ash, a contralto. It's Carol who turns out to be the culprit. Boucher, who was an expert on opera, gifted Ellery with his own knowledge that deep contraltos can sing tenor when, as in wartime, there are not enough male singers, and that when they do they are called tenorettes. Manny Lee rejected the synopsis but Boucher later attached the same clue to a different plot in Synopsis #22, which Lee transformed into "The Peddler of Death" (December 5, 1945) but which Boucher had called (I kid you not) "The Three Tenors."

In Synopsis #15, "The Quisling Quarterback," Ellery tries to find out whether the FBI is right in suspecting a college football player, who is also a nuclear physics genius, of being in league with the Nach Niederlage movement, a conspiracy among surviving Nazis to establish a Fourth Reich. Then Dr. Hohenfeld, the refugee scientist in charge of atomic research at the university, is murdered and Ellery solves the crime in rapid order, although apparently not to the satisfaction of Manny Lee, who thought the censors would keep the script off the air. Lee likewise rejected Boucher's next synopsis, #16, "The Unbirthday Present." A war correspondent who is writing the inside story behind his overseas experiences tells Ellery that three men – a German, an Englishman and a Spaniard – are in the Nach Niederlage movement. The three find out that their covers have been blown and draw straws to see who will kill the correspondent, who is eliminated by a bomb delivered to him as a gift on a day that apparently had no meaning in his life that would justify a gift. I am probably giving away too much if I reveal that Manny rejected this one because the gimmick was "too Catholic."

Everything Boucher submitted during 1946 and the first half of 1947 was accepted by Lee, paid for, and turned into a script – sometimes, as we've seen above, a script with only a distant resemblance to Boucher's original. Then in the summer of 1947 Manny turned down three in a row. In synopsis #61, "May Tenth," Ellery visits a small city and is asked by the chief of police to persuade lawyer and city councilman George Drummond to cast his deciding vote in favor of a tough new anti-gambling ordinance. Drummond vanishes and the ordinance is defeated by one vote. Later, as the Drummonds' furniture is being delivered to their new house, the lawyer's body is found inside a roll of carpet. Eventually the local gambling czar, Knife Nickson, is shot to death, leaving the message MAY 10 scratched into his desk with his knife. Those who think they know what the words mean can check their deduction by turning to the synopsis itself, which is printed later in this book.

In Synopsis #62, "The Modern Fagin," Ellery tries to uncover the mysterious person who is organizing the boys at a prep school into a jewelry theft ring. The Fagin character turns out to be the head of the school, who is a fanatic on the subject of spelling reform, and at the climax Ellery has to figure out the secret combination to a safe before a time bomb inside it goes off. The combination turns out to be the "reformed" spelling of his own name: KWEEN.

In synopsis #63, "The Giant at Large," a jewelry store is robbed in broad daylight by an unseen thief who, judging by the thumbprint he left behind, must be eight feet tall. More robberies follow, each one with the same gigantic thumbprint left behind. The prime suspect is one Herman the Horror but Ellery as usual pins the crimes on someone less likely. Boucher's synopsis, which is also printed later in this book, includes an aside in which he assures Manny that he has personally seen the phenomenon on which the plot hangs. The main intellectual challenge Ellery faces is finding the criminal's secret hideaway merely from the clue that the address would be of interest to a detective. Try to guess this one before you turn to the synopsis itself!

The three final unused synopses came in only a short while before the series was earmarked for cancellation, but the reasons they were rejected were substantive. Perhaps the wildest and craziest of all the Boucher synopses is #71, "The King of the Jungle." Ellery and Nikki are flying back to the U.S. from the Republic of San Pedro (there's that Sherlockian allusion again!) on a private plane piloted by fugitive Dick Hymson, whom Ellery has tricked into returning to the States. The plane crashes in the Central American jungle. Ellery, Nikki and Hymson are found by natives who speak with perfect British accents and brought to King Leo, who decides to make Nikki his next wife. Hymson tells Ellery that an old enemy of his named Jones is among them and will probably kill him. Ellery and Hymson stage a boxing match, telling the stupid natives that this is how white men determine who is superior, and thus manipulate Leo into agreeing to box with Ellery himself. While that match is going on, Hymson is murdered. Knowing Hymson has never been to England, Ellery deduces that the murderer is the one tribesman he's heard using American locutions. In a letter of February 4, 1948, Lee told Boucher: "There are so many things wrong with it from my standpoint that frankly, Tony, I don't know what the hell to say about it. I wouldn't dare put it on the air – I'd laugh it off myself."

Somewhat better but still not very good is #73, "The Hostages to Fortune." Nikki cracks up and her doctor prescribes a quiet resort hotel in upstate New York. In a long letter to Ellery she describes the place and its guests: a rich woman loaded with jewels, house detective Dave Dunlop and his wife and 4-year-old son, two enigmatic men named Hadley and Turk. Ellery recognizes the last two as criminals and joins Nikki at the hotel. On a canoeing trip they exchange I-love-yous. When they return, the lights at the hotel have all gone out and Mrs. Fortescue's diamond is missing, as is 4-year-old Butch Dunlop. Ellery eventually concludes that Dave Dunlop was forced by the kidnappers of his son to steal the jewel for them. Dave shoots himself, then tells Ellery that the hiding place of the diamond is "Right Ellen, Left Eighty." This Ellery deduces to mean "Right LN, Left AT," the combination to a safe. Lee rejected the synopsis on the ground that child kidnapping was a taboo subject for radio.

The last of all the Boucher synopses, which is also printed in this book, is by far the best of those that never made it to the air. In #77, "The Green-Eyed Murder," Ellery and Nikki are invited to dinner at the home of Senator Lewis Moore, who accuses Ellery of having an affair with his wife Dessa when he finds her compact in Ellery's coat. Dessa has a private meeting with Ellery in which she says she's on the verge of a crack-up because someone has been planting false rumors that have turned her husband into a paranoid. The rumors lead Ellery to a dead man and clues indicating that it was the senator who killed him. Lee told Boucher he couldn't use this one because any script involving a paranoid U.S. senator would inevitably be rejected by the network.

Many of Anthony Boucher's countless contributions to the mystery genre he knew and loved so well are amply documented and fondly appreciated, but his contributions to the Ellery Queen saga, between the late spring of 1945 and May 1948 when the series went off the air, have been nowhere near as well known and widely discussed as they deserve to be. Perhaps now he'll receive the credit he should have had all along.

**Photo above: Hugh Marlowe and Marian Shockley during the rehearsals.**

# CHAPTER TEN

# After the Last Performance

It was the end of Ellery Queen as a star of U.S. radio but far from the end of his detective career. Indeed Fred Dannay and Manny Lee were at the peak of their powers as writers when the Queen show left the air, and their next two novels, *Ten Days' Wonder* (1948) and *Cat of Many Tails* (1949), are among their finest. Manny and Kaye Lee returned to the east coast and made their new home in suburban Connecticut, first in Westport, later on a rustic 63-acre estate in Roxbury. By 1954 they were raising a total of eight children. Manny had been a city boy but he took to the life of a country gentleman as if to the manor born, buying a station wagon for the family, keeping chickens and cows, helping make butter and pasteurized milk for home consumption, planning a garden, declaring his property a game preserve, adding to his collections of stamps and medals and phonograph records. In his workroom, a small converted cottage on his grounds that had been a schoolhouse in the Revolutionary War era, he continued his primary job of fleshing out Fred's synopses into the later novels of Queen's third period, in which complex deductive puzzlement was fused with in-depth characterizations, magnificently detailed evocations of place and mood, and occasional ventures into social concern. For many of his vivid details he drew on family and friends. "My mother would use pet words and mannerisms that would frequently appear in his books," said Manny and Kaye's oldest daughter, Christopher Rebecca Lee. "When I was a teenager it would wreck it for me. I'd be reading about this glamorous woman and then out would come one of my mother's phrases." Among the best Queen novels of this time were *The Origin of Evil* (1951) with its strong Darwinian motifs, *The Glass Village* (1954) with its anti-McCarthy overtones, and the gerontological *Inspector Queen's Own Case* (1956). When not busy on a novel, Manny recast old EQ radio scripts into short stories that sold at top prices to periodicals like *This Week*. The noise level of his collaborations with Fred Dannay remained as high as ever. Manny's son Rand Lee was an ear-witness to some of the fights. "Often I would pick up the phone, hoping the line was free, and put down the receiver moments later with Dad's and Fred's arguing voices still ringing in my ears. On one occasion, Dad threw down a plot outline and exclaimed, 'He gives me the most ridiculous characters to work with and expects me to make them realistic!'"

It was a productive enough but relaxed and varied existence, and Manny, who was never a workaholic like Fred, seemed to thrive on it. "Dad didn't act like a famous author," Rand recalls. "He watched baseball on TV in his shorts and T-shirt; he hated parties and had to be blackmailed into wearing a tie." At one of those parties he was cornered by a fanatical Queen devotee and fell asleep in his chair while she gushed at him. When he gave a talk at the local school, his daughter Christopher's fifth grade teacher was dumbfounded to discover that "Ellery Queen" was not at all the prototype WASP hunk she had always imagined but a short stocky Jew wearing overalls and red socks. Manny took an increasingly active role in Roxbury's civic life, serving during 1957-58 as Justice of the Peace, later beating his playwright neighbor Arthur Miller in an election for a seat on the Library Board.

Meanwhile the self-styled country bumpkin Fred Dannay was settling into the suburban Larchmont life with his second wife, Hilda. But tragedy invaded their existence

55

when, in 1948, Hilda gave birth to their first and only child. As Fred explained during the 1979 Carroll College interview:

> "[Stephen] was born prematurely at seven months and weighing less than two pounds. He was the miracle baby of Doctors Hospital in New York City. We didn't realize for about a year that he – that the boy had had brain damage at birth. And the brain damage was so severe that the child, who had an absolutely angelic face, never walked and never talked . . . I was aware long before my wife that one of these days the tragedy would be capped by the death of that child. Actually he lived till he was six years old."

It is to the short unhappy life of Stephen Dannay that we owe the pervasive birth-death themes in several Queen novels, beginning with *Cat of Many Tails* (1949), which grew out of an anecdote told to Fred by one of the infant's doctors over dinner in a hospital cafeteria. Fred's response to grief was to drown himself in work. He continued to edit numerous anthologies of mystery fiction and the monthly issues of *EQMM*, to create the detailed synopses for Manny to expand into novels and stories, and to donate long hours as an officer of the Mystery Writers of America organization.

By this point in the authors' joint career, Ellery Queen had all but become a synonym for American detective, and even though radio drama was breathing its last gasp, Ellery was introduced to an even larger audience through the new medium of television. Three separate Queen series were seen on TV during the fifties: a live 30-minute program (1950-52) starring Richard Hart and, after Hart's death, Lee Bowman; a syndicated half-hour film series (1955-56) with radio's first Ellery, Hugh Marlowe, recreating his role; and a live 60-minute series in color (1958-59) starring George Nader, who was replaced after the show switched to videotape by Lee Philips. But Fred and Manny didn't involve themselves with TV as they had with radio, and the teledramas contained little if anything of the authentic Queen.

It was also during the fifties that, as a kind of therapy against his son's impending death, Fred wrote his only novel without Manny. In *The Golden Summer* (1953), published under his birth-name of Daniel Nathan, Fred's therapeutic strategy was to evoke the contentment of his own vanished childhood, with the hope of erasing from his mind the anguish of his middle life. It's a heavily autobiographical novel, set in Elmira during the summer of 1915 and describing the business adventures of a skinny and bespectacled 10-year-old named Danny Nathan, who's a physical weakling but shrewd and nimble-witted enough to talk himself out of any spot and to manipulate his playmates out of their loose change. *The Golden Summer* amounts to a book-length double entendre: the season of innocent security and peace, the season Danny made $4.73 from his duller contemporaries. Commercially the book was a disaster, but in Fred's brutally honest portrait of himself we can see the key to the entire Ellery Queen universe to come, including the image of Ellery I as the weak-eyed young genius who dominates his environment by the force of his mind.

In 1957 Ellery was again heard on the radio, not in the United States but on a six-week summer series broadcast in England over the BBC and based on a half dozen of the earliest Queen short stories. And the next year came the final novel of Queen's third period, *The Finishing Stroke* (1958), in which Fred and Manny nostalgically recreated the young manhood of Ellery himself. The time is 1929, shortly after the publication of the author-detective's first novel – which happens to be titled *The Roman Hat Mystery* – and the signals are clear all through this elegy to "the lovely past" that the cousins were retiring as mystery writers. Fred sold the University of Texas his collection of detective short story volumes and wound up spending two semesters on the campus as a professor of creative writing.

After a short sabbatical from fiction writing, the workaholic Dannay wanted to work on more Ellery Queen novels but was stymied when Lee developed writer's block and was unable to do his share of any more collaborations. Eventually the cousins' literary agent arranged for Lee's function to be taken over by other authors, unknown in the mystery field but with high reputations in science fiction. The fourth and final period of Queen books began auspiciously with *The Player On the Other Side* (1963), written by Theodore Sturgeon from Dannay's lengthy synopsis. The next few Queens were expanded from Fred's outlines by Avram Davidson, but then Manny Lee overcame his block and collaborated with Fred on Ellery's last adventures as he had on the earliest. The fourth-period Queens are marked by a zest for experiment within the strict deductive tradition and a retreat from all semblance of plausibility into what Fred liked to call "Fun and Games," i.e. a potpourri of stylized plots and characters and dozens of motifs recycled from earlier Queen fiction. During period four Queen also returned to radio, in name at least, with *Ellery Queen's Minute Mysteries*, a syndicated package of literally hundreds of 60-second whodunits with which neither Fred nor Manny had a thing to do beyond endorsing the checks for permitting the use of their creation.* Most of these vignettes are so silly they've been reported to cause outbreaks of the giggles among personnel of the radio stations where they are aired, but until the early 1980s when the licenses to broadcast them were terminated, they could still be heard around the country in odd moments of the broadcast day.

In the late 1960s Manny Lee suffered a series of heart attacks and, on doctor's orders, took off a great deal of weight. It didn't save him. On April 2, 1971, the 65-year-old Lee had another attack and died on the way to the Waterbury hospital. He never saw a copy of Ellery's last adventure, *A Fine and Private Place* (1971). He also missed Claude Chabrol's 1970 French movie based on *Ten Days' Wonder* and featuring Orson Welles and Anthony Perkins, and Universal's 2-hour film adaptation of *Cat of Many Tails* as a pilot for a proposed TV series starring Peter Lawford and Harry Morgan as Ellery and the Inspector. Cinematically he didn't miss much.

Manny and I had been corresponding for a while but I had met him only once, just before the 1970 Mystery Writers of America dinner, which was the last public function he and Fred attended together. We had arranged to meet "under the clock" in the lounge of the Biltmore Hotel where the dinner was being held. When we were introduced to each other, a young man who happened to be sitting nearby jumped up at the sound of his name and ran over and pumped his hand and whooped: "Manfred B. Lee! I think you're the

---

* At least 520 minute mysteries were produced and syndicated, issued on reel-to-reel format, and produced by Creative Marketing and Communications Corp. in Cincinnati, Ohio. Up to four box sets were issued, each containing 129, 130 and/or 131 episodes each. Originally issued in 7 ½ ips. Mono (not Stereo). Set one was released in November 1965 with episodes 1 to 130. Set two was released in April 1966 with episodes 131 to 259. Set three was released in September 1966 with episodes 260 to 390. Set four was released in February of 1967 with episodes 391 to 520. Bill Owen (same author team of Buxton & Owen who wrote *The Big Broadcast, 1920 - 50*) played the role of Ellery in the mysteries.

greatest writer that ever lived!" To which Manny replied, peering owlishly at the intruder: "That doesn't say much for your taste, does it?" For me that was the essential Manny Lee – genial, earthy, frank and unpretentious. I would have given much to have known him better.

At first Fred Dannay planned to continue the Queen novels, either alone or with a new partner. But then on the heels of Manny's death a new tragedy invaded Fred's life. In 1972, 27 years after his first wife Mary had died of cancer, his second wife Hilda did likewise. And with her death Fred himself began dying by inches. Each time I visited him during the next few years he seemed to have shrunk in his chair a little more. A photograph of him taken by Santi Visalli in 1973 shows the empty, devastated face of a man waiting to die. The only thing that kept him functioning, he told me, was the inexorable work schedule demanded of him by *EQMM*. I couldn't help feeling that his days were numbered.

And then he met the third woman in his life. At a dinner party he happened to be introduced to Rose Koppel, a recently widowed artist who worked at Manhattan's Ethical Culture School. In November 1975 they were married, and Rose literally saved her 70-year-old husband's life. He had always been a private person, so much so that after almost thirty years in the house on Byron Lane many of his closest neighbors still had no idea what he did for a living. Rose de-privatized him as no other person before her had ever succeeded in doing, and made it possible for him to enjoy his role as elder statesman of mystery fiction that time and the deaths of most of his contemporaries had bestowed on him.

The years of Fred's third marriage opened up countless opportunities for media exposure. First there was NBC-TV's weekly 60-minute film series (1975-76), set in the late 1940s and starring Jim Hutton and David Wayne as Ellery and Inspector Queen. The night the first episode was broadcast, Fred told *Playboy*, "I happened to be home alone, and when I saw [Hutton] on the screen I had the most curious reaction. I had the feeling I was seeing myself, years and years ago." The series was only the beginning of Fred's late-blooming career as a media personality. During the next few years he received so much public attention – guest lectures at the University of California, two appearances on TV's *Dick Cavett Show*, superstar treatment at the International Crime Writers' Congress held in New York early in 1978 (at which Fred and Rose were seen dancing cheek-to-cheek at 3:00 a.m.), interviews with *Playboy* and *People* and dozens of other periodicals, testimonial dinners celebrating the fiftieth anniversary of the publication of *The Roman Hat Mystery*, an honorary doctoral degree from Carroll College, a lavish trip to Tokyo for the premiere of a Japanese movie based on *Calamity Town* and to Stockholm for the 1981 International Crime Writers' Congress – that it was a miracle he accomplished any work at all. He gave up the idea of breaking in a new collaborator and writing more Ellery Queen novels, saying that it would be disloyal to Manny's memory, but continued to edit both *EQMM* and a prodigious number of hard-cover and paperback anthologies. After he turned 75, however, his health began to deteriorate and he was forced to curtail more and more of his work. He was hospitalized twice and then, late in the summer of 1982, a third time. That Labor Day weekend his heart stopped.

For me his death meant not only the end of a great tradition in detective fiction and of an exciting and fruitful editor-writer interaction but also the end of an infinitely precious friendship. Many of our viewpoints and interests were different but our feeling for the literature of crime brought us together and gave birth to our feeling for each other.

We shared heartbreak and triumph, happy times and sad. But for me the best times were when we'd talk, hour after hour, about the writers who had preceded Fred and those who were his contemporaries and those who were coming up after him and, as I got older, some who were coming up after me. I never felt so much a part of a living tradition as I did on those occasions. He was the closest to a grandfather I've known. Without him I would never have written a word of fiction worth reading. Now the excitement of his presence lives only in memories.

And how about the others? What ever happened to the rest of the people most closely associated with *The Adventures of Ellery Queen* following their time with the series?

Discharged from the Navy with a Bronze Star after the war, George Zachary resumed his career as a producer-director in radio. His marriage to Marian Shockley broke up soon after his return to civilian life. He produced *The Ford Theater* for NBC during the 1947-48 season and, as we've already seen, recycled one of the earliest 60-minute Ellery Queen scripts as an episode of the series on January 4, 1948. As radio declined and television began to grow, Zachary changed media, working on the production of early TV series like NBC's comedy *The Life of Riley*. Eventually he and his second wife relocated to Sarasota, Florida where in May 1964, at age 52, he died of a heart attack.

Hugh Marlowe continued acting both on the stage (for example, opposite Gertrude Lawrence in *Lady in the Dark*) and in movies (including key roles in *Twelve O'Clock High*, 1949, with Gregory Peck and in the Academy-Award winning *All About Eve*, 1950, with Bette Davis). In 1955-56 he played Ellery in the 32-episode syndicated telefilm series *The New Adventures of Ellery Queen*, and also gave a fine performance on the other side of the law as a suave, corrupt district attorney's investigator in *Illegal* (1955), starring Edward G. Robinson. His best-known role in later life was the patriarch of the principal family in NBC-TV's daytime serial *Another World*. On May 2, 1982, at age 71, he died of a heart attack in his Manhattan home.

In 1946 Marian Shockley married radio actor Clayton "Bud" Collyer, best known as the star of the long-running *The Adventures of Superman* series but also active in a variety of soap operas and game shows. She appeared with Collyer in series like *Road to Life* and *The Guiding Light* and moved into TV with him in the early fifties. In the late 1960s they were living in Greenwich, Connecticut but after Collyer's death in 1969 Shockley moved to Westlake Village, California where she served on the board of a local adoption agency. She died on December 14, 1981.

Both during and after his years as Inspector Queen, Santos Ortega had the title roles in other radio detective series of the 1940s including *Perry Mason*, *Nero Wolfe* and *Charlie Chan*. In 1956 he signed with CBS to play Grandpa Hughes in that network's new daytime serial, *As The World Turns*, and was still in the part twenty years later when, at age 76, he took a brief trip to Florida and suddenly died there.

Ted de Corsia, who was Sergeant Velie on the Queen series for most of its duration, was promoted to the top of the police ladder when he took over the role of Commissioner Weston in *The Shadow*. In the late forties he made the transition to movie acting with his performances as heavies in two memorable "films noir" of 1948: Orson Welles' *The Lady From Shanghai* and Jules Dassin's *The Naked City*. During the 1949-50 season he starred as a Scotland Yard inspector in the CBS radio series *Pursuit*. During the fifties and sixties he enjoyed a prolific career in both movies and TV. He died in 1973.

Sydney Smith's post-EQ years were filled with acting assignments on the stage, in radio and for early television. He later moved to the West Coast and was featured in several movies such as *No Time for Sergeants* (1958) with Andy Griffith and *Some Came Running* (1958) with Frank Sinatra. He wasn't proud of his film period, which he described in a letter to me as the time when he "toiled among the whores." Returning to school, he earned a Master's degree when he was over 50 and began a new career as Associate Professor of Theatre at Northern Illinois University. He retired in 1976 and moved to Washington, where he acted off and on with the Seattle Rep until his death in March 1978.

Richard Coogan, who replaced Smith as Ellery Queen but lasted only a few months in the part, was one of the first radio actors to leave that medium and make his mark on television. Children whose parents bought their first set soon after World War II may remember him as star of the live sci-fi series *Captain Video* during its first season (1949-50). Later he starred as Marshal Matt Wayne on *The Californians* (1957-59). He remains in astonishingly good health and will turn 88 not long before this book is published.

Lawrence Dobkin, who replaced Coogan as Ellery, is also still alive and well, as witness his introduction to this book. After radio's golden age he continued to act on TV but devoted most of his time to directing. Among the dozens of series to which he contributed episodes are *The Rifleman*, *77 Sunset Strip*, *The Donna Reed Show*, *Tarzan*, *Barnaby Jones* and *The Waltons*.

As radio slowly died, Anthony Boucher spent progressively less time writing mystery stories and scripts and more time reviewing the mystery fiction of others, a sideline which he'd started in 1941 for the San Francisco *Chronicle*. Ten years later he landed the most prestigious crime reviewing position in the United States, the proprietorship of the New York *Times Book Review's* "Criminals at Large" column. His *Times* work is generally considered the finest body of mystery criticism there is. He continued as *Times* reviewer, while simultaneously turning out a mountain of other editorial and critical work, until April 1968 when at the unbearably early age of 56 he died of lung cancer.

One by one the lights go out, the lives go out, the memories fade to black. Ellery Queen's first radio adventure was broadcast four years before I was born, and I was five when the series was canceled. I never heard a single episode "live" yet, thanks to the miracle of audio tape and the easier-to-take-for-granted miracle of print, I can almost believe that I listened to it every week. *The Adventures of Ellery Queen* was part of the golden age of a very special medium which deeply affected the lives of those who were instructed and entertained by it. And, as I hope I've demonstrated, the series decisively shaped many of the subsequent novels and stories of the cousins who created the show. This book is my way of saying to the ghosts of Fred Dannay and Manny Lee and George Zachary and Hugh Marlowe and Sydney Smith and all the others, and to the survivors like Richard Coogan and Larry Dobkin: "Thanks for the memories."

# THREE ELLERY QUEEN RADIO SYNOPSES

## Anthony Boucher

# THE ADVENTURE OF MAY TENTH

**Anthony Boucher synopsis #61**

CHARACTERS:

EQ

NP

Joe Bauer, police chief

Mary Drummond, wife of George Drummond, city councilman

Harold Harding, mayor

Harvey Gilbert, city councilman

"Knife" Nickson, gambling racketeer

moving men, councilmen, etc

SCENE 1:    El & Nikki are visiting a small city, scene of a former triumph or two. They drop in on their old friend, Police Chief Bauer, who is not unlike Insp Q.  To El's "How goes things?"–

CHIEF:    Not so good, and you've showed up at the right time, Ellery.  Seems to me you get on pretty well with George Drummond?

EL:  He's a good lawyer.  I've met him in court several times.

CHIEF:    Well, the city's been having trouble with gambling, and our city ordinances aren't tight enough to take care of it.   The City Attorney and I worked out a new ordinance that's really got teeth in it.  It's coming up before the Council tonight.  Now part of the council is new boys from the reform slate – they're OK.  But the holdovers are pretty much tied in with the gambling crowd.  It'll be close, and George's vote'll decide it – only nobody knows where he stands.

EL:   There was a time, Chief, when I'd have said this was politics and I'd have nothing to do with it.  But I've learned now that no man who's out to clean up our cities can stay clear of politics.  Come on, Nikki – we're going to get and deliver George Drummond's vote.

SCENE 2:   In front of the Drummond house.  Chaos.  The D's are moving.  The van is in front of the house, and men are swarming like ants.  B g of grunts & commands.

HEAD MOVER:  Mrs. Drummond's inside some place.  Don't know where *he* is.

MAN:  Boss sent me over – said you could use another hand here.

HEAD MOVER:  You're damn tooting.  (TO EL) I think you'll find her in the front room.

They find her, and very distraite she is.  Nikki is all feminine sympathy, especially as they start trying to find George.  Some confusion of looking over the house for him in the midst of bumps and noises.

HEAD MOVER:  We're knocking off for lunch now, Mrs. D.  See you in a half hour.

MRS. D:  Ouf!  Now we'll have a little peace.  I don't know how we accumulated so much *stuff*.  We're going to just get it into the van today – then we'll stay at a hotel tonight and unload at the new house tomorrow.  George! (BUT STILL NO SIGN OF HIM) Drat him! He stayed away from the office to help me, and I'll bet he's just sneaked away someplace.

She and Nikki get together on if that isn't just like a man, but El, as they leave, is worried.

EL:  I don't know, Nikki.  But when a man's vote may determine the political future of a city, and he vanishes unexpectedly – I see trouble ahead.

SCENE 3:  City council chamber – Mayor Harding, platitudinous progressive, presiding. Councilman Gilbert, a slickly domineering article, speaks briefly against the new ordinance, and it's defeated by one vote.

CHIEF:  Drummond could've made it a tie, and the Mayor's deciding vote would have passed it – Harding's a stuffed shirt but OK.

"Knife" Nickson, whose voice is the essence of cold calm menace, passes by with a taunting insult to the Chief and a sneer at Ellery, warning him to keep his nose out of this city.

CHIEF: That's the biggest crook we've got, and he means that threat, Ellery.  I'll try to protect you, but if Nickson's out for you . . .

EL:  I've been threatened before.  And I'm staying here till I find out what happened to George Drummond.

SCENE 4: The Drummonds' new house. B g of unloading.

MRS. D (ALMOST IN HYSTERICS):  And he never showed up at the hotel last night.

I can understand his walking out on the moving, but never a word. . . if he went off on a toot I'll never forgive him. . .

EL: Neither should the citizens. . .

And it is at this point that the movers drop an extra heavy carpet and out rolls the body of George Drummond.
COMMERCIAL

SCENE 5: Same, later

CHIEF: I don't think he was supposed to die, Ellery. He was stunned and stuffed in there. With the van locked up overnight, he'd be safely kept from the crucial council meeting, and no harm done. Only he went and suffocated.

EL: It's murder anyway. How about this extra man that joined you?

HEAD MOVER: The boss says he didn't send anybody. He was a good worker though.

EL: Can you describe him?

HEAD MOVER: Hell, I usually saw him buried under a load. He was just a guy – how would I know?

EL; There's one lead, chief. He did handle a lot of this stuff, and a mover's hands are unusually sweaty and dirty. There'll be good prints – and if we get the prints of the regular crew and eliminate them. . .

SCENE 6: Chez Nickson.

NIKKI: There isn't anything that looks deader than a nightspot in the daytime, is there?

EL: The prints checked fine with Chet Given, one of Knife Nickson's henchmen. The Knife must've put him on the job.

A very sinister henchman shows them into Knife's office. This whole sequence is straight out of a Chandler story. Maybe if you want El could pull some bravura like removing the henchman's rod with judo. Nickson is taut, quiet and deadly. Throughout the scene he plays solitaire mumbletypeg with the knife that gives him his sobriquet; its thuds, as he tosses it up and lets it land on the desk, punctuate the dialog. It's obvious that the Knife is in this up to his ears and scared now that what was meant as a harmless snatch has turned into murder. But he's as imperturbable as he can be, says that he's sent Given away on a little vacation, and again warns Ellery to clear the hell out.

SCENE 7: Police HQ

64

EL: There's no whodunit angle on this, Chief. There's no question the Knife's responsible. The puzzle is how to clean things up. I want you to talk the Mayor into calling an extraordinary session of the Council, to reconsider the ordinance in the light of events, and to draft a petition to the Governor requesting state militia and martial law if necessary to clean out this nest of rats.

CHIEF: I think the Mayor'll go for that, Ellery. And it doesn't look like we can pin anything on the Knife any other way.
Phone interrupts with a report that the Knife's been found murdered.

SCENE 8: Nickson's office.

The Knife is very dead – shot in the chest. And there's a dying message. With his everpresent knife he scrawled on the desk: MAY 10. We go into a montage of Nikki working on the phone, talking to Mrs. D, to the reference librarian, to the Mayor, and everybody for possible meanings. We learn that the tenth of May is the Drummonds' wedding anniversary, the date of the last city elections, and the day that Hitler invaded the Lowlands – none of which helps very much. Especially since the Knife was a brutally direct type – not at all the type of Queen character who takes pleasure in making it hard to solve his murder.

SCENE 9: Extraordinary session of the council. Shocking events have brought about many political shifts. Despite strenuous efforts of Councilman Gilbert, Harding swings it with a big speech, including among other flowers the sentence: "The deaths of common criminals do not concern us so deeply; they were men who lived beyond the law and died beyond the law. But the death of our dear friend and colleague, George Drummond – a death maneuvered and machinated for purely political motives – "

NIKKI (AS THE NEW PROGRAM IS BEING CARRIED): This is fine for a clean-up; but who killed the Knife? There must be somebody behind him yet.

CHIEF (FADING In): Better come outside, El. News for you. (AS THE DOOR CUTS OFF THE COUNCIL'S NOISE) We found Chet Given all right. His little vacation wasn't a very healthy one. We found him wrapped in baling wire, his skull bashed in, and tossed on the city dump. Pretty touch of irony there from somebody.

NIKKI: But who's behind it all? And what does May tenth mean?

EL: Now I know.

JURY SPOT

SOLUTION

Maybe the denouement could be staged in the council session – that might be fun.

Anyway:

EL:  We agreed that the Knife had a direct mind, and that May tenth as a clue could only have some subtle indirect meaning.  Therefore the Knife did not intend to write May tenth. Nikki, how do you spell May tenth?

NIKKI:  M A Y one zero.

EL:  Or:  M A Y O, with a straight line inserted.  The Knife started, very simply, to scratch his murderer's name, or rather title:  M A Y O R.  He collapsed before the R. The killer returned to the office, perhaps for papers that revealed his tie-in with Nickson.  He saw the message.  He couldn't erase those cuts in the wood.  So he simply added one straight line which changed the unmistakable M A Y O into the highly cryptic May 10.  (He may even have had a malicious knowledge of my weakness for such puzzles.)

MAYOR:  This is preposterous.  You mean to imply that I –

EL:  The dying message would be bad enough, Mayor Harding.  There's no other way to interpret it.  But you made one other slip.  Just now you referred to "the deaths of common criminals" and said "*they* were *men* who lived and died beyond the law."  At that time all of us knew only of the Knife's death – it was after that that even I learned that Given had been bumped.  Only some one tied into the criminal set-up could have known.  Your professed "liberalism" has been a cover for the nastiest connections; I've more respect for an honest rat like Councilman Gilbert.

And the Mayor cracks, and peace and justice are restored to the community.

# THE ADVENTURE OF THE GIANT AT LARGE

## Anthony Boucher synopsis #63

CHARACTERS:

EQ

NP

Insp Q

Sgt V

Brian Derwent, a jewel-designer

Herman the Horror, a mug

various jewelers, police and others

SCENE 1: A small jeweler's shop. The proprietor is wishing good luck to a young engaged couple.

JEWELER: Wear the diamond in good health, young lady. And I hope you'll remember this shop when you're ready for the wedding ring. (AD LIB GOODBYES AND DOOR CLOSE OFF) (TO HIMSELF) Nice young people. Now we'll just put these diamonds back in the –

VOICE (TONELESS UNRECOGNIZABLE WHISPER, COLDLY MENACING): No you don't. Don't turn around. Just set the tray down and –

JEWELER: Who are you?

VOICE: I said don't turn around!

JEWELER; Where did you –

VOICE: All right. You asked for it.

THUD, GROAN & SLUMP OF BODY

VERY SHORT BRIDGE TO

JEWELER: And that's the last I know, Sergeant. I just started to turn my head when he sapped me.

VELIE:  Scooped up a pocketful of diamond rings and made a clean getaway. . . Damnedest daring daylight robbery I've seen in years.  Well, boys?  No luck on the prints, I suppose?

FINGERPRINT MAN:  Look. . . uh. . . Sergeant, I. . .

VELIE:  Well?  Get a print?

FING:  Well, yes, but. . .  Come over here, Sgt.  You better take a look at this yourself.

VELIE (LONG LOW WHISTLE):  I'll be a monkey's uncle. . . !  This is one for the Inspector!  And maybe even the Maestro!

SCENE 2:  Police HQ.

INSP:  There you are, Ellery.  Cleanest, most successful robbery you can imagine, but he left one thumb print.

EL:  They always slip up once.

INSP (DRILY):  The ones we catch do, at least.  But look at the print.

NIKKI:  Let me see. . .  My, it's big, isn't it?

INSP:  Big?  You haven't any better words than that?  I've checked this thumbprint against the standard indexes for thumb size proportionate to body size.  If the man who left this print is constructed according to any human pattern, he's at least eight feet tall.

EL:  A giant?  Well, I can't imagine an easier case for you, Dad.  This is a natural for police methods – no 8-foot criminal is ever going to slip through a police dragnet.

SCENE 3:  Montage, either of flash episodes or of headlines and/or radio commentators, indicating spreading success of The Giant through a half-dozen robberies – all equally daring and all characterized by a single thumb-print.

SCENE 4:  Police HQ.

INSP:  They're riding me like hell, son.  I haven't had a minute's peace since The Giant started to work.  Look in through the door there.

NIKKI:  What a strange looking lot of men!  And all so enormous!

INSP:  We've pulled in every known or suspected crook over six feet.  The patrolmen have orders to pick up anybody extra large on a vag charge.  Not a single print checks.

EL; You know, Dad, that doesn't surprise me. It seems to me you're missing the obvious meaning of this print.

INSP: And what may that be, pray tell?

VELIE (BURSTING IN): Phone call from 57$^{th}$ & Madison – looks like another Giant job.

EL: Deal me in, Dad. I'm coming along.

SCENE 5: Jewelry store.

VELIE: Same like usual, Maestro. He slips in and hides –

EL: Must be a little difficult hiding that size, mustn't it?

VELIE: Well, he does – until the shop's empty except for one clerk. Then he gets to work. And here's the print.

EL: Hmmm. A Giant's print, as ever was. But who's this with Dad?

INSP: Ellery, this is Dan Mannering of the Continental Detective Agency. Tell him, Dan.

MANNERING: There's three shops side by side here, see, Mr. Queen. All jewelry, and they haven't got any back entrances. So they went in together and hired me. I sit in the building across the street and keep an eye on the three shops and buzz 'em if anybody big goes in. Well, I've been watching this shop from the time the boss got here till the cops arrived. And nobody over five ten went in the one door.

INSP: So he's not only The Giant. He's also The Invisible Man.

COMMERCIAL

SCENE 6: Same, picking up from last line.

EL: And I said this was a simple case for police routine! But let me point out, Dad, that –

DERWENT: Mr. Queen? I'm Brian Derwent – I own the jewelry shop next door. I wonder if I might talk with you a moment about this plague that's befallen our business.

INSP: If you've got any police information, Derwent –

DERWENT: No, it's just that. . . I hope you won't mind if Mr. Queen steps next door with me?

INSP: Run along, son. (FADING) Dan, if I hadn't known you as an operative for twenty years. . .

FOOTSTEPS

DERWENT (A TRIFLE TWITTERY): I hope your father doesn't feel hurt, Mr. Queen. But I'm not used to dealing with the police. I can't even read mystery stories – and in a business like mine reputation is so important. I thought that if I could talk with a. . . well, with a gentleman like you. . .

EL: I assure you Dad's equally much of a gentleman – and so is every member of the Finest. But if it makes you more comfortable. . .

DOOR

DERWENT: Here is my. . . well, if I may be immodest, my treasure-house.

NIKKI: Ellery! This is the most wonderfully imaginative jewelry I've ever seen!

DERWENT: Ahhmm! Thank you. I do flatter myself I have a certain touch. . .

EL: You mean you make these fascinating pieces yourself?

DERWENT: I understand the dubiety in your voice. You look at my empty sleeve and think how can a one-armed man be such a craftsman. I assure you that working out my own techniques was no simple problem, but the results. . .

NIKKI: Yummmm! Ellery, I hope you're remembering it's less than three months till Christmas.

EL: Now what is it you wanted to tell me?

DERWENT: I. . . well, I must confess that I have had certain. . . ah. . . underworld contacts. Every jeweler has. Criminals rolling in money come in with wild orders to fill for their girls.

NIKKI: I would wind up on the side of the law.

DERWENT: That is how I happened once to have seen Herman the Horror. Does the name mean anything to you, Mr. Q?

EL: No.

DERWENT: He's an enormous glandular monstrosity – ripe for a sideshow – who works as a muscleman for various criminals. And three times I've seen him lurking in this district of jewelers. The last time I summoned up courage to follow him – to a bar in Yorkville where he seemed well known. I thought you should know. . .

El is interested and D gives him the address.

DERWENT: Dear me! Here it is after five on a Friday and I'm still in New York. I must scurry away for my weekend of silence on a peak in Connecticut.

EL: Can we get in touch with you if anything comes of this lead?

DERWENT: Not till Monday at this shop. I have never given my rural address to anyone in New York – I must have a weekend of peace. Though I regret it in this case – it's an address a detective would enjoy. But please do see me Monday – I'm having a showing Monday night of my newest creations, and I do want your protection – and let me know if you find Herman the Horror.

SCENE 7: Police HQ.

INSP: This Yorkville lead sounds good. Velie's following it up – he's supposed to phone in about now.

EL: But dad, look. This thumbprint is always left. Therefore we're supposed to find it. Therefore it must mean something other than it seems to. Could it be a forgery?

INSP: I think of things sometimes too, son. I've had the best men in the dept checking that. A: they find traces of dirt and sweat and pore-marks. B: the print's never quite the same twice. It's positively not from any fake stamp – it's the changing sweaty imprint of a real human thumb.

NIKKI (HESITANTLY): When you smash your thumb with a hammer it gets all swollen –

INSP: And the print gets distorted – whorls and loops all out of natural symmetry. This is perfectly natural. Damnit, where is Velie?

EL: He was supposed to check in when?

INSP: Almost twenty minutes ago, and you know Velie. Hey son, where you going?

EL: Yorkville.

SCENE 8: Bar b g

EL: TOUGH): But I gotta see Herman, see? I got a job for him. (CRACKLE OF BILLS) This roll's just the advance – and there's a piece of it for you.

71

Bartender gives in, takes him back to Herman.

EL: Look, Herman, I got a better deal for you than the jewelry pitch.

HERMAN (MORTIMER SNERD OVERAMPLIFIED): How you know about that? Say, I seen your pitcher. . . You're. . . you're a son of a cop. Me, I eat cops for breakfast, see. Looky here.

EL: Velie!

HERMAN: Naw, he ain't dead – yet. But you both will be soon.

LUNGE, STRUGGLE, CRASHES, FINAL DEAFENING THUD

El: And judo works even on Giants.

SCENE 9: Police HQ

VELIE: Jeez, Maestro, I can't thank you. The big lug jumps me and what can I do?

INSP: I think this does it, son. His story's pretty thin. Says he got a C-note in an envelope with a note saying he should lurk around that jewelry district.

EL: Which could be true – and a clever red-herring on the part of the criminal.

At which point the fingerprint report arrives: Herman is not the Giant.

SCENE 10: Music up into b g of party.

DERWENT: I'm so glad you all could come. I'm so terribly afraid of The Giant tonight – especially since Herman turned out not to be. All my finest pieces are here. And please, *please* watch out. (HE FADES ADLIBBING GREETINGS TO OTHER GUESTS)

EL: Nikki, I've got a strange job for you. Get Derwent alone and flirt with him – flirt like crazy. (NIKKI'S REACTIONS CAN BE IMAGINED) And above all – get him to kiss you.

NIKKI: But why?

EL: I think you'll find out.

Party babble up – What wonderful jewelry, etc –

Nikki follows instructions, plays up to Derwent like anything, finally succeeds in a kiss.

NIKKI (STARTLED): Oh!

DERWENT: What? Oh. Damn that Queen. I should've suspected. . .

NIKKI: Suspected what?

DERWENT: That he'd arranged that kiss so that you would feel the arm under my empty sleeve. Well, all I can do is to see that you don't report back to him. Come on. This isn't a finger in your ribs – not even The Giant's Thumb.

NIKKI: You can't take me out of here. There are police guards – you asked for them yourself.

DERWENT: And don't you think they'll let Miss Porter through, with escort? And if you don't say the right words, dear – something may happen to your ribs.

SCENE 11: Still party b g.

INSP: Where's Derwent? Doesn't he frequent his own party?

EL: Is he gone? And Nikki with him –

They check with a guard. Nikki left with Derwent.

Insp queries a distraught Ellery.

EL: When a case turns on a thumb-print, I suspect a man one of whose hands I never see, even a supposedly one-armed man – and especially when that man put us on the false trail of Herman. I tried to have Nikki check – and now she's caught.

SCENE 12: Derwent's hide-out.

DERWENT: And here we are, Miss Porter, nice and cosy – or may I call you Nikki now that we are doomed to live together?

NIKKI: You beast!

DERWENT: My dear, has none of Mr. Queen's imagination rubbed off on you? But now that we are home I can take off my coat with its empty sleeve and show you – You see, I do have another arm. And on that arm I have a hand, and on that hand I have a thumb . . . Look.

NIKKI: It's a double thumb – two upper bones and two thumbnails!

DERWENT: But turn it over – only *one* thumbprint! And that the thumbprint of a

Giant! It was clever of Queen to suspect my empty sleeve – but not clever enough. Now I have you. . . and I assure you I have no intention of harming anyone so lovely. I shall simply keep you – until Queen arranges for my escape to Central America, with The Giant's loot.

SCENE 13:  Fast car b g

EL:  I can see what he's planning – to bargain Nikki against a promise of immunity. The only way to get ourselves out of a moral dilemma is to find her at once. I'm sure he headed for his Connecticut hangout – he said he'd never given that address to anyone.

INSP:  So we just head for Connecticut and find it?

EL:  But we know the city. He said, "I must scurry away for my weekend of silence on a peak in Connecticut." What could that mean but the famous line from Keats' sonnet, "Silent upon a peak in. . . *Darien*"?

VELIE:  So we just search every house in Darien?

EL:  But I told you the rest of that conversation. We even know the street address.

JURY SPOT

SOLUTION

Derwent preparing a message to Queen and threatening Nikki, interrupted by the arrival of The U S Marines. Excitement, incl wonder at Derwent's astonishing thumb.

NIKKI:  But how did you know where to find me?

EL:  Derwent said this was "an address a detective would enjoy." Now connoisseurs of crime may know such addresses as 110A Piccadilly for Lord Peter Wimsey, or E 38$^{th}$ St for Philo Vance, or even W 87$^{th}$ for me and Dad. But Derwent also said he knew nothing about mysteries. What is the only address that a non-enthusiast would know and associate with detectives? Only one possible one – the address of the greatest detective in history--and that is precisely where I found you in Darien – at 221 Baker St.

NOTE A:  The thing of a double thumb having a single print is absolutely correct; I personally know such a case. If it were saved for solution, it might be unfair; but since it comes before, it should be OK.

NOTE B:  To go out of one's way to avoid complications with DPSC [Denis Conan Doyle, son of Sir Arthur and one of his literary executors], it might be well, as I have done in the last speech above, to avoid the actual name of Sh-rl-ck H-lmes.

# THE ADVENTURE OF THE GREEN-EYED MURDER

**Anthony Boucher synopsis #77**

CHARACTERS:

EQ

NP

Insp. Q

Sgt V

Senator Lewis Moore

Dessa, his wife

Dr. James Ogden, his friend

Emily, his wife

SCENE 1: El & Nikki arriving at the Moores.

EL: I know you'll like the Moores, Nikki. Not only is the Senator one of the finest men we've ever had in Washington, but he's a swell guy. And as for his wife – (He goes into raptures which Nikki barely tolerates).

They are greeted by Dessa, who is as warm and charming as El predicted. But as she and Nikki are being introduced, Lewis Moore appears – and a marked strain is noticeable.

LEWIS: Let me take your coat, Queen.

DESSA: And of course you know the Ogdens, Ellery. Miss Porter, Dr. Ogden, Mrs. Ogden . . .

James Ogden is a trifle too affable, Emily light and fluttery. As social badinage is getting under way, Lewis returns storming.

LEWIS (IN A COLD RAGE): I found this in your coat, Queen.

DESSA: Why it's my compact!

LEWIS: The one I gave you for an engagement present. The one you said you lost in the subway. And I find it – (HARD) Have you an explanation for this, Queen?

75

With the Ogdens trying to interpose and soothe, the scene turns really nasty. Lewis begins to rage about how he's known damned well all along what's been going on between Queen and his wife, and after this little proof he will thank Queen to get the hell out of his house.

NIKKI (AS THEY LEAVE): Just like you said. Nice charming people.

EL: Nikki, I swear I don't understand what can have done this to Lewis.

NIKKI: By the way. . . uh. . . where did you get that compact?

EL: I don't know. Of course I've been seeing a lot of Dessa--she's Secretary of this World Federation Institute I'm so interested in--and I suppose she might have. . .

NIKKI: You know, I'd almost like to believe your Senator. It'd at least prove you could be human.

SCENE 2: Cocktail lounge b g.

DESSA (LAUGHING NOT TOO CONVINCINGLY): I do almost feel clandestine meeting you like this, Ellery.

EL: But I couldn't come to the house, and I do have to talk to you.

He questions her about Lewis, and finds out nothing more than that he has been acting very queerly lately – frowns of suspicion, lifted eyebrows at El's name and so on. She's on the verge of a crack-up herself – obviously whole-heartedly in love with her husband and shocked by his suspicions.

EMILY (FADING IN IN A GREAT FLUTTER): Dessa, I couldn't help seeing you and I do want to warn you. I ran into Lewis and he says you weren't home and he knows you're with Ellery and he's going to find you and it's all so foolish because here you are (SUDDENLY TRAILING OFF FLATLY). . . with Ellery. . .

EL: It's not foolish. It's damned dangerous. Someone's been putting ideas into Lewis' head.

Lewis bursts in. There is a dead silence of several beats. Then

LEWIS (COLDLY): I'll send someone to the house for my things, Dessa. You can refer any messages for me to the Plaza; I'll be staying there from now on. We can discuss the legal aspects later.

Dessa starts to protest.

76

EL (ASIDE TO EMILY): Come on. Let's leave them alone – for what good it'll do with Lewis in this mood.

EMILY: And to think it's all over that silly old compact. I remember all about that now. I found it in our sofa after Dessa was there and James said I should give it to him to give back to her.

EL: James! Tell me, Emily, does James have any. . . grudge against Lewis?

EMILY: Why they're just the best of friends. Even when James didn't get that federal appointment he'd counted on so for years he said that's politics, isn't it and he'd cleave to Lewis like a brother.

EL: Cleave to, or simply cleave? Thanks, Emily. I think I know what to do now – if it isn't too late.

SCENE 3: Chez Queen.

EL: So that explains the compact, Nikki. Dr. James Ogden planted it on me. Obviously he also planted the rumors that have been driving Lewis nuts.

NIKKI: Did you see this in Winchell tonight? "What bigtime politico is so embroiled with personal problems that he's neglecting his fence-building? And whose divorce suit is apt to embarrass his fall campaign?"

EL: This could ruin Lewis. Now if I can find out Ogden's motives and expose him. . .

NIKKI: I've got an idea too. Did you say Lewis was at the Plaza?

SCENE 4: Plaza bar. Nikki picks up Lewis and they start to hit it off beautifully as fellow sufferers. He suggests dinner and the theater.

NIKKI: Wonderful! There's one thing I've been dying to see. Do you suppose a Senator can wangle tickets for that sold-out revival of Othello?

SCENE 5: Chez Ogden. El gets rid of Emily and starts pitching it to James. James tries to stall a bit, trying to interest such an omnivorous amateur as Ellery in his mildly notable numismatic collection, but finally he breaks down.

JAMES: All right. I hate Lewis. We were boys together. I worked hard – slaved my way through medical college – what am I? A not very successful doctor. . . Lewis was the gay dog, the mixer – he quit college and began taking politics seriously – and look where he is now. I thought I'd get my own back when this big Federal medical appointment came up. The deal was that Lewis was to have the appointment as reward for his work in committee. So he appoints that damned Yeshkowitz – on the supposed

77

grounds that he's a far better doctor and administrator. We know why it was – strictly to get the Jewish vote . . . and stab me in the back. I'm sick of Lewis—I knew his weak spot; he's always worried about being twelve years older than Dessa – and I decided to smash him.

EL: But why pick me?

JAMES: Because you're – hell, because you're a do-gooder – a professional model of virtue. You needed smearing. You got it. It won't do you any good when this breaks-- it'll fix you with the public and incidentally with that cute little tart of a secretary--

El socks him in the jaw and walks out.

SCENE 6: Queen apt. Nikki has induced Lewis to come there for a nightcap.

LEWIS (MUCH SOFTENED): You're a clever girl, Miss Porter. Shakespeare wrote everything, didn't he? Even what's been happening to me. I see now what a fool I've been.

El comes in. Lewis makes a warm and handsome apology and hurries home to Dessa.

EL: I'm still worried about Ogden, though. There are horrible depths of bitterness in that man. I've a feeling we haven't heard the last of him. . .

SCENE 7: Chez Ogden.

NIKKI (LITTLE VOICE): Well, Ellery, I guess we've heard the last of Ogden now.

VELIE: I ain't ever seen 'em much deader, Miss Porter.

EL: You can discount that day-old bruise on the chin, dad. I gave him that myself. Now tell me the rest.

All this is late afternoon of the day following the last scenes. The man in the apt below was disturbed by feeble thumps coming from Ogden's study. He got the janitor to break in and found Ogden dying – died before an ambulance arrived and without talking. But he kept pointing at where he'd set out two coins from his collection – a Japanese copper piece and a French 20-franc gold piece. Knifed to death – knife just missing heart, died of internal hemorrhage, giving him long enough to root out the coins, which bear his prints and traces of blood. Knife lying some distance away – handle rubbed on rug to wipe off prints. Emily was out shopping when it all happened (she says). She and James had had a terrible fight last night about the compact business.

INSP: I don't know what political repercussions this'll have in the dept, but we've got to go grill a Senator.

78

SCENE 8: Chez Moore.

Lewis, just after having regained his happiness, is on the verge of cracking again.

LEWIS: God knows I had reason enough to kill him, Inspector, but –

Time-check: Ogden was found at 5: 15. Couldn't have lived more than fifteen minutes with that wound, therefore murder around 5.   At 5 Dessa was at a movie – no corroboration.

LEWIS:  I was around here all afternoon, catching up on the letters I've been neglecting while. . .

INSP:  Any phone calls to check your time?

LEWIS:  I had a long distance call in to talk some party business with George Outland in San Francisco – it finally came through.  But I've no idea what time – I was working hard.

(NOTE:  If you'd like really to use George, who is a reasonably well-known name nationally in Demo politics, I'm sure I could arrange clearance.  He's a great mystery fan, and would probably be thrilled to death.)

SCENE 9:  HQ

INSP:  Well, we've checked with Outland.  He noticed the time – it was almost exactly 3 o'clock.

NIKKI:  And there's 3 hours' difference in our times, so that'd be 6 here.  It doesn't clear him.

INSP:  And we've had a man from the museum look at these coins and--

EL:  Oh yes.  I figured the coins long ago.  Yes, now we know who killed James Ogden.

JURY SPOT & SOLUTION

EL:  A small Japanese copper coin, as any crossword puzzle solver knows, is a sen.  A French 20-franc gold piece is a louis.

NIKKI:  Sen. . . Senator.  Louis. . . Lewis.  (SADLY) Senator Lewis. . .  Just when I'd decided he really was nice. . .

EL:  *But*:  The murder took place at 5.  At 3 o'clock in SF, George Outland was talking to Lewis on a call the phone company traces to Lewis' own phone.  And we've read,

79

even in the papers back here, that California is suffering the worst power shortage in her history and has gone on daylight saving time. The time difference is now only *two* hours – -not 3, Nikki – and Outland was talking to Lewis at precisely the time of the murder!

INSP: Then the "dying message" is a fake!

EL: Precisely. I wondered all along why a man should leave such a message in a study equipped with writing materials, but you can never tell what victims on this show do in their last moments. But who left the fake? We found on those coins only Ogden's prints, unsmudged, with traces of his own blood. He left the fake himself – after stabbing himself and using his medical knowledge to just miss the heart. He let himself die slowly, to have time to wipe the knife and plant his "dying message" – using his last seconds, he hoped, finally to accomplish his perverted objective of destroying Senator Lewis Moore. And, of course, using the "dying message" technique rather than a plain written message because he knew I'd investigate the case and would fall for my own brilliant deductions from the coins.

**Photo above: Manny Lee and Kaye Brinker Lee with granddaughter Anne Steinfield during the summer of 1965. Photo courtesy of Anne Steinfield Sohboff.**

# QUEEN IN THE SHADOW'S PARLOR

## William Nadel

Around the time Ellery Queen made his debut as both the detective in *The Roman Hat Mystery* and the joint byline of his creators Fred Dannay and Manny Lee, the radio production company of McKnight & Jordan was founded by author-actress-director Edith Meiser, her husband Tom McKnight, and NBC executive Wally Jordan. In 1930 this company brought to radio the print medium's pre-eminent detective character, Sherlock Holmes, and the character who was to become the most celebrated sleuth of the airwaves, The Shadow. In his first incarnation, which lasted (with several interruptions) from July 31, 1930 until the end of the 1934-35 season, "The Shadow" was merely a sinister voice (first James LaCurto, then Frank Readick, finally LaCurto again) whose function was to narrate tales of mystery and suspense adapted from the latest issue of Street & Smith's Detective Story Magazine. The character excited such curiosity that Street & Smith commissioned Walter B. Gibson to convert him into the hero of what turned into a long series of pulp action novels. Then in 1937 Gibson's version of the character became the inspiration for a "new" radio series, still packaged by McKnight & Jordan – albeit with close supervision from the sponsor and its advertising agency – and with 22-year-old Orson Welles playing wealthy dilettante Lamont Cranston and his crime-fighting alter ego "The Shadow." Welles portrayed the weird figure with the power to cloud men's minds during the 26 episodes of the 1937-38 season and 25 of the 26 segments of the summer 1938 season, then left the part to concentrate on the *Mercury Theater of the Air* which was his major radio work at the time.

When the series returned in the fall of 1938, *The Shadow* was portrayed by Bill Johnstone. And during that first of Johnstone's five seasons in the part, among the scriptwriters who created his adventures were the cousins Fred Dannay and Manny Lee who were known throughout the mystery-loving world as Ellery Queen. Edith Meiser was script editor for the series. Fifty years later, she told me: "We hired the Queen cousins to write our top mystery show. I had read their stories and was only too glad to have them working for us. We handed them model scripts and they went to work. After editing the results, I would send the finished scripts to Ruthrauff & Ryan [the advertising agency]."

The Ruthrauff & Ryan executives who directed and produced *The Shadow* at this time were Nathan Tufts and Wilson "Bill" Tuttle. Copies of the final scripts were also sent to Street & Smith, the publishers of *The Shadow Magazine*, and those copies are now at the library of Syracuse University. Unfortunately, all scripts before the fall of 1939 bear no author credits. The files of McKnight & Jordan must have contained paperwork revealing how many of the 26 scripts broadcast during the 1938-39 season were written by Dannay and Lee but that information vanished long ago when the firm was liquidated.

So how many of those scripts did the cousins write? Probably eight and possibly eleven. I arrived at this answer by a two-step process. First, I eliminated the scripts that can be attributed to others who are known to have written for *The Shadow* that season. Episodes that center on horror and mad scientists were the domain of Alonzo Deen Cole, while Jerry Devine's forte was revenge and retribution and Arch Oboler was a master of the "supernormal." One of the scripts not eliminated by this process we know was written by Brian Byrne because he got credit when it was reused some years later. Any or all of the scripts that have survived this winnowing process may have been written by Dannay and Lee.

But some of those can be eliminated for another reason. In the summer and fall of 1938, before being hired for *The Shadow*, Fred and Manny had written some scripts for *Alias Jimmy Valentine*, a series about a reformed safecracker that was packaged by Frank and Anne Hummert's Air Features production company. The Hummerts were afraid of losing their "trade secrets" to rival companies and therefore did not like their writers to work for others while on the Hummert payroll. They also didn't like to give authors credit for their scripts. Since the only *Alias Jimmy Valentine* script which did credit Fred and Manny was broadcast on November 21, 1938, that was probably their last work for the company. Once they had finished that script – about six to eight weeks before its airdate, the usual time gap between submission of a script and broadcast – they were free to work for McKnight & Jordan. Therefore their first script for *The Shadow* could be no earlier than November.

The first episode broadcast that month was "Shyster Payoff" (November 6, 1938), which pits *The Shadow* against a crooked lawyer and does not fit the style or tone of Alonzo Deen Cole or Jerry Devine, who clearly had written the earlier scripts that season. More likely than not it was the work of Dannay and Lee. The Shadow's next adventure, "Black Rock" (November 13, 1938), deals with a "con man" type and suggests the scripts Fred and Manny had previously written for *Alias Jimmy Valentine*. "Murder in E Flat" (December 4, 1938) with its many musical references hints at the cousins even more strongly since music was Manny Lee's hobby.

Three of the episodes broadcast around this time – "Fountain of Death" (November 27, 1938), "Murder by Rescue" (December 11, 1938) and "Give Us This Day" (December 25, 1938) – are not available for examination. Whether any of these were written by the cousins there is no way of determining at this time. The next episode that does seem to be by Fred and Manny is "Valley of the Living Dead" (January 22, 1939), in which Lamont Cranston makes a speech about social injustice that is rare on *The Shadow* but echoes Manny Lee's strong "social consciousness" as it was manifested in many of the later Ellery Queen novels and radio scripts. "The Ghost of Captain Bayloe" (February 5, 1939) is one of the season's most literary scripts, a sea adventure told as a radio movie, with links both to the cousins' brief stints in Hollywood before becoming involved with radio and to Fred Dannay's well-known love for juvenile adventure sagas like *Treasure Island*.

More social comments in the Manny Lee vein are heard in "Friend of Darkness" (February 19, 1939) and "Can the Dead Talk?" (March 19, 1939), making them likely candidates for authorship by the cousins. Between those two came "Sabotage by Air" (March 5, 1939), an unusual spy thriller about radio recordings that convey hidden messages when played at faster than normal speed. The plot so bothered actor Sidney Slon that he went to producer-director Bill Tuttle after the broadcast and begged for a chance to write for *The Shadow*, claiming that he could turn out better scripts than those he was acting in. Little did he know that some of those scripts, probably including the one he had just finished acting in, were the work of perhaps the finest American mystery writers of their time. Eventually Slon himself replaced Edith Meiser as script editor on *The Shadow*.

By then of course Dannay and Lee had finished their apprenticeship in radio and launched their own Ellery Queen series, whose long run is traced week by week in the log that follows.

# ELLERY QUEEN RADIO LOG

## Francis M. Nevins & Martin Grams, Jr.

# SEASON ONE

EPISODE #1 **"THE GUM-CHEWING MILLIONAIRE"** Broadcast on June 18, 1939
Guests: Peter Arno (cartoonist), Ruth McKenney (playwright), Lee T. Smith,
and Frederick Chase Taylor (radio personality known as Colonel Stoopnagle).
Written by Frederic Dannay and Manfred B. Lee.
Produced and directed by George Zachary.
Music composed and conducted by Bernard Herrmann.
Announcer: Ken Roberts.
Story: Ellery receives a friendly letter from a complete stranger, asking him to recommend a nurse, and is soon trying to solve the bludgeon murder of a crippled, gum-loving, will-changing old tyrant.

**Trivia, etc.** The script for this premiere episode of the series was later adapted (not by Dannay and Lee) into the novelette *The Murdered Millionaire* (Whitman Better Little Books, 1942). A 30-minute version of the script was broadcast on May 25 and 27, 1944, as "The Great Chewing Gum Mystery" (Episode #179).

EPISODE #2 **"THE LAST MAN CLUB"** Broadcast on June 25, 1939
Guests: Ed Gardner (radio producer/director), Gelett Burgess (writer),
Princess A. Kropotkin (Russian refugee), and Deems Taylor (music critic).
Written by Frederic Dannay and Manfred B. Lee.
Produced and directed by George Zachary.
Music composed and conducted by Bernard Herrmann.
Announcer: Ken Roberts.
Story: After witnessing a hit-and-run death, Ellery and Nikki follow the victim's dying message along a trail that leads him to an artist, a bartender, a fashion designer, and the affairs of a survivor-take-all group to which the dead man belonged.

**Trivia, etc.** The script for this episode was adapted (not by Dannay and Lee) into the novelette *The Last Man Club* (Whitman Better Little Books, 1940). The episode was rerun under the same title on February 18, 1940 (Episode #36). A 30-minute version of the script was broadcast on January 6 and 8, 1944, as "The Disaster Club" (Episode #159).

EPISODE #3 **"THE FALLEN ANGEL"** Broadcast on July 2, 1939
Guests: William H. Barton, Jr., Christopher Coates, Francesca La Monte,
and Pauline Simmons.
Written by Frederic Dannay and Manfred B. Lee.
Produced and directed by George Zachary.
Music composed and conducted by Bernard Herrmann.
Announcer: Ken Roberts.
Story: On a Fourth of July weekend, Nikki pulls Ellery into the problems of a girl friend who recently married an aging tycoon and moved into the family mansion and apparently into a sexual relationship with her husband's artistic younger brother. Then murder enters the picture.

**Trivia, etc.** A 30-minute version of the script for this episode was broadcast on NBC's *Molle Mystery Theater*, June 14, 1946. The script was later adapted by Dannay and Lee into the short story "The Fallen Angel" (*Ellery Queen's Mystery Magazine*, July 1951; collected in *Calendar of Crime*, 1952).

EPISODE #4  **"NAPOLEON'S RAZOR"**  Broadcast on July 9, 1939
     Guests: Craig Earl (host of radio's *Professor Quiz* program), Betty Garde (singer), Lillian Hellman (playwright), and Herman Shumlin (Broadway producer).
     Written by Frederic Dannay and Manfred B. Lee.
     Produced and directed by George Zachary.
     Music composed and conducted by Bernard Herrmann.
     Announcer: Ken Roberts.
     Story: Ellery tries to solve a transcontinental train murder that involves a traveling salesman, a faded movie star, a professor and an old razor.

     **Trivia, etc.** A 30-minute version of this script was broadcast on June 22 and 24, 1944, as "The Corpse in Lower Five" (Episode #183).

EPISODE #5  **"THE IMPOSSIBLE CRIME"**  Broadcast on July 16, 1939
     Guests: Jane Franklin, Mrs. Mary E. Hamilton, Michael Krozier, and John J. Martin.
     Written by Frederic Dannay and Manfred B. Lee.
     Produced and directed by George Zachary.
     Music composed and conducted by Bernard Herrmann.
     Announcer: Ken Roberts.
     Story: unknown.

EPISODE #6  **"GEORGE SPELVIN, MURDERER"**  Broadcast on July 23, 1939
     Guests: Katharine Albert (playwright), Dale Eunson (playwright), Constance Smith, and John S. Young (radio announcer).
     Written by Frederic Dannay and Manfred B. Lee.
     Produced and directed by George Zachary.
     Music composed and conducted by Bernard Herrmann.
     Announcer: Ken Roberts.
     Story: Ellery tackles a murder case in which, even after he knows everything about the killer, he knows nothing.

EPISODE #7  **"THE BAD BOY"**  Broadcast on July 30, 1939
     Guests: Daisy Amoury, Lewis Birdseye, Helen Leighty, and Dr. Lloyd B. Sharp (all New York child welfare officials).
     Written by Frederic Dannay and Manfred B. Lee.
     Produced and directed by George Zachary.
     Music composed and conducted by Bernard Herrmann.
     Announcer: Ken Roberts.
     Story: Ellery visits an old brownstone overlooking Washington Square and tries to solve the murder of a hateful old woman who was poisoned by arsenic in a serving of rabbit stew and found dead in her bed with several dozen live bunnies loose in the room.

     **Trivia, etc.** Beginning October 4, 1947, NBC premiered a new anthology series entitled *The Ford Theater*, with George Zachary directing the first season's worth of hour-long episodes. One of those episodes was a restaging of "The Bad Boy" (January 4, 1948), with Hugh Marlowe, Ted de Corsia and Santos Ortega playing the lead roles.

EPISODE #8  **"THE FLYING NEEDLE"**  Broadcast on August 6, 1939
     Guests: E.L. Bragdon, Leonard Carlton, Dinty Doyle, and Joe Ranson.
     Written by Frederic Dannay and Manfred B. Lee.
     Produced and directed by George Zachary.

Music composed and conducted by Bernard Herrmann.

Announcer: Ken Roberts.

Story: Ellery investigates a murder committed with a poisoned needle that flew through the air from an apparently invisible source.

**Trivia, etc.** A 30-minute version of the script for this episode was broadcast on February 3 and 5, 1944, as "The Murder on the Air" (Episode #163).

EPISODE #9 **"THE WANDERING CORPSE"** Broadcast on August 13, 1939

Guests: Howard Barlow, Johnny Green, Raymond Paige, and Mark Warnow (all bandleaders).

Written by Frederic Dannay and Manfred B. Lee.

Produced and directed by George Zachary.

Music composed and conducted by Bernard Herrmann.

Announcer: Ken Roberts.

Story: Ellery joins his father and Sergeant Velie in an investigation that involves election fraud and a newly elected District Attorney whose body is found in a Turkish bath.

**Trivia, etc.** A 30-minute version of the script for this episode was broadcast on November 2 and 4, 1944, as "The Election Day Murder" (Episode #202).

EPISODE #10 **"THE THIRTEENTH CLUE"** Broadcast on August 20, 1939

Guests: Henry Casler, James Crayhon, Don Doherty, and Margaret Bourke-White (all news photographers).

Written by Frederic Dannay and Manfred B. Lee.

Produced and directed by George Zachary.

Music composed and conducted by Bernard Herrmann.

Announcer: Ken Roberts.

Story: Ellery investigates a series of thefts from a Broadway sideshow and the murder of a midget who died of a rattlesnake bite in a locked room.

**Trivia, etc.** A 30-minute version of the script for this episode was broadcast on February 17 and 19, 1944, as "The Squirrel Woman" (Episode #165).

EPISODE #11 **"THE SECRET PARTNER"** Broadcast on August 27, 1939

Guests: Lois Doyle, Buster Holfer, Estelle Levy (radio actress), and Arthur Ross (radio emcee).

Written by Frederic Dannay and Manfred B. Lee.

Produced and directed by George Zachary.

Music composed and conducted by Leith Stevens.

Announcer: Ken Roberts.

Story: Ellery and Nikki become involved in a plot to smuggle diamonds from the Netherlands into the United States in shipments of tulip bulbs.

**Trivia, etc.** The script for this episode was later adapted (not by Dannay and Lee) into a serialized comic book, given away weekly at Gulf Oil stations during May and June of 1940.

EPISODE #12 **"THE MILLION DOLLAR FINGER"** Broadcast on September 3, 1939

Guests: Tony Sarg (illustrator), Dean Cornwell (painter), Ruth Garth (industrial designer), and Suzanne Silvercruys (sculptor).

Written by Frederic Dannay and Manfred B. Lee.

Produced and directed by George Zachary.
Music composed and conducted by Leith Stevens.
Announcer: Ken Roberts.
Story: Ellery investigates murder among a group of starving artists in Greenwich Village.

EPISODE #13  **"THE THREE R'S"**  Broadcast on September 10, 1939
Guests: four undergraduates from Midwest colleges.
Written by Frederic Dannay and Manfred B. Lee.
Produced and directed by George Zachary.
Music composed and conducted by Leith Stevens.
Announcer: Ken Roberts.
Story: As the new school year begins, Ellery is hired by the administrators of Barlowe College to locate one of its faculty, a Poe scholar who vanished in the Ozarks during the summer.

**Trivia, etc.** This episode was broadcast only on the West Coast. The Queen show's time slot on the East Coast was given over to a 60-minute version of "Peter Ibbetson" by Orson Welles and his Mercury Theater players, with guest star Helen Hayes.

A 30-minute version of the script for this episode was broadcast on September 14 and 16, 1944, as "The College Crime" (Episode #195). The script was later adapted by Dannay and Lee into the short story "The Three Rs" (*Ellery Queen's Mystery Magazine*, September 1946; collected in *Calendar of Crime*, 1952).

EPISODE #14  **"THE BLUE CURSE"**  Broadcast on September 17, 1939
Guests: four winners of a write-in contest.
Written by Frederic Dannay and Manfred B. Lee.
Produced and directed by George Zachary.
Music composed and conducted by Lyn Murray.
Announcer: Ken Roberts.
Story: unknown.

**Trivia, etc.** This episode too was broadcast only on the West Coast. Listeners in the East heard Orson Welles and his Mercury Theater cast in a 60-minute adaptation of a popular novel for *The Campbell Playhouse*. The episode was repeated under the same title on February 4, 1940 (Episode #34).

EPISODE #15  **"THE LOST TREASURE"**  Broadcast on September 24, 1939
West Coast Guests: Camilla Boone, James Edwards, Hugh Hawley, and Esther Tyler.
East Coast Guests: Dean Cornwell (commercial artist), Ruth Garth
(industrial designer), Tony Sarg (illustrator), and Suzanne Silvercruys (sculptor).
Written by Frederic Dannay and Manfred B. Lee.
Produced and directed by George Zachary.
Music composed and conducted by Lyn Murray.
Announcer: Ken Roberts.
Story: A retired explorer, on whose private island Captain Kidd is rumored to have buried part of his treasure, asks Ellery to investigate his niece's new husband. When Ellery arrives on the island, he runs into a treasure hunt and the murder of his host.

**Trivia, etc.** This episode was repeated as "Captain Kidd's Bedroom" on February 11, 1940 (Episode #35). A 30-minute version of the script was broadcast on April 27 and 29, 1944, as "The Buried Treasure" (Episode #175). The script for this episode was later adapted by Dannay and Lee into the short story "The Needle's Eye" (*Ellery Queen's Mystery Magazine*, August 1951; collected in *Calendar of Crime*, 1952).

**EPISODE #16**    **"THE WOMAN FROM NOWHERE"**    Broadcast on October 1, 1939
Guests:  Wally Butterworth and Parks Johnson (co-hosts of radio's *Vox Pop* program)
and four audience members.
Written by Frederic Dannay and Manfred B. Lee.
Produced and directed by George Zachary.
Music composed and conducted by Lyn Murray.
Announcer: Ken Roberts.
Story: Ellery investigates when a pawnbroker and his family, moving from one house
to another, find the body of an unknown woman in a trunk from their basement.

**EPISODE #17**    **"THE MOTHER GOOSE MURDERS"**    Broadcast on October 8, 1939
Guests:  four audience members.
Written by Frederic Dannay and Manfred B. Lee.
Produced and directed by George Zachary.
Music composed and conducted by Lyn Murray.
Announcer: Ken Roberts.
Story:  Ellery probes a series of nursery-rhyme killings in an old hotel.

**EPISODE #18**    **"THE MARCH OF DEATH"**    Broadcast on October 15, 1939
Guest:  Harry Kurnitz (crime novelist/screenwriter).
Written by Frederic Dannay and Manfred B. Lee.
Produced and directed by George Zachary.
Music composed and conducted by Lyn Murray.
Announcer: Ken Roberts.
Story:  Ellery encounters murder and a dying message while trying to help a
department-store magnate find three scattered children.

**EPISODE #19**    **"THE HAUNTED CAVE"**    Broadcast on October 22, 1939
Guests:  four members of the CBS staff and Radio City Music Hall.
Written by Frederic Dannay and Manfred B. Lee.
Produced and directed by George Zachary.
Music composed and conducted by Lyn Murray.
Announcer: Ken Roberts.
Story:  Ellery is invited to a lodge in the Adirondacks where a serial strangler had
operated a century before.  Soon after, Ellery becomes involved in a new murder-by-strangulation
mystery when a psychic investigator is found dead inside a cave that no one else could have
entered because there is only one set of footprints.

**Trivia, etc.**  The script for this episode was later adapted (not by Dannay and Lee but
with their permission) into the short story "The Haunted Cave" (*Radio & Television Mirror*, May
1940). A 30-minute version of the script was broadcast on April 13 and 15, 1944, as "Dead
Man's Cavern" (Episode #173).

**EPISODE #20**    **"THE DEAD CAT"**    Broadcast on October 29, 1939
Guests:  unknown.
Written by Frederic Dannay and Manfred B. Lee.
Produced and directed by George Zachary.
Music composed and conducted by Lyn Murray.
Announcer: Ken Roberts.
Story:  Ellery and Nikki attend a Halloween party in cat costumes and stay to find out
who cut the throat of one of the guests in pitch darkness during a game of "Murder."

**Trivia, etc.** This was the first of four consecutive episodes in which the guest armchair detectives were not celebrities but audience members selected on the basis of letters they wrote.

A 30-minute version of the script for this episode was broadcast on June 1 and 3, 1944, as "The Murder Game" (Episode #180). The script was later adapted by Dannay and Lee into the short story "The Dead Cat" (*Ellery Queen's Mystery Magazine*, October 1946; collected in *Calendar of Crime*, 1952).

EPISODE #21   **"THE PICTURE PUZZLE"**   Broadcast on November 5, 1939
Guests: unknown.
Written by Frederic Dannay and Manfred B. Lee.
Produced and directed by George Zachary.
Music composed and conducted by Lyn Murray.
Announcer: Ken Roberts.
Story: Ellery tries to decipher a message in a painting on the wall of a prison cell that provides the clue to where an executed bank robber hid a fortune in stolen bonds.

**Trivia, etc.** A 30-minute version of the script for this episode was broadcast on April 6 and 8, 1944, as "The Painted Problem" (Episode #172).

Sometime during November 1939 the series experienced its first cast change when Ted de Corsia replaced Howard Smith in the role of Sergeant Velie. De Corsia continued in that part until April 1947.

EPISODE #22   **"THE CELLINI CUP"**   Broadcast on November 12, 1939
Guests: unknown.
Written by Frederic Dannay and Manfred B. Lee.
Produced and directed by George Zachary.
Music composed and conducted by Lyn Murray.
Announcer: Ken Roberts.
Story: Ellery is visited by an irate man who claims that an art dealer cheated him out of a priceless Cellini cup. Two nights later the cup is stolen from the art dealer's son in total darkness and Ellery tries to deduce who the thief was and how he vanished.

**Trivia, etc.** The script for this episode was later adapted (not by Dannay and Lee and without their permission) into the short story "Here is a Mystery" (*Radio Guide*, January 26, 1940). Although the purpose of the magazine feature was to call attention to deserving radio programs and personalities, the way the editors went about it greatly offended Dannay and Lee. Soon after the short story appeared in print, the magazine offered an apology.

A 30-minute version of the script was broadcast on May 4 and 6, 1944, as "The Thief in the Dark" (Episode #176).

EPISODE #23   **"THE TELL-TALE BOTTLE"**   Broadcast on November 19, 1939
Guests: unknown.
Written by Frederic Dannay and Manfred B. Lee.
Produced and directed by George Zachary.
Music composed and conducted by Lyn Murray.
Announcer: Ken Roberts.
Story: While delivering Thanksgiving food baskets to the poor, Ellery and Nikki blunder into a cocaine-pushing operation and murder.

**Trivia, etc.** The script for this episode was later adapted by Dannay and Lee into the short story "The Telltale Bottle" (*Ellery Queen's Mystery Magazine*, November 1946; collected in *Calendar of Crime*, 1952).

EPISODE #24 **"THE LOST CHILD"** Broadcast on November 26, 1939
    Guests: four unidentified celebrities.
    Written by Frederic Dannay and Manfred B. Lee.
    Produced and directed by George Zachary.
    Music composed and conducted by Lyn Murray.
    Announcer: Ken Roberts.
    Story: Ellery encounters a mysterious letter and a negligent nurse while searching for a child who disappeared as its parents were about to divorce.

    **Trivia, etc.** The script for this episode was later adapted by Dannay and Lee into the short story "Kidnaped!" (*This Week*, July 8, 1951; collected as "Child Missing!" in *Queen's Bureau of Investigation*, 1955). A 30-minute version of the script was broadcast on May 7 and 9, 1942, as "The Missing Child" (Episode #85).

EPISODE #25 **"THE MAN WHO WANTED TO BE MURDERED"** December 3, 1939
    Guests: four unidentified celebrities.
    Written by Frederic Dannay and Manfred B. Lee.
    Produced and directed by George Zachary.
    Music composed and conducted by Lyn Murray.
    Announcer: Ken Roberts.
    Story: A wheelchair-bound old gambler deliberately tempts his brother, his nephew, his niece and his doctor into trying to murder him when he executes a will dividing most of his estate among them if he dies within one week but leaving everything to charity if he lives longer. Then the old man makes a $25,000 bet that Ellery can't solve his murder.

    **Trivia, etc.** The script for this episode was later adapted (not by Dannay and Lee but with their permission) into the short story "The Man Who Wanted to Be Murdered" (*Radio and Television Mirror*, August 1940).

EPISODE #26 **"THE BLACK SECRET"** Broadcast on December 10, 1939
    Guests: four unidentified celebrities.
    Written by Frederic Dannay and Manfred B. Lee.
    Produced and directed by George Zachary.
    Music composed and conducted by Lyn Murray.
    Announcer: Ken Roberts.
    Story: Ellery and Nikki become clerks in a rare-book emporium while trying to solve the theft of some priceless volumes, but then the co-owner of the store is murdered.

    **Trivia, etc.** A 30-minute version of this episode was broadcast on June 8 and 10, 1944, as "The Dark Secret" (Episode #181).

EPISODE #27 **"THE THREE SCRATCHES"** Broadcast on December 17, 1939
    Guests: four unidentified celebrities.
    Written by Frederic Dannay and Manfred B. Lee.
    Produced and directed by George Zachary.
    Music composed and conducted by Lyn Murray.
    Announcer: Ken Roberts.
    Story: unknown.

EPISODE #28 **"THE SWISS NUTCRACKER"** Broadcast on December 24, 1939
    Guests: four unidentified celebrities.

Written by Frederic Dannay and Manfred B. Lee.
Produced and directed by George Zachary.
Music composed and conducted by Lyn Murray.
Announcer: Ken Roberts.
Story: While snowbound at a new England house party, Ellery investigates first the thefts of a nutcracker and a Santa Claus suit and then the disappearance of a valuable diamond at a time when everyone in the house has an alibi.

EPISODE #29   **"THE SCORPION'S THUMB"**   Broadcast on December 31, 1939
Guests:  four unidentified celebrities.
Written by Frederic Dannay and Manfred B. Lee.
Produced and directed by George Zachary.
Music composed and conducted by Lyn Murray.
Announcer: Ken Roberts.
Story:  Near the end of the year, Ellery is asked to look into an embezzlement from a Wall Street brokerage house. Then a partner in the firm dies of a poisoned cocktail during a New Year's Day party and Ellery tries to deduce the murderer's identity.

**Trivia, etc.** The script for this episode was later adapted (not by Dannay and Lee but with their permission) into the short story "The Scorpion's Thumb" (*Radio and Television Mirror*, December 1940).

EPISODE #30   **"THE DYING SCARECROW"**   Broadcast on January 7, 1940
Guests:   Marge Kerr, Russell Markert (promoter), George Shoemaker, and Helen Sioussat (radio producer/director).
Written by Frederic Dannay and Manfred B. Lee.
Produced and directed by George Zachary.
Music composed and conducted by Lyn Murray.
Announcer: Ken Roberts.
Story: Ellery, Inspector Queen, Sergeant Velie and Nikki are driving through midwestern farm country one summer when they stop to take home movies of a picturesque scarecrow. To their surprise they find a badly knifed man inside the scarecrow outfit. Six months later Ellery and his entourage return to the same area during a blizzard and encounter the same man again, this time dead and concealed inside a snowman in the farmyard.

**Trivia, etc.** A 30-minute version of this script was broadcast on January 20 and 22, 1944, as "The Scarecrow and the Snowman" (Episode #161).

EPISODE #31      **"THE WOMAN IN BLACK"**      Broadcast on January 14, 1940
Guests: unknown.
Written by Frederic Dannay and Manfred B. Lee.
Produced and directed by George Zachary.
Music composed and conducted by Lyn Murray.
Announcer: Ken Roberts.
Story: Ellery looks into the legend of a ghost haunting the family of an English novelist.

**Trivia, etc.** A 30-minute version of the script for this episode was broadcast on March 16 and 18, 1944, as "The Circular Clues" (Episode #169).

EPISODE #32    **"THE ANONYMOUS LETTERS"**    Broadcast on January 21, 1940
    East Coast guests:  George and Martha Washington, Napoleon Bonaparte, Benjamin
    Franklin, and Robert E. Lee (five ordinary people who happened to have the
    same names as five famous historical figures).
    Written by Frederic Dannay and Manfred B. Lee.
    Produced and directed by George Zachary.
    Music composed and conducted by Lyn Murray.
    Announcer: Ken Roberts.
    Story: unknown.

EPISODE #33    **"THE DEVIL'S VIOLIN"**    Broadcast on January 28, 1940
    Guests:  four people named John Smith.
    Written by Frederic Dannay and Manfred B. Lee.
    Produced and directed by George Zachary.
    Music composed and conducted by Lyn Murray.
    Announcer: Ken Roberts.
    Story:  Ellery encounters a violin virtuoso and child prodigy who are refugees from
Austria, and sets out to save their priceless Stradivarius from a bearded man with dark glasses
and a limp, who calls himself John Smith.

    **Trivia, etc.**  A 30-minute version of this script was broadcast on March 9 and 11,
1944, as "Wanted: John Smith" (Episode #168).

EPISODE #34    **"THE BLUE CURSE"**    Broadcast on February 4, 1940
    Guest:  Donald Cook (movie and radio actor).
    Written by Frederic Dannay and Manfred B. Lee.
    Produced and directed by George Zachary.
    Music composed and conducted by Lyn Murray.
    Announcer: Ken Roberts.
    Story: same as Episode #14.

    **Trivia, etc.**  This was a rerun of Episode #14, "The Blue Curse" (September 17, 1939),
which had not previously been heard on the East Coast.

EPISODE #35    **"CAPTAIN KIDD'S BEDROOM"**    Broadcast on February 11, 1940
    Guests:  unknown.
    Written by Frederic Dannay and Manfred B. Lee.
    Produced and directed by George Zachary.
    Music composed and conducted by Lyn Murray.
    Announcer: Ken Roberts.
    Story:  same as Episode #15.

    **Trivia,  etc.**  This was a rerun of Episode #15, "The Lost Treasure" (September 24,
1939), which had not previously been heard on the East Coast.

EPISODE #36    **"THE LAST MAN CLUB"**    Broadcast on February 18, 1940
    Guests:  unknown.
    Written by Frederic Dannay and Manfred B. Lee.
    Produced and directed by George Zachary.
    Music composed and conducted by Lyn Murray.
    Announcer: Ken Roberts.
    Story:  same as Episode #2.

**Trivia, etc.** This was a rerun of Episode #2, "The Last Man Club" (June 25, 1939). It was also the final radio adventure of Ellery Queen in the hour-long format. After this week all episodes of the series were 30 minutes long.

EPISODE #37   **"THE OLD SOLDIERS"**   Broadcast on February 25, 1940
　　　　Guests: unknown.
　　　　Written by Frederic Dannay and Manfred B. Lee.
　　　　Produced and directed by George Zachary.
　　　　Music composed and conducted by Lyn Murray.
　　　　Announcer: Ken Roberts.
　　　　Story: unknown.


**Trivia, etc.** This was not only the first 30-minute episode of the series but also the first in which Arthur Allen took over for Robert Strauss in the role of Doc Prouty.

EPISODE #38   **"THE WHISTLING CLOWN"**   Broadcast on March 3, 1940
　　　　Guests: unknown.
　　　　Written by Frederic Dannay and Manfred B. Lee.
　　　　Produced and directed by George Zachary.
　　　　Music composed and conducted by Lyn Murray.
　　　　Announcer: Ken Roberts.
　　　　Story: Ellery looks into the death of a circus clown who was found hanged in his dressing room.

EPISODE #39   **"THE THREE FISHBOWLS"**   Broadcast on March 10, 1940
　　　　Guests: unknown.
　　　　Written by Frederic Dannay and Manfred B. Lee.
　　　　Produced and directed by George Zachary.
　　　　Music composed and conducted by Lyn Murray.
　　　　Announcer: Ken Roberts.
　　　　Story: Ellery investigates a theft from the display case of a Chinese antiquity dealer soon after he gave fishbowls to three of his customers.

EPISODE #40   **"THE SILVER BALL"**   Broadcast on March 17, 1940
　　　　Guests: unknown.
　　　　Written by Frederic Dannay and Manfred B. Lee.
　　　　Produced and directed by George Zachary.
　　　　Music composed and conducted by Lyn Murray.
　　　　Announcer: Ken Roberts.
　　　　Story: unknown.


**Trivia, etc.** The script for this episode was repeated on March 23 and 25, 1944, as "The Glass Ball" (Episode #170).

EPISODE #41   **"THE WIZARD'S CAT"**   Broadcast on March 24, 1940
　　　　Guests: unknown.
　　　　Written by Frederic Dannay and Manfred B. Lee.
　　　　Produced and directed by George Zachary.
　　　　Music composed and conducted by Lyn Murray.
　　　　Announcer: Ken Roberts.
　　　　Story: Ellery probes the murder of a Wall Street wizard who was poisoned on a train.

EPISODE #42 **"THE EMPEROR'S DICE"**   Broadcast on March 31, 1940
Guests: unknown.
Written by Frederic Dannay and Manfred B. Lee.
Produced and directed by George Zachary.
Music composed and conducted by Lyn Murray.
Announcer: Ken Roberts.
Story: Ellery visits a sinister old house and investigates the apparent ten-year-old murder of a millionaire collector of gambling devices.

**Trivia, etc.** The script for this episode was repeated on August 31 and September 2, 1944, as "The Dead Man's Bones" (Episode #193). The script was later adapted by Dannay and Lee into the short story "The Emperor's Dice" (*Ellery Queen's Mystery Magazine*, April 1951; collected in *Calendar of Crime*, 1952).

EPISODE #43 **"THE FORGOTTEN MEN"**   Broadcast on April 7, 1940
Guests: unknown.
Written by Frederic Dannay and Manfred B. Lee.
Produced and directed by George Zachary.
Music composed and conducted by Lyn Murray.
Announcer: Ken Roberts.
Story: unknown.

EPISODE #44 **"THE YELLOW PIGEON"**   Broadcast on April 14, 1940
Guests: unknown.
Written by Frederic Dannay and Manfred B. Lee.
Produced and directed by George Zachary.
Music composed and conducted by Lyn Murray.
Announcer: Ken Roberts.
Story: Ellery probes the case of a racketeer who was killed by a poisoned cigarette soon after being informed on by a stool pigeon.

EPISODE #45 **"THE POKER CLUB"**   Broadcast on April 21, 1940
Guests: unknown.
Written by Frederic Dannay and Manfred B. Lee.
Produced and directed by George Zachary.
Music composed and conducted by Lyn Murray.
Announcer: Ken Roberts.
Story: Ellery investigates a murder that grew out of a poker game following a performance of Shakespeare's *Julius Caesar*.

**Trivia, etc.** This episode was broadcast from 8:00 to 8:30 p.m. EST, a time slot the series used only this week. It was also the final episode to feature the character of Doc Prouty in the continuing cast.
This episode was repeated on April 22 and 24, 1943, as "The Deadly Game" (Episode #122).

EPISODE #46 **"THE DOUBLE TRIANGLE"**   Broadcast on April 28, 1940
Guests: unknown.
Written by Frederic Dannay and Manfred B. Lee.
Produced and directed by George Zachary.
Music composed and conducted by Lyn Murray.

Announcer: Bert Parks.

Sponsor: Gulf Oil.

Story: Ellery tries to locate the mysterious lover who is romancing the wife of a volatile young bookkeeper but his efforts to keep the husband from murdering the lover culminate in his becoming a virtual eyewitness to the killing of his wife.

**Trivia, etc.** This was the first episode of the *Ellery Queen* series to be sponsored. Gulf Gasoline and Oil had sponsored a Sunday evening program entitled *The Gulf Screen Guild Theater*, a variety program in which the guest stars donated their fees to the Motion Picture Relief Fund. Beginning April 28, that program went off the air for the summer. Gulf Oil, however, continued to sponsor the time slot and *Ellery Queen* moved into it to accommodate, thereby gaining its first sponsor. This was also the first episode in which Bert Parks served as announcer.

This episode was repeated under the same title on July 8 and 10, 1943 (Episode #133). The script for this episode was published in *The Case Book of Ellery Queen* (1945).

### EPISODE #47 "THE MAN WHO COULD DOUBLE THE SIZE OF DIAMONDS"

Broadcast on May 5, 1940

Guests: unknown.

Written by Frederic Dannay and Manfred B. Lee.

Produced and directed by George Zachary.

Music composed and conducted by Lyn Murray.

Announcer: Bert Parks.

Sponsor: Gulf Oil.

Story: Ellery investigates the murder of an eccentric scientist who claims to have discovered a chemical process for growing diamonds and also probes the impossible theft of four such stones from a locked and heavily guarded vault.

**Trivia, etc.** The script for this episode was published in *Ellery Queen's Mystery Magazine*, May 1943. The episode was repeated under the same title on July 15 and 17, 1943 (Episode #134).

### EPISODE #48 "THE FIRE BUG"   Broadcast on May 12, 1940

Guests: unknown.

Written by Frederic Dannay and Manfred B. Lee.

Produced and directed by George Zachary.

Music composed and conducted by Lyn Murray.

Announcer: Bert Parks.

Sponsor: Gulf Oil.

Story: Ellery looks into a series of suspicious blazes in his neighborhood, each of which destroyed a building owned by the same man.

**Trivia, etc.** The script for this episode was published in *Ellery Queen's Mystery Magazine*, March 1943. The episode was repeated under the same title on July 22 and 24, 1943 (Episode #135).

### EPISODE #49 "THE HONEYMOON HOUSE"   Broadcast on May 19, 1940

Guest: Arthur Mann (sports writer).

Written by Frederic Dannay and Manfred B. Lee.

Produced and directed by George Zachary.

Music composed and conducted by Lyn Murray.

Announcer: Bert Parks.

Sponsor: Gulf Oil.

Story: Ellery tries to solve the wedding-night murder of a munitions manufacturer's daughter who married the son of her father's business rival.

**Trivia, etc.** This episode was repeated under the same title on July 29 and 31, 1943 (Episode #136). The script was published in *The Case Book of Ellery Queen*, 1945.

EPISODE #50 **"THE MOUSE'S BLOOD"** Broadcast on May 26, 1940

Guests: unknown.

Written by Frederic Dannay and Manfred B. Lee.

Produced and directed by George Zachary.

Music composed and conducted by Lyn Murray.

Announcer: Bert Parks.

Sponsor: Gulf Oil.

Story: Ellery happens to be outside the house where a blackmailer is stabbed to death by one of the four athletes who were to have made payoffs to the dead man that night.

**Trivia, etc.** The script for this episode was published in *Ellery Queen's Mystery Magazine*, September 1942, and was later anthologized in *The Fireside Mystery Book*, ed. Frank Owen, 1947. The episode was repeated under the same title on August 5 and 7, 1943 (Episode #137).

EPISODE #51 **"THE FOUR MURDERERS"** Broadcast on June 2, 1940

Guests: Louis Connolly (newspaperman) and Mary Rhinehart (stenographer).

Written by Frederic Dannay and Manfred B. Lee.

Produced and directed by George Zachary.

Music composed and conducted by Lyn Murray.

Announcer: Bert Parks.

Sponsor: Gulf Oil.

Story: unknown.

**Trivia, etc.** This episode was repeated under the same title on August 12 and 14, 1943 (Episode #138).

EPISODE #52 **"THE GOOD SAMARITAN"** Broadcast on June 9, 1940

Guests: unknown.

Written by Frederic Dannay and Manfred B. Lee.

Produced and directed by George Zachary.

Music composed and conducted by Lyn Murray.

Announcer: Bert Parks.

Sponsor: Gulf Oil.

Story: Ellery hunts the elusive benefactor who has been sending stolen $100 bills to the needy tenants of a certain tenement building.

**Trivia, etc.** The script for this episode was published in *Ellery Queen's Mystery Magazine*, November 1942. This episode was repeated under the same title on August 19 and 21, 1943 (Episode #139).

EPISODE #53 **"THE MYSTERIOUS TRAVELERS"** Broadcast on June 16, 1940

Guest: Muriel Frizzell (supervisor).

Written by Frederic Dannay and Manfred B. Lee.

Produced and directed by George Zachary.
Music composed and conducted by Lyn Murray.
Announcer: Bert Parks.
Sponsor: Gulf Oil.
Story: Ellery investigates the death of a businessman who apparently committed suicide in his office while three men from Persia, Ceylon and the Fiji Islands who claimed he had wronged them were waiting to see him.

**Trivia, etc.** This episode was repeated under the same title on August 26 and 28, 1943 (Episode #140).

EPISODE #54   **"THE DARK CLOUD"**   Broadcast on June 23, 1940
Guests: unknown.
Written by Frederic Dannay and Manfred B. Lee.
Produced and directed by George Zachary.
Music composed and conducted by Lyn Murray.
Announcer: Bert Parks.
Sponsor: Gulf Oil.
Story: unknown.

**Trivia, etc.** This episode was repeated under the same title on September 2 and 4, 1943 (Episode #141).

EPISODE #55   **"THE BLIND BULLET"**   Broadcast on June 30, 1940
Guest: Fred Hogan (telephone maintenance man).
Written by Frederic Dannay and Manfred B. Lee.
Produced and directed by George Zachary.
Music composed and conducted by Lyn Murray.
Announcer: Bert Parks.
Sponsor: Gulf Oil.
Story: Ellery is hired to protect a ruthless tycoon from an anonymous enemy who has threatened to kill the magnate at a precise minute on a precise day. When the murderer carries out his threat in a pitch-black railroad tunnel, Ellery tries to figure out how the crime could have taken place in total darkness.

**Trivia, etc.** The script for this episode was published in *Ellery Queen's Mystery Magazine*, September 1943. The episode was repeated under the same title on September 9 and 11, 1943 (Episode #142).

EPISODE #56   **"THE FALLEN GLADIATOR"**   Broadcast on July 7, 1940
Guests: unknown.
Written by Frederic Dannay and Manfred B. Lee.
Produced and directed by George Zachary.
Music composed and conducted by Lyn Murray.
Announcer: Bert Parks.
Sponsor: Gulf Oil.
Story: After attending a world heavyweight championship boxing match, Ellery discovers the dethroned champ's body in a parking lot.

**Trivia, etc.** The script for this episode was adapted by Dannay and Lee from their short story "Mind Over Matter" (*Blue Book*, October 1939; collected in *The New Adventures of Ellery Queen*, 1940). The episode was repeated under its original radio title on September 16 and 18, 1943 (Episode #143).

EPISODE #57 **"THE FRIGHTENED STAR"** Broadcast on July 14, 1940
West Coast Guest: Mitzi Cumming.
East Coast Guest: Dr. Henry R. Junemann (dentistry professor).
Written by Frederic Dannay and Manfred B. Lee.
Produced and directed by George Zachary.
Music composed and conducted by Lyn Murray.
Announcer: Bert Parks.
Sponsor: Gulf Oil.
Story: Ellery investigates the locked-room death of a Hollywood actress who mysteriously went into retirement at the height of her popularity.

**Trivia, etc.** The script for this episode was published in *Ellery Queen's Mystery Magazine*, Spring 1942. This episode was repeated under the same title on October 21 and 23, 1943 (Episode #148).

EPISODE #58 **"THE TREASURE HUNT"** Broadcast on July 21, 1940
Guest: Carol Bruce (vocalist).
Written by Frederic Dannay and Manfred B. Lee.
Produced and directed by George Zachary.
Music composed and conducted by Lyn Murray.
Announcer: Bert Parks.
Sponsor: Gulf Oil.
Story: Ellery searches for a rope of pearls that one of the house guests of a retired general stole from his daughter's bedroom, and devises a treasure-hunting game to catch the thief in a psychological trap.

**Trivia, etc.** The script for this episode was adapted by Dannay and Lee from their short story "The Treasure Hunt" (*Detective Story*, December 1935; collected in *The New Adventures of Ellery Queen*, 1940). The episode was repeated under the same title on September 23 and 25, 1943 (Episode #144).

EPISODE #59 **"THE BLACK SHEEP"** Broadcast on July 28, 1940
Guests: Marjorie Allen (soprano) and Benny Baker (comedian).
Written by Frederic Dannay and Manfred B. Lee.
Produced and directed by George Zachary.
Music composed and conducted by Lyn Murray.
Announcer: Bert Parks.
Sponsor: Gulf Oil.
Story: When a masked thief steals a $15,000 payroll from the owner of a mill in the village of Fallboro and the owner's surly stepson is arrested for the crime of circumstantial evidence, the young man's distraught mother appeals to Ellery for help.

**Trivia, etc.** This episode was repeated on September 21 and 23, 1944, as "The Robber of Fallboro" (Episode #196). The script was later adapted by Dannay and Lee into the short story "The Accused" (*Today's Family*, February 1953; collected as "The Robber of Wrightsville" in *Queen's Bureau of Investigation*, 1955).

EPISODE #60 **"THE FATAL MILLION"** Broadcast on August 4, 1940
Guest: Doris Sharp (radio casting director).
Written by Frederic Dannay and Manfred B. Lee.
Produced and directed by George Zachary.

Music composed and conducted by Lyn Murray.
Announcer: Bert Parks.
Sponsor: Gulf Oil.
Story: Ellery hunts the impersonator who murdered the owner of a chain of roadside restaurants, posed as his victim during a secret sales transaction and walked away with $1,000,000 in a suitcase.

**Trivia, etc.** This episode was repeated on August 17 and 19, 1944, as "The Man Who Wanted Cash" (Episode #191).

EPISODE #61 **"THE INVISIBLE CLOCK"** Broadcast on August 11, 1940
Guest: Andrew S. Telep (newspaper editor).
Written by Frederic Dannay and Manfred B. Lee.
Produced and directed by George Zachary.
Music composed and conducted by Lyn Murray.
Announcer: Bert Parks.
Sponsor: Gulf Oil.
Story: Ellery and Nikki attend a society ball where a clock is heard ticking where no clock exists and a priceless ruby disappears.

**Trivia, etc.** This episode, whose working title was "The Mysterious Clock," was repeated under its final title on September 28 and 30, 1944 (Episode #197). The script was published in *The Case Book of Ellery Queen*, 1945.

EPISODE #62 **"THE MEANEST MAN IN THE WORLD"** Broadcast on August 18, 1940
Guests: unknown.
Written by Frederic Dannay and Manfred B. Lee.
Produced and directed by George Zachary.
Music composed and conducted by Lyn Murray.
Announcer: Bert Parks.
Sponsor: Gulf Oil.
Story: Ellery and Nikki serve side by side as jurors at the trial of a destitute man charged with having plunged a paperknife into the back of a vicious miser's neck. Reading the evidence as no one else has, Ellery leaps from the jury box, cross examines the witnesses himself, and extracts a confession in open court from the real murderer.

**Trivia, etc.** The script for this episode was published in *Ellery Queen's Mystery Magazine*, July 1942. This episode was repeated on August 3 and 5, 1944, as "The Man Without a Heart" (Episode #189).

EPISODE #63 **"THE PHARAOH'S CURSE"** Broadcast on August 25, 1940
Guests: unknown.
Written by Frederic Dannay and Manfred B. Lee.
Produced and directed by George Zachary.
Music composed and conducted by Lyn Murray.
Announcer: Bert Parks.
Sponsor: Gulf Oil.
Story: Ellery travels to Egypt to investigate the violent deaths of several members of an archaeological expedition.

**Trivia, etc.** This episode was repeated on July 6 and 8, 1944, as "The Egyptian Tomb" (Episode #185).

EPISODE #64 **"BOX 13"** Broadcast on September 1, 1940
        Guests: unknown.
        Written by Frederic Dannay and Manfred B. Lee.
        Produced and directed by George Zachary.
        Music composed and conducted by Lyn Murray.
        Announcer: Bert Parks.
        Sponsor: Gulf Oil.
        Story: unknown.

EPISODE #65 **"THE PICNIC MURDER"** Broadcast on September 8, 1940
        Guests: unknown.
        Written by Frederic Dannay and Manfred B. Lee.
        Produced and directed by George Zachary.
        Music composed and conducted by Lyn Murray.
        Announcer: Bert Parks.
        Sponsor: Gulf Oil.
        Story: Ellery tries to clear a small-town mayor who is the prime suspect when his wife's supposed lover is killed during a Sunday picnic in the park.

        **Trivia, etc.** This episode was repeated on August 24 and 26, 1944, as "The Mayor and the Corpse" (episode #192).

EPISODE #66 **"THE DISAPPEARING MAGICIAN"** Broadcast on September 15, 1940
        Guests: unknown.
        Written by Frederic Dannay and Manfred B. Lee.
        Produced and directed by George Zachary.
        Music composed and conducted by Lyn Murray.
        Announcer: Bert Parks.
        Sponsor: Gulf Oil.
        Story: When the decrepit old house owned by four ex-vaudevillians is threatened with foreclosure, the magician among the quartet issues a challenge to a sharp businessman who has made a standing offer of $25,000 for any illusionist's trick he can't solve within 24 hours. The magician claims he can disappear from the house while it's surrounded by policemen and enlists Ellery, Inspector Queen and dozens of cops for the feat.

        **Trivia, etc.** This episode was repeated on November 4 and 6, 1943, as "The Vanishing Magician" (Episode #150).

EPISODE #67 **"THE MARK OF CAIN"** Broadcast on September 22, 1940
        Guests: unknown.
        Written by Frederic Dannay and Manfred B. Lee.
        Produced and directed by George Zachary.
        Music composed and conducted by Lyn Murray.
        Announcer: Bert Parks.
        Sponsor: Gulf Oil.
        Story: Ellery, Inspector Queen, Sergeant Velie and Nikki pose as servants in an attempt to prevent murder among the heirs of eccentric millionaire John Cain.

        **Trivia, etc.** The script for this episode, whose initial working title was "The House of Cain," was published in *The Pocket Mystery Reader*, ed. Lee Wright , 1942. This episode was repeated on August 10 and 12, 1944, as "The Three Hands" (Episode #190).
        After this week the series went off the air, returning fifteen months later but now on NBC and with Carleton Young rather than Hugh Marlowe as Ellery.

# SEASON TWO

EPISODE #68  **"THE SONG OF DEATH"**
> Broadcast on January 8, 1942 (West Coast).
> Guests: Frank Buck (explorer) and Dorothy McGuire (actress).
> Broadcast on January 10, 1942 (East Coast).
> Guests: Neysa McMein (illustrator/poster artist) and Frederick Chase Taylor (radio's Colonel Stoopnagle).
> Written by Frederic Dannay and Manfred B. Lee.
> Produced and directed by George Zachary.
> Announcer: Ernest Chappell.
> Organ music: Charles Paul.
> Sponsor: Bromo-Seltzer.
> Story: While tracing the source of some counterfeit $100 bills, Ellery visits a night club and becomes involved in the murder of a female FBI agent.

EPISODE #69  **"THE INVISIBLE CLUE"**
> Broadcast on January 15, 1942 (West Coast).
> Guests: Charles Herbert (radio producer/composer) and Mark Warnow (radio orchestra conductor).
> Broadcast on January 17, 1942 (East Coast).
> Guests: Meyer Davis (orchestra leader) and Ham Fisher (cartoonist).
> Written by Frederic Dannay and Manfred B. Lee.
> Produced and directed by George Zachary.
> Announcer: Ernest Chappell.
> Organ music: Charles Paul.
> Sponsor: Bromo-Seltzer.
> Story: When Ellery receives a letter from a terrified man asking to be awakened at 7:00 the next morning, he is plunged into the search for a criminal who can't be seen by human eyes.

> **Trivia, etc.** The script for this episode was published in *Adventures in Radio*, ed. Margaret Cuthbert, 1945. The episode was repeated on January 15, 1948 as "The Terrified Man" (Episode #336).

EPISODE #70  **"THE PATIENT MURDERER"**
> Broadcast on January 22, 1942 (West Coast).
> Guests: Aubrey Waller Cook (pianist) and Bea Wain (radio singer).
> Broadcast on January 24, 1942 (East Coast).
> Guests: Lois January (actress) and George Jessel (comedian).
> Written by Frederic Dannay and Manfred B. Lee.
> Produced and directed by George Zachary.
> Announcer: Ernest Chappell.
> Organ music: Charles Paul.
> Sponsor: Bromo-Seltzer.
> Story: Inspector Queen asks Ellery to help him solve the murders of four men – a realtor, a lawyer, a meat packer and a judge – each of whom was found stabbed to death with a note beside him reading "Patient Murderer."

EPISODE #71  **"THE FIFTY-SECOND CARD"**
> Broadcast on January 29, 1942 (West Coast).
> Guests: A. Finn and M. Kingsley.

Broadcast on January 31, 1942 (East Coast).
Guests: Norman Corwin (radio writer) and Gypsy Rose Lee (stripper/actress).
Written by Frederic Dannay and Manfred B. Lee.
Announcer: Ernest Chappell.
Organ music: Charles Paul.
Sponsor: Bromo-Seltzer.
Story: Ellery uses a deck of cards to solve the murder of a blackmailer who was demanding huge final payments from each of the four people he'd been victimizing for years.

## EPISODE #72 "THE IMAGINARY MAN"
Broadcast on February 5, 1942 (West Coast).
Guests: Mel Ott (baseball star) and Hank Worden (actor).
Broadcast on February 7, 1942 (East Coast).
Guests: Frank Forrest (singer) and Lucille Manners (singer).
Written by Frederic Dannay and Manfred B. Lee.
Announcer: Ernest Chappell.
Organ music: Charles Paul.
Sponsor: Bromo-Seltzer.
Story: Soon after a woman asks Ellery to save her from being killed by her uncle, her cousin is found dead in her car, a victim of carbon monoxide poisoning.

## EPISODE #73 "THE ST. VALENTINE'S KNOT"
Broadcast on February 12, 1942 (West Coast).
Guests: Lady Hardwicke (wife of actor Sir Cedric Hardwicke) and Mary Lewis (Metropolitan Opera soprano).
Broadcast on February 14, 1942 (East Coast).
Guests: D. Fritsch and Parks Johnson (host of radio's *Vox Pop* program).
Written by Frederic Dannay and Manfred B. Lee.
Announcer: Ernest Chappell.
Organ music: Charles Paul.
Sponsor: Bromo-Seltzer.
Story: Ellery investigates when a retired actress at a sanitarium for show business people is murdered by poisoned chocolates.

## EPISODE #74 "GEORGE WASHINGTON'S DOLLAR"
Broadcast on February 19, 1942 (West Coast).
Guests: Mr. and Mrs. Parks Johnson (of radio's *Vox Pop* program).
Broadcast on February 21, 1942 (East Coast).
Guests: Gilda Gray (actress) and Joe Howard (musician).
Written by Frederic Dannay and Manfred B. Lee.
Announcer: Ernest Chappell.
Organ music: Charles Paul.
Sponsor: Bromo-Seltzer.
Story: Ellery is challenged to find a rare coin which Washington is believed to have buried on a remote Pennsylvania farm in 1791.

**Trivia, etc.** The script for this episode was later adapted by Dannay and Lee into the short story "The President's Half Disme" (*Ellery Queen's Mystery Magazine*, February 1947; collected in *Calendar of Crime*, 1952).

EPISODE #75 **"THE OLD WITCH"**
  Broadcast on February 26, 1942 (West Coast).
  Guests: Vicki Baum (novelist) and Howard Dietz (theatrical producer).
  Broadcast on February 28, 1942 (East Coast).
  Guests: Heinie Dorner (tenor) and E.B. Locker.
  Written by Frederic Dannay and Manfred B. Lee.
  Announcer: Ernest Chappell.
  Organ music: Charles Paul.
  Sponsor: Bromo-Seltzer.
  Story: Ellery finds murder when Sergeant Velie asks his help in combating Witch Hazel, a demented old woman in Velie's apartment building who's been terrorizing the neighborhood children, including Velie's daughter, by threatening to put spells on them.

EPISODE #76 **"THE MISSING TUMBLER"**
  Broadcast on March 5, 1942 (West Coast).
  Guests: Blue Barron (orchestra leader) and Bill Stern (radio sportscaster).
  Broadcast on March 7, 1942 (East Coast).
  Guests: Aubrey Waller Cook (pianist) and Mayor Harter (Harter via phone).
  Written by Frederic Dannay and Manfred B. Lee.
  Announcer: Ernest Chappell.
  Organ music: Charles Paul.
  Sponsor: Bromo-Seltzer.
  Story: Ellery tries to solve the murder of a sports columnist who was about to expose three celebrities in three different sports who were fixing sporting events.

EPISODE #77 **"THE INCOME TAX ROBBERY"**
  Broadcast on March 12, 1942 (West Coast).
  Guests: George Jessel (comedian) and Mayor E. Reilly (Reilly via phone).
  Broadcast on March 14, 1942 (East Coast).
  Guests: M. Hedstrom and Mayor Jackson (Jackson via phone).
  Written by Frederic Dannay and Manfred B. Lee.
  Announcer: Ernest Chappell.
  Organ music: Charles Paul.
  Sponsor: Bromo-Seltzer.
  Story: When a luckless private eye reports the theft of all his income tax records 48 hours before the March 15 filing deadline, Ellery takes a hand and finds himself investigating a case of blackmail and murder.

  **Trivia, etc.** The script for this episode was later adapted by Dannay and Lee into the short story "The Ides of Michael Magoon" (*Ellery Queen's Mystery Magazine*, March 1947; collected in *Calendar of Crime*, 1952).

EPISODE #78 **"THE OUT-OF-ORDER TELEPHONE"**
  Broadcast on March 19, 1942 (West Coast).
  Guests: G.F. Donahoe and M.S. McDermott.
  Broadcast on March 21, 1942 (East Coast).
  Guests: F.E. Conaty and G.S. Miller.
  Written by Frederic Dannay and Manfred B. Lee.
  Announcer: Ernest Chappell.
  Organ music: Charles Paul.
  Sponsor: Bromo-Seltzer.
  Story: A telephone clue helps Ellery solve the murder of the owner of a so-called beauty salon that was actually a front for a racket.

EPISODE #79   **"THE SERVANT PROBLEM"**
> Broadcast on March 26, 1942 (West Coast).
> Guests: John Allen (radio newscaster) and Jim Ameche (radio actor).
> Broadcast on March 28, 1942 (East Coast).
> Guests: Leo G. Carroll (actor) and Judith Evelyn (actress).
> Written by Frederic Dannay and Manfred B. Lee.
> Announcer: Ernest Chappell.
> Organ music: Charles Paul.
> Sponsor: Bromo-Seltzer.
> Story: unknown.

EPISODE #80   **"THE BLACK SYNDICATE"**
> Broadcast on April 2, 1942 (West Coast).
> Guests: Mayor A. Rossi (via phone) and Lois Wilson (actress).
> Broadcast on April 4, 1942 (East Coast).
> Guests: Judge S. McDevitt and Selena Royle (actress).
> Written by Frederic Dannay and Manfred B. Lee.
> Announcer: Ernest Chappell.
> Organ music: Charles Paul.
> Sponsor: Bromo-Seltzer.

Story:   Blake, the head of an export firm, directs his four partners – Llewellyn in London, Arnot in Paris, Casini in Berne and Kotch in Istanbul – to shut down their branches of the business and send all the proceeds to him in New York where the money will be evenly divided among the five at a meeting.   Ellery is called in when both Blake and the money disappear.

> **Trivia, etc.** It was during rehearsals for this episode that featured actress Kaye Brinker met Manfred B. Lee, whom she married three months later.

EPISODE #81   **"ELLERY QUEEN, SWINDLER"**
> Broadcast on April 9, 1942 (West Coast).
> Guests: Bill Johnson (orchestra leader) and Allen Prescott (radio comedian).
> Broadcast on April 11, 1942 (East Coast).
> Guests: Marian Anderson (singer) and Arthur Murray (dance instructor).
> Written by Frederic Dannay and Manfred B. Lee.
> Announcer: Ernest Chappell.
> Organ music: Charles Paul.
> Sponsor: Bromo-Seltzer.

Story:   Ellery and his French comrade Jallet work out a gem-switching maneuver to recover the $4,000 that jeweler Adolf Humperdinck legally stole from one of his employees.

> **Trivia, etc.** The script for this episode was published in *Rogues' Gallery*, ed. Ellery Queen, 1945.

EPISODE #82   **"THE SUPERSTITIOUS CLIENT"**
> Broadcast on April 16, 1942 (West Coast).
> Guests: L. Brophy and Mayor Z. Leymel (Leymel via phone).
> Broadcast on April 18, 1942 (East Coast).
> Guests: Mrs. Octavus Roy Cohen (wife of author) and Mayor R. Perkins.
> Written by Frederic Dannay and Manfred B. Lee.
> Announcer: Ernest Chappell.

Organ music: Charles Paul.

Sponsor: Bromo-Seltzer.

Story: Ellery is called in to investigate a series of weird events that befell his client just before moving into the house he designed especially to ward off all sorts of supernatural threats.

## EPISODE #83    "THE MILLIONAIRES' CLUB"
Broadcast on April 23, 1942 (West Coast).

Guests: Bernardine Flynn (radio actress/announcer) and Otto Soglow (cartoonist).

Broadcast on April 25, 1942 (East Coast).

Guests: L. Brophy and Ward Greene (author).

Written by Frederic Dannay and Manfred B. Lee.

Announcer: Ernest Chappell.

Organ music: Charles Paul.

Sponsor: Bromo-Seltzer.

Story: Ellery takes a hand when the four members of a subgroup within a larger club of twelve rich men are threatened by what seems to be a series of fatal accidents.

**Trivia, etc.** This episode was repeated on December 28 and 30, 1944, as "The Inner Circle" (Episode #210). The script was later adapted by Dannay and Lee into the short story "The Inner Circle" (*Ellery Queen's Mystery Magazine*, January 1947; collected in *Calendar of Crime*, 1952).

## EPISODE #84    "THE LIVING CORPSE"
Broadcast on April 30, 1942 (West Coast).

Guests: N.W. Lathan and Mayor E. Reilly (Reilly via phone).

Broadcast on May 2, 1942 (East Coast).

Guests: Shirley Booth (actress) and Ed Gardner (star of radio's *Duffy's Tavern*).

Written by Frederic Dannay and Manfred B. Lee.

Announcer: Ernest Chappell.

Organ music: Charles Paul.

Sponsor: Bromo-Seltzer.

Story: Nikki finds a corpse in an apartment closet while helping her out-of-town friend find a place to stay. The corpse vanishes before Ellery arrives, then reappears as a living man who in turn is murdered.

## EPISODE #85    "THE MISSING CHILD"
Broadcast on May 7, 1942 (West Coast).

Guests: Shep Fields (orchestra leader) and Mrs. Joy Lyons.

Broadcast on May 9, 1942 (East Coast).

Guests: Lawrence E. Spivak (publisher) and Bea Wain (radio singer).

Written by Frederic Dannay and Manfred B. Lee.

Announcer: Ernest Chappell.

Organ music: Charles Paul.

Sponsor: Bromo-Seltzer.

Story: same as Episode #24, "The Lost Child" (November 26, 1939).

## EPISODE #86    "THE GREEN HAT"
Broadcast on May 14, 1942 (West Coast).

Guests: a "jury" of servicemen.

Broadcast on May 16, 1942 (East Coast).
Guests: a so-called "blue-ribbon jury."
Written by Frederic Dannay and Manfred B. Lee.
Announcer: Ernest Chappell.
Organ music: Charles Paul.
Sponsor: Bromo-Seltzer.
Story: Ellery investigates when the bodyguard of an industrial tycoon turned wartime Federal bureaucrat is found murdered at a Washington victory ball, clutching a piece of crepe paper in his hand.

## EPISODE #87　"THE THREE IOU'S"

Broadcast on May 21, 1942 (West Coast).
Guests: R. Porterfield and Earl Young (radio newscaster).
Broadcast on May 23, 1942 (East Coast).
Guests: Alice Marble (radio sportscaster) and Mayor E.J. Reilly (Reilly via phone).
Written by Frederic Dannay and Manfred B. Lee.
Announcer: Ernest Chappell.
Organ music: Charles Paul.
Sponsor: Bromo-Seltzer.
Story: Ellery investigates the murder of a loan shark who carried in his pocket the IOUs of three people to whom he had lent money.

## EPISODE #88　"THE OLD MEN"

Broadcast on May 28, 1942 (West Coast).
Guests: Joan Caulfield (actress) and Emery Deutsch (bandleader).
Broadcast on May 30, 1942 (East Coast).
Guests: D. Lind and Judge J.T. Mahoney.
Written by Frederic Dannay and Manfred B. Lee.
Announcer: Ernest Chappell.
Organ music: Charles Paul.
Sponsor: Bromo-Seltzer.
Story: Ellery tries to solve a series of Memorial Day deaths among the last surviving Union Army veterans in a tiny Pennsylvania town.

**Trivia, etc.** The script for this episode was later adapted by Dannay and Lee into the short story "As Simple As ABC" (*Ellery Queen's Mystery Magazine*, May 1951; collected as "The Gettysburg Bugle" in *Calendar of Crime*, 1952).

## EPISODE #89　"THE DOG FIRES"

Broadcast on June 4, 1942 (West Coast).
Guests: Joan Edwards (singer/actress) and J. Scheeter.
Broadcast on June 6, 1942 (East Coast).
Guests: Warren Hull (actor/radio announcer) and Joana Leschin (concert pianist).
Written by Frederic Dannay and Manfred B. Lee.
Announcer: Ernest Chappell.
Organ music: Charles Paul.
Sponsor: Bromo-Seltzer.
Story: Ellery pursues a pyromaniac with a penchant for setting fires in pet shops.

EPISODE #90  **"THE JUNE BRIDE"**
>Broadcast on June 11, 1942 (West Coast).
>Guests: Lois January (actress) and Lem Ward (painter/woodcarver).
>Broadcast on June 13, 1942 (East Coast).
>Guests: C. Agar and Jack McManus (newspaper editor).
>Written by Frederic Dannay and Manfred B. Lee.
>Announcer: Ernest Chappell.
>Organ music: Charles Paul.
>Sponsor: Bromo-Seltzer.
>Story: Ellery attends a wedding when the lovely and wealthy bride, whose violent-tempered ex-boyfriend had threatened to kill her rather than see her marry another man, drops dead seven minutes after the ceremony.

>**Trivia, etc.** The script for this episode was later adapted by Dannay and Lee into the short story "The Medical Finger" (*Ellery Queen's Mystery Magazine*, June 1951; collected in *Calendar of Crime*, 1952).

EPISODE #91  **"THE GOLF MURDER"**
>Broadcast on June 18, 1942 (West Coast).
>Guests: Alphonso d'Artega (bandleader) and Kay Lorraine (vocalist).
>Broadcast on June 20, 1942 (East Coast).
>Guests: Joan Edwards (singer/actress) and Conrad Thibault (singer).
>Written by Frederic Dannay and Manfred B. Lee.
>Announcer: Ernest Chappell.
>Organ music: Charles Paul.
>Sponsor: Bromo-Seltzer.
>Story: Ellery investigates the murder of an executive on a private golf course.

EPISODE #92  **"THE MIDNIGHT VISITOR"**
>Broadcast on June 25, 1942 (West Coast).
>Guests: James and Dorothy Kilgallen (journalists).
>Broadcast on June 27, 1942 (East Coast).
>Guests: E. Allardice and A. Simon.
>Written by Frederic Dannay and Manfred B. Lee.
>Announcer: Ernest Chappell.
>Organ music: Charles Paul.
>Sponsor: Bromo-Seltzer.
>Story: Ellery and Nikki find everything but peace and quiet when they accept an invitation for a quiet weekend in the country.

EPISODE #93  **"THE AIR RAID WARDEN"**
>Broadcast on July 2, 1942 (West Coast).
>Guests: D. Mich and Benay Venuta (singer/actress).
>Broadcast on July 4, 1942 (East Coast).
>Guests: Clyde Barrie (baritone) and Dick Stabile (bandleader).
>Written by Frederic Dannay and Manfred B. Lee.
>Announcer: Ernest Chappell.
>Organ music: Charles Paul.
>Sponsor: Bromo-Seltzer.
>Story: While accompanying Nikki on her rounds as an air raid warden, Ellery sees the warden responsible for an adjoining beat enter a house from which he never comes out.

# SEASON THREE

**EPISODE #94    "THE WORLD SERIES CRIME"**
>Broadcast on October 8, 1942 (West Coast).
>Guests: unknown.
>Broadcast on October 10, 1942 (East Coast).
>Guests: George McManus (comic strip artist) and Benay Venuta (singer/actress).
>Written by Frederic Dannay and Manfred B. Lee.
>Announcer: Ernest Chappell.
>Organ music: Charles Paul.
>Sponsor: Bromo-Seltzer.
>Story: Three hours before the seventh game of the Series, the "Eagles" team hires Ellery to break the jinx on its powerhouse hitter "Sparky" by retrieving his lucky bat, Uncle Sam, which was stolen the morning after game three.

>**Trivia, etc.** This episode was repeated under the same title on September 30 and October 2, 1943 (Episode #145). In 1985 the Japanese house of Gogaku Shunjusha published the script for this episode as a booklet, with notes in Japanese to help youths in that country who were studying English.

**EPISODE #95    "MR. X"**
>Broadcast on October 15, 1942 (West Coast).
>Guests: Harriet Van Horne (newspaper columnist) and G. Parsons.
>Broadcast on October 17, 1942 (East Coast).
>Guests: A. Ames and G. Parsons.
>Written by Frederic Dannay and Manfred B. Lee.
>Announcer: Ernest Chappell.
>Organ music: Charles Paul.
>Sponsor: Bromo-Seltzer.
>Story: Ellery investigates the death of a recluse who had turned his apartment into a fortress and shut himself inside.

**EPISODE #96    "THE POLISH REFUGEE"**
>Broadcast on October 22, 1942 (West Coast).
>Guests: unknown.
>Broadcast on October 24, 1942 (East Coast).
>Guests: R. Day, Jr. and Oscar Serlin (theatrical producer).
>Written by Frederic Dannay and Manfred B. Lee.
>Announcer: Ernest Chappell.
>Organ music: Charles Paul.
>Sponsor: Bromo-Seltzer.
>Story: Ellery tries to help a refugee countess who recently escaped from Nazi-occupied Poland.

**EPISODE #97    "THE WITCH'S BROOM"**
>Broadcast on October 29, 1942 (West Coast).
>Guests: P.C. Mason and M/Sgt. W.P. Berkley.
>Broadcast on October 31, 1942 (East Coast).
>Guests: John Van Druten (playwright) and Flora Robson (actress).

Written by Frederic Dannay and Manfred B. Lee.
Announcer: Ernest Chappell.
Organ music: Charles Paul.
Sponsor: Bromo-Seltzer.
Story:  While paying a Halloween visit to an old friend of his father's who is serving as chief of police in a small town, Ellery investigates an alleged witch and her broomstick.

EPISODE #98   **"THE FATAL LETTER"**
Broadcast on November 5, 1942  (West Coast).
Guests:  Sgt. Vance and Sgt. L. White.
Broadcast on November 7, 1942  (East Coast).
Guests:  Jerry Lester (comedian) and Lucille Manners (singer).
Written by Frederic Dannay and Manfred B. Lee.
Announcer: Ernest Chappell.
Organ music: Charles Paul.
Sponsor: Bromo-Seltzer.
Story: Ellery tries to solve the murder of a man who was blackmailing three politicians for money to pay his gambling debts.

EPISODE #99   **"THE POET'S TRIANGLE"**
Broadcast on November 12, 1942  (West Coast).
Guests: D. London and Lanny Ross (singer).
Broadcast on November 14, 1942  (East Coast).
Guests: Les Brown (bandleader) and E. Lyon.
Written by Frederic Dannay and Manfred B. Lee.
Announcer: Ernest Chappell.
Organ music: Charles Paul.
Sponsor: Bromo-Seltzer.
Story:  unknown.

EPISODE #100   **"THE BALD-HEADED GHOST"**
Broadcast on November 19, 1942  (West Coast).
Guests:  unknown.
Broadcast on November 21, 1942  (East Coast).
Guests: Eva Gabor (actress) and Dr. R.A. Button.
Written by Frederic Dannay and Manfred B. Lee.
Announcer: Ernest Chappell.
Organ music: Charles Paul.
Sponsor: Bromo-Seltzer.
Story:  Ellery becomes involved with an apparently supernatural crime while trying to save Nikki from the clutches of a womanizing actor.

EPISODE #101   **"THE THREE MOTHERS"**
Broadcast on November 26, 1942  (West Coast).
Guests:  Bernard Geis (publisher) and C. Marr.
Broadcast on November 28, 1942  (East Coast).
Guests:  unknown.
Written by Frederic Dannay and Manfred B. Lee.
Announcer: Ernest Chappell.
Organ music: Charles Paul.
Sponsor: Bromo-Seltzer.

Story: Ellery tries to figure out which of three women is the mother of a baby who was found eight months earlier on a fourth woman's doorstep, but as soon as he has solved that problem the real mother is murdered.

**Trivia, etc.** This episode, whose original working title was "The Dead Man's Chest," was repeated on January 22, 1947 as "Queen Solomon" (Episode #306).

### EPISODE #102   "THE MAN IN THE TAXI"
Broadcast on December 3, 1942 (West Coast).
Guests: L. Guy and M. Hayes.
Broadcast on December 5, 1942 (East Coast).
Guests: Sally Rand (fan dancer) and Barry Wood (singer/musician).
Written by Frederic Dannay and Manfred B. Lee.
Announcer: Ernest Chappell.
Organ music: Charles Paul.
Sponsor: Bromo-Seltzer.
Story: Ellery investigates the murder of a playboy who for reasons of his own was working as a cab driver when he was stabbed to death in his taxi.

### EPISODE #103   "THE GYMNASIUM MURDER"
Broadcast on December 10, 1942 (West Coast).
Guests: Irving Caesar (Broadway composer) and Lady Hardwicke (wife of actor Sir Cedric Hardwicke).
Scheduled for East Coast broadcast on December 12, 1942 but pre-empted
by a football game.
Written by Frederic Dannay and Manfred B. Lee.
Announcer: Ernest Chappell.
Organ music: Charles Paul.
Sponsor: Bromo-Seltzer.
Story: Ellery tries to clear a boxer who is charged with murder after his opponent, who died in the ring, is discovered to have been drugged.

**Trivia, etc.** This episode was broadcast on both East and West Coasts under the same title on August 21, 1946 (Episode #290).

### EPISODE #104   "THE YELLOW LEDGER"
Broadcast on December 17, 1942 (West Coast).
Guests: Walter B. Gibson (author and creator of *The Shadow*) and Choo Choo Johnson (hobo musician).
Broadcast on December 19, 1942 (East Coast).
Guests: L. Sullivan and Hank Worden (actor).
Written by Frederic Dannay and Manfred B. Lee.
Announcer: Ernest Chappell.
Organ music: Charles Paul.
Sponsor: Bromo-Seltzer.
Story: Ellery takes the place of a wounded FBI agent and deliberately walks into a trap while on the way to Washington with a ledger containing evidence against a Nazi spy ring.

**Trivia, etc.** The script for this episode, whose original working title was "Ellery Queen's Greatest Case," was later adapted by Dannay and Lee into the short story "The Black Ledger" (*This Week*, January 26, 1952; collected in *Queen's Bureau of Investigation*, 1955).

EPISODE #105  **"THE RED AND GREEN BOXES"**
>Broadcast on December 24, 1942  (West Coast).
>Guests:  A. Ames and Capt. Don Saxon.
>Broadcast on December 26, 1942  (East Coast).
>Guests:  Ann Corio (stripper/actress) and P. Schoenstein.
>Written by Frederic Dannay and Manfred B. Lee.
>Announcer: Ernest Chappell.
>Organ music: Charles Paul.
>Sponsor: Bromo-Seltzer.
>Story: Ellery investigates a Christmas mystery involving the theft of a red box
containing a ruby and the substitution of a green box containing a paste emerald.

EPISODE #106  **"THE MAN WHO WAS MURDERED BY INSTALLMENTS"**
>Broadcast on December 31, 1942  (West Coast).
>Guests:  V. Carol and H. Thompson.
>Broadcast on January 2, 1943  (East Coast).
>Guests:  Walter Compton (radio host) and Peggy Wood (actress).
>Written by Frederic Dannay and Manfred B. Lee.
>Announcer: Ernest Chappell.
>Organ music: Charles Paul.
>Sponsor: Bromo-Seltzer.
>Story:  When a wealthy old man is shot first in the arm and then in the leg, Ellery
investigates the old man's two nephews and his niece, all but one of whom have been secretly
disinherited.

>**Trivia, etc.** This episode was repeated on April 22, 1948 as "Murder by Installments"
(Episode #350).

EPISODE #107  **"THE SINGING RAT"**
>Broadcast on January 7, 1943  (West Coast).
>Guests: Ann Corio (stripper/actress) and A.D. McKelvey.
>Broadcast on January 9, 1943  (East Coast).
>Guests:  Jean Holloway (radio writer) and Frank Luther (radio announcer).
>Written by Frederic Dannay and Manfred B. Lee.
>Produced and directed by Bruce Kamman.
>Announcer: Ernest Chappell.
>Organ music: Charles Paul.
>Sponsor: Bromo-Seltzer.
>Story:  Ellery investigates when a hollowed-out cigarette containing a document that
incriminates four suspected racketeers disappears from Inspector Queen's office.

EPISODE #108  **"MR. SHORT AND MR. LONG"**
>Broadcast on January 14, 1943  (West Coast).
>Guests:  John G. Chapman (New York *Daily News* drama critic) and C.G. Kimball.
>Broadcast on January 16, 1943  (East Coast).
>Guests:  Joan Edwards (singer/actress) and B. Yost.
>Written by Frederic Dannay and Manfred B. Lee.
>Produced and directed by Bruce Kamman.
>Announcer: Ernest Chappell.
>Organ music: Charles Paul.
>Sponsor: Bromo-Seltzer.

Story: A bedridden Ellery tries to figure out how a man could have stepped out of his house, returned for an umbrella and then managed never to be seen again.

**Trivia, etc.** The script for this episode was published as "The Disappearance of Mr. James Phillimore" in *The Misadventures of Sherlock Holmes*, ed. Ellery Queen, 1944.

## EPISODE #109  "THE FAIRY TALE MURDER"
Broadcast on January 21, 1943 (West Coast).
Guests: William Fawcett (magazine publisher) and I. Thirer.
Broadcast on January 23, 1943 (East Coast).
Guests: B. Briskam and P. Schoenstein.
Written by Frederic Dannay and Manfred B. Lee.
Produced and directed by Bruce Kamman.
Announcer: Ernest Chappell.
Organ music: Charles Paul.
Sponsor: Bromo-Seltzer.
Story: Nikki impersonates both Little Red Riding Hood and a frightened old woman as Ellery tries to solve a poison murder where the suspects are three big bad wolves.

## EPISODE #110  "TOM, DICK AND HARRY"
Broadcast on January 28, 1943 (West Coast).
Guests: Helen Barton (visitor from San Diego) and Harry Conover (modeling agency owner).
Broadcast on January 30, 1943 (East Coast).
Guests: Bob Allen (singer) and F. Mercer.
Written by Frederic Dannay and Manfred B. Lee.
Produced and directed by Bruce Kamman.
Announcer: Ernest Chappell.
Organ music: Charles Paul.
Sponsor: Bromo-Seltzer.
Story: Ellery is summoned to Washington and asked by a high government official to find out how the Japanese learned about a secret U.S. convoy they ambushed on the high seas and why the captured enemy commander was carrying a note that read "Ellery Q."

**Trivia, etc.** The script for this episode was published as "The Murdered Ship" in *Ellery Queen's Mystery Magazine*, July 1943, and in *The Saint's Choice, Volume 7: Radio Thrillers*, ed. Leslie Charteris, 1946.

## EPISODE #111  "THE SECRET ENEMY"
Broadcast on February 4, 1943 (West Coast).
Guests: T. Dugan and J. Hogan.
Broadcast on February 6, 1943 (East Coast).
Guests: Harry Conover (modeling agency owner) and Candy Jones (model).
Written by Frederic Dannay and Manfred B. Lee.
Produced and directed by Bruce Kamman.
Announcer: Ernest Chappell.
Organ music: Charles Paul.
Sponsor: Bromo-Seltzer.
Story: Ellery pursues a strange avenger from the past who is responsible for the murder of an entire family.

EPISODE #112   **"THE BROKEN STATUES"**
      Broadcast on February 11, 1943 (West Coast).
      Guests: S.A. McCabe and Capt. Don Saxon.
      Broadcast on February 13, 1943 (East Coast).
      Guests: Joan Edwards (actress) and Abe Lyman (bandleader).
      Written by Frederic Dannay and Manfred B. Lee.
      Produced and directed by Bruce Kamman.
      Announcer: Ernest Chappell.
      Organ music: Charles Paul.
      Sponsor: Bromo-Seltzer.
      Story: Ellery tries to figure out why someone is going around smashing an amateur sculptor's feeble attempts to copy some of the world's greatest statues.

EPISODE #113   **"THE TWO SWORDSMEN"**
      Broadcast on February 18, 1943 (West Coast).
      Guests: Pvt. M. Kaplan and J.M. Ross.
      Broadcast on February 20, 1943 (East Coast).
      Guests: Bob Bruce (radio actor) and Herb Shriner (humorist).
      Written by Frederic Dannay and Manfred B. Lee.
      Produced and directed by Bruce Kamman.
      Announcer: Ernest Chappell.
      Organ music: Charles Paul.
      Sponsor: Bromo-Seltzer.
      Story: unknown.

EPISODE #114   **"THE ONE-LEGGED MAN"**
      Broadcast on February 25, 1943 (West Coast).
      Guests: J. Crowley and C. Hughes.
      Broadcast on February 27, 1943 (East Coast).
      Guests: W. Evans and S.A. McCabe.
      Written by Frederic Dannay and Manfred B. Lee.
      Produced and directed by Bruce Kamman.
      Announcer: Ernest Chappell.
      Organ music: Charles Paul.
      Sponsor: Bromo-Seltzer.
      Story: Ellery visits a munitions plant on a government assignment to investigate mysterious one-legged tracks in the snow within a sealed courtyard, but the case becomes one of sabotage and murder when the head of the plant is killed by a booby-trapped pencil.

      **Trivia, etc.** The script for this episode was published in *Ellery Queen's Mystery Magazine*, November 1943.

EPISODE #115   **"NUMBER THIRTEEN DREAM STREET"**
      Broadcast on March 4, 1943 (West Coast).
      Guests: Nanette Fabray (actress) and Luana Walters (actress).
      Broadcast on March 6, 1943 (East Coast).
      Guests: Nancy Kelly (actress) and Ed Sullivan (newspaper columnist).
      Written by Frederic Dannay and Manfred B. Lee.
      Produced and directed by Bruce Kamman.
      Announcer: Ernest Chappell.
      Organ music: Charles Paul.
      Sponsor: Bromo-Seltzer.

Story: Ellery tries to help an actress locate her uncle, who has been writing letters to her from a fictitious address.

## EPISODE #116   "THE INCREDIBLE MURDER"

Broadcast on March 11, 1943  (West Coast).
Guests:  J.A. Knight and Helen Twelvetrees (actress).
Broadcast on March 13, 1943  (East Coast).
Guests:  William Prince (actor) and John Shuttleworth (fictitious radio host).
Written by Frederic Dannay and Manfred B. Lee.
Produced and directed by Bruce Kamman.
Announcer: Ernest Chappell.
Organ music: Charles Paul.
Sponsor: Bromo-Seltzer.
Story: Ellery visits the state penitentiary's death house to investigate the murder of a man who was about to be legally executed.

## EPISODE #117   "THE BOY DETECTIVES"

Broadcast on March 18, 1943  (West Coast).
Guests:  Jerry Lester (comedian) and H. Mueller.
Broadcast on March 20, 1943  (East Coast).
Guests:  Frank Forrest (tenor) and M. Reich.
Written by Frederic Dannay and Manfred B. Lee.
Produced and directed by Bruce Kamman.
Announcer: Ernest Chappell.
Organ music: Charles Paul.
Sponsor: Bromo-Seltzer.
Story: Ellery tries to help two youthful messengers who find themselves involved with desperate criminals inside a nut store.

**Trivia, etc.** The original working title for this episode was "The Great Nut Mystery."

## EPISODE #118   "THE CIRCUS TRAIN"

Broadcast on March 25, 1943  (West Coast).
Guests:  Bob Bruce (radio actor) and G.I. Giles.
Broadcast on March 27, 1943  (East Coast).
Guests:  G.R. Crowley and F. Beverley Kelley (circus publicity director).
Written by Frederic Dannay and Manfred B. Lee.
Produced and directed by Bruce Kamman.
Announcer: Ernest Chappell.
Organ music: Charles Paul.
Sponsor: Bromo-Seltzer.
Story: Ellery, Nikki, Inspector Queen and Sergeant Velie are traveling from Chicago back to New York in the passenger car of a circus train when the show proprietor's skull is bashed in by the circus giant's shoe and three $10,000 bills vanish from the speeding train.

## EPISODE #119   "THE HUMAN WEAPON"

Broadcast on April 1, 1943  (West Coast).
Guests:  Alphonso d'Artega (bandleader) and N. Bodanya.
Broadcast on April 3, 1943  (East Coast).
Guests:  Jerry Lester (comedian) and B. O'Neill.
Written by Frederic Dannay and Manfred B. Lee.

Produced and directed by Bruce Kamman.
Announcer: Ernest Chappell.
Organ music: Charles Paul.
Sponsor: Bromo-Seltzer.
Story: Ellery investigates the murder of a woman whose husband recently escaped from the insane asylum to which she had had him committed.

**Trivia, etc.** This episode was repeated on March 4, 1948 under the same title (Episode #343).

## EPISODE #120 "THE THREE MUSKETEERS"
Broadcast on April 8, 1943 (West Coast).
Guests: Doris McFerrin (magazine editor) and Leonard Sillman (Broadway producer).
Broadcast on April 10, 1943 (East Coast).
Guests: Lois January (actress) and C. Johnson.
Written by Frederic Dannay and Manfred B. Lee.
Produced and directed by Bruce Kamman.
Announcer: Ernest Chappell.
Organ music: Charles Paul.
Sponsor: Bromo-Seltzer.
Story: When a man about to cash a lottery ticket dies suddenly due to a slow-acting poison, Ellery tries to identify the murderer among three suspects who, following the Dumas characters' motto "One for all and all for one," are covering up for each other.

## EPISODE #121 "PHARAOH JONES' LAST CASE"
Broadcast on April 15, 1943 (West Coast).
Guests: Dorothy Arzner (movie director) and Bill Johnson (orchestra leader).
Broadcast on April 17, 1943 (East Coast).
Guests: Brenda Forbes (movie actress) and F. Sammis.
Written by Frederic Dannay and Manfred B. Lee.
Produced and directed by Bruce Kamman.
Announcer: Ernest Chappell.
Organ music: Charles Paul.
Sponsor: Bromo-Seltzer.
Story: unknown.

## EPISODE #122 "THE DEADLY GAME"
Broadcast on April 22, 1943 (West Coast).
Guests: B. Juengst and N. Shafer.
Broadcast on April 24, 1943 (East Coast).
Guests: Virginia Gilmore (actress) and John Nanovic (pulp-magazine editor).
Written by Frederic Dannay and Manfred B. Lee.
Produced and directed by Bruce Kamman.
Announcer: Ernest Chappell.
Organ music: Charles Paul.
Sponsor: Bromo-Seltzer.
Story: same as Episode #45, "The Poker Club" (April 21, 1940).

## EPISODE #123 "THE THREE GIFTS"
Broadcast on April 29, 1943 (West Coast).
Guests: J. Fox and C. Post.

Broadcast on May 1, 1943 (East Coast).
Guests: G. Gilbert and Jimmy Jemail (newspaper gossip columnist).
Written by Frederic Dannay and Manfred B. Lee.
Produced and directed by Bruce Kamman.
Announcer: Ernest Chappell.
Organ music: Charles Paul.
Sponsor: Bromo-Seltzer.
Story: Ellery takes a hand when crime begins to intrude on the placid life of a little old man whose one desire is to bring happiness to three people he's never seen.

## EPISODE #124  "THE EYE PRINT"
Broadcast on May 6, 1943 (West Coast).
Guests: Lee Dixon and Celeste Holm (movie actress).
Broadcast on May 8, 1943 (East Coast).
Guests: Joan Caulfield (actress) and Richard Widmark (actor).
Written by Frederic Dannay and Manfred B. Lee.
Produced and directed by Bruce Kamman.
Announcer: Ernest Chappell.
Organ music: Charles Paul.
Sponsor: Bromo-Seltzer.
Story: Ellery becomes involved in the bizarre case of a skeleton found in the hunting lodge of a wealthy family which had sentenced one of its members to stay there for a year after being caught embezzling money.

## EPISODE #125  "THE BARBARIC MURDER"
Broadcast on May 13, 1943 (West Coast).
Guests: A. Connolly and Bretaigne Windust (stage and movie director).
Broadcast on May 15, 1943 (East Coast).
Guests: K. Cravens and Alexander Kirkland (movie actor).
Written by Frederic Dannay and Manfred B. Lee.
Produced and directed by Bruce Kamman.
Announcer: Ernest Chappell.
Organ music: Charles Paul.
Sponsor: Bromo-Seltzer.
Story: Ellery investigates the murder of an archaeologist and the disappearance of an emerald he brought back from South America.

## EPISODE #126  "THE FORTUNE TELLER"
Broadcast on May 20, 1943 (West Coast).
Guests: Patricia Peardon (radio actress) and Mayor E. Reilly.
Broadcast on May 22, 1943 (East Coast).
Guests: K. Hughes and M. May.
Written by Frederic Dannay and Manfred B. Lee.
Produced and directed by Bruce Kamman.
Announcer: Ernest Chappell.
Organ music: Charles Paul.
Sponsor: Bromo-Seltzer.
Story: Ellery tries to save a wealthy spinster from a gypsy fortune teller who seems able to predict the future with uncanny accuracy.

EPISODE #127 **"THE DEATH TRAPS"**
  Broadcast on May 27, 1943 (West Coast).
  Guests: Ruth McDevitt (radio actress) and L. Rollins.
  Broadcast on May 29, 1943 (East Coast).
  Guests: P. Lawrence and Guy Lombardo (bandleader).
  Written by Frederic Dannay and Manfred B. Lee.
  Produced and directed by Bruce Kamman.
  Announcer: Ernest Chappell.
  Organ music: Charles Paul.
  Sponsor: Bromo-Seltzer.
  Story: Ellery becomes involved with a young woman required by a relative's will to
live in a house which somebody else in the family has rigged with a series of death traps.

  **Trivia, etc.** This episode was repeated on January 29, 1948 as "The Death House"
(Episode #338).

EPISODE #128 **"THE KILLER WHO WAS GOING TO DIE"**
  Broadcast on June 3, 1943 (West Coast).
  Guests: R. Burton and J. Bellows.
  Broadcast on June 5, 1943 (East Coast).
  Guests: Nellie Revell (radio personality) and B. Yost.
  Written by Frederic Dannay and Manfred B. Lee.
  Produced and directed by Bruce Kamman.
  Announcer: Ernest Chappell.
  Sponsored by Bromo-Seltzer.
  Organ music: Charles Paul.
  Sponsor: Bromo-Seltzer.
  Story: Ellery investigates when a ruthless womanizer who broke many hearts is
murdered in a reducing cabinet.

EPISODE #129 **"CRIME, INC."**
  Broadcast on June 10, 1943 (West Coast).
  Guests: Guy Lombardo (bandleader) and Arleen Whelan (actress).
  Broadcast on June 12, 1943 (East Coast).
  Guests: Mia Slavenska (ballerina) and D. Thimor.
  Written by Frederic Dannay and Manfred B. Lee.
  Produced and directed by Bruce Kamman.
  Announcer: Ernest Chappell.
  Organ music: Charles Paul.
  Sponsor: Bromo-Seltzer.
  Story: Ellery tries to deduce which member of a six-person crime cartel killed the
group's leader just before the police were to arrest all of them.

  **Trivia, etc.** A condensed version of the script for this episode was published as "The
Crime Corporation" (*Story Digest*, November 1946).

EPISODE #130 **"THE MAN WITH THE RED BEARD"**
  Broadcast on June 17, 1943 (West Coast).
  Guests: Virginia Field (actress) and Norman Tokar (radio actor).
  Broadcast on June 19, 1943 (East Coast).
  Guests: Joe Besser (comedian) and Gypsy Rose Lee (stripper/actress).

Written by Frederic Dannay and Manfred B. Lee.
Produced and directed by Bruce Kamman.
Announcer: Ernest Chappell.
Organ music: Charles Paul.
Sponsor: Bromo-Seltzer.
Story: Ellery tries to recover money intended for the USO that was stolen from an insurance agent.

EPISODE #131 **"SERGEANT VELIE'S REVENGE"**
Broadcast on June 24, 1943 (West Coast).
Guests: Christine Ayers (showgirl) and William Fawcett (magazine publisher).
Broadcast on June 26, 1943 (East Coast).
Guests: Virginia Field (actress) and Norman Tokar (radio actor).
Written by Frederic Dannay and Manfred B. Lee.
Produced and directed by Bruce Kamman.
Announcer: Ernest Chappell.
Organ music: Charles Paul.
Sponsor: Bromo-Seltzer.
Story: unknown.

EPISODE #132 **"THE HIDDEN CRIME"**
Broadcast on July 1, 1943 (West Coast).
Guest: J. Deering and Dr. A.B. Hecht.
Broadcast on July 3, 1943 (East Coast).
Guests: James Montgomery Flagg (magazine illustrator) and Harriet Van Horne (newspaper columnist).
Written by Frederic Dannay and Manfred B. Lee.
Produced and directed by Bruce Kamman.
Announcer: Ernest Chappell.
Organ music: Charles Paul.
Spnsor: Bromo-Seltzer.
Story: Ellery tries to solve a crime so clever that no one knows exactly what it is.

EPISODE #133 **"THE DOUBLE TRIANGLE"**
Broadcast on July 8, 1943 (West Coast).
Guests: Harry Von Zell (actor) and Fred Waring (bandleader).
Broadcast on July 10, 1943 (East Coast).
Guests: Phil Baker (radio comedian) and Donna Dae (singer).
Written by Frederic Dannay and Manfred B. Lee.
Produced and directed by Bruce Kamman.
Announcer: Ernest Chappell.
Organ music: Charles Paul.
Sponsor: Bromo-Seltzer.
Story: same as Episode #46 (April 28, 1940).

**Trivia, etc.** This was the first of 13 rerun episodes. Sometime during August 1943 Carleton Young left the role of Ellery and was replaced by Sydney Smith. A few weeks later, sometime in September, Marian Shockley was replaced in the role of Nikki by Helen Lewis.

EPISODE #134 **"THE MAN WHO COULD DOUBLE THE SIZE OF DIAMONDS"**
Broadcast on July 15, 1943 (West Coast).
Guests: M. Davis and W. Doble.

Broadcast on July 17, 1943 (East Coast).
Guests: Joan Edwards (singer/actress) and R. Mealand.
Written by Frederic Dannay and Manfred B. Lee.
Produced and directed by Bruce Kamman.
Announcer: Ernest Chappell.
Organ music: Charles Paul.
Sponsor: Bromo-Seltzer.
Story: same as Episode #47 ( May 5, 1940).

EPISODE #135 **"THE FIRE BUG"**
Broadcast on July 22, 1943 (West Coast),
Guests: Pvt. J. Fink and John Wayne (movie star).
Broadcast on July 24, 1943 (East Coast).
Guests: Janet Blair (actress) and Paula Stone (actress).
Written by Frederic Dannay and Manfred B. Lee.
Produced and directed by Bruce Kamman.
Announcer: Ernest Chappell.
Organ music: Charles Paul.
Sponsor: Bromo-Seltzer.
Story: same as Episode #48 (May 12, 1940).

EPISODE #136 **"THE HONEYMOON HOUSE"**
Broadcast on July 29, 1943 (West Coast).
Guests: Virginia Gilmore (actress) and F. Hornaday.
Broadcast on July 31, 1943 (East Coast).
Guests: Ann Corio (stripper/actress) and Paul Lavalle (orchestra conductor).
Written by Frederic Dannay and Manfred B. Lee.
Produced and directed by Bruce Kamman.
Announcer: Ernest Chappell.
Organ music: Charles Paul.
Sponsor: Bromo-Seltzer.
Story: same as Episode #49 (May 19, 1940).

EPISODE #137 **"THE MOUSE'S BLOOD"**
Broadcast on August 5, 1943 (West Coast).
Guests: Ann Corio (stripper/actress) and Jay C. Flippen (actor).
Broadcast on August 7, 1943 (East Coast).
Guests: M. Davis and Mary Small (vocalist).
Written by Frederic Dannay and Manfred B. Lee.
Produced and directed by Bruce Kamman.
Announcer: Ernest Chappell.
Organ music: Charles Paul.
Sponsor: Bromo-Seltzer.
Story: same as Episode #50 (May 26, 1940).

EPISODE #138 **"THE FOUR MURDERERS"**
Broadcast on August 12, 1943 (West Coast).
Guests: Paul Lavalle (orchestra conductor) and Paula Stone (actress).
Broadcast on August 14, 1943 (East Coast).
Guests: Jay Jostyn (actor) and Danton Walker (newspaper columnist).
Written by Frederic Dannay and Manfred B. Lee.

Produced and directed by Bruce Kamman.
Announcer: Ernest Chappell.
Organ music: Charles Paul.
Sponsor: Bromo-Seltzer.
Story: same as Episode #51 (June 2, 1940).

### EPISODE #139    "THE GOOD SAMARITAN"
Broadcast on August 19, 1943 (West Coast).
Guests: Jan Kiepura (opera singer) and Danton Walker (newspaper columnist).
Broadcast on August 21, 1943 (East Coast).
Guests: Rajah Raboid (stage magician) and Ralph Edwards (media emcee).
Written by Frederic Dannay and Manfred B. Lee.
Produced and directed by Bruce Kamman.
Announcer: Ernest Chappell.
Organ music: Charles Paul.
Sponsor: Bromo-Seltzer.
Story: same as Episode #52 (June 9, 1940).

### EPISODE #140    "THE MYSTERIOUS TRAVELERS"
Broadcast on August 26, 1943 (West Coast).
Guests: Otto Preminger (movie director) and Rajah Raboid (stage magician).
Broadcast on August 28, 1943 (East Coast).
Guests: F.B. Beddow and C.C. Connel.
Written by Frederic Dannay and Manfred B. Lee.
Produced and directed by Bruce Kamman.
Announcer: Ernest Chappell.
Organ music: Charles Paul.
Sponsor: Bromo-Seltzer.
Story: same as Episode #53 (June 16, 1940).

### EPISODE #141    "THE DARK CLOUD"
Broadcast on September 2, 1943 (West Coast).
Guests: Ezra MacIntosh (radio producer/director) and I.T. Miller.
Broadcast on September 4, 1943 (East Coast).
Guests: Christine Ayers (showgirl) and Spike Jones (bandleader).
Written by Frederic Dannay and Manfred B. Lee.
Produced and directed by Bruce Kamman.
Announcer: Ernest Chappell.
Organ music: Charles Paul.
Sponsor: Bromo-Seltzer.
Story: same as Episode #54 (June 23, 1940).

### EPISODE #142    "THE BLIND BULLET"
Broadcast on September 9, 1943 (West Coast).
Guests: Candy Jones (model) and Spike Jones (bandleader).
Broadcast on September 11, 1943 (East Coast).
Guests: Richard Coogan (radio actor) and Julie Stevens (radio actress).
Written by Frederic Dannay and Manfred B. Lee.
Produced and directed by Bruce Kamman.
Announcer: Ernest Chappell.
Organ music: Charles Paul.
Sponsor: Bromo-Seltzer.
Story: same as Episode #55 (June 30, 1940).

EPISODE #143   **"THE FALLEN GLADIATOR"**
>Broadcast on September 16, 1943 (West Coast).
>Guests: Jack Dolph (author) and Dave Rubinoff (violinist).
>Broadcast on September 18, 1943 (East Coast).
>Guests: Don Dunphy (sports announcer) and John Wayne (movie star).
>Written by Frederic Dannay and Manfred B. Lee.
>Produced and directed by Bruce Kamman.
>Announcer: Ernest Chappell.
>Organ music: Charles Paul.
>Sponsor: Bromo-Seltzer.
>Story: same as Episode #56 (July 7, 1940).

EPISODE #144   **"THE TREASURE HUNT"**
>Broadcast on September 23, 1943 (West Coast).
>Guests: Jackie Kelk (radio actor) and Mary Small (vocalist).
>Broadcast on September 25, 1943 (East Coast).
>Guests: "Senator" Ed Ford, Harry Hershfield, and Joe Laurie, Jr. (three of the four joke experts on radio's *Can You Top This?*).
>Written by Frederic Dannay and Manfred B. Lee.
>Produced and directed by Bruce Kamman.
>Announcer: Ernest Chappell.
>Organ music: Charles Paul.
>Sponsor: Bromo-Seltzer.
>Story: same as Episode #58 (July 21, 1940).

EPISODE #145   **"THE WORLD SERIES CRIME"**
>Broadcast on September 30, 1943 (West Coast).
>Guests: Don Dunphy (sports announcer) and Al Schacht (baseball coach).
>Broadcast on October 2, 1943 (East Coast).
>Guests: Art Flynn (sportswriter), Ken Sears (ball player) and Joe Gordon (ball player).
>Written by Frederic Dannay and Manfred B. Lee.
>Produced and directed by Bruce Kamman.
>Announcer: Ernest Chappell.
>Organ music: Charles Paul.
>Sponsor: Bromo-Seltzer.
>Story: same as Episode #94 (October 10, 1942).

# SEASON FOUR

EPISODE #146   **"THE MAN WITH 10,000 ENEMIES"**
>Broadcast on October 7, 1943 (West Coast).
>Guests: B. Cash and Hope Emerson (actress).
>Broadcast on October 9, 1943 (East Coast).
>Guests: P. Browning and M. Little.
>Written by Frederic Dannay and Manfred B. Lee.
>Produced and directed by Bruce Kamman.
>Announcer: Ernest Chappell.
>Organ music: Charles Paul.
>Sponsor: Bromo-Seltzer.
>Story: unknown.

EPISODE #147   **"THE HOPELESS CASE"**
Broadcast on October 14, 1943  (West Coast).
Guests:  Vic Carroll and M. E. Keeler.
Broadcast on October 16, 1943  (East Coast).
Guests:  Nadine Conner (singer) and Mayor C.V. Mooney.
Written by Frederic Dannay and Manfred B. Lee.
Produced and directed by Bruce Kamman.
Announcer: Ernest Chappell.
Organ music: Charles Paul.
Sponsor: Bromo-Seltzer.
Story:  Ellery tries to save a man who insists on his innocence in a poison murder despite having been accused by the dying victim himself.

EPISODE #148   **"THE FRIGHTENED STAR"**
Broadcast on October 21, 1943  (West Coast).
Guests:  Earl Carroll (theatrical producer) and Beryl Wallace (showgirl/actress).
Broadcast on October 23, 1943  (East Coast).
Guests:  H. Goldman and Edythe Wright (vocalist).
Written by Frederic Dannay and Manfred B. Lee.
Produced and directed by Bruce Kamman.
Announcer: Ernest Chappell.
Organ music: Charles Paul.
Sponsor: Bromo-Seltzer.
Story: same as Episode #57 (July 14, 1940).

EPISODE #149   **"THE STOLEN REMBRANDT"**
Broadcast on October 28, 1943  (West Coast).
Guests:  Eric Blore (actor) and W. Shaw.
Broadcast on October 30, 1943  (East Coast).
Guests:  C.S. Foster and H.S. Palmer.
Written by Frederic Dannay and Manfred B. Lee.
Produced and directed by Bruce Kamman.
Announcer: Ernest Chappell.
Organ music: Charles Paul.
Sponsor: Bromo-Seltzer.
Story:  unknown.

EPISODE #150   **"THE VANISHING MAGICIAN"**
Broadcast on November 4, 1943  (West Coast).
Guests:  B. Pemberton and Linda Watkins (radio actress).
Broadcast on November 6, 1943  (East Coast).
Guests:  Edward Pawley (actor) and S. Bigman (*Time* magazine editor).
Written by Frederic Dannay and Manfred B. Lee.
Produced and directed by Bruce Kamman.
Announcer: Ernest Chappell.
Organ music: Charles Paul.
Sponsor: Bromo-Seltzer.
Story:  same as Episode #66, "The Disappearing Magician" (September 15, 1940).

**Trivia, etc.** This was the last episode in which Helen Lewis played Nikki Porter. The following week Marian Shockley, the original Nikki, returned to the part.

## EPISODE #151 "THE THREE DOLLAR ROBBERY"

Broadcast on November 11, 1943 (West Coast).
Guests: Fran Carlon (radio actress) and Edward Pawley (actor).
Broadcast on November 13, 1943 (East Coast)
Guests: Linda Watkins (radio actress) and E. McGrane.
Written by Frederic Dannay and Manfred B. Lee.
Produced and directed by Bruce Kamman.
Announcer: Ernest Chappell.
Organ music: Charles Paul.
Sponsor: Bromo-Seltzer.
Story: Ellery is offered $5,000 if he can find a rare $3 gold piece that was stolen during a card game.

## EPISODE #152 "THE BULLET-PROOF MAN"

Broadcast on November 18, 1943 (West Coast).
Guests: Mrs. F. Cooper, Virginia Field (actress), and Ed Sullivan (newspaper columnist).
Broadcast on November 20, 1943 (East Coast).
Guests: Warren Hull and Parks Johnson (co-hosts of the *Vox Pop* program).
Written by Frederic Dannay and Manfred B. Lee.
Produced and directed by Bruce Kamman.
Announcer: Ernest Chappell.
Organ music: Charles Paul.
Sponsor: Bromo-Seltzer.
Story: Ellery investigates a murder among the bizarre tenants of a new office building that is not yet officially open and discovers that loose talk by soldiers (while drinking soda pop!) caused the death of American troops.

**Trivia, etc.** The Office of War Information syndicated various episodes of *Ellery Queen* for troops fighting overseas. The episodes were recorded and edited by the World Lateral Transcription Company, which deleted both the Bromo-Seltzer commercials and the armchair detectives' discussions, leaving a 15-minute drama. Public service announcements were added live. This is one of the two such episodes that survive on tape.

## EPISODE #153 "THE TRAIN THAT VANISHED"

Broadcast on November 25, 1943 (West Coast).
Guests: B. Berg and Lt. V. Perring.
Broadcast on November 27, 1943 (East Coast).
Guests: J.C. Cullen and Jack Dempsey (former boxer).
Written by Frederic Dannay and Manfred B. Lee.
Produced and directed by Bob Steel.
Announcer: Ernest Chappell.
Organ music: Charles Paul.
Sponsor: Bromo-Seltzer.
Story: Ellery tries to solve the riddle of why a notorious gangster bothered to steal a child's toy train.

## EPISODE #154 "THE DYING MESSAGE"

Broadcast on December 2, 1943 (West Coast).
Guests: Arthur and Kathryn Murray (dance instructors).
Broadcast on December 4, 1943 (East Coast).

Guests: J.L. Stewart and V.S. Wange.
Written by Frederic Dannay and Manfred B. Lee.
Produced and directed by Bob Steel.
Announcer: Ernest Chappell.
Organ music: Charles Paul.
Sponsor: Bromo-Seltzer.
Story: Ellery tries to solve the murder of a college professor who left as his dying message the word "me."

## EPISODE #155   "THE MAN WHO PLAYED DEAD"

Broadcast on December 9, 1943 (West Coast).
Guests: D. Caulson and Ginni Young (vocalist).
Broadcast on December 11, 1943 (East Coast).
Guests: Arthur and Kathryn Murray (dance instructors).
Written by Frederic Dannay and Manfred B. Lee.
Produced and directed by Bob Steel.
Announcer: Ernest Chappell.
Organ music: Charles Paul.
Sponsor: Bromo-Seltzer.
Story: Ellery is hired by an insurance company to look into an apparent automobile accident which left nothing of the car's passengers except a few cinders.

## EPISODE #156   "THE UNLUCKY MAN"

Broadcast on December 16, 1943 (West Coast).
Guests: S. Bigman (*Time* magazine editor) and M. Thompson.
Broadcast on December 18, 1943 (East Coast).
Guests: Ted Collins (Columbia Records talent scout) and Earl Wilson (newspaper columnist).
Written by Frederic Dannay and Manfred B. Lee.
Produced and directed by Bob Steel.
Announcer: Ernest Chappell.
Organ music: Charles Paul.
Sponsor: Bromo-Seltzer.
Story: unknown.

## EPISODE #157   "THE DAUPHIN'S DOLL"

Broadcast on December 23, 1943 (West Coast).
Guests: Sgt. R. Carlson and Pvt. V. Ellis.
Broadcast on December 25, 1943 (East Coast).
Guests: Pvt. I. Bassett and Pfc. P. Grove.
Written by Manfred B. Lee.
Produced and directed by Bob Steel.
Announcer: Ernest Chappell.
Organ music: Charles Paul.
Sponsor: Bromo-Seltzer.
Story: Ellery joins forces with Inspector Queen and dozens of policemen to protect a valuable doll with a diamond crown from a thief who has announced that he'll make the figure vanish while it's on exhibit at a major department store, on the day before Christmas.

**Trivia, etc.** Lee told Anthony Boucher in a letter of August 10, 1946 that he alone wrote the script for this episode, with no input from Dannay. Lee later adapted the script into the short story "The Dauphin's Doll" (*Ellery Queen's Mystery Magazine*, December 1948; collected in *Calendar of Crime*, 1952).

EPISODE #158   **"THE INVISIBLE FOOTPRINTS"**
Broadcast on December 30, 1943  (West Coast).
Guests:  Joan Brooks (vocalist) and Ben Grauer (radio announcer).
Broadcast on January 1, 1944  (East Coast).
Guests:  Pamela Kellino (actress) and A. Reynolds.
Written by Frederic Dannay and Manfred B. Lee.
Produced and directed by Bob Steel.
Announcer: Ernest Chappell.
Organ music: Charles Paul.
Sponsor: Bromo-Seltzer.
Story:  Ellery encounters a strange old shipping tycoon as he tries to figure out how a human being could walk through freshly fallen snow without leaving tracks.

EPISODE #159   **"THE DISASTER CLUB"**
Broadcast on January 6, 1944  (West Coast).
Guests:  John Boles (actor) and Agatha Christie (mystery writer).
Broadcast on January 8, 1944  (East Coast).
Guests:  Joan Brooks (vocalist) and George McManus (comic strip artist).
Written by Frederic Dannay and Manfred B. Lee.
Produced and directed by Bob Steel.
Announcer: Ernest Chappell.
Organ music: Charles Paul.
Sponsor: Bromo-Seltzer.
Story:  same as Episode #2, "The Last Man Club" (June 25, 1939).

EPISODE #160   **"THE MISCHIEF MAKER"**
Broadcast on January 13, 1944  (West Coast).
Guests:  Bill O'Connor (radio announcer) and E.M. Smith.
Broadcast on January 15, 1944  (East Coast).
Guests:  G. Beane and P. Cusack.
Written by Frederic Dannay and Manfred B. Lee.
Produced and directed by Bob Steel.
Announcer: Ernest Chappell.
Organ music: Charles Paul.
Sponsor: Bromo-Seltzer.
Story: Ellery investigates a series of anonymous poison pen letters written to the residents of a single apartment building.

EPISODE #161   **"THE SCARECROW AND THE SNOWMAN"**
Broadcast on January 20, 1944  (West Coast).
Guests:  Jeanne Cagney (actress) and P. Cusack.
Broadcast on January 22, 1944  (East Coast).
Guests:  Bill O'Connor (radio announcer) and Gloria Swanson (actress).
Written by Frederic Dannay and Manfred B. Lee.
Produced and directed by Bob Steel.
Announcer: Ernest Chappell.
Organ music: Charles Paul.
Sponsor: Bromo-Seltzer.
Story:  same as Episode #30, "The Dying Scarecrow" (January 7, 1940).

EPISODE #162   **"THE FAMILY GHOST"**
>Broadcast on January 27, 1944  (West Coast).
>Guests:  Marc Connelly (playwright) and Martha Scott (actress).
>Broadcast on January 29, 1944  (East Coast).
>Guests:  Howard W. Blakeslee (science editor) and Mrs. Blakeslee.
>Written by Frederic Dannay and Manfred B. Lee.
>Produced and directed by Bob Steel.
>Announcer: Ernest Chappell.
>Organ music: Charles Paul.
>Sponsor: Bromo-Seltzer.
>Story:  Ellery investigates the case of a ghost who apparently can be shot and wounded
but not killed.

EPISODE #163   **"THE MURDER ON THE AIR"**
>Broadcast on February 3, 1944  (West Coast).
>Guests:  Eddie Mayehoff (comedian) and Bea Wain (singer).
>Broadcast on February 5, 1944  (East Coast).
>Guests:  Agatha Christie (mystery writer) and Edith Head (costume designer).
>Written by Frederic Dannay and Manfred B. Lee.
>Produced and directed by Bob Steel.
>Announcer: Ernest Chappell.
>Organ music: Charles Paul.
>Sponsor: Bromo-Seltzer.
>Story:  same as Episode #8, "The Flying Needle" (August 6, 1939).

EPISODE #164   **"THE PROBLEM CHILD"**
>Broadcast on February 10, 1944  (West Coast).
>Guests:  P. Lawrence and John Shuttleworth (fictitious radio host).
>Broadcast on February 12, 1944  (East Coast).
>Guests:  Ben Grauer (radio announcer) and J. Tucker.
>Written by Frederic Dannay and Manfred B. Lee.
>Produced and directed by Bob Steel.
>Announcer: Ernest Chappell.
>Organ music: Charles Paul.
>Sponsor: Bromo-Seltzer.
>Story:  unknown.

EPISODE #165   **"THE SQUIRREL WOMAN"**
>Broadcast on February 17, 1944  (West Coast).
>Guests:  Brenda Forbes (radio actress) and Candy Jones (model).
>Broadcast on February 19, 1944  (East Coast).
>Guests:  Admiral Y. Sterling and Benay Venuta (singer/actress).
>Written by Frederic Dannay and Manfred B. Lee.
>Produced and directed by Bob Steel.
>Announcer: Ernest Chappell.
>Organ music: Charles Paul.
>Sponsor: Bromo-Seltzer.
>Story:  same as Episode #10, "The Thirteenth Clue" (August 20, 1939).

EPISODE #166  **"THE BLACK JINX"**
    Broadcast on February 24, 1944 (West Coast).
    Guests: Irene Bordoni (singer) and Al Trace (singer/songwriter).
    Broadcast on February 26, 1944 (East Coast).
    Guests: Eddie Dowling (Broadway producer) and Helen Menken (radio actress).
    Written by Frederic Dannay and Manfred B. Lee.
    Produced and directed by Bob Steel.
    Announcer: Ernest Chappell.
    Organ music: Charles Paul.
    Sponsor: Bromo-Seltzer.
    Story: unknown.

EPISODE #167  **"THE RED CROSS"**
    Broadcast on March 2, 1944 (West Coast).
    Guests: Arlene Francis (actress) and Lucy Monroe (singer).
    Broadcast on March 4, 1944 (East Coast).
    Guests: Helen Hayes (actress) and Lindsay MacHarrie (radio director).
    Written by Frederic Dannay and Manfred B. Lee.
    Produced and directed by Bob Steel.
    Announcer: Ernest Chappell.
    Organ music: Charles Paul.
    Sponsor: Bromo-Seltzer.
    Story: unknown.

EPISODE #168  **"WANTED: JOHN SMITH"**
    Broadcast on March 9, 1944 (West Coast).
    Guests: Aubrey Waller Cook (pianist) and June Vincent (actress).
    Broadcast on March 11, 1944 (East Coast).
    Guests: Irene Bordoni (singer) and Stan Lomax (baseball player).
    Written by Frederic Dannay and Manfred B. Lee.
    Produced and directed by Bob Steel.
    Announcer: Ernest Chappell.
    Organ music: Charles Paul.
    Sponsor: Bromo-Seltzer.
    Story: same as Episode #33, "The Devil's Violin" (January 28, 1940).

EPISODE #169  **"THE CIRCULAR CLUES"**
    Broadcast on March 16, 1944 (West Coast).
    Guests: Joan Edwards (singer/actress) and B. Yost.
    Broadcast on March 18, 1944 (East Coast).
    Guests: Connee Boswell (singer) and Xavier Cugat (bandleader).
    Written by Frederic Dannay and Manfred B. Lee.
    Produced and directed by Bob Steel.
    Announcer: Ernest Chappell.
    Organ music: Charles Paul.
    Sponsor: Bromo-Seltzer.
    Story: same as Episode #31, "The Woman in Black" (January 14, 1940).

EPISODE #170  **"THE GLASS BALL"**
    Broadcast on March 23, 1944 (West Coast).
    Guests: Nanette Fabray (actress) and Mrs. I. Gerhard.

Broadcast on March 25, 1944 (East Coast).
Guests: John G. Chapman (New York *Daily News* radio critic) and S. Schulman.
Written by Frederic Dannay and Manfred B. Lee.
Produced and directed by Bob Steel.
Announcer: Ernest Chappell.
Organ music: Charles Paul.
Sponsor: Bromo-Seltzer.
Story: same as episode #40, "The Silver Ball" (March 17, 1940).

EPISODE #171   **"THE CASE ELLERY QUEEN COULDN'T SOLVE"**
Broadcast on March 30, 1944 (West Coast).
Guests: H. Duval and P. Yung.
Broadcast on April 1, 1944 (East Coast).
Guests: J. Clyde and Dick Todd (vocalist).
Written by Frederic Dannay and Manfred B. Lee.
Produced and directed by Bob Steel.
Announcer: Ernest Chappell.
Organ music: Charles Paul.
Sponsor: Bromo-Seltzer.
Story: Ellery tries to unravel the mystery surrounding a cache of famous rubies that had been lost for almost half a century.

EPISODE #172   **"THE PAINTED PROBLEM"**
Broadcast on April 6, 1944 (West Coast).
Guests: I. Munson and Ya Ching Lee.
Broadcast on April 8, 1944 (East Coast).
Guests: Milton Cross (*Metropolitan Opera* radio host) and Marc Lawrence (actor).
Written by Frederic Dannay and Manfred B. Lee.
Produced and directed by Bob Steel.
Announcer: Ernest Chappell.
Organ music: Charles Paul.
Sponsor: Bromo-Seltzer.
Story: same as Episode #21, "The Picture Puzzle" (November 5, 1939).

EPISODE #173   **"DEAD MAN'S CAVERN"**
Broadcast on April 13, 1944 (West Coast).
Guests: F. Beverley Kelley (circus publicity director) and Marc Lawrence (actor).
Broadcast on April 15, 1944 (East Coast).
Guests: Dale Carnegie (motivational speaker) and Ted Fio Rito (musician).
Written by Frederic Dannay and Manfred B. Lee.
Produced and directed by Bob Steel.
Announcer: Ernest Chappell.
Organ music: Charles Paul.
Sponsor: Bromo-Seltzer.
Story: same as Episode #19, "The Haunted Cave" (October 22, 1939).

EPISODE #174   **"THE LETTERS OF BLOOD"**
Broadcast on April 20, 1944 (West Coast).
Guests: M. Gateson and B. Vlavianos.
Broadcast on April 22, 1944 (East Coast).
Guests: P. Fears and George McManus (comic strip artist).

Written by Frederic Dannay and Manfred B. Lee.
Produced and directed by Bob Steel.
Announcer: Ernest Chappell.
Organ music: Charles Paul.
Sponsor: Bromo-Seltzer.
Story: Ellery sends radio messages to a South Pacific airbase, Latin America and Teheran as he tries to unravel the dying message left by a murdered millionaire.

## EPISODE #175 "THE BURIED TREASURE"
Broadcast on April 27, 1944 (West Coast).
Guests: A. Lesser and P. Fears.
Broadcast on April 29, 1944 (East Coast).
Guests: Mrs. I. Gerhard and Clayton Rawson (mystery writer).
Written by Frederic Dannay and Manfred B. Lee.
Produced and directed by Bob Steel.
Announcer: Ernest Chappell.
Organ music: Charles Paul.
Sponsor: Bromo-Seltzer.
Story: same as Episode #15, "The Lost Treasure" (September 24, 1939).

## EPISODE #176 "THE THIEF IN THE DARK"
Broadcast on May 4, 1944 (West Coast).
Guests: M. Gardner and J.C. Lewis (radio producer).
Broadcast on May 6, 1944 (East Coast).
Guests: R. Watson/A. Pope, and Martin Kosleck (actor).
Written by Frederic Dannay and Manfred B. Lee.
Produced and directed by Bob Steel.
Announcer: Ernest Chappell.
Organ music: Charles Paul.
Sponsor: Bromo-Seltzer.
Story: same as Episode #22, "The Cellini Cup" (November 12, 1939).

**Trivia, etc.** Several scenes from this episode were broadcast as an Armed Forces Radio Service sneak preview and survive on tape.

## EPISODE #177 "THE CHINESE PUZZLE"
Broadcast on May 11, 1944 (West Coast).
Guests: A. Fisher and Rex Harrison (actor).
Broadcast on May 13, 1944 (East Coast)
Guests: John J. Anthony (fictitious radio host) and Rose Marie Lombardo (radio singer).
Written by Frederic Dannay and Manfred B. Lee.
Produced and directed by Bob Steel.
Announcer: Ernest Chappell.
Organ music: Charles.Paul.
Sponsor: Bromo-Seltzer.
Story: A series of strange unsigned messages sends Ellery off on a hunt for a mysterious Chinese, a secret bundle and the person who committed a murder in a theatrical boardinghouse.

EPISODE #178  **"THE BOTTLE OF WINE"**
      Broadcast on May 18, 1944  (West Coast).
      Guests:  Marjorie Lord (actress) and S. Schuyler.
      Broadcast on May 20, 1944  (East Coast).
      Guests:  J. Brice and J. McGurrin.
      Written by Frederic Dannay and Manfred B. Lee.
      Produced and directed by Bob Steel.
      Announcer: Ernest Chappell.
      Organ music: Charles Paul.
      Sponsor: Bromo-Seltzer.
      Story:  Ellery explores the connection between a rare bottle of Chateau d'Yquem and several crimes including murder.

EPISODE #179  **"THE GREAT CHEWING GUM MYSTERY"**
      Broadcast on May 25, 1944  (West Coast).
      Guests:  Henry Daniell (actor) and Lou Frankel.
      Broadcast on May 27, 1944  (East Coast).
      Guests:  E.S. Friendly and Vincent Lopez (bandleader).
      Written by Frederic Dannay and Manfred B. Lee.
      Produced and directed by Bob Steel.
      Announcer: Ernest Chappell.
      Organ music: Charles Paul.
      Sponsor: Bromo-Seltzer.
      Story:  same as Episode #1, "The Gum-Chewing Millionaire" (June 18, 1939).

EPISODE #180  **"THE MURDER GAME"**
      Broadcast on June 1, 1944  (West Coast).
      Guests:  John Archer (actor) and Carol Thurston (actress).
      Broadcast on June 3, 1944  (East Coast).
      Guests:  B. Kaplan and Rose Marie (actress).
      Written by Frederic Dannay and Manfred B. Lee.
      Produced and directed by Bob Steel.
      Announcer: Ernest Chappell.
      Organ music: Charles Paul.
      Sponsor: Bromo-Seltzer.
      Story:  same as Episode #20, "The Dead Cat" (October 29, 1939).

      **Trivia, etc.** The 60-minute drama "The Dead Cat" was broadcast just before Halloween of 1939 and dealt with a murder at a Halloween party. In this 30-minute version, broadcast several months before Halloween of 1944, the murder takes place during a game at Nikki's birthday party.

EPISODE #181  **"THE DARK SECRET"**
      Broadcast on June 8, 1944  (West Coast).
      Guest:  Royal Arch Gunnison (radio reporter).
      Broadcast on June 10, 1944  (East Coast).
      Guests:  G. Greentree and Carol Thurston (actress).
      Written by Frederic Dannay and Manfred B. Lee.
      Produced and directed by Bob Steel.
      Announcer: Ernest Chappell.
      Organ music: Charles Paul.
      Sponsor: Bromo-Seltzer.
      Story:  same as Episode #26, "The Black Secret" (December 10, 1939).

Trivia, etc. Several scenes from this episode were broadcast as an Armed Forces Radio Service sneak preview and survive on tape.

EPISODE #182   "THE BLUE CHIP"
>Broadcast on June 15, 1944  (West Coast).
>Guest:  Jane Cowl (actress).
>Broadcast on June 17, 1944  (East Coast).
>Guest:  Roland Young (actor).
>Written by Frederic Dannay and Manfred B. Lee.
>Produced and directed by Bob Steel.
>Announcer: Ernest Chappell.
>Organ music: Charles Paul.
>Sponsor: Bromo-Seltzer.
>Story: Ellery, Inspector Queen and Nikki are paying a weekend visit to Sergeant
Velie's summer home when a taxicab deposits a corpse on the doorstep.

EPISODE #183   "THE CORPSE IN LOWER FIVE"
>Broadcast on June 22, 1944  (West Coast).
>Guest:  M. Rognadahl.
>Broadcast on June 24, 1944  (East Coast).
>Guest:  C. Halliday.
>Written by Frederic Dannay and Manfred B. Lee.
>Produced and directed by Bob Steel.
>Announcer: Ernest Chappell.
>Organ music: Charles Paul.
>Sponsor: Bromo-Seltzer.
>Story:  same as Episode #4, "Napoleon's Razor" (July 9, 1939).

EPISODE #184   "THE DEVIL'S HEAD"
>Broadcast on June 29, 1944  (West Coast)
>Guest:  Claudia Morgan (radio actress).
>Broadcast on July 1, 1944  (East Coast)
>Guest:  Hildegarde (radio singer).
>Written by Frederic Dannay and Manfred B. Lee.
>Produced and directed by Bob Steel.
>Announcer: Ernest Chappell.
>Organ music: Charles Paul.
>Sponsor: Bromo-Seltzer.
>Story:  Ellery visits a mansion on the East River known as the House of the Four Devils
and tries to find out who has made several attempts on the owner's life.

EPISODE #185   "THE EGYPTIAN TOMB"
>Broadcast on July 6, 1944  (West Coast).
>Guest:  Michael Whalen (actor).
>Broadcast on July 8, 1944  (East Coast).
>Guest:  Royal Arch Gunnison (radio reporter).
>Written by Frederic Dannay and Manfred B. Lee.
>Produced and directed by Bob Steel.
>Announcer: Ernest Chappell.
>Organ music: Charles Paul.
>Sponsor: Bromo-Seltzer.
>Story:  same as Episode #63, "The Pharaoh's Curse" (August 25, 1940).

## EPISODE #186    "THE FOUL TIP"

Broadcast on July 13, 1944 (West Coast).
Guest: C. LaTorre.
Broadcast on July 15, 1944 (East Coast).
Guest: Michael Whalen (actor).
Written by Frederic Dannay and Manfred B. Lee.
Produced and directed by Bob Steel.
Announcer: Ernest Chappell.
Organ music: Charles Paul.
Sponsor: Bromo-Seltzer.
Story: While attending a big-league baseball game, Ellery is drawn into the case of a Western movie star who dies when, after being asked to sign some autographs, he's handed a pencil coated with poison.

## EPISODE #187    "THE YANG PIECE"

Broadcast on July 20, 1944 (West Coast).
Guest: Major George Fielding Eliot (military analyst).
Broadcast on July 22, 1944 (East Coast).
Guest: Colonel John Stilwell (retired Army officer).
Written by Frederic Dannay and Manfred B. Lee.
Produced and directed by Bob Steel.
Announcer: Ernest Chappell.
Sponsored by Bromo-Seltzer.
Organ music: Charles Paul.
Sponsor: Bromo-Seltzer.
Story: Ellery investigates a series of bizarre incidents surrounding an old Chinese curio dealer.

## EPISODE #188    "THE FOUR PRISONERS"

Broadcast on July 27, 1944 (West Coast).
Guest: Dr. F.E. Long.
Broadcast on July 29, 1944 (East Coast).
Guest: Claudia Morgan (radio actress).
Written by Frederic Dannay and Manfred B. Lee.
Produced and directed by Bob Steel.
Announcer: Ernest Chappell.
Organ music: Charles Paul.
Sponsor: Bromo-Seltzer.
Story: unknown.

## EPISODE #189    "THE MAN WITHOUT A HEART"

Broadcast on August 3, 1944 (West Coast).
Guest: Jane Russell (actress).
Broadcast on August 5, 1944 (East Coast).
Guest: Jane Cowl (actress).
Written by Frederic Dannay and Manfred B. Lee.
Produced and directed by Bob Steel.
Announcer: Ernest Chappell.
Organ music: Charles Paul.
Sponsor: Bromo-Seltzer.
Story: same as Episode #62, "The Meanest Man in the World" (August 18, 1940).

EPISODE #190   **"THE THREE HANDS"**
>Broadcast on August 10, 1944  (West Coast).
>Guest:  Dorothy Hart (actress).
>Broadcast on August 12, 1944  (East Coast).
>Guest:  Major George Fielding Eliot (military analyst).
>Written by Frederic Dannay and Manfred B. Lee.
>Produced and directed by Bob Steel.
>Announcer: Ernest Chappell.
>Organ music: Charles Paul.
>Sponsor: Bromo-Seltzer.
>Story:  same as Episode #67, "The Mark of Cain" (September 22, 1940).

EPISODE #191   **"THE MAN WHO WANTED CASH"**
>Broadcast on August 17, 1944  (West Coast).
>Guest:  John Mills (actor).
>Broadcast on August 19, 1944  (East Coast).
>Guest:  Bill Stern (sportscaster).
>Written by Frederic Dannay and Manfred B. Lee.
>Produced and directed by Bob Steel.
>Announcer: Ernest Chappell.
>Organ music: Charles Paul.
>Sponsor: Bromo-Seltzer.
>Story:  same as Episode #60,  "The Fatal Million" (August 4, 1940).

EPISODE #192   **"THE MAYOR AND THE CORPSE"**
>Broadcast on August 24, 1944  (West Coast).
>Guest:  John Conte (radio announcer).
>Broadcast on August 26, 1944  (East Coast).
>Guest:  Joan Edwards (singer/actress).
>Written by Frederic Dannay and Manfred B. Lee.
>Produced and directed by Bob Steel.
>Announcer: Ernest Chappell.
>Organ music: Charles Paul.
>Sponsor: Bromo-Seltzer.
>Story:  same as Episode #65, "The Picnic Murder" (September 8, 1940).

EPISODE #193   **"THE DEAD MAN'S BONES"**
>Broadcast on August 31, 1944  (West Coast).
>Guest:  Earl Wilson (newspaper columnist).
>Broadcast on September 2, 1944  (East Coast).
>Guest:  Fred Waring (bandleader).
>Written by Frederic Dannay and Manfred B. Lee.
>Produced and directed by Bob Steel.
>Announcer: Ernest Chappell
>Organ music: Charles Paul.
>Sponsor: Bromo-Seltzer.
>Story:  same as Episode #42, "The Emperor's Dice" (March 31, 1940).

EPISODE #194   **"THE DISAPPEARING CATS"**
>Broadcast on September 7, 1944  (West Coast).
>Guest:  Allan Jones (singer/actor).

Broadcast on September 9, 1944 (East Coast).
Guest: W. Peterson.
Written by Frederic Dannay and Manfred B. Lee.
Produced and directed by Bob Steel.
Announcer: Ernest Chappell.
Organ music: Charles Paul.
Sponsor: Bromo-Seltzer.
Story: unknown.

EPISODE #195   **"THE COLLEGE CRIME"**
Broadcast on September 14, 1944 (West Coast).
Guest: Captain J. Chase.
Broadcast on September 16, 1944 (East Coast).
Guest: Josephine Antoine (soprano).
Written by Frederic Dannay and Manfred B. Lee.
Produced and directed by Bob Steel.
Announcer: Ernest Chappell.
Organ music: Charles Paul.
Sponsor: Bromo-Seltzer.
Story: same as Episode #13, "The Three Rs" (September 10, 1939).

EPISODE #196   **"THE ROBBER OF FALLBORO"**
Broadcast on September 21, 1944 (West Coast).
Guest: Cornel Wilde (actor).
Broadcast on September 23, 1944 (East Coast).
Guest: V.E. Chenea.
Written by Frederic Dannay and Manfred B. Lee.
Produced and directed by Bob Steel.
Announcer: Ernest Chappell.
Organ music: Charles Paul.
Sponsor: Bromo-Seltzer.
Story: same as Episode #59, "The Black Sheep" ( July 28, 1940).

EPISODE #197   **"THE INVISIBLE CLOCK"**
Broadcast on September 28, 1944 (West Coast).
Guests: J. Holton, C. Choiniere.
Broadcast on September 30, 1944 (East Coast).
Guest: Lt. E. Mallon.
Written by Frederic Dannay and Manfred B. Lee.
Produced and directed by Bob Steel.
Announcer: Ernest Chappell.
Organ music: Charles Paul.
Sponsor: Bromo-Seltzer.
Story: same as Episode #61, "The Invisible Clock" (August 11, 1940).

# SEASON FIVE

EPISODE #198   **"THE CAFE SOCIETY CASE"**
Broadcast on October 5, 1944 (West Coast).
Guest: W. Peterson.

Broadcast on October 7, 1944 (East Coast).

Guests: Joe Laurie, Jr., "Senator" Ed Ford, and Harry Hershfield (three of the four joke experts on radio's *Can You Top This?*).

Written by Frederic Dannay and Manfred B. Lee.

Produced and directed by Bob Steel.

Announcer: Ernest Chappell.

Organ music: Charles Paul.

Sponsor: Bromo-Seltzer.

Story: Ellery tries to determine which of three patrician gentlemen is responsible for a drowning at a palatial summer home.

### EPISODE #199 "CLEOPATRA'S SNAKE"

Broadcast on October 12, 1944 (West Coast).

Guest: Ken Sobol (author).

Broadcast on October 14, 1944 (East Coast).

Guest: Armand Denis (explorer/documentary filmmaker).

Written by Frederic Dannay and Manfred B. Lee.

Produced and directed by Bob Steel.

Announcer: Ernest Chappell.

Organ music: Charles Paul.

Sponsor: Bromo-Seltzer.

Story: Ellery gets himself entangled in a mystery involving both ancient Egypt and modern experimental television.

### EPISODE #200 "THE AIRPORT DISASTERS"

Broadcast on October 19, 1944 (West Coast).

Guest: unknown.

Broadcast on October 21, 1944 (East Coast).

Guest: Vaughn Monroe (singer).

Written by Frederic Dannay and Manfred B. Lee.

Produced and directed by Bob Steel.

Announcer: Ernest Chappell.

Organ music: Charles Paul.

Sponsor: Bromo-Seltzer.

Story: Ellery tries to break up a sabotage ring assigned to wreck airplanes carrying important passengers just as Inspector Queen takes off in a plane targeted for destruction.

**Trivia, etc.** Apparently this episode was pre-empted on the West Coast.

### EPISODE #201 "THE UNFORTUNATE FISHERMAN"

Broadcast on October 26, 1944 (West Coast).

Guest: Leonard Levinson (radio writer).

Broadcast on October 28, 1944 (East Coast).

Guest: S. Kerr.

Written by Frederic Dannay and Manfred B. Lee.

Produced and directed by Bob Steel.

Announcer: Ernest Chappell.

Organ music: Charles Paul.

Sponsor: Bromo-Seltzer.

Story: Ellery, Inspector Queen and Nikki encounter a mystery while on a fishing trip in the North Woods.

EPISODE #202   **"THE ELECTION DAY MURDER"**
> Broadcast on November 2, 1944  (West Coast).
> Guest:  Aline MacMahon (actress).
> Broadcast on November 4, 1944  (East Coast).
> Guest:  N. Siegel.
> Written by Frederic Dannay and Manfred B. Lee.
> Produced and directed by Bob Steel.
> Announcer: Ernest Chappell.
> Organ music: Charles Paul.
> Sponsor: Bromo-Seltzer.
> Story:  same as Episode #9, "The Wandering Corpse" (August 13, 1939).

EPISODE #203   **"THE BOOBY TRAP"**
> Broadcast on November 9, 1944  (West Coast).
> Guest:  Peter Donald (radio comedian).
> Broadcast on November 11, 1944  (East Coast).
> Guest:  Nora Stirling (radio writer).
> Written by Frederic Dannay and Manfred B. Lee.
> Produced and directed by Bob Steel.
> Announcer: Ernest Chappell.
> Organ music: Charles Paul.
> Sponsor: Bromo-Seltzer.

Story:  After appearing on a radio quiz program whose host can identify almost any literary allusion, Ellery finds the man murdered by a booby-trapped copy of *Alice in Wonderland*. Ellery then tries to deduce why the victim pulled down books by Shaw, Shakespeare, Whitman and Ulysses S. Grant from his shelves before he died.

**Trivia, etc.** The script for this episode was later adapted by Dannay and Lee into the short story "Enter Ellery Queen" (*Argosy,* June 1960; collected as "Mystery at the Library of Congress" in *Queen's Experiments in Detection,* 1968).

EPISODE #204   **"THE RIGHT END"**
> Broadcast on November 16, 1944  (West Coast).
> Guest:  Tom Slater (radio host).
> Broadcast on November 18, 1944 (East Coast).
> Guest:  Red Barber (sportscaster).
> Written by Frederic Dannay and Manfred B. Lee.
> Produced and directed by Bob Steel.
> Announcer: Ernest Chappell.
> Organ music: Charles Paul.
> Sponsor: Bromo-Seltzer.

Story:  Ellery comes out of the grandstands to play detective when a football star is found dead between the halves of a gridiron classic.

EPISODE #205   **"THE THESPIS CLUB"**
> Broadcast on November 23, 1944  (West Coast).
> Guest:  unknown.
> Broadcast on November 25, 1944  (East Coast).
> Guest:  Fannie Hurst (novelist).
> Written by Frederic Dannay and Manfred B. Lee.
> Produced and directed by Bob Steel.
> Announcer: Ernest Chappell.
> Organ music: Charles Paul.

Sponsor: Bromo-Seltzer.

Story: Ellery investigates when a newly marketed health drink proves to be fatal.

**Trivia, etc.** The original working title for this episode was "The Taste Test." Fannie Hurst was hosting her own anthology series *Fannie Hurst Presents,* broadcast over ABC Radio on Saturday mornings, and in fact had hosted an episode earlier on the day she appeared as a guest on the Queen show.

### EPISODE #206   "THE GLASS SWORD"
Broadcast on November 30, 1944 (West Coast).
Guest: Jeanne Cagney (actress).
Broadcast on December 2, 1944 (East Coast).
Guest: Rouben Mamoulian (movie director).
Written by Frederic Dannay and Manfred B. Lee.
Produced and directed by Bob Steel.
Announcer: Ernest Chappell.
Organ music: Charles Paul.
Sponsor: Bromo-Seltzer.
Story: unknown.

### EPISODE #207   "THE STICKPIN AND THE RING"
Broadcast on December 7, 1944 (West Coast).
Guest: Victor Jory (actor).
Broadcast on December 9, 1944 (East Coast).
Guest: Ilka Chase (actress).
Written by Frederic Dannay and Manfred B. Lee.
Produced and directed by Bob Steel.
Announcer: Ernest Chappell.
Organ music: Charles Paul.
Sponsor: Bromo-Seltzer.
Story: Ellery tries to expose an astrologer who makes a habit of accurately predicting disasters.

### EPISODE #208   "DEATH ON SKATES"
Broadcast on December 14, 1944 (West Coast).
Guest: Barry Sullivan (actor).
Broadcast on December 16, 1944 (East Coast).
Guest: Frank Graham (radio announcer).
Written by Frederic Dannay and Manfred B. Lee.
Produced and directed by Bob Steel.
Announcer: Ernest Chappell.
Organ music: Charles Paul.
Sponsor: Bromo-Seltzer.
Story: unknown.

### EPISODE #209   "THE TOY CANNON"
Broadcast on December 21, 1944 (West Coast).
Guest: Neil Hamilton (actor).
Broadcast on December 23, 1944 (East Coast).
Guest: Harriet Van Horne (radio critic/newspaper columnist).
Written by Frederic Dannay and Manfred B. Lee.

Produced and directed by Bob Steel.
Announcer: Ernest Chappell.
Organ music: Charles Paul.
Sponsor: Bromo-Seltzer.
Story: unknown.

EPISODE #210   **"THE INNER CIRCLE"**
Broadcast on December 28, 1944 (West Coast).
Guest: R. Daigh.
Broadcast on December 30, 1944 (East Coast).
Guest: Luise Rainer (actress).
Written by Frederic Dannay and Manfred B. Lee.
Produced and directed by Bob Steel.
Announcer: Ernest Chappell.
Organ music: Charles Paul.
Sponsor: Bromo-Seltzer.
Story: same as Episode #83, "The Millionaires' Club" (April 23 and 25, 1942).

**Trivia, etc.** This was the final episode sponsored by Bromo-Seltzer. Three weeks later the series would return with a new sponsor (Anacin), a new evening (Wednesday instead of Thursday), a new network (CBS, where it had started, instead of NBC) and a new Nikki (Barbara Terrell replacing Marian Shockley).

EPISODE #211   **"THE DIAMOND FENCE"**   Broadcast on January 24, 1945
Guest: Janet Blair (actress).
Written by Tom Everitt and Manfred B. Lee.
Produced and directed by Bob Steel.
Announcer: Don Hancock.
Organ music: unknown.
Sponsor: Anacin.
Story:   Ellery investigates the murder of a middleman for stolen gems and the disappearance of five diamond rings from the scene of the crime under impossible circumstances.

EPISODE #212   **"THE SEVEN THOUSAND VICTIMS"**   Broadcast on January 31, 1945
Guest: George Givot (actor).
Written by Tom Everitt and Manfred B. Lee.
Produced and directed by Bob Steel.
Announcer: Don Hancock.
Organ music: unknown.
Sponsor: Anacin.
Story:   Ellery tries to find out who tried to destroy an Army transport carrying 7,000 wounded soldiers to New York by shutting down the guiding beacon of an isolated lighthouse off the Long Island shore.

EPISODE #213   **"THE LOST CARD"**   Broadcast on February 7, 1945
Guest: Dean F. Willey (railroad executive).
Written by Tom Everitt and Manfred B. Lee.
Produced and directed by Bob Steel.
Announcer: Don Hancock.
Organ music: unknown.
Sponsor: Anacin.

139

Story: On a train from Boston to New York, a wealthy old man is murdered during a card game and one of the cards from the deck is found missing. Among the passengers on the train is Ellery, who tries to solve the crime.

EPISODE #214 **"THE WINE MACHINE"** Broadcast on February 14, 1945
    Guest: Howard W. Blakeslee (science editor).
    Written by Tom Everitt and Manfred B. Lee.
    Produced and directed by Bob Steel.
    Announcer: Don Hancock.
    Organ music: unknown.
    Sponsor: Anacin.
    Story: Ellery encounters murder while accompanying a wealthy potential investor to the demonstration of a new invention which an eccentric scientist claims can age wine in a matter of minutes.

EPISODE #215 **"THE CRIME IN THE SNOW"** Broadcast on February 21, 1945
    Guest: Ted Husing (sportscaster).
    Written by Tom Everitt and Manfred B. Lee.
    Produced and directed by Bob Steel.
    Announcer: Don Hancock.
    Organ music: unknown.
    Sponsor: Anacin.
    Story: While Ellery and Nikki are enjoying a weekend at a ski lodge, a corpse is discovered in the snow.

EPISODE #216 **"THE SECRET WEAPON"** Broadcast on February 28, 1945
    Guest: H.W. Roden (mystery writer).
    Written by Tom Everitt and Manfred B. Lee.
    Produced and directed by Bob Steel.
    Announcer: Don Hancock.
    Organ music: unknown.
    Sponsor: Anacin.
    Story: Ellery investigates a case of sabotage in a war plant where a German refugee scientist is developing a new weapon to defeat the Nazis.

EPISODE #217 **"THE RARE STAMP"** Broadcast on March 7, 1945
    Guest: Dick Powell (movie star).
    Written by Tom Everitt and Manfred B. Lee.
    Produced and directed by Bob Steel.
    Announcer: Don Hancock.
    Organ music: unknown.
    Sponsor: Anacin.
    Story: Ellery takes a hand when a retired judge with a valuable stamp collection receives a threatening note and is shot at by an unknown gunman.

EPISODE #218 **"THE POISONED SLIPPER"** Broadcast on March 14, 1945
    Guest: Earl Wilson (newspaper columnist).
    Written by Tom Everitt and Manfred B. Lee.
    Produced and directed by Bob Steel.
    Announcer: Don Hancock.
    Organ music: unknown.
    Sponsor: Anacin.

Story: Ellery tries to solve the murder of a New York newspaper's city editor in the paper's busy newsroom.

EPISODE #219  **"THE SWORD OF DAMOCLES"**  Broadcast on March 21, 1945
    Guest: Milo Boulton (radio host).
    Written by Tom Everitt and Manfred B. Lee.
    Produced and directed by Bob Steel.
    Announcer: Don Hancock.
    Organ music: unknown.
    Sponsor: Anacin.
    Story: Ellery pits his wits against an invisible killer who has turned from collecting old books and paintings to amassing historic weapons and instruments of torture.

EPISODE #220  **"THE RED DEATH"**  Broadcast on March 28, 1945
    Guest: Jane Wyatt (actress).
    Written by Tom Everitt and Manfred B. Lee.
    Produced and directed by Bob Steel.
    Announcer: Don Hancock.
    Organ music: unknown.
    Sponsor: Anacin.
    Story: Ellery investigates a murder apparently committed by a horse at a big-time rodeo.

EPISODE #221  **"THE LUCKY SAILOR"**  Broadcast on April 4, 1945
    Guest: F. Beverley Kelley (circus publicity director).
    Written by _____ and Manfred B. Lee.
    Produced and directed by Bob Steel.
    Announcer: Don Hancock.
    Organ music: unknown.
    Sponsor: Anacin.
    Story: Clues tattooed on a sailor lead Ellery to a pair of dice and a mysterious tombstone.

EPISODE #222  **"THE MUSICAL MURDER"**  Broadcast on April 11, 1945
    Guest: Anne Fromer (magazine editor).
    Written by Tom Everitt and Manfred B. Lee.
    Produced and directed by Bob Steel.
    Announcer: Don Hancock.
    Organ music: unknown.
    Sponsor: Anacin.
    Story: Ellery investigates a murder stemming from a feud among rival songwriters.

EPISODE #223  **"THE CRIME THAT WASN'T POSSIBLE"**  Broadcast on April 18, 1945
    Guest: Monroe Wheeler (art critic/book designer).
    Written by Frederic Dannay and Manfred B. Lee.
    Produced and directed by Bob Steel.
    Announcer: Don Hancock.
    Organ music: unknown.
    Sponsor: Anacin.
    Story: Ellery takes a hand when a bold thief announces that he'll steal a priceless masterpiece from a well-guarded art museum on a certain day and then carries out his promise.

**Trivia, etc.** *The Adventures of Ellery Queen* was not broadcast on April 25, 1945 due to a news special on the San Francisco Conference of the United Nations. From 7:30 to 8:00 p.m. EST, almost every major radio station broadcast President Truman's historic speech at the opening plenary session of the United Nations Conference on International Organization.

EPISODE #224  **"THE KEY TO THE MYSTERY"**  Broadcast on May 2, 1945
        Guest: Jo-Carroll Dennison (actress).
        Written by Frederic Dannay and Manfred B. Lee.
        Produced and directed by Bob Steel.
        Announcer: Don Hancock.
        Organ music: unknown.
        Sponsor: Anacin.
        Story: Ellery tries to help a glamorous movie star when an anonymous blackmailer threatens to go public with an old film unless she pays him off.

EPISODE #225  **"THE MURDERED MOTHS"**  Broadcast on May 9, 1945
        Guest: Jack Gaver (author).
        Written by Frederic Dannay and Manfred B. Lee.
        Produced and directed by Bob Steel.
        Announcer: Don Hancock.
        Organ music: unknown.
        Sponsor: Anacin.
        Story: Ellery investigates an elopement that leads to tragedy and murder.

EPISODE #226  **"THE DANGEROUS RACE"**  Broadcast on May 16, 1945
        Guest: Orlo Robertson (sports editor).
        Written by Frederic Dannay and Manfred B. Lee.
        Produced and directed by Bob Steel.
        Announcer: Don Hancock.
        Organ music: unknown.
        Sponsor: Anacin.
        Story: Ellery encounters murder at the racetrack while trying to protect a valuable horse.

EPISODE #227  **"THE MAN IN THE PILLBOX"**  Broadcast on May 23, 1945
        Guest: Ted R. Gamble (Director of War Finance).
        Written by Frederic Dannay and Manfred B. Lee.
        Produced and directed by Bob Steel.
        Announcer: Don Hancock.
        Organ music: unknown.
        Sponsor: Anacin.
        Story: Ellery and Nikki are in a boat drifting on a peaceful lake when someone takes a shot at them from a pillbox-like structure on an island in the lake's center.

EPISODE #228  **"THE RUNAWAY HUSBAND"**  Broadcast on May 30, 1945
        Guest: James Montgomery Flagg (magazine illustrator).
        Written by Frederic Dannay and Manfred B. Lee.
        Produced and directed by Bob Steel.
        Announcer: Don Hancock.
        Organ music: unknown.
        Sponsor: Anacin.

Story: Ellery investigates the disappearance of a man who runs a model agency.

**EPISODE #229 "THE IRON WOMAN"** Broadcast on June 6, 1945
   Guest: Annamary Dickey (Metropolitan Opera star).
   Written by Frederic Dannay and Manfred B. Lee.
   Produced and directed by Bob Steel.
   Announcer: Don Hancock.
   Organ music: unknown.
   Sponsor: Anacin.
   Story: Ellery is called in when a socialite famous for her athletic skills becomes the victim of a series of diabolically planned sports accidents.

**EPISODE #230 "THE CORPSE OF MR. ENTWHISTLE"** Broadcast on June 13, 1945
   Guest: Gladys Swarthout (opera singer).
   Repeat performance guest: Ted R. Gamble (Director of War Finance).
   Written by Anthony Boucher and Manfred B. Lee.
   Produced and directed by Bob Steel.
   Announcer: Don Hancock.
   Organ music: unknown.
   Sponsor: Anacin.
   Story: Ellery is consulted by a newspaperwoman who found professional blackmailer Ezra Entwhistle in his soundproof office with three bullets in his body, one on top of the other.

   **Trivia, etc.** This was the first of more than 70 episodes for which the distinguished mystery writer and critic Anthony Boucher wrote the synopses that Manfred B. Lee expanded into scripts.

**EPISODE #231 "THE ABSENT AUTOMATIC"** Broadcast on June 20, 1945
   Guest: Col. Joseph S. Snyder (executive officer of Camp Kilmer).
   Repeat performance guest: Joan Tetzel (actress).
   Written by Anthony Boucher and Manfred B. Lee.
   Produced and directed by Bob Steel.
   Announcer: Don Hancock.
   Organ music: unknown.
   Sponsor: Anacin.
   Story: A Pulitzer Prize-winning biographer comes to Ellery for help after he finds threatening notes in his mailbox. Later he comes back claiming he's just killed his jealous secretary, who was about to shoot him. But when Ellery arrives he finds neither the gun nor the alleged threatening letters.

**EPISODE #232 "MR. 1 AND MR. 2"** Broadcast on June 27, 1945
   Guest: Bennett Cerf (publisher/raconteur).
   Repeat performance guest: Victor Moore (actor).
   Written by _____ and Manfred B. Lee.
   Produced and directed by Bob Steel.
   Announcer: Don Hancock.
   Organ music: unknown.
   Sponsor: Anacin.
   Story: A reclusive multimillionaire is murdered after asking Ellery to find out which of the two men who have shown up on his doorstep is genuinely his son, who ran away from home almost thirty years earlier.

EPISODE #233   **"NIKKI'S RICH UNCLE"**   Broadcast on July 4, 1945
>    Guest:  George Frazier (magazine editor).
>    Written by Anthony Boucher and Manfred B. Lee.
>    Produced and directed by Bob Steel.
>    Announcer: Don Hancock.
>    Organ music: unknown.
>    Sponsor: Anacin.
>    Story:  Ellery comes to the rescue when Nikki is suspected of murdering the man who showed up in her life, claiming to be her wealthy uncle.

EPISODE #234   **"THE SHIPYARD RACKET"**   Broadcast on July 11, 1945
>    Guest:  George Lait (war correspondent).
>    Written by _____ and Manfred B. Lee.
>    Produced and directed by Bob Steel.
>    Announcer: Don Hancock.
>    Organ music: unknown.
>    Sponsor: Anacin.
>    Story:  Ellery probes the murder of a shipyard personnel manager who was challenging a racketeer with a hold on his workers.

EPISODE #235   **"THE GENTLEMAN BURGLAR"**   Broadcast on July 18, 1945
>    Guests:  Wendy Barrie (actress) and Fred Uttal (radio quizmaster).
>    Written by Anthony Boucher and Manfred B. Lee.
>    Produced and directed by Bob Steel.
>    Announcer: Don Hancock.
>    Organ music: unknown.
>    Sponsor: Anacin.
>    Story:  Ellery is caught red-handed by Sergeant Velie when he turns safecracker and tries to open a private vault.

>    **Trivia, etc.** This was the last episode in which Barbara Terrell played Nikki Porter. She was replaced the following week by Gertrude Warner.

EPISODE #236   **"THE TORTURE VICTIM"**   Broadcast on July 25, 1945
>    Guest:  Julie Gibson (actress).
>    Written by Anthony Boucher and Manfred B. Lee.
>    Produced and directed by Bob Steel.
>    Announcer: Don Hancock.
>    Organ music: unknown.
>    Sponsor: Anacin.
>    Story:  Ellery becomes involved in a baffling mystery that begins when a sheet is found with the message "They're Torturing Me" written in blood.

EPISODE #237   **"NICK THE KNIFE"**   Broadcast on August 1, 1945
>    Guest:  Gertrude Niesen (Broadway actress).
>    Repeat performance guest:  Thomas Lockhart (Coast Guardsman).
>    Written by Anthony Boucher and Manfred B. Lee.
>    Produced and directed by Bob Steel.
>    Announcer: Don Hancock.
>    Organ music: unknown.
>    Sponsor: Anacin.
>    Story:  Ellery tries to identify the sociopath who has slashed the wrists and faces of more than thirty beautiful women on Manhattan's night streets.

**Trivia, etc.** This episode was repeated on April 15, 1948 as "The Slicer" (Episode #349).

EPISODE #238   **"THE CLUE IN C MAJOR"**   Broadcast on August 8, 1945
　　　Guest:  Evelyn Keyes (actress).
　　　Written by Anthony Boucher and Manfred B. Lee.
　　　Produced and directed by Bob Steel.
　　　Announcer: Don Hancock.
　　　Organ music: unknown.
　　　Sponsor: Anacin.
　　　Story:  Ellery tries to solve a murder committed while he and Nikki are weekend guests in an eccentric French composer's Connecticut home.

EPISODE #239   **"THE TIME OF DEATH"**   Broadcast on August 15, 1945
　　　Guest:  Sally Eilers (actress).
　　　Written by Anthony Boucher and Manfred B. Lee.
　　　Produced and directed by Bob Steel.
　　　Announcer: Don Hancock.
　　　Organ music: unknown.
　　　Sponsor: Anacin.
　　　Story:  Ellery is consulted by a dying old millionaire who fears that after his death someone in the household of his only son and sole heir will kill the son for his inheritance. Sure enough, the son is murdered almost immediately after the father's natural death.

# SEASON SIX

EPISODE #240   **"THE MAN WHO WAS AFRAID"**   Broadcast on September 5, 1945
　　　Guest:  Jonah J. Goldstein (New York judge).
　　　Written by Anthony Boucher and Manfred B. Lee.
　　　Produced and directed by Bob Steel.
　　　Announcer: Don Hancock.
　　　Organ music: unknown.
　　　Sponsor: Anacin.
　　　Story:  Ellery encounters a distinguished actor who is obsessed by the idea that he actually is the homicidal character he portrays.

EPISODE #241   **"THE BLUE EGG"**   Broadcast on September 12, 1945
　　　Guest:  Virginia MacWatters (opera singer).
　　　Written by Frederic Dannay and Manfred B. Lee.
　　　Produced and directed by Bob Steel.
　　　Announcer: Don Hancock.
　　　Organ music: unknown.
　　　Sponsor: Anacin.
　　　Story:  A British detective comes to Ellery for help when the priceless sapphire that he was hired to take back to England vanishes under impossible circumstances.

**Trivia, etc.** This script was one of several written by Dannay and Lee before Dannay's departure from the series and held in reserve by Lee against emergencies. The episode was repeated under the same title on February 26, 1948 (Episode #342).

EPISODE #242   **"THE LOST SOUL"**   Broadcast on September 19, 1945
Guest:  Shep Fields (musician).
Written by Anthony Boucher and Manfred B. Lee.
Produced and directed by Bob Steel.
Announcer: Don Hancock.
Organ music: unknown.
Sponsor: Anacin.
Story:  Ellery goes after the vandal who slashed to ribbons a recent painting after the artist who executed it announces that he'll never paint again.

EPISODE #243   **"THE GREEN HOUSE"**   Broadcast on September 26, 1945
Guest:  George V. Denny, Jr. (associate director of the New York League for Political Education).
Written by Anthony Boucher and Manfred B. Lee.
Produced and directed by Bob Steel.
Announcer: Don Hancock.
Organ music: unknown.
Sponsor: Anacin.
Story:  Ellery is kidnapped and taken to the kingdom of Serakia where the despotic dictator Marshal Zah demands that he find out who stabbed his wife in the back.

EPISODE #244   **"ELLERY QUEEN, CUPID"**   Broadcast on October 3, 1945
Guest:  Edith Spencer (radio personality known as Aunt Jenny).
Written by Anthony Boucher and Manfred B. Lee.
Produced and directed by Bob Steel.
Announcer: Don Hancock
Organ music: unknown.
Sponsor: Anacin
Story:  Ellery tries to discover which of the veterans who frequent a creative arts studio for returning servicemen is sending anonymous love notes to a plain woman who works there.

EPISODE #245   **"THE KID GLOVE KILLER"**   Broadcast on October 10, 1945
Guest:  Eddie Dowling (Broadway producer).
Repeat performance guest:  Carol Stone (Broadway actress).
Written by Anthony Boucher and Manfred B. Lee.
Produced and directed by Bob Steel.
Announcer: Don Hancock.
Organ music: unknown.
Sponsor: Anacin.
Story:  Ellery tries to track down a masked criminal who committed murder in order to steal a box of black kid gloves from a men's store.

EPISODE #246   **"THE OTHER MAN"**   Broadcast on October 17, 1945
Guest:  Jan Clayton (actress).
Repeat performance guest:  Danton Walker (newspaper columnist).
Written by Anthony Boucher and Manfred B. Lee.
Produced and directed by Bob Steel.
Announcer: Don Hancock.
Organ music: unknown.
Sponsor: Anacin.
Story:  Ellery investigates a murder at an exclusive masquerade ball where each of the 52 guests came dressed as a playing card.

EPISODE #247 **"THE REPENTANT THIEF"** Broadcast on October 24, 1945
Guest: Commander Henry H. Hale (U.S. Navy officer).
Written by Anthony Boucher and Manfred B. Lee.
Produced and directed by Bob Steel.
Announcer: Don Hancock.
Organ music: unknown.
Sponsor: Anacin.
Story: Ellery and Nikki run into a mystery when their car runs out of gasoline during a heavy rainstorm and they take shelter in a strange house on a mountain.

EPISODE #248 **"THE HALLOWE'EN MURDER"** Broadcast on October 31, 1945
Guest: Edward Everett Horton (actor).
Written by Anthony Boucher and Manfred B. Lee.
Produced and directed by Bob Steel.
Announcer: Don Hancock.
Organ music: unknown.
Sponsor: Anacin.
Story: Ellery and Nikki set out for a night of fun at an old-fashioned Hallowe'en party but wind up having to solve a murder when a guest is poisoned during a game of bobbing for apples.

EPISODE #249 **"THE MESSAGE IN RED"** Broadcast on November 7, 1945
Guest: Victor Jory (actor).
Written by Anthony Boucher and Manfred B. Lee.
Produced and directed by Bob Steel.
Announcer: Don Hancock.
Organ music: unknown.
Sponsors: Anacin, Hill's Cold Tablets.
Story: When three women – a public stenographer, a manuscript reader for a publishing house, and a French maid – are all shot to death on the same night with the same gun, Ellery concludes that someone is out to drop a certain incriminating document down the memory hole of everyone who's seen it.

EPISODE #250 **"THE HAPPY MARRIAGE"** Broadcast on November 14, 1945
Guests: Joseph Curtin and Alice Frost (stars of radio's *Mr. and Mrs. North*, appearing here as their characters).
Written by Anthony Boucher and Manfred B. Lee.
Produced and directed by Bob Steel.
Announcer: Don Hancock.
Organ music: unknown.
Sponsor: Anacin.
Story: Ellery tries to solve a murder arising from an apparently blissful marriage that is in reality miserable.

EPISODE #251 **"THE APE'S BOSS"** Broadcast on November 21, 1945
Guest: unknown.
Written by Anthony Boucher and Manfred B. Lee.
Produced and directed by Bob Steel.
Announcer: Don Hancock.
Organ music: unknown.
Sponsor: Anacin.

Story: Ellery tries to identify the secret mastermind giving orders to moronic Ape Loogan, the ostensible leader of a gang whose crimes are terrorizing the city.

EPISODE #252 **"THE DOODLE OF MR. O'DREW"** Broadcast on November 28, 1945
Guest: Vera Zorina (dancer/actress).
Written by Anthony Boucher and Manfred B. Lee.
Produced and directed by Bob Steel.
Announcer: Don Hancock.
Organ music: unknown.
Sponsor: Anacin.
Story: Ellery tries to figure out which of the show-business hopefuls who had been cheated by a crooked talent scout got even by killing him.

EPISODE #253 **"THE PEDDLER OF DEATH"** Broadcast on December 5, 1945
Guest: Helen Hayes (actress).
Written by Anthony Boucher and Manfred B. Lee.
Produced and directed by Bob Steel.
Announcer: Don Hancock.
Organ music: unknown.
Sponsor: Anacin.
Story: The leader of a jazz band asks Ellery to figure out which member of his combo has been supplying his lead singer with narcotics, but the singer is murdered before Ellery can question him.

EPISODE #254 **"THE MAN WITH TWO FACES"** Broadcast on December 12, 1945
Guest: Major General Emmanuel E. Lombard (retired French army officer).
Repeat performance guest: Vera Zorina (dancer/actress).
Written by Anthony Boucher and Manfred B. Lee.
Produced and directed by Bob Steel.
Announcer: Don Hancock.
Organ music: unknown.
Sponsor: Anacin.
Story: A woman comes to Ellery for help when she begins to suspect that the veteran who came back to her after the war, with a new face created by plastic surgery in Europe, is not her husband but an impostor. Then that man is stabbed to death and a second man shows up claiming to be married to the woman.

EPISODE #255 **"THE CURIOUS THEFTS"** Broadcast on December 19, 1945
Guest: Ralph Morgan (actor).
Repeat performance guest: Virginia Vale (actress).
Written by _____ and Manfred B. Lee.
Produced and directed by Bob Steel.
Announcer: Don Hancock.
Organ music: unknown.
Sponsor: Anacin.
Story: A well-known novelist whose marriage is tottering comes to Ellery for help when his household is plagued by a rash of bizarre pilferings culminating in murder.

**Trivia, etc.** A condensed version of the script for this episode was published in *Story Digest,* September 1946.

148

EPISODE #256   **"THE MAN WHO LOVED MURDERS"**   Broadcast on December 26, 1945
      Guest: Jean Sablon (vocalist).
      Written by Anthony Boucher and Manfred B. Lee.
      Produced and directed by Bob Steel.
      Announcer: Don Hancock.
      Organ music: unknown.
      Sponsor: Anacin.
      Story: Ellery investigates the murder of Gregory Snye, who loved murders so much that he made a habit of manipulating others into committing them.

EPISODE #257   **"THE LOST HOARD"**   Broadcast on January 2, 1946
      Guest: Saul Pett (newspaper columnist).
      Written by Anthony Boucher and Manfred B. Lee.
      Produced and directed by Bob Steel.
      Announcer: Don Hancock.
      Organ music: unknown.
      Sponsor: Anacin.
      Story: Ellery visits a small town in upstate New York to hunt for the ransom from an old kidnapping.

EPISODE #258   **"THE VARIOUS DEATHS OF MR. FRAYNE"**   Broadcast on Jan. 9, 1946
      Guest: Arthur Godfrey (radio emcee).
      Written by Anthony Boucher and Manfred B. Lee.
      Produced and directed by Bob Steel.
      Announcer: Don Hancock.
      Organ music: unknown.
      Sponsor: Anacin.
      Story: A once best-selling novelist suffering from writer's block tells Ellery that he'll soon be murdered but asks that the killer not be punished. Ellery believes the author is planning to commit suicide under circumstances that will look like murder so that his life insurance policy will not be voided.  Then the man does apparently kill himself, but under circumstances that look exactly like suicide.

EPISODE #259   **"THE GREEN EYE"**   Broadcast on January 16, 1946
      Guest: Morgan Conway (actor).
      Written by Anthony Boucher and Manfred B. Lee.
      Produced and directed by Bob Steel.
      Announcer: Don Hancock.
      Organ music: unknown.
      Sponsor: Anacin.
      Story: Ellery pursues an international criminal who leaves an eye drawn in green ink at the scene of each of his jewel robberies.

EPISODE #260   **"THE LOVELY RACKETEER"**   Broadcast on January 23, 1946
      Guest: James L. Cox (inventor).
      Written by _____ and Manfred B. Lee.
      Produced and directed by Bob Steel.
      Announcer: Don Hancock.
      Organ music: unknown.
      Sponsor: Anacin.
      Story: Ellery probes the murder of a female robber who was killed by one of the three men in her criminal organization.

EPISODE #261   **"ELLERY QUEEN'S TRAGEDY"**   Broadcast on January 30, 1946
>   Guest: unknown.
>   Written by Anthony Boucher and Manfred B. Lee.
>   Produced and directed by Bob Steel.
>   Announcer: Don Hancock.
>   Organ music: unknown.
>   Sponsor: Anacin.
>   Story: Two men show up in New York, each claiming to be a famous French mystery writer for whom a fortune in wartime US royalties is waiting. Ellery becomes involved when the impostor shoots Inspector Queen and leaves him near death.

>   **Trivia, etc.** Lee's script radically changed Boucher's synopsis for this episode, adding the element of the near-fatal attack on Ellery's father because Santos Ortega, who played the Inspector, was taking a leave of absence from the series and had to be written out of this script and those for the next several weeks as well.

EPISODE #262   **"THE FIFTEENTH FLOOR"**   Broadcast on February 6, 1946
>   Guest: Marjorie Rambeau (actress).
>   Written by Tom Everitt and Manfred B. Lee.
>   Produced and directed by Bob Steel.
>   Announcer: Don Hancock.
>   Organ music: unknown.
>   Sponsor: Anacin.
>   Story: Ellery tries to track down an ex-convict who's determined to find and kill the mysterious person who informed on him.

EPISODE #263   **"THE LIVING DEAD"**   Broadcast on February 13, 1946
>   Guest: Belita (ice skater/actress).
>   Repeat performance guest: James L. Cox (inventor).
>   Written by Anthony Boucher and Manfred B. Lee.
>   Produced and directed by Bob Steel.
>   Announcer: Don Hancock.
>   Organ music: unknown.
>   Sponsor: Anacin.
>   Story: An old friend asks Ellery to investigate an almost 40-year-old murder which has led the woman he loves to move into the musty old home where all the suspects continue to live.

EPISODE #264   **"THE THREE FENCERS"**   Broadcast on February 20, 1946
>   Guest: Willie Mosconi (pool expert).
>   Repeat performance guest: Eugene List (pianist).
>   Written by Anthony Boucher and Manfred B. Lee.
>   Produced and directed by Bob Steel.
>   Announcer: Don Hancock.
>   Organ music: unknown.
>   Sponsor: Anacin.
>   Story: Ellery investigates the murder of a female fencer from France who was stabbed to death with a foil.

EPISODE #265   **"THE NINTH MRS. POOK"**   Broadcast on February 27, 1946
>   Guest: Craig Rice (mystery writer).
>   Repeat performance guest: Dick Joy (radio announcer).

Written by Anthony Boucher and Manfred B. Lee.
Produced and directed by Bob Steel.
Announcer: Don Hancock.
Organ music: unknown.
Sponsor: Anacin.
Story: Ellery and Nikki discover that their fellow guests at a resort include a man who has made a career out of marrying women and killing them for their money and his most recent wife, who has made her own career out of marrying and killing men. When their honeymoon cottage burns to the ground, Ellery tries to determine which of them died first.

EPISODE #266   **"THE PHANTOM SHADOW"**   Broadcast on March 6, 1946
Guest: Alfred Eichler (advertising executive/mystery writer).
Repeat performance guest: Jean Meegan (newspaperwoman).
Written by Anthony Boucher and Manfred B. Lee.
Produced and directed by Bob Steel.
Announcer: Don Hancock.
Organ music: unknown.
Sponsor: Anacin.
Story: While temporarily substituting on a night secretarial job for a girlfriend, Nikki calls Ellery and claims she's just witnessed a murder through a window of the law office directly across the street from her. But when the police search that office they find no sign of a body or a struggle and no evidence of a crime at all.

EPISODE #267   **"THE CLUE OF THE ELEPHANT"**   Broadcast on March 13, 1946
Guest: Betty Forsling (*Newsweek* radio editor).
Repeat performance guest: Sam Spiegel (movie producer).
Written by Anthony Boucher and Manfred B. Lee.
Produced and directed by Bob Steel.
Announcer: Don Hancock.
Organ music: unknown.
Sponsor: Anacin.
Story: Thirty years after some circus people stranded in South America found a hoard of Mayan gold and formed a survivor-take-all tontine, murders begin to strike the group and a pregnant pachyderm helps Ellery find the solution.

EPISODE #268   **"THE MAN WHO WAITED"**   Broadcast on March 20, 1946
Guest: Orson Welles (actor/director).
Written by Frederic Dannay and Manfred B. Lee.
Produced and directed by Bob Steel.
Announcer: Don Hancock.
Organ music: unknown.
Sponsor: Anacin.
Story: Ellery tries to figure out which of three payroll robbers recently released from prison killed the fourth member of their gang, who betrayed his comrades and stole the loot.

**Trivia, etc.** This was another of the scripts written before Fred Dannay left the series and held back by Manny Lee in case of emergency. The script was later adapted by Dannay and Lee into the short story "Cold Money" (*This Week*, March 20, 1952; collected in *Queen's Bureau of Investigation*, 1955).

EPISODE #269 **"THE ARMCHAIR DETECTIVE"** Broadcast on March 27, 1946
Guest: Pvt. Pat Berkeley (wounded soldier).
Written by Anthony Boucher and Manfred B. Lee.
Produced and directed by Bob Steel.
Announcer: Don Hancock.
Organ music: unknown.
Sponsor: Anacin.
Story: When the guest armchair detective is found poisoned while the *Ellery Queen* show is on the air, Ellery finds the solution to the murder before the show finishes.

**Trivia, etc.** This episode was repeated under the same title on March 18, 1948 (Episode #345).

EPISODE #270 **"THE DEATH WISH"** Broadcast on April 3, 1946
Guest: Con Colleano (circus trapeze artist).
Repeat performance guests: six of the "Goldwyn Girls."
Written by Anthony Boucher and Manfred B. Lee.
Produced and directed by Bob Steel.
Announcer: Don Hancock.
Organ music: unknown.
Sponsor: Anacin.
Story: Ellery encounters a man who claims he committed a hit-and-run but can't prove it because the alleged body has vanished. Eventually he comes to suspect that the body may have been stolen by a famous actor who's on the brink of a nervous breakdown.

EPISODE #271 **"THE GIRL WHO COULDN'T GET MARRIED"** Broadcast April 10, 1946
Guest: Carolyn Rolland (magazine editor).
Written by Anthony Boucher and Manfred B. Lee.
Produced and directed by Bob Steel.
Announcer: Don Hancock.
Organ music: unknown.
Sponsor: Anacin.
Story: Investigating the case of a woman whose intended husbands keep dying just before the wedding, Ellery suspects that the apparently natural deaths were murders and, in order to trap the killer, pretends to be engaged to the woman himself.

EPISODE #272 **"NIKKI PORTER, MURDER VICTIM"** Broadcast on April 17, 1946
Guests: six of the "Goldwyn Girls."
Written by Anthony Boucher and Manfred B. Lee.
Produced and directed by Bob Steel.
Announcer: Don Hancock.
Organ music: unknown.
Sponsor: Anacin.
Story: After an epidemic of jewel-robbery murders, Ellery finds Nikki shot under circumstances which indicate that she had seen someone who wanted to give Ellery evidence about the crimes. Then while she's recovering in the hospital, someone wearing a surgical mask and gown tries to kill her again.

**Trivia, etc.** Ellery solves this one by figuring out why the criminal continued to wear the surgical mask after disposing of the rest of the medical garb. Boucher did not invent the plot gimmick himself but found it in "De Muerte Natural," a short story by Mexican writer Rafael Bernal, and paid Bernal $100 for letting him use it.

EPISODE #273 **"THE MAN WHO BOUGHT ONE GRAPE"** Broadcast April 24, 1946
Guest: James P. Markham (Texan).
Repeat performance guest: James H. Pepkin (Texan).
Written by Anthony Boucher and Manfred B. Lee.
Produced and directed by Bob Steel.
Announcer: Don Hancock.
Organ music: unknown.
Sponsor: Anacin.
Story: Ellery tries to figure out why an eccentric one-eyed millionaire has been buying one and only one grape a day from an Italian fruit vendor. The millionaire tells Ellery that he's been putting the grapes in his empty eye socket as substitutes for his irreplaceable glass eye which has been stolen. Then the thief is found murdered.

**Trivia, etc.** Two Texans were chosen as guest armchair sleuths for this episode because Boucher, who among countless other talents was a poker expert, made the solution to the murder center on a poker hand known as the blaze which is peculiar to that state.

EPISODE #274 **"THE RHUBARB SOLUTION"** Broadcast on May 1, 1946
Guest: Joan Edwards (singer).
Repeat performance guest: Saul Pett (newspaper columnist).
Written by Anthony Boucher and Manfred B. Lee.
Produced and directed by Bob Steel.
Announcer: Don Hancock.
Organ music: unknown.
Sponsor: Anacin.
Story: A dollar bill with a message written on it in nail polish helps Ellery find a farm woman who vanished shortly before she was to come into an inheritance.

EPISODE #275 **"THE NINE MILE CLUE"** Broadcast on May 8, 1946
Guest: Red Barber (sportscaster).
Repeat performance guest: Muriel Babcock (magazine editor).
Written by Richard Manoff and Manfred B. Lee.
Produced and directed by Bob Steel.
Announcer: Don Hancock
Organ music: unknown.
Sponsor: Anacin.
Story: Ellery and Nikki stop off in a small town for needed auto repairs. Then the garage owner is killed and Ellery's car is involved in the crime.

EPISODE #276 **"THE CRIME IN DARKNESS"** Broadcast on May 15, 1946
Guest: Vernon Pope (magazine editor).
Repeat performance guest: Margaret Whiting (singer).
Written by Tom Everitt and Manfred B. Lee.
Produced and directed by Bob Steel.
Announcer: Don Hancock.
Organ music: unknown.
Sponsor: Anacin.
Story: Ellery probes the case of a man who sees with his mind and uses telepathy instead of his eyes.

EPISODE #277   **"THE HOLLYWOOD MURDER CASES"**   Broadcast on May 22, 1946
Guest: Elsa Miranda (the "Chiquita Banana" girl).
Repeat performance guest: Lucille Ball (actress).
Written by Anthony Boucher and Manfred B. Lee.
Produced and directed by Bob Steel.
Announcer: Don Hancock.
Organ music: unknown.
Sponsor: Anacin.
Story: Ellery comes to Hollywood with Nikki to write a screenplay based on the murder of a famous director at the dawn of talking pictures. He discovers another director who claims he has a piece of film soundtrack that implicates a famous actress in the crime. Then the soundtrack is stolen and the second director is murdered.

EPISODE #278   **"THE LAUGHING WOMAN"**   Broadcast on May 29, 1946
Guest: Francis Lederer (actor).
Repeat performance guest: John Reed King (radio announcer).
Written by Anthony Boucher and Manfred B. Lee.
Produced and directed by Bob Steel.
Announcer: Don Hancock.
Organ music: unknown.
Sponsor: Anacin.
Story: Ellery tries to find out why a neurotic woman has left her husband to take up with a racketeer. Then the racketeer is murdered and the cuckolded husband is prime suspect.

EPISODE #279   **"MR. WARREN'S PROFESSION"**   Broadcast on June 5, 1946
Guest: Dorothy Dunn (contest winner from Ohio).
Repeat performance guest: Barbara Lewis (secretary).
Written by Anthony Boucher and Manfred B. Lee.
Produced and directed by Bob Steel.
Announcer: Don Hancock.
Organ music: unknown.
Sponsor: Anacin.
Story: Ellery investigates the murder of a professional blackmailer who had a habit of making puns based on book titles and whose last act before dying was to ring a bell over and over.

EPISODE #280   **"THE GREAT SPY PUZZLE"**   Broadcast on June 12, 1946
Guest: John Reed King (radio announcer).
Repeat performance guest: Archie Mayo (movie director).
Written by Frederic Dannay and Manfred B. Lee.
Produced and directed by Bob Steel.
Announcer: Don Hancock.
Organ music: unknown.
Sponsor: Anacin.
Story: A young man comes to Ellery and offers him the fragments of a mysterious piece of paper but is killed in the dark in front of both Ellery and Nikki before he can explain the paper's meaning. Seeing the words "Ft. Haust" on one of the fragments, Ellery suspects he's in the middle of an atomic espionage case. Then he discovers that there is no such place as Fort Haust.

**Trivia, etc.** This was yet another of the scripts Manny Lee held in reserve against emergencies after Fred Dannay left the series.

EPISODE #281   **"COKEY AND THE PIZZA"**   Broadcast on June 19, 1946
>   Guest:  Elsa Miranda (the "Chiquita Banana" girl).
>   Repeat performance guest:  Francis Lederer (actor).
>   Written by Anthony Boucher and Manfred B. Lee.
>   Produced and directed by Bob Steel.
>   Announcer: Don Hancock.
>   Organ music: unknown.
>   Sponsor: Anacin.

Story:  Ellery tries to figure out how a fugitive gangster holed up in a room above an Italian restaurant is being supplied with cocaine. Then the gangster is killed by someone who is described as looking like a penguin.

EPISODE #282   **"THE DOUBLE DIE"**   Broadcast on June 26, 1946
>   Guests: Joseph Curtin and Alice Frost (stars of radio's *Mr. and Mrs. North* and appearing here as their characters).
>   Written by Anthony Boucher and Manfred B. Lee.
>   Produced and directed by Bob Steel.
>   Announcer: Don Hancock.
>   Organ music: unknown.
>   Sponsor: Anacin.

Story:  An honest gambler asks Ellery to find out which of his henchmen is using loaded dice but  before Ellery can begin investigating he's summoned to Indiana to look into the matter of why his phone number was found in the hotel room of a vanished corpse. While Ellery is gone his gambler client is murdered, leaving a dying message in the form of a pair of dice turned up to show threes.

EPISODE #283   **"THE WAR BRIDE"**   Broadcast on July 3, 1946
>   Guest: Dolores Moran (actress).
>   Repeat performance guest:  Richard Long (actor).
>   Written by Richard Manoff and Manfred B. Lee.
>   Produced and directed by Bob Steel.
>   Announcer: Don Hancock.
>   Organ music: unknown.
>   Sponsor: Anacin.

Story:  Ellery tries to help an ex-soldier who's determined to marry the young French woman he met overseas despite being threatened with murder if he does.

EPISODE #284   **"THE CONFIDENTIAL BUTLER"**   Broadcast on July 10, 1946
>   Guest:  W.C. Siple (air freight executive).
>   Repeat performance guest:  Sunny Skylar (songwriter).
>   Written by Frederic Dannay and Manfred B. Lee.
>   Produced and directed by Bob Steel.
>   Announcer: Don Hancock.
>   Organ music: unknown.
>   Sponsor: Anacin.

Story:  Ellery uses a tea-brewing clue to solve the murder of a butler who was blackmailing three of his former employers.

**Trivia, etc.** This is yet another of the Dannay-Lee scripts completed before Dannay left the series.

EPISODE #285   **"THE ULTRA-MODERN MURDER"**   Broadcast on July 17, 1946
        Guest:  Alan Baxter (actor).
        Repeat performance guest:  Ed Hall (newspaper editor).
        Written by Anthony Boucher and Manfred B. Lee.
        Produced and directed by Bob Steel.
        Announcer: Don Hancock.
        Organ music: unknown.
        Sponsor: Anacin.
        Story:  Ellery investigates the case of a woman who entered a surrealist art studio in the
dark, pulled on a light cord made from a snake's tail, and was shot to death by an antique dueling
pistol in the hand of a statue of Venus facing the door.

EPISODE #286   **"THE GOLDEN KEY"**   Broadcast on July 24, 1946
        Guest:  Ben Hecht (author).
        Repeat performance guest:  Maxwell Hamilton (magazine editor).
        Written by Tom Everitt and Manfred B. Lee.
        Produced and directed by Bob Steel.
        Announcer: Don Hancock.
        Organ music: unknown.
        Sponsor: Anacin.
        Story:  Ellery uses a Phi Beta Kappa key to track down the person who's been trying to
kill three young college students.

EPISODE #287  **"THE MAN WHO GOT AWAY WITH MURDER"** Broadcast July 31, 1946
        Guest:  Ray Bolger (dancer/actor).
        Written by Anthony Boucher and Manfred B. Lee.
        Produced and directed by Bob Steel.
        Announcer: Don Hancock.
        Organ music: unknown.
        Sponsor: Anacin.
        Story:  A lawyer who blames Ellery for the failure of his political ambitions gets even
by phoning and confessing to a wave of recent murders, then claiming that the caller was an
impostor so that Ellery looks foolish. Then the lawyer is himself stabbed to death.

EPISODE #288   **"THE FIRST NIGHT"**   Broadcast on August 7, 1946
        Guest:  Milton Berle (comedian).
        Repeat performance guest:  Joan Edwards (singer).
        Written by Tom Everitt and Manfred B. Lee.
        Produced and directed by Bob Steel.
        Announcer: Don Hancock.
        Organ music: unknown.
        Sponsor: Anacin.
        Story:  On a seaside vacation, Ellery becomes involved in a mystery affecting a summer
theater company.

EPISODE #289   **"BIS TO CAL"**   Broadcast on August 14, 1946
        Guest:  Paula Stone (actress).
        Repeat performance guest:  Benny Baker (comedian).
        Announcer: Don Hancock.
        Written by Anthony Boucher and Manfred B. Lee.
        Produced and directed by Bob Steel.

Organ music: unknown.

Sponsor: Anacin.

Story: A treacherous financier comes to Ellery for help when his daughter is kidnapped and a ransom note is delivered with her thumbprint in blood. Ellery comes to suspect that the woman has faked her own abduction in order to collect the money her father had reneged on donating to a school for the blind.

EPISODE #290 **"THE GYMNASIUM MURDER"** Broadcast on August 21, 1946

Guests: Warren Hull and Parks Johnson (co-hosts of radio's *Vox Pop* program).

Written by Frederic Dannay and Manfred B. Lee.

Produced and directed by Bob Steel.

Announcer: Don Hancock.

Organ music: unknown.

Sponsor: Anacin.

Story: same as Episode #103, "The Gymnasium Murder" (October 10 and 12, 1942).

EPISODE #291 **"THE DOOMED MAN"** Broadcast on August 28, 1946

Guest: Marsha Hunt (actress).

Written by Frederic Dannay and Manfred B. Lee.

Produced and directed by Bob Steel.

Announcer: Don Hancock.

Organ music: unknown.

Sponsor: Anacin.

Story: Ellery uses a candlestick clue to clear a young man who's been charged with the murder of his father, the patriarch of a family with a long tradition of leaving all property to the next generation in equal shares.

**Trivia, etc.** This was the last of the Dannay-Lee scripts that Lee had kept in reserve against emergencies. After this episode the series went off the air for six weeks. When it returned, Charlotte Keane replaced Gertrude Warner in the role of Nikki.

# SEASON SEVEN

EPISODE #292 **"ELLERY QUEEN, CRIMINAL"** Broadcast on October 9, 1946

Guest: Jean Sablon (vocalist).

Written by Anthony Boucher and Manfred B. Lee.

Produced and directed by Bob Steel.

Announcer: Don Hancock.

Sponsor: Anacin.

Story: While on the trail of a clever thief and impersonator, Ellery is beaten up and held prisoner in a hotel room with a woman as his guard. When he returns to New York Nikki doesn't recognize him. and he's accused of being an impostor. Then the woman who held him is killed in a room full of dust.

**Trivia, etc.** The October 16, 1946 broadcast was pre-empted by a news special on the Nuremberg war crimes trials.

EPISODE #293 **"THE WOMAN WHO DIED SEVERAL TIMES"** Broadcast Oct. 23, 1946

Guest: John Carradine (actor).

Written by Anthony Boucher and Manfred B. Lee.
Produced and directed by Bob Steel.
Announcer: Don Hancock.
Organ music: unknown.
Sponsors: Anacin, Hill's Cold Tablets, BiSoDol Mints.
Story:  A politician confesses to Ellery that he's just shot and killed his conniving mistress. When they go to her apartment they find her alive and well and learn that she had goaded the man into firing at her with blanks. Later the woman takes up with a well-known book reviewer and he too claims he shot her to death. But this time she's really dead.

**Trivia, etc.**  At some point in the series between this episode and Episode #307, broadcast at the end of January 1947, three of the four members of the regular cast were replaced, with Richard Coogan taking over from Sydney Smith as Ellery, Bill Smith from Santos Ortega as Inspector Queen, and Ed Latimer from Ted de Corsia as Sergeant Velie. The recently hired Charlotte Keane continued as Nikki.

Guest armchair detective John Carradine commented during this broadcast, which was sponsored in part by Anacin, that he needed an aspirin!

### EPISODE #294   "ELLERY QUEEN'S RIVAL"   Broadcast on October 30, 1946

Guest:  Rear Admiral H.B. Miller (retired Navy officer).
Written by Anthony Boucher and Manfred B. Lee.
Produced and directed by Bob Steel.
Announcer: Don Hancock.
Organ music: unknown.
Sponsors: Anacin, Hill's Cold Tablets, BiSoDol Mints.
Story:  Nikki goes out on a date with Larry Kinnaire, another writer of detective stories, and comes upon a locked room murder. When a second locked room killing occurs, Ellery attempts to impress Nikki by solving the crimes before Larry can.

### EPISODE #295   "THE CRIME OF INSPECTOR QUEEN"   Broadcast November 6, 1946

Guest:  Paul Douglas (actor).
Written by Anthony Boucher and Manfred B. Lee.
Produced and directed by Bob Steel.
Announcer: Don Hancock.
Organ music: unknown.
Sponsors: Anacin, Hill's Cold Tablets, BiSoDol Mints.
Story:  Ellery accompanies his father to Los Angeles to pick up Joe Krupp, an accused killer willing to testify against his crime bosses.  On the train back to the east coast Krupp is murdered and Inspector Queen is the prime suspect.

**Trivia, etc.** Guest armchair detective Paul Douglas correctly named the murderer this week.

### EPISODE #296   "THE UNEASY VOYAGE"   Broadcast on November 13, 1946

Guest:  Carmina Freeman (editorial director of *Baffling Detective* magazine).
Written by Tom Everitt and Manfred B. Lee.
Produced and directed by Bob Steel.
Announcer: Don Hancock.
Organ music: unknown.
Sponsors: Anacin, Hill's Cold tablets, BiSoDol Mints.

Story: Ellery boards an ocean liner in hopes of preventing the murder of a French patriot, who is poisoned soon after a professional killer is identified as being on board.

Trivia, etc. Guest armchair detective Carmina Freeman presented an award to the program at the episode's end. "Ellery" announced that as of next week's program the guest armchair detective would be contacted by telephone from among the listeners.

EPISODE #297 **"THE PRIZEFIGHTER'S BIRTHDAY"** Broadcast November 20, 1946
The guest armchair detective was reached by telephone in Columbus, Ohio.
Written by Richard Manoff and Manfred B. Lee.
Produced and directed by Bob Steel.
Announcer: Don Hancock.
Organ music: unknown.
Sponsors: Anacin, Hill's Cold Tablets, BiSoDol Mints.
Story: Ellery investigates when a professional prizefighter is almost murdered by a package bomb after defying gangsters who have told him to throw his twenty-sixth fight or else.

EPISODE #298 **"THE BLACKMAIL VICTIM"** Broadcast on November 27, 1946
The guest armchair detective was reached by telephone in Chicago, Illinois.
Written by Tom Everitt and Manfred B. Lee.
Produced and directed by Bob Steel.
Announcer: Don Hancock.
Organ music: unknown.
Sponsors: Anacin, Hill's Cold Tablets, BiSoDol Mints.
Story: A drunken journalist claims he will kill people at random unless he is paid $25,000 which Ellery is to deliver. When the criminal escapes after concealing the money in the morgue, Ellery tries to figure out the hiding place.

EPISODE #299 **"ELLERY QUEEN, GIGOLO"** Broadcast on December 4, 1946
The guest armchair detective was reached by telephone in Cambridge, Massachusetts.
Written by Anthony Boucher and Manfred B. Lee.
Produced and directed by Bob Steel.
Announcer: Don Hancock.
Organ music: unknown.
Sponsors: Anacin, Hill's Cold Tablets, BiSoDol Mints.
Story: Ellery goes undercover to investigate an escort service that seems to be behind a series of jewel robberies. When the woman who ran the service is murdered in the street, Ellery uses a chesspiece found in her hand to solve the crime.

EPISODE #300 **"THE OLD MAN'S DARLING"** Broadcast on December 11, 1946
The guest armchair detective was reached by telephone in Indiana.
Written by Richard Manoff and Manfred B. Lee.
Produced and directed by Bob Steel.
Announcer: Don Hancock.
Organ music: unknown.
Sponsors: Anacin, Hill's Cold Tablets, BiSoDol Mints.
Story: Ellery is offered $5,000 for a children's fund if he'll determine whether or not old John Spuyten's attractive young nurse has been stealing valuables from the house. Then the nurse is murdered.

EPISODE #301   **"THE HURRICANE THAT COMMITTED A MURDER"**   Dec. 18, 1946
The guest armchair detective was reached by telephone.
Written by Tom Everitt and Manfred B. Lee.
Produced and directed by Bob Steel.
Announcer: Don Hancock.
Organ music: unknown.
Sponsors: Anacin, Hill's Cold Tablets, BiSoDol Mints.
Story:  Ellery tries to solve the murder of a dope peddler in a waterfront boarding house which was blown up by a bomb triggered by a barometer and an approaching hurricane.

EPISODE #302   **"ELLERY QUEEN, SANTA CLAUS"**   Broadcast on December 25, 1946
The guest armchair detective was a housewife reached by telephone in
Jersey City, New Jersey.
Written by Tom Everitt and Manfred B. Lee.
Produced and directed by Bob Steel.
Announcer: Don Hancock.
Organ music: unknown.
Sponsors: Anacin, Hill's Cold Tablets, BiSoDol Mints.
Story:  Trying to prove the innocence of a man on death row, Ellery investigates a $1,000 diamond ring on the finger of a movie theatre box office clerk and a department store Santa Claus who is knifed to death.

   **Trivia, etc.** This episode was repeated under the same title on December 25, 1947 (Episode #333).

EPISODE #303   **"THE UNHAPPY NEW YEAR"**   Broadcast on January 1, 1947
The guest armchair detective was reached by telephone in Old Greenwich, Connecticut.
Written by Anthony Boucher and Manfred B. Lee.
Produced and directed by Bob Steel.
Announcer: Don Hancock.
Organ music: unknown.
Sponsors: Anacin, Hill's Cold Tablets, BiSoDol Mints.
Story:  An unhappy advertising man, married to a radio writer, threatens suicide when his life seems to be going downhill.  Just before he kills himself, somebody tries to shoot him. This case is solved not by Ellery but by Inspector Queen.

   **Trivia, etc.** This episode was repeated under the same title on January 1, 1948 (Episode #334).

EPISODE #304   **"THE MAN WHO COULD VANISH"**   Broadcast on January 8, 1947
The guest armchair detective was reached by phone in Arlington, Virginia.
Written by Anthony Boucher and Manfred B. Lee.
Produced and directed by Bob Steel.
Announcer: Don Hancock.
Organ music: unknown.
Sponsors: Anacin, Hill's Cold Tablets, BiSoDol Mints.
Story:  Ellery investigates when a certain Mr. Revenant enters the police station, confesses to Sergeant Velie that he has committed a murder, and claims that he can disappear at will---which he proceeds to do as soon as he's put in jail.

   **Trivia, etc.** This was the first in a package of *Ellery Queen* episodes that were restaged in Australia with local actors and local commercials, syndicated throughout that continent. Grace Gibson produced and John Saul directed. The Australian version of this episode survives on tape.

EPISODE #305  **"THE LOLLIPOP MURDERS"**  Broadcast on January 15, 1947
The guest armchair detective was reached by telephone.
Written by Tom Everitt and Manfred B. Lee.
Produced and directed by Bob Steel.
Announcer: Don Hancock.
Organ music: unknown.
Sponsors: Anacin, Hill's Cold Tablets, BiSoDol Mints.
Story:  Ellery is forced to go out on a gangster's yacht and solve the murder of a woman whose last act before dying was to stuff a wrapped lollipop in her mouth.

EPISODE #306  **"QUEEN SOLOMON"**  Broadcast on January 22, 1947
The guest armchair detective was reached by telephone in Baltimore, Maryland.
Written by Frederic Dannay and Manfred B. Lee.
Produced and directed by Bob Steel.
Announcer: Don Hancock.
Organ music: unknown.
Sponsors: Anacin, Hill's Cold Tablets, BiSoDol Mints.
Story:  same as episode #101, "The Three Mothers" (November 26 and 28, 1942).

EPISODE #307  **"THE STONE AGE DETECTIVE"**  Broadcast on January 29, 1947
The guest armchair detective was reached by telephone in Detroit, Michigan.
Written by Tom Everitt and Manfred B. Lee.
Produced and directed by Bob Steel.
Announcer: Don Hancock.
Organ music: unknown.
Sponsors: Anacin, Hill's Cold Tablets, BiSoDol Mints.
Story:  Ellery investigates the murder of an 84-year-old man who hired a famous scientist to develop a way to extend his life and had a primitive tribesman with strange powers as his bodyguard.

**Trivia, etc.** After this episode the show returned to a policy of having celebrities as guest armchair detectives.

EPISODE #308  **"THE HUNTED HOUSE"**  Broadcast on February 5, 1947
Guest:  Victor Jory (actor).
Written by Richard Manoff and Manfred B. Lee.
Produced and directed by Bob Steel.
Announcer: Don Hancock.
Organ music: unknown.
Sponsors: Anacin, Hill's Cold Tablets, BiSoDol Mints.
Story:  Desperate to rent an apartment during the housing shortage, Sergeant Velie finds himself photographed in an incriminating pose and blackmailed.  Murder soon follows, and Ellery comes to the aid of his friend.

**Trivia, etc**. This was the last episode in which Ellery was played by Richard Coogan. He was replaced the following week by Lawrence Dobkin.

EPISODE #309  **"THE GREEN GORILLAS"**  Broadcast on February 12, 1947
Guest:  Jose Ferrer (actor).
Written by Tom Everitt and Manfred B. Lee.
Produced and directed by Bob Steel.

161

Announcer: Don Hancock.
Organ music: unknown.
Sponsor: Anacin.
Story: Ellery enlists teen-ager Bob Brown to help him identify the hidden young mastermind who is frightening neighborhood boys into joining his "Green Gorillas" gang.

**Trivia, etc.** This episode was repeated under the same title on June 1, 1947 (Episode #319).

EPISODE #310  **"THE BIG BRAIN"**  Broadcast on February 19, 1947
Guest: Jean Parker (actress).
Written by Tom Everitt and Manfred B. Lee.
Produced and directed by Bob Steel.
Announcer: Bill Cullen.
Organ music: unknown.
Sponsor: Anacin.
Story: On a visit to Florida, Ellery and Nikki become involved with murder and an Argentine businessman who is out to buy big-league American baseball players.

EPISODE #311 **"THE STRANGE DEATH OF MR. ENTRICSON"** Broadcast Feb. 26, 1947
Guest: June Knight (actress).
Written by Tom Everitt and Manfred B. Lee.
Produced and directed by Bob Steel.
Announcer: Don Hancock.
Organ music: unknown.
Sponsor: Anacin.
Story: Ellery investigates the locked-room murder of an elderly lawyer who had been hired by four racketeers to incorporate them legally.

EPISODE #312  **"NIKKI PORTER, KILLER"**  Broadcast on March 5, 1947
Guest: Alfred Drake (actor).
Written by Ken Crossen and Manfred B. Lee.
Produced and directed by Bob Steel.
Announcer: Don Hancock.
Organ music: unknown.
Sponsor: Anacin.
Story: Ellery comes to the rescue when Nikki, suffering from amnesia, steps off a train just as the loot from a bank robbery disappears from her compartment and a man is found murdered.

EPISODE #313  **"THE CROOKED MAN"**  Broadcast on March 12, 1947
Guests: Warren Hull and Parks Johnson  (co-hosts of the *Vox Pop* program).
Written by Anthony Boucher and Manfred B. Lee.
Produced and directed by Bob Steel.
Announcer: Don Hancock.
Organ music: unknown.
Sponsor: Anacin.
Story: Ellery frames himself for Nikki's murder in order to trap a blackmailing private eye several of whose victims have killed themselves. But the head of the blackmail ring has put all the evidence in a safe rigged with a time bomb. Knowing only that the clue to the safe's combination is in the second verse of the nursery rhyme "Simple Simon," Ellery struggles to solve the riddle before the bomb goes off.

EPISODE #314   **"THE SPECIALIST IN COPS"**   Broadcast on March 19, 1947
  Guest:  Bela Lugosi (actor).
  Written by Anthony Boucher and Manfred B. Lee.
  Produced and directed by Bob Steel.
  Announcer: Don Hancock.
  Organ music: unknown.
  Sponsor: Anacin.
  Story:  Captured by gangster Nutsy Yapp, whose specialty is killing police officers for
hire, Ellery tries to let Inspector Queen know where he's being held prisoner despite the fact that
the note Yapp allows him to write his father is being censored.

  **Trivia, etc.** The first half of this episode exists on tape. The guest armchair detective is
billed as one Joan Barton.

EPISODE #315   **"THE TEN THOUSAND DOLLAR BILL"**   Broadcast on March 26, 1947
  Guest:  Ted Malone (poetry reader).
  Written by Tom Everitt and Manfred B. Lee.
  Produced and directed by Bob Steel.
  Announcer: Don Hancock.
  Organ music: unknown.
  Sponsors: Anacin, Hill's Cold tablets, BiSoDol Mints.
  Story:  A drunk with a thick bankroll causes Ellery and Nikki to spend an evening at a
country inn where they have to contend with a disappearance, an embezzlement, and a man found
murdered with a $10,000 bill in his hand.

EPISODE #316   **"THE MAN WHO MURDERED A CITY"**   Broadcast on April 2, 1947
  Guests:  Andre Baruch (radio announcer) and Bea Wain (singer).
  Supporting cast:  Ted Osborne.
  Written by Anthony Boucher and Manfred B. Lee.
  Produced and directed by Bob Steel.
  Announcer: Don Hancock.
  Organ music: unknown.
  Sponsors: Anacin, BiSoDol Mints, Kolynos Toothpaste.
  Story:  Ellery sets out to expose the identity of "The Buzzer," a hidden mastermind
who has taken control of a municipal government because the citizens didn't bother to vote.

EPISODE #317   **"THE BIG FIX"**   Broadcast on April 9, 1947
  Guest: unknown.
  Written by Richard Manoff and Manfred B. Lee.
  Produced and directed by Bob Steel.
  Announcer: Don Hancock.
  Organ music: unknown.
  Sponsors: Anacin, BiSoDol Mints.
  Story:  Ellery probes the murder of compulsive gambler Larry "Hot" Lipps, who was
killed shortly after his doctor told him he would die a natural death within a few weeks.

EPISODE #318   **"THE REDHEADED BLONDE BRUNETTE"**   Broadcast April 16, 1947
  Guest:  Arthur Godfrey (radio personality).
  Supporting cast:  Kaye Brinker.
  Written by Tom Everitt and Manfred B. Lee.
  Produced and directed by Bob Steel.
  Announcer: Don Hancock.

Organ music: unknown.

Sponsors: Anacin, Hill's Cold Tablets, BiSoDol Mints.

Story: Ellery tries to solve the murder of a night-club singer who married several military men to get their allotment checks and insurance.

**Trivia, etc.** After this episode the series went on hiatus for six weeks. During that time it moved from the east to the west coast and from CBS back to NBC. On the program's return, George Matthews took over from Ed Latimer as Sergeant Velie.

EPISODE #319 **"THE GREEN GORILLAS"** Broadcast on June 1, 1947

West Coast guest: Nina Foch (actress).

East Coast guest: Dorothy Gordon (radio producer).

Written by Tom Everitt and Manfred B. Lee.

Produced and directed by Tom Victor.

Announcer: Don Hancock.

Organ music: Chet Kingsbury.

Sponsors: Anacin, Freezone, Kolynos Toothpaste.

Story: same as Episode # 309, "The Green Gorillas" (February 12, 1947).

EPISODE #320 **"THE SKY PIRATES"** Broadcast on June 8, 1947

West Coast guest: Marion Bell (vocalist).

East Coast guest: Cy Steinhauser (radio editor of the Pittsburgh *Press*).

Written by Tom Everitt and Manfred B. Lee.

Produced and directed by Tom Victor.

Announcer: Don Hancock.

Organ music: Chet Kingsbury.

Sponsors: Anacin, Freezone, Kolynos Toothpaste.

Story: Ellery tries to frustrate two air pirates who have held up a transatlantic airliner, shot one of the passengers, robbed all the others and plan to bail out over the ocean.

**Trivia, etc.** Following this broadcast the series went off the air for a seven-week summer hiatus, replaced by *The Dave Garroway Show*. On its return, Ed Latimer reclaimed the role of Sergeant Velie from George Matthews.

## SEASON EIGHT

EPISODE #321 **"THE ATOMIC MURDER"** Broadcast on August 3, 1947

West Coast guest: Fay McKenzie (actress).

East Coast guest: Eddie Dowling (Broadway producer).

Written by Tom Everitt and Manfred B. Lee.

Produced and directed by Tom Victor.

Announcer: Don Hancock.

Organ music: Chet Kingsbury.

Sponsors: Anacin, Freezone, Kolynos Toothpaste.

Story: Ellery investigates the attempted assassination of a famous atomic scientist and the murder of the scientist's wife, with the prime suspects being escaped Nazis who were friends of the notorious Martin Bormann.

EPISODE #322 **"THE FOOLISH GIRLS"** Broadcast on August 10, 1947

West Coast guest: Eddie Dowling (Broadway producer).

East Coast guest:  Marion Bell (vocalist).
Written by Tom Everitt and Manfred B. Lee.
Produced and directed by Tom Victor.
Announcer: Don Hancock.
Organ music: Chet Kingsbury.
Sponsors: Anacin, Freezone, Kolynos Toothpaste.
Story:  Ellery becomes involved when some teen-age girls insist on visiting the same bar that was frequented by a 17-year-old friend of theirs before her murder.

EPISODE #323   **"MURDER FOR AMERICANS"**   Broadcast on August 17, 1947
West Coast guest:  Jeffrey Lynn (actor).
East Coast guest:  Patrice Munsel (singer).
Written by Anthony Boucher and Manfred B. Lee.
Produced and directed by Tom Victor.
Announcer: Don Hancock.
Organ music: Chet Kingsbury.
Sponsors: Anacin, Freezone, Kolynos Toothpaste.
Story:  While visiting an upstate city that is being flooded with pamphlets attacking Jews, Catholics and blacks, Ellery is asked by a 10-year-old Jewish girl to find her vanished friend, the daughter of an Irish cop.

**Trivia, etc.**  Guest armchair detective Patrice Munsel correctly guessed the killer's identity.

EPISODE #324   **"THE RATS WHO WALKED LIKE MEN"**   Broadcast August 24, 1947
West Coast guest:  J. Franken.
East Coast guest:  G. Gaghan.
Written by Tom Everitt and Manfred B. Lee.
Produced and directed by Tom Victor.
Announcer: Don Hancock.
Organ music: Chet Kingsbury.
Sponsors: Anacin, Freezone, Kolynos Toothpaste.
Story:  Ellery is framed for the murder of a broken-down press agent who had been hired by three gangsters to get good publicity for them.

EPISODE #325   **"THE KING'S HORSE"**   Broadcast on August 31, 1947
West Coast guest:  John Emery (actor).
East Coast guest:  Pam Camp (Miss Arkansas of 1947).
Written by Tom Everitt and Manfred B. Lee.
Produced and directed by Tom Victor.
Announcer: Don Hancock.
Organ music: Chet Kingsbury.
Sponsors: Anacin, Freezone, Kolynos Toothpaste.
Story:  Ellery uses a newsreel to solve the murder of the king of Uridia, who was killed by a bomb at the racetrack.

EPISODE #326   **"NUMBER THIRTY-ONE"**   Broadcast on September 7, 1947
West Coast guest:  Kent Smith (actor).
East Coast guest:  Sonya Stein (radio editor of the Washington *Post*).
Written by Tom Everitt and Manfred B. Lee.
Produced and directed by Tom Victor.

165

Announcer: Don Hancock.

Organ music: Chet Kingsbury.

Sponsors: Anacin, Freezone, Kolynos Toothpaste.

Story: Ellery tries to crack the secret of international mystery man George Arcaris's success at smuggling diamonds into the Port of New York and also to solve the murder of a young black man who was the servant of a Manhattan socialite.

**Trivia, etc.** Guest armchair detective Sonya Stein correctly guessed the killer's identity.

EPISODE #327  **"TRAGEDY IN BLUE"**  Broadcast on September 14, 1947

West Coast guest: Danton Walker (newspaper columnist).

East Coast guest: Jean Sablon (baritone).

Written by Tom Everitt and Manfred B. Lee.

Produced and directed by Tom Victor.

Announcer: Don Hancock.

Organ music: Chet Kingsbury.

Sponsors: Anacin, Freezone, Kolynos Toothpaste.

Story: Ellery becomes involved with three Blue sisters, whose Broadway and radio careers are threatened by a shadowy man from their past. Then Zona Blue collapses after performing a singing commercial and her evil husband is found with his throat cut.

EPISODE #328  **"THE MAN WHO SQUARED THE CIRCLE"**  Broadcast Sept. 21, 1947

West Coast guest: George Frazier (newspaper columnist).

East Coast guests: Warren Hull and Parks Johnson (co-hosts of Radio's *Vox Pop*).

Written by Anthony Boucher and Manfred B. Lee.

Produced and directed by Tom Victor.

Announcer: Don Hancock.

Organ music: Chet Kingsbury.

Sponsors: Anacin, Freezone, Kolynos Toothpaste.

Story: Ellery is consulted by a famous mathematician who claims to have squared the circle but says that the papers demonstrating his proof have been stolen. Then the mathematician is assaulted and leaves a cryptic clue to his attacker.

**Trivia, etc.** This was the final episode sponsored by Anacin and the various products its company manufactured. The series went off the air for two months, returning on the ABC network, with no sponsor at all, and with three of the four regular cast members replaced. Herb Butterfield took over as Inspector Queen, Alan Reed as Sergeant Velie and Virginia Gregg as Nikki Porter. Lawrence Dobkin continued to play Ellery.

EPISODE #329  **"THE SAGA OF RUFFY RUX"**  Broadcast on November 27, 1947

Guest: McCullah St. Johns.

Supporting cast: Luis Van Rooten (Ruffy Rux), Jack Petruzzi (Glitch), Charles Seel (Protherick), Paul Frees (Mac), Jack Webb (Reno).

Written by Anthony Boucher and Manfred B. Lee.

Produced and directed by Dick Woollen.

Announcer: Paul Masterson.

Organ music: Rex Koury.

Story: Ellery is pitted against a gangster who talks like Elmer Fudd and has a habit of constantly jingling the two silver dollars he carries for luck.

EPISODE #330    "_____"    Broadcast on December 4, 1947
      Guest: unknown.
      Written by Frederic Dannay and Manfred B. Lee.
      Produced and directed by Dick Woollen.
      Announcer: Paul Masterson
      Organ music: Rex Koury.
      Story: unknown.

**Trivia, etc.** Manny Lee told Anthony Boucher in a letter that the episode to be broadcast this week would be a rerun of an old Dannay-Lee script, but which one is not known.

EPISODE #331    **"NIKKI PORTER, BRIDE"**    Broadcast on December 11, 1947
      Guest:  Zuma Palmer (columnist for the Hollywood *Citizen-News*).
      Supporting cast:  Joseph Kearns, Maxine Marx, Edward Marr, Eleanor Audley, Myra Marsh.
      Written by Anthony Boucher and Manfred B. Lee.
      Produced and directed by Dick Woollen.
      Announcer: Paul Masterson.
      Organ music: Rex Koury.
      Story:  Nikki quits her job with Ellery in anger and plans to marry Hobart Grimman, a known bigamist and a fraud. Ellery becomes involved when Grimman is shot during the ceremony.

EPISODE #332    **"THE MELANCHOLY DANE"**    Broadcast on December 18, 1947
      Guest:  Dick Williams (west coast editor of *Pic Magazine*).
      Supporting cast:  Stacy Harris, Eleanor Audley, Paul Frees, Georgia Ellis, Earl Lee, Willis Bouchey.
      Written by Anthony Boucher and Manfred B. Lee.
      Produced and directed by Dick Woollen.
      Announcer: Paul Masterson.
      Organ music: Rex Koury.
      Story:   Ellery tries to solve a murder with a strong resemblance to the plot of Shakespeare's *Hamlet*: Willis Dane's mother marries his uncle Claude immediately after his father's sudden death and Willis is accused of murder when Claude is found poisoned.

EPISODE #333    **"ELLERY QUEEN, SANTA CLAUS"**    Broadcast on December 25, 1947
      Guest: Fabius Friedman (west coast editor of *Radio Best* magazine).
      Written by Tom Everitt and Manfred B. Lee.
      Produced and directed by Dick Woollen.
      Announcer: Paul Masterson.
      Organ music: Rex Koury.
      Story:  same as Episode #302, "Ellery Queen, Santa Claus" (December 25, 1946).

**Trivia, etc.** Either this rerun or that of the following week marked the last appearance of Virginia Gregg as Nikki Porter. She was replaced in the part by Kaye Brinker, who in private life was Mrs. Manfred B. Lee.

EPISODE #334    **"THE UNHAPPY NEW YEAR"**    Broadcast on January 1, 1948
      Guest: unknown.
      Written by Anthony Boucher and Manfred B. Lee.
      Produced and directed by Dick Woollen.

Announcer: Paul Masterson.

Organ music: Rex Koury.

Story: same as Episode #303, "The Unhappy New Year" (January 1, 1947).

EPISODE #335 **"THE HEAD HUNTER"** Broadcast on January 8, 1948

Guest: Alice Canfield.

Supporting cast: William Conrad, Luis Van Rooten, Charles McGraw, Tony Barrett.

Written by Anthony Boucher and Manfred B. Lee.

Produced and directed by Dick Woollen.

Announcer: Paul Masterson.

Organ music: Rex Koury.

Story: Ellery tries to uncover the identity of the mysterious "Head Man," who has murdered two gamblers and is hunting more of them.

EPISODE #336 **"THE TERRIFIED MAN"** Broadcast on January 15, 1948

Guest: Jerry Devine (radio scriptwriter/producer/director).

Supporting cast: John Brown.

Written by Frederic Dannay and Manfred B. Lee.

Produced and directed by Dick Woollen.

Announcer: Paul Masterson.

Organ music: Rex Koury.

Story: Same as Episode #69, "The Invisible Clue" (January 15 and 17, 1942).

EPISODE #337 **"THE PRIVATE EYE"** Broadcast on January 22, 1948

Guest: Henry Morgan (radio comedian/quizmaster).

Written by Anthony Boucher and Manfred B. Lee.

Produced and directed by Dick Woollen.

Announcer: Paul Masterson.

Organ music: Rex Koury.

Story: Ellery and sadistic private eye Cam Clubb apply their different methods of sleuthing to the murder of a statesman in exile from a mythical Balkan country.

**Trivia, etc.** This was the last episode in which Ellery was portrayed by Lawrence Dobkin. He was replaced the following week by Howard Culver, the last actor to play the part on network radio.

EPISODE #338 **"THE DEATH HOUSE"** Broadcast on January 29, 1948

Guest: Erskine Johnson (Hollywood columnist).

Supporting cast: Lurene Tuttle, Earl Lee, Ralph Moody, Wilms Herbert, Ira Grossel.

Written by Frederic Dannay and Manfred B. Lee.

Produced and directed by Dick Woollen.

Announcer: Paul Masterson.

Organ music: Rex Koury.

Story: same as Episode #127, "The Death Traps" (May 27 and 29, 1943).

**Trivia, etc.** Guest armchair detective Erskine Johnson correctly guessed the identity of the killer this week. Actor Ira Grossel, who played a supporting role, is better known as Jeff Chandler.

EPISODE #339 **"BUBSY"** Broadcast on February 5, 1948

Guest: Charles "Buddy" Rogers (movie actor/producer).

Supporting cast: Paul Frees, Edwin Max, Eleanor Audley, Jack Petruzzi, Peter Leeds, Harald Dyrenfurth.

Written by _____ and Manfred B. Lee.
Produced and directed by Dick Woollen.
Announcer: Paul Masterson.
Organ music: Rex Koury.
Story: Ellery and Nikki are kidnapped by a moronic hired assassin who threatens to kill them both unless Ellery can figure out the identity of the assassin's hidden employer.

**Trivia, etc.** Hollywood actor/producer Charles "Buddy" Rogers correctly guessed the killer's identity this week.

EPISODE #340 **"A QUESTION OF COLOR"** Broadcast on February 12, 1948
Guest: Edith Gwynn (Hollywood columnist).
Supporting cast: Roy Candy, James Edwards, Willis Bouchey, Roy Glenn,
Frankie Lynn, Edith Wilson, Earl Smith.
Written by Anthony Boucher and Manfred B. Lee.
Produced and directed by Dick Woollen.
Announcer: Paul Masterson.
Organ music: Rex Koury.
Story: Ellery tries to help a young black boxer who has been manipulated by gamblers into a bout he can't win.

**Trivia, etc.** Guest armchair detective Edith Gwynn correctly guessed the identity of the culprit this week.

EPISODE #341 **"THE OLD SINNER"** Broadcast on February 19, 1948
Guest: Virginia MacPherson (writer for United Press syndicate)
Supporting cast: Tom Collins, Fay Baker, Wilms Herbert, Stacy Harris, Ralph Moody.
Written by Anthony Boucher and Manfred B. Lee.
Produced and directed by Dick Woollen.
Announcer: Paul Masterson.
Organ music: Rex Koury.
Story: Ellery investigates when an asthmatic old black-sheep uncle is promptly but not fatally poisoned after returning to blackmail family members over a seven-year-old Minnesota murder.

EPISODE #342 **"THE BLUE EGG"** Broadcast on February 26, 1948
Guest: Seymour Nebenzal (movie producer)
Supporting cast: Frank Lovejoy, Gene Leonard.
Written by Frederic Dannay and Manfred B. Lee.
Produced and directed by Dick Woollen.
Announcer: Paul Masterson.
Organ music: Rex Koury.
Story: same as Episode #241, "The Blue Egg" (September 12, 1945).

EPISODE #343 **"THE HUMAN WEAPON"** Broadcast on March 4, 1948
East Coast guest: Joan Barton (actress).
West Coast guest: John Nelson (radio emcee).
Supporting cast: Luis Van Rooten, Lurene Tuttle, Anne Stone, Rye Billsbury.
Written by Frederic Dannay and Manfred B. Lee.
Produced and directed by Dick Woollen.
Announcer: Paul Masterson.

Organ music: Rex Koury.

Story: same as Episode # 119, "The Human Weapon" (April 1 and 3, 1943).

EPISODE #344   **"THE LYNCHING OF MR. CUE"**   Broadcast on March 11, 1948
Guest: Kirk Douglas (actor).
Supporting cast: William Conrad, Edwin Max, Willis Bouchey, Buddy Gray,
Georgia Backus.
Written by Anthony Boucher and Manfred B. Lee.
Produced and directed by Dick Woollen.
Announcer: Paul Masterson.
Organ music: Rex Koury.
Story: Ellery is arrested and threatened with a lynch mob when he passes through the small town of Guff City and through a comedy of errors is mistaken for a non-existent gangster known as Scarface Ellery Cue.

EPISODE #345   **"THE ARMCHAIR DETECTIVE"**   Broadcast on March 18, 1948
Guest: Sheilah Graham (newspaper columnist).
Supporting cast: Joan Banks, Bill Johnstone, Charles Seel, Anne Morrison,
Joseph Kearns.
Written by Anthony Boucher and Manfred B. Lee.
Produced and directed by Dick Woollen.
Announcer: Paul Masterson.
Organ music: Rex Koury.
Story: same as Episode # 269, "The Armchair Detective" (March 27, 1946).

EPISODE #346   **"THE FARMER'S DAUGHTER"**   Broadcast on March 25, 1948
Guest: Agnes Moorehead (actress).
Supporting cast: Anne Morrison, Jeff Chandler, Luis Van Rooten, Earl Keen.
Written by Anthony Boucher and Manfred B. Lee.
Produced and directed by Dick Woollen.
Announcer: Paul Masterson.
Organ music: Rex Koury.
Story: Ellery and Nikki run into danger when they visit a farm which is also enjoying a visit from an escaped convict.

EPISODE #347   **"THE VANISHING CROOK"**   Broadcast on April 1, 1948
Guest: Arlene Rogers (winner of the "America's Champion Movie Fan" contest).
Supporting cast: Jack Webb, Joan Banks, Eric Snowden, Paul Frees.
Written by _____ and Manfred B. Lee.
Produced and directed by Dick Woollen.
Announcer: Paul Masterson.
Organ music: Rex Koury.
Story: Ellery helps his father find an English jewel thief who managed to disappear just before the police broke in on him.

**Trivia, etc.** This was a repeat of an as yet unidentified episode from earlier in the series.

EPISODE #348   **"THE K.I. CASE"**   Broadcast on April 8, 1948
Guest: Jimmy Starr (motion picture editor of the Los Angeles *Herald-Express*).
Supporting cast: Jay Novello, Luis Van Rooten, Rye Billsbury, Betty Lou Gerson,
Frank Lovejoy.

Written by Anthony Boucher and Manfred B. Lee.
Produced and directed by Dick Woollen.
Announcer: Paul Masterson.
Organ music: Rex Koury.
Story: Ellery investigates the murder of a racketeer who, just before being killed, said "KI" over the phone to the great detective.

EPISODE #349 **"THE SLICER"** Broadcast on April 15, 1948
Guest: Gene Handsaker (Hollywood columnist).
Written by Anthony Boucher and Manfred B. Lee.
Produced and directed by Dick Woollen.
Announcer: Paul Masterson.
Organ music: Rex Koury.
Story: same as Episode #237, "Nick the Knife" (August 1, 1945).

EPISODE #350 **"MURDER BY INSTALLMENTS"** Broadcast on April 22, 1948
Guest: Mel Blanc (voice of movie cartoon characters).
Supporting cast: Paul Frees, Robert Griffin, Bob Lewis, Charles Seel, Frances Chaney.
Written by Frederic Dannay and Manfred B. Lee.
Produced and directed by Dick Woollen.
Announcer: Paul Masterson.
Organ music: Rex Koury.
Story: same as Episode #106, "The Man Who Was Murdered by Installments" (December 31, 1942 and January 2, 1943).

**Trivia, etc.** Either this week's episode or that of the following week was the last in which Ellery was portrayed by Lawrence Dobkin. The part was taken over by Howard Culver for the final few episodes of the series' nine-year run.
Guest armchair detective Mel Blanc correctly guessed the killer's identity this week.

EPISODE #351 **"THE THREE FROGS"** Broadcast on April 29, 1948
Guest: Florabel Muir (columnist for *Daily Variety*).
Written by Anthony Boucher and Manfred B. Lee.
Produced and directed by Dwight Hauser.
Announcer: Paul Masterson.
Organ music: Rex Koury.
Story: When Nikki sets out to reform a juvenile delinquent she finds hiding in her apartment, her project meshes with Ellery's hunt for a Faginesque criminal known as The Frog, who has organized a youth gang for criminal purposes.

EPISODE #352 **"ONE DIAMOND"** Broadcast on May 6, 1948
Guest: Peggy Lee (singer).
Supporting cast: Sidney Miller, Eric Snowden, Wilms Herbert, Willis Bouchey, Joan Banks.
Written by Anthony Boucher and Manfred B. Lee.
Produced and directed by Dwight Hauser.
Announcer: Paul Masterson.
Organ music: Rex Koury.
Story: Ellery investigates the murder of germ-phobic millionaire Mark Gallows and the puzzle of why the killer wasn't able to correctly read the simple map showing the hiding place of the famous Gallows Diamond.

EPISODE #353   **"NIKKI PORTER, STARLET"**   Broadcast on May 13, 1948
  Guest:  Harve Fischman (former Quiz Kid).
  Written by Anthony Boucher and Manfred B. Lee.
  Produced and directed by Dwight Hauser.
  Announcer: Paul Masterson.
  Organ music: Rex Koury.
  Story:  same as Episode #252, "The Doodle of Mr. O'Drew" (November 28, 1945).

EPISODE #354   **"MISERY MIKE"**   Broadcast on May 20, 1948
  Guest:  Cliff Arquette (radio actor).
  Supporting cast: Sidney Miller (Misery Mike), Barney Phillips (Coogle),
  Anne Stone (Doris), Tony Barrett (Swint), Louis Merrill (Solassi),
  Barney Phillips (Manager), Herb Butterfield (German), Tony Barrett (Reporter).
  Written by Anthony Boucher and Manfred B. Lee.
  Produced and directed by Dwight Hauser.
  Announcer: Paul Masterson.
  Organ music: Rex Koury.
  Accordion music: Ernie Felice.
  Story:  Ellery probes the murder of an accordion-playing criminal with a penchant for
blackmailing opera singers.

EPISODE #355   "_____"   Broadcast on May 27, 1948
  Guest:  Sam Abbott.
  Written by _____ and Manfred B. Lee.
  Produced and directed by Dwight Hauser.
  Announcer: Paul Masterson.
  Organ music: Rex Koury.
  Story:  Ellery becomes involved in a case with overtones of racial prejudice.

  **Trivia, etc.**  This last of Ellery's radio adventures was a repeat of a previous episode,
but both its new title and its original source remain unidentified.

## APPENDIX A:  AUTHOR! AUTHOR!

Fred Dannay and Manny Lee created this cross between a game show and a panel show and sold it to the Mutual radio network, where it debuted two and a half months before *The Adventures of Ellery Queen* premiered on CBS.  A surprising number of the guest authors who matched wits each week with Fred and Manny remain well-known names today.  A few of them, including Ruth McKenney, Vicki Baum and John G. Chapman, also guested on *Ellery Queen* and will be found in the "Biographies in Brief" section later in this book.

*Author! Author!*'s first time slot on Mutual was Friday evenings between 8:30 and 9:00 P.M. EST.  The guests who appeared with "Mr. Ellery" and "Mr. Queen" were as follows.

April 7, 1939      Carl Van Doren and Ruth McKenney

April 14, 1939     Carl Van Doren and Ruth McKenney

April 21, 1939     Morris Ernst and Dorothy Parker

April 28, 1939     Quentin Reynolds and Alfred Kreymborg

May 5, 1939        Frank Sullivan and Carl Van Doren

May 12, 1939       Carl Van Doren

May 19, 1939       Ludwig Bemelmans and Alice Duer Miller

May 26, 1939       Lorenz Hart and Henry Pringle

June 2, 1939       Mark Van Doren and Frank Case

June 9, 1939       Dorothy Parker and Donald Ogden Stewart

At this point the program moved from Friday to Monday evening, 9:30-10:00 P.M. EST

June 12, 1939      Stanley Walker and Heywood Broun

June 19, 1939      George S. Kaufman and Moss Hart

June 26, 1939      Dawn Powell and Erskine Caldwell

July 3, 1939       Vicki Baum and Bayard Veiller

July 10, 1939      MacKinlay Kantor and Gelett Burgess

| July 17, 1939 | Phil Stong and William Blake |
|---|---|
| July 24, 1939 | Conrad Bercovici and Thyra Samter Winslow |
| July 31, 1939 | John G. Chapman and Lucius Beebe |
| Aug. 7, 1939 | Pre-empted by baseball |
| Aug. 14, 1939 | Carl Carmer, John G. Chapman, Bayard Veiller and Heywood Broun |
| Aug. 21, 1939 | Gladys Shelley, William Blake, Heywood Broun and John G. Chapman |

On August 28 the program was pre-empted by a news report from London about the imminent beginning of World War II.

| Sept. 4, 1939 | Heywood Broun and John G. Chapman |
|---|---|
| Sept. 11, 1939 | William C. White, Heywood Broun, John G.Chapman, and Alice Leone-Moats |
| Sept. 18, 1939 | Heywood Broun, John G. Chapman, Sigmund Spaeth, and Pietro di Donato |
| Sept. 25, 1939 | Heywood Broun, John G. Chapman, Morris Ernst, and Samuel Liebowitz |
| Oct. 2, 1939 | Heywood Broun, John G. Chapman, Henry Pringle, and C.V.R. Thompson |
| Oct. 9, 1939 | Heywood Broun, John G. Chapman, Dawn Powell and James Thurber |
| Oct. 16, 1939 | Vicki Baum and Lewis Gannett |
| Oct. 23, 1939 | Vicki Baum, Lillian Hellman, and Vincent McHugh |
| Oct. 30, 1939 | Lin Yutang and Col. Theodore Roosevelt Jr. |

At this point the program moved to an earlier Monday evening time slot, 8:00-8:30 P.M. EST.

| Nov. 6, 1939 | Guests unknown |
|---|---|
| Nov. 13, 1939 | Guests unknown |

Nov. 20, 1939    Paul Whiteman, Henry Pringle, and Samson Raphaelson

Nov. 27, 1939    Vicki Baum and W.E. Woodward

Dec. 4, 1939     James Thurber, Henry Pringle and Carl Van Doren

Dec. 11, 1939    Meyer Berger and H.I. Phillips

Dec. 18, 1939    Sarah Hay and Raymond Holden

Dec. 25, 1939    Fred Schwade Jr., Claude H. Bishop, and Sigmund Spaeth

On New Year's Day of 1940 *Author! Author!* was pre-empted for a special musical program.

Jan. 8, 1940     Sarah Hay, Raymond Holden, and Maurice Dekobra

Jan. 15, 1940    Col. Theodore Roosevelt Jr., and Morris Ernst

Jan. 22, 1940    Frank Case, Oliver La Farge, Maurice Dekobra,
                 and Alfred Kreymborg

Jan. 29, 1940     Helen Huntington Smith and Edna Lee Bocker

Feb. 5, 1940     Carveth Wells, John Bakeless, Oliver La Farge, and Helen Hull

Feb. 12, 1940    Oliver La Farge, Frank Case, and Helen Huntington Smith

175

# APPENDIX B: NETWORKS, TIME SLOTS AND SPONSORS

**SEASON ONE (episodes 1-13 – June 18, 1939-September 10, 1939)**
| | | | |
|---|---|---|---|
| CBS | Sunday | 8:00 - 9:00 P.M. EST | sustained |

**SEASON ONE (episodes 14-36 – September 17, 1939-February 18, 1940)**
| | | | |
|---|---|---|---|
| CBS | Sunday | 10:00 - 11:00 P.M. EST | sustained |

**SEASON ONE (episodes 37-44 – February 25, 1940-April 14, 1940)**
| | | | |
|---|---|---|---|
| CBS | Sunday | 10:00 - 10:30 P.M. EST | sustained |

**SEASON ONE (episode 45 – April 21, 1940)**
| | | | |
|---|---|---|---|
| CBS | Sunday | 8:00 - 8:30 P.M. EST | sustained |

**SEASON ONE (episodes 46-67 – April 28, 1940-September 22, 1940)**
| | | | |
|---|---|---|---|
| CBS | Sunday | 7:30 - 8:00 P.M. EST | Gulf Oil |

**SEASON TWO (episodes 68-93 – January 8, 1942 - July 2/4, 1942)**
**SEASON THREE (episodes 94-145 – Oct. 8/10, 1942 – Sept. 30/October 2, 1943)**
**SEASON FOUR (episodes 146-197 – October 7/9, 1943-September 28/30, 1944)**
**SEASON FIVE (episodes 198-210 – October 5/7, 1944-December 28/30, 1944)**
| | | | |
|---|---|---|---|
| NBC | Thursday | 9:30 - 10:00 P.M. PST (West) | Bromo-Seltzer |
| NBC | Saturday | 7:30 - 8:00 P.M. EST (East) | Bromo-Seltzer |

**SEASON FIVE (episodes 211-239 – January 24, 1945-August 15, 1945)**
**SEASON SIX (episodes 240-291 – September 5, 1945-August 28, 1946)**
**SEASON SEVEN (episodes 292-318 – October 9, 1946-April 16, 1947)**
| | | | |
|---|---|---|---|
| CBS | Wednesday | 7:30 - 8:00 P.M. EST | Anacin |

**SEASON SEVEN (episodes 319-320 – June 1, 1947-June 8, 1947)**
**SEASON EIGHT (episodes 321-328 – August 3, 1947-September 21, 1947)**
| | | | |
|---|---|---|---|
| NBC | Sunday | 6:30 - 7:00 P.M. EST | Anacin |

**SEASON EIGHT (episodes 329-338 – November 27, 1947-January 29, 1948)**
| | | | |
|---|---|---|---|
| ABC | Thursday | 7:30 - 8:00 P.M. EST | sustained |

**SEASON EIGHT (episodes 339-355 – February 5, 1948-May 27, 1948)**
| | | | |
|---|---|---|---|
| ABC | Thursday | 8:30 - 9:00 P.M. EST | sustained |

# THE REGULAR CAST

*As Ellery Queen, As Nikki Porter, As Inspector Queen, As Sergeant Velie, and Doc Prouty.*

**SEASON ONE (episodes 1-20 minimum, 1-24 maximum –
June 18, 1939-Oct. __ or Nov. __, 1939)**
Hugh Marlowe, Marian Shockley, Santos Ortega, Howard Smith, and Robert Strauss.

**SEASON ONE (episodes 21-36 maximum, 25-36 minimum –
Nov. __ or Dec. __, 1939-Feb. 18, 1940)**
Hugh Marlowe, Marian Shockley, Santos Ortega, Ted de Corsia, and Robert Strauss.

**SEASON ONE (episodes 37-45 – Feb. 25, 1940-April 21, 1940)**
Hugh Marlowe, Marian Shockley, Santos Ortega, Ted de Corsia, and Arthur Allen

Note: At this point the regular character of Doc Prouty was dropped from the series.
*Cast: As Ellery Queen, As Nikki Porter, As Inspector Queen, and As Sergeant Velie.*

**SEASON ONE (episodes 46-67 – April 28, 1940-Sept. 22, 1940)**
Hugh Marlowe, Marian Shockley, Santos Ortega, and Ted de Corsia.

**SEASON TWO (episodes 68-93 – Jan. 8, 1942-July 2/4, 1942)**
**SEASON THREE (episodes 94-136 minimum, 94-140 maximum –
Oct. 8, 1942-July __ or Aug. __, 1943)**
Carleton Young, Marian Shockley, Santos Ortega, and Ted de Corsia.

**SEASON THREE (episodes 137-145 maximum, 141-145 minimum –
Aug. __ or Sept. __, 1943-Sept. 30/Oct. 2, 1943)**
Sydney Smith, Marian Shockley, Santos Ortega, and Ted de Corsia.

**SEASON FOUR (episodes 146-150 – Oct. 7/9, 1943-Nov. 4/6, 1943)**
Sydney Smith, Helen Lewis, Santos Ortega, and Ted de Corsia.

**SEASON FOUR (episodes 151-197 – Nov. 11/13, 1943-Sept. 28/30, 1944)**
**SEASON FIVE (episodes 198-210 – Oct. 5/7, 1944-Dec. 28/30, 1944)**
Sydney Smith, Marian Shockley, Santos Ortega, and Ted de Corsia.

**SEASON FIVE (episodes 211-235 – Jan. 24, 1945-July 18, 1945)**
Sydney Smith, Barbara Terrell, Santos Ortega, and Ted de Corsia.

177

**SEASON FIVE (episodes 236-239 – July 25, 1945-Aug. 15, 1945)**
**SEASON SIX (episodes 240-291 – Sept. 5, 1945-Aug. 28, 1946)**
Sydney Smith, Gertrude Warner, Santos Ortega, and Ted de Corsia.

**SEASON SEVEN (episodes 292-??? – Oct. 9, 1946-???)**
Sydney Smith, Charlotte Keane, Santos Ortega, and Ted de Corsia.

**SEASON SEVEN (episodes ???-308 – ???-Feb. 5, 1947)**
Richard Coogan, Charlotte Keane, Bill Smith, and Ed Latimer.

**SEASON SEVEN (episodes 309-318 – Feb. 12, 1947-April 16, 1947)**
Lawrence Dobkin, Charlotte Keane, Bill Smith, and Ed Latimer.

**SEASON SEVEN (episodes 319-320 – June 1, 1947-June 8, 1947)**
Lawrence Dobkin, Charlotte Keane, Bill Smith, and George Matthews.

**SEASON EIGHT (episodes 321-328 – Aug. 3, 1947-Sept. 21, 1947)**
Lawrence Dobkin, Charlotte Keane, Bill Smith, and Ed Latimer.

**SEASON EIGHT (episodes 329-332 minimum, 329-334 maximum –**
**Nov. 27, 1947-Dec. __, 1947 or Jan. __, 1948)**
Lawrence Dobkin, Virginia Gregg, Herb Butterfield, and Alan Reed.

**SEASON EIGHT (episodes 333-351 maximum, 335-350 minimum –**
**Dec. __, 1947 or Jan. __, 1948-April 22 or 29, 1948)**
Lawrence Dobkin, Kaye Brinker, Herb Butterfield, and Alan Reed.

**SEASON EIGHT (episodes 351-355 maximum, 352-355 minimum –**
**April 29 or May 5, 1948-May 27, 1948)**
Howard Culver, Kaye Brinker, Herb Butterfield, and Alan Reed.

# THE COMPETITION

This appendix is for those who might be curious about the programs *The Adventures of Ellery Queen* went up against during its years on radio. At least on the East Coast, most of the programs the other national networks scheduled in EQ's time slot offered either music or news and commentary.

## ELLERY QUEEN ON CBS

June 18, 1939 - September 10, 1939
| | |
|---|---|
| NBC | *The Chase and Sanborn Hour* |
| Blue | Various musical segments |
| Mutual | Continuing Forums: "The Alien Bills" |

September 24, 1939 - April 14, 1940
| | |
|---|---|
| NBC | *The Spitalny All-Girl Orchestra* |
| Blue | European Commentaries/*Readings by Cheerio* |
| Mutual | *The Good-Will Hour* |

April 21, 1940
| | |
|---|---|
| NBC | *The Chase and Sanborn Hour* |
| Blue | *Margaret Daum Sings* |
| Mutual | Special Forum: "The Relief Program" |

April 28, 1940 - June 30, 1940
| | |
|---|---|
| NBC | *The Band Wagon Music Program* |
| Blue | *The Fisk Jubilee Choir* |
| Mutual | News |

July 7, 1940 - September 22, 1940
| | |
|---|---|
| NBC | *The Band Wagon Music Program* |
| Blue | *World's Fair Music Program* |
| Mutual | News |

## ELLERY QUEEN ON NBC

January 10, 1942 - February 7, 1942
| | |
|---|---|
| CBS | Various concert orchestras |
| Blue | *Little Ol' Hollywood* |
| Mutual | News |

February 14, 1942 - April 4, 1942
| | |
|---|---|
| CBS | Various concert orchestras |
| Blue | *The Message of Israel* |
| Mutual | News |

April 11, 1942 - May 9, 1942
CBS            *Tillie the Toiler*
Blue           *The Message of Israel*
Mutual         News

May 16, 1942 - July 4, 1942
CBS            *Tillie the Toiler*
Blue           Various concert orchestras *
Mutual         News and commentary

October 10, 1942 - October 17, 1942
CBS            *Soldiers With Wings*
Blue           Special Democracy Programs
Mutual         News and commentary with Arthur Hale

October 24, 1942
CBS            *Soldiers With Wings*
Blue           *Swap Night*
Mutual         News and commentary with Arthur Hale

October 31, 1942
CBS            *Thanks to the Yanks* starring Bob Hawk
Blue           *Swap Night*
Mutual         News and commentary with Arthur Hale

November 7, 1942 - November 21, 1942
CBS            *Thanks to the Yanks* starring Bob Hawk
Blue           *Sing for Dough*
Mutual         News and commentary with Arthur Hale

November 28, 1942
CBS            *Thanks to the Yanks* starring Bob Hawk
Blue           *The Message From Israel*
Mutual         News and commentary with Arthur Hale

December 5, 1942 - December 19, 1942
CBS            *Thanks to the Yanks* starring Bob Hawk
Blue           *The Green Hornet*
Mutual         News and commentary with Arthur Hale


* A special lecture, "An American University," replaced the Blue Network's musical program on May 23, 1942.

December 26, 1942 - January 16, 1943
CBS             *Thanks to the Yanks* starring Bob Hawk
Blue            *War Bond Specials* with all-star casts
Mutual          News and commentary with Arthur Hale

January 23, 1943 - January 30, 1943
CBS             *Thanks to the Yanks* starring Bob Hawk
Blue            *The Strange Dr. Karnac*
Mutual          News and commentary with Arthur Hale

February 6, 1943 - April 24, 1943
CBS             *Thanks to the Yanks* starring Bob Hawk
Blue            *The Danny Thomas Variety Show*
Mutual          News and commentary with Arthur Hale

May 1, 1943
CBS             *Thanks to the Yanks* starring Bob Hawk
Blue            *Breakfast at Sardi's*
Mutual          News and commentary with Arthur Hale

May 8, 1943 - May 22, 1943
CBS             *Thanks to the Yanks* starring Bob Hawk
Blue            *History Is Fun*
Mutual          News and commentary with Arthur Hale

May 29, 1943 - July 3, 1943
CBS             *Thanks to the Yanks* starring Bob Hawk
Blue            *Enough–And On Time*
Mutual          News and commentary with Arthur Hale

July 10, 1943 - August 14, 1943
CBS             Various orchestras
Blue            *Enough –And On Time*
Mutual          News and commentary with Arthur Hale

August 21, 1943 - August 28, 1943
CBS             *Suspense*
Blue            *Army Service Forces Presents*
Mutual          News and commentary with Arthur Hale

September 4, 1943 - October 2, 1943
CBS             *The Colonel Stoopnagle Show*
Blue            *What's New?*
Mutual          News and commentary with Arthur Hale

October 9, 1943 - February 26, 1944
CBS          *Thanks to the Yanks* starring Bob Hawk
Blue          *What's New?*
Mutual      News and commentary with Arthur Hale

March 4, 1944 - June 24, 1944
CBS          *Thanks to the Yanks* starring Bob Hawk
Blue          Various musical presentations
Mutual      News and commentary with Arthur Hale

July 1, 1944 - August 26, 1944
CBS          *Mrs. Miniver*
Blue          Various musical presentations
Mutual      News and commentary with Arthur Hale

September 2, 1944 - September 9, 1944
CBS          *Mrs. Miniver*
Blue          *Slanguage Quiz*
Mutual      News and commentary with Arthur Hale

September 16, 1944 - December 30, 1944
CBS          *America in the Air*
Blue          *On Stage, Everybody*
Mutual      News and commentary with Arthur Hale

## ELLERY QUEEN ON CBS

January 24, 1945 - April 18, 1945
May 2, 1945 - August 15, 1945
September 5, 1945 - September 12, 1945

NBC            Roth Orchestra and Chorus
Blue/ABC    *The Lone Ranger* *
Mutual        *Can You Top This?* (One exception: Mutual offered a studio program
                  on September 12, 1945)

September 19, 1945 - October 10, 1945
NBC            *Red Barber's Star Revue*
ABC            *The Lone Ranger*
Mutual        News and commentary with Cecil Brown **


* As of June 14, 1945, The Blue Network officially became ABC.
** Mutual offered a special, "Railroads: A Look Ahead" on October 3, 1945.

October 17, 1945 - February 20, 1946
NBC             *Red Barber's Star Revue*
ABC             *The Lone Ranger*
Mutual          News and commentary with Frank Singiser

February 27, 1946 - March 27, 1946
NBC             Various musical performances *
ABC             *The Lone Ranger*
Mutual          News and commentary with Frank Singiser

April 3, 1946
NBC             Various musical performances *
ABC             *The Lone Ranger*
Mutual          Harold G. Hoffman, talk and commentary

April 10, 1946
NBC             *Backstage at the Circus*
ABC             *The Lone Ranger*
Mutual          Harold G. Hoffman, talk and commentary

April 17, 1946 - May 29, 1946
NBC             Various musical performances *
ABC             *The Lone Ranger*
Mutual          Harold G. Hoffman, talk and commentary

June 5, 1946
NBC             Various musical performances *
ABC             *The Lone Ranger*
Mutual          *Battle of the Commentators* with Cecil Brown

June 12, 1946 - June 26, 1946
NBC             *Around the Town*
ABC             *The Lone Ranger*
Mutual          *Battle of the Commentators* with Cecil Brown

July 3, 1946 - August 28, 1946
NBC             *Claims Agent*
ABC             *The Lone Ranger*
Mutual          *Battle of the Commentators* with Cecil Brown


* Performing on a rotating basis were The Jack Harris Orchestra, The Erskine Hawkins Orchestra, The Blue Barron Orchestra and The Mills Brothers.

October 9, 1946, October 23, 1946 - November 6, 1946
NBC       *The Barry Wood Show*
ABC       *The Lone Ranger*
Mutual    *Battle of the Commentators* with Cecil Brown

December 4, 1946
NBC       *The Barry Wood Show*
ABC       *The Lone Ranger*
Mutual    Lowell Thomas, interviewed

December 11, 1946 - December 25, 1946
NBC       *The Barry Wood Show*
ABC       *The Lone Ranger*
Mutual    *The Listener Reports*

January 1, 1947
NBC       *The Barry Wood Show*
ABC       *The Lone Ranger*
Mutual    News with Vandeventer

January 8, 1947 - February 5, 1947
NBC       *The Barry Wood Show*
ABC       *The Lone Ranger*
Mutual    *The Listener Reports*

February 12, 1947 - April 2, 1947
NBC       *The Barry Wood Show*
ABC       *The Lone Ranger*
Mutual    *Strange As It Seems*

April 9, 1947 - April 16, 1947
NBC       *The Blue Barron Orchestra*
ABC       *The Lone Ranger*
Mutual    *Strange As It Seems*

## ELLERY QUEEN ON NBC

June 1, 1947 - June 8, 1947
CBS       *Kate Smith's Serenade*
ABC       *The Greatest Story Ever Told*
Mutual    *Nick Carter, Master Detective*

August 3, 1947 - August 10, 1947
CBS       *Sound Off* with the Warnow Orchestra
ABC       *The Greatest Story Ever Told*
Mutual    *Nick Carter, Master Detective*

August 17, 1947 - September 21, 1947
CBS         *The Pause That Refreshes*
ABC         *The Greatest Story Ever Told*
Mutual      *Nick Carter, Master Detective*


# ELLERY QUEEN ON ABC

November 27, 1947
CBS         *Club 15* with Bob Crosby
NBC         *The Guy Lombardo Orchestra*
Mutual      Wendell Noble, news

December 4, 1947 - January 22, 1948
CBS         *Club 15* with Bob Crosby
NBC         *Hollywood Open House*
Mutual      Wendell Noble, news

January 29, 1948 - March 18, 1948
CBS         *Mr. Keen, Tracer of Lost Persons*
NBC         *The George Burns and Gracie Allen Show*
Mutual      *The Ray Bloch Orchestra*

March 25, 1948 - May 27, 1948
CBS         *Mr. Keen, Tracer of Lost Persons*
NBC         *The Burns and Allen Show*
Mutual      *The Great Talent Hunt* (also known as *The Big Talent Hunt*)

185

# APPENDIX C: BIOGRAPHIES IN BRIEF: THE REGULARS

## 1. ELLERY QUEEN

Hugh Marlowe, the first actor to play Ellery on radio, was born Hugh Hipple in Philadelphia on January 30, 1911 and made his radio debut in 1931 as an announcer on Davenport, Iowa's WHO-WOC. Over the next few years he was heard on *Amateur Gentleman, Shell Chateau* and *Hollywood Hotel.* He made his Broadway debut in 1936 and his Hollywood debut a year later. He played Ellery on radio from the series' beginning (June 18, 1939) until the end of its first season (September 22, 1940), a total of 36 hour-long episodes and 31 that ran half an hour. During a little more than four months of the time he played Ellery one evening a week he could also be heard five times a week in the daytime serial *Brenda Curtis*, playing attorney Jim Curtis whose wife sacrifices her career as an actress to marry him. Less than two years after leaving *Ellery Queen*, Marlowe starred as Dr. Benjamin Ordway in another radio mystery series, *The Crime Doctor.* On Broadway he appeared with Gertrude Lawrence in *Lady in the Dark*; in the movies he had meaty roles opposite Gregory Peck in *Twelve O'Clock High* (1949), Bette Davis in *All About Eve* (1950) and Edward G. Robinson in *Illegal* (1955). He returned as Ellery on the 32-episode filmed TV series *The New Adventures of Ellery Queen* (1955-56) but his longest-running television role was as Jim Matthews in the daytime serial *Another World*, a part he played for almost 13 years. He died of a heart attack on May 2, 1982 at age 71.

*The Adventures of Ellery Queen* was off the air from late September 1940 until January 8, 1942, when it returned with Carleton Young in the role of Ellery. Young was born in Westfield, N.Y. on May 26, 1907. After studying drama at Carnegie Institute he toured with a stock company and later appeared in several Broadway productions. He made his radio debut in 1935 and had continuing roles in several daytime serials like *Carol Kennedy's Romance, Second Husband, Trouble House* and *Hilltop House.* He played Ellery between January 1942 and August 1943, about 70 30-minute episodes in all. In the years after his stint as the master detective he starred in two other radio mystery series, playing movie producer/ amateur sleuth Jim Laughton in *Hollywood Mystery Time* (1944-45) and lawyer/undercover crimefighter Philip Gault in *The Whisperer* (1951). After radio was displaced by television he played John Bates on *Leave It to Beaver.* Young died of cancer on July 11, 1971 at age 64.

In August 1943 Young signed a Hollywood contract and left the series. He was replaced as Ellery by Sydney Smith. Born in 1909, Smith had played supporting roles on daytime serials including *Abie's Irish Rose* and *Life Can Be Beautiful* and crime series like *Gang Busters.* He had also been host and narrator on the mystery anthology series Crime Club. He played Ellery for approximately forty months, longer than any other actor in any medium. After leaving the series he continued to act on the stage, on radio and TV and in movies. In his fifties he went back to school, earned a Master's degree and began a new career as Associate Professor of Theatre at Northern Illinois University. He retired in 1976, moved to the state of Washington and died there on March 4, 1978 at the age of 68.

The next Ellery Queen was a radio actor who had appeared on the show one evening in September 1943, serving as a guest armchair detective and matching wits with Sydney Smith whom he would eventually replace. Richard Coogan was born in Short Hills, N.J. on April 4, 1914, and played supporting roles on radio series such as *Molle Mystery Theater, The Mysterious Traveler* and *Hour of Mystery* before taking over the role of Ellery late in 1946. While portraying the master detective one evening a week he was also playing Abie on the daytime serial *Abie's Irish Rose*. In February 1947 Coogan was let go from *Ellery Queen* and soon afterward transitioned from radio to television, where he is best known for having starred in the live science-fiction series *Captain Video* (1949-50) and in the filmed Western series *The Californians* (1957-59). He is in his late eighties today and still miraculously healthy and active.

Coogan's replacement as Ellery was Lawrence Dobkin, who was born in New York City on September 16, 1919 and began acting on radio while still in high school, continuing to appear on the Yankee network while attending Yale drama school. Later he had regular parts on several radio mystery series – including *The Adventures of Nero Wolfe, The Man from Homicide* and *The Saint* – and also appeared in movies including the film noir classic *D.O.A.* (1949). During the 1950s he moved from radio to television, first as an actor and then as a director, contributing episodes to dozens of series including *The Rifleman, 77 Sunset Strip, The Donna Reed Show, Tarzan, Barnaby Jones* and *The Waltons*. He is still alive today and has written the introduction to this book.

The last actor to play Ellery on network radio was Howard Culver, who had the part only four or five weeks when the show was canceled. Culver was born in Colorado on June 2, 1918 but grew up in California. He debuted on radio in 1936 and carved out a dual career in the medium as both actor and newscaster. In the years before his brief stint as Ellery Queen he had appeared regularly on *The Hour of St. Francis* (despite its name a 15-minute dramatic series on religious themes) and *Strange Wills* and had hosted *We Deliver the Goods*, a musical variety show on which all the entertainers were seamen. After the cancellation of *Ellery Queen* Culver starred in the Western series *Straight Arrow*, served as narrator on the revived version of *Chandu, The Magician*, and had the male lead on *Defense Attorney*, playing not a lawyer but the newspaperman lover of the woman (Mercedes McCambridge) who had the title role. He died of meningitis on August 5, 1984 at age 66.

## 2. NIKKI PORTER

Fred Dannay and Manny Lee created the character of Ellery's secretary/girlfriend Nikki Porter expressly for radio at the urging of George Zachary, the original producer/director of the series. The first actress to play the part was Marian Shockley, who was born in Kansas City, Missouri on October 10, 1908. While a student majoring in history at the University of Missouri she was offered an acting job with a stock company. She made her Broadway debut in *Dear Old Darling* (1936). On radio she was heard on daytime dramas like *Abie's Irish Rose, Road of Life* and *My True Story* before Zachary offered her the part of Nikki.

187

Shockley and Zachary were married in October 1939 and the Nikki character was written out of at least two scripts so the newlyweds could have a honeymoon. Except for that interruption she played Nikki opposite Hugh Marlowe's Ellery throughout the series' first season, from June 1939 till September 1940, 67 episodes in all. When the series returned to the air in January 1942 with Carleton Young as Ellery, Shockley returned as Nikki and stayed in the part until September 1943. Less than two months later she again took over as Nikki and kept the role until the last broadcast of 1944. She and George Zachary were divorced after World War II and Shockley married actor Clayton "Bud" Collyer, who was best known on radio as the star of *Superman*. After Collyer's death in 1969, Shockley took up various humanitarian causes. She died on December 14, 1981.

Shockley's replacement as Nikki was Helen Lewis. Among the daytime serials on which Lewis had regular parts are *Kate Hopkins, Angel of Mercy, Ma Perkins* and *Road to Life*. In the mystery field she played Tess Trueheart on *Dick Tracy*. After less than two months as Nikki she was replaced by her own predecessor in the part, Marian Shockley.

For the 25 episodes broadcast between late January and mid-July of 1945, Nikki was portrayed by Barbara Terrell. Little about her career is known, but she later played the female lead in the daytime serial *We Love and Learn*.

Terrell's replacement was Gertrude Warner, who kept the part for 86 episodes broadcast between late July 1945 and late August 1946. Born in West Hartford, Connecticut on April 2, 1917, Warner had made her radio debut in 1935 on her hometown station WTIC. Four years later she joined the cast of the daytime serials *Against the Storm* and *Valiant Lady*. Later she starred in *The Man I Married, Joyce Jordan, M.D.* and *Ellen Randolph*. After leaving *Ellery Queen* she played the lead in the daytime serial *Whispering Streets*. She was the last actress to play Margot Lane on *The Shadow* and also the last to play Della Street on *Perry Mason*. After radio faded away Warner taught acting at Weist-Barron School and Oberlin College. She died in New York City on January 26, 1986.

*Ellery Queen* went on hiatus after the episode heard on August 28, 1946. When it returned for a seventh season on October 9, Nikki was played by Charlotte Keane. Little is known about her career beyond the fact that she had a continuing role in the daytime serial *Backstage Wife*. Keane continued as Nikki until the last sponsored episode of the series, broadcast September 21, 1947.

After another hiatus the series returned on a sustaining basis, with Virginia Gregg now playing Nikki. Gregg was born in Harrisburg, Illinois on March 6, 1916 and started out as a bass viola player with the Pasadena Symphony. She and five other young women formed a group known as the Singing Strings which was heard on the CBS and Mutual radio networks. Among the series on which she appeared are *The Jack Benny Program, Escape, Lum & Abner, Philip Marlowe, T-Man, The Line-Up* and *Dragnet*. She had continuing parts on *Let George Do It, Dr. Kildare* and *Richard Diamond, Private Detective*. Her stint as Nikki lasted only for about five or six weeks. She continued to act on radio and TV until her death of lung cancer on September 15, 1986 at the age of 70.

From January 8, 1948 until the last episode of *Ellery Queen* at the end of May, Nikki was portrayed by Kaye Brinker. Born in Seattle, Washington in 1915, Brinker had hosted her own radio talk show, *True to Life* (1939-40), and had been the announcer on *Poetic Melodies*. Among the daytime serials in which she had supporting roles are *Joyce Jordan, M.D., Our Gal Sunday, Everywoman* and *We, The Abbotts*. She starred in the daytime drama *Manhattan Mother* and was the announcer on *Romance*. She married Ellery Queen co-creator Manfred B. Lee in 1943. After Manny's death in 1971 she moved first to Florida and finally to County Cork, Ireland, where she died on May 11, 1991.

## 3. INSPECTOR RICHARD QUEEN

The first actor to play Ellery's father on radio was Santos Ortega, who was born on June 30, 1899 and whose ability to assume almost any accent guaranteed that he'd be one of the first to be called whenever a radio script called for an ethnic. Ortega holds the distinction of having lasted longer in his role than any other regular on *Ellery Queen*, a total of almost 7 ½ years from the first episode of the series until late in 1946. His other contributions to the radio mystery genre are huge. He was the first actor to play the radio version of *Perry Mason* and also starred in *Nero Wolfe, Bulldog Drummond* and *The Adventures of Charlie Chan*, not to mention his stint as Commissioner Weston on *The Shadow*. As Dr. Doom he hosted the anthology series *It's Murder* and as Inspector Slade he narrated the puzzles that audience members were challenged to solve on the short-lived quiz show *Who Dun It?* His last major starring role on radio was in *Hannibal Cobb* (1950-51). In 1956 he signed with CBS-TV to play Grandpa Hughes on the daytime serial *As The World Turns* and was still in the part twenty years later when he took a brief trip to Fort Lauderdale, Florida and, on April 10, 1976, died there.

Ortega's replacement as Inspector Queen was Bill Smith, who played the role for about nine months between late 1946 and September 1947. Smith had had regular roles on daytime radio serials like *The Brighter Day* and *Stella Dallas*. In the mystery genre he was featured on *The Adventures of the Thin Man*. After his stint on *Ellery Queen* he joined the cast of *Thousand Dollar Reward*, a program on which the actors presented a murder mystery which was followed up by a random telephone call to a listener who received the titular prize if he or she could identify the culprit.

Several weeks into *Ellery Queen*'s eighth and final season on radio, the role of Inspector Queen was taken over by Herb Butterfield, who played criminals, cops and victims on countless mystery programs including *Crime Classics, Mystery in the Air, Broadway Is My Beat, Pete Kelly's Blues* and *The Man from Homicide*. He was also in the regular cast of *Dangerous Assignment* and *The Halls of Ivy*. Butterfield continued as Ellery's father until the Queen series went off the air at the end of May 1948. He died on May 2, 1957 at age 61.

## 4. SERGEANT VELIE

Howard Smith, radio's first Sergeant Velie, was born in Attleboro, Massachusetts on August 12, 1894. He made his professional acting debut in 1915 and his first radio appearance on *The Collier Hour* in 1928. He worked with Orson Welles on *The Campbell Playhouse*, with Al Jolson on *Shell Chateau*, and had continuing roles on *The Aldrich Family, Pretty Kitty Kelly* and *Dick Tracy*. Among the series on which he played supporting roles over the years are *Crime Doctor, Mr. District Attorney, Eno Crime Clues, Gang Busters, The Shadow, The Lux Radio Theater* and *The March of Time*. Like countless other radio actors, Smith moved from that medium into television in the 1950s. He died of a heart attack on January 10, 1968 at age 73.

Four or five months after *Ellery Queen* debuted on radio, Smith was replaced by Ted de Corsia, who played Sergeant Velie for the next seven years. Born in Brooklyn on September 29, 1905, Edward Gildea de Corsia enjoyed a long acting career in vaudeville, radio, movies and TV. On radio he starred on *Captain Courage* and *McGarry and his Mouse* and played Commissioner Weston on *The Shadow*. After his long run on *Ellery Queen* he starred as Inspector Peter Black on *Pursuit* and was heard regularly on the mystery-adventure series *Christopher London*. He also appeared in more than 30 movies, usually playing a brutal thug like his character Garza in *The Naked City* (1948). He died on April 11, 1973 at age 67.

In the fall of 1946 the part of Sergeant Velie was taken over by Ed Latimer, a utility actor who kept very busy in radio during the 1930s and 1940s. Among the series in which he had continuing roles are *Nick Carter, Master Detective The Romance of Helen Trent* and *House in the Country*. During World War II he starred in the half-hour drama series *Wings for the Martins*, which was designed to inform parents about the problems of raising children, and also in *Hasten the Day*, a 15-minute serial about the home front in wartime, produced under the auspices of the Office of War Information. Latimer continued as Sergeant Velie on *Ellery Queen* until September of 1947 except for two weeks in June.

During those two weeks the sergeant was portrayed by George Matthews. Not much is known about Matthews' career in radio but he co-starred on the Mutual boxing series *Fight Camp* in the summer of 1941 and, after his short short tenure as Velie, had a continuing part on *Hearts in Harmony*, a series about a USO volunteer entertainer.

From late November of 1947 until *Ellery Queen* left the airwaves in May 1948, Alan Reed played Velie. Born Teddy Bergman in New York City on August 20, 1907, Reed worked on Broadway with Alfred Lunt and Lynn Fontanne but appeared much more frequently on radio. During the 1940s he played the Irish cop Clancy on *Duffy's Tavern* and the Runyonesque cab driver Shrevie on *The Shadow*, and for a brief while had his own program, *The Falstaff Show*, a 15-minute comedy/variety series heard three times a week over ABC. On television he supplied the voice of Fred Flintstone on *The Flintstones*. He died on June 14, 1977.

# 5. DOC PROUTY

The medical examiner character who appeared in the vast majority of Ellery Queen novels and short stories didn't last too long on radio – only long enough to be played by two actors. The first of these was Robert Strauss, who was born in New York City on November 8, 1913 and entered radio in the early 1930s. On *The Tattered Man* (1933-34) he told stories to an audience of juveniles. He played a variety of hillbilly characters in radio series like *Heart Throbs of the Hills, Grits and Gravy* and *Mrs. Wiggs of the Cabbage Patch*. After leaving *Ellery Queen* in mid-February of 1940 he had supporting roles in a large number of other radio series including *The Aldrich Family, The Damon Runyon Theater, Famous Jury Trials, Snow Village Sketches* and *Howie Wing*. His best-known role was not on radio but in the movie *Stalag 17* (1953) where he played a homesick GI in a German prison camp. He died from complications of a stroke on February 20, 1975 at age 61.

His replacement as Doc Prouty was Arthur Allen, who was born in Gowanda, New York on April 18, 1881 and appeared regularly in movies and stage plays as well as on radio. In late 1929 and early 1930 he and Louis Mason co-starred on their own music program, *The Schradertown Band*. Between 1934 and 1936 he co-starred with Parker Fennelly on the 15-minute series *Big Ben Dream Dramas*. Not long before taking over as Doc Prouty, Allen rejoined Fennelly for the 30-minute series *Four Corners, U.S.A.* The role of Prouty was dropped after Allen had played the part in nine episodes. He went on to supporting roles in series like *Gibbs and Finney, General Delivery* and *The Bishop and the Gargoyle*. During World War II he and Parker Fennelly teamed up yet again as co-stars of the comedy series *Masters of Down East*. Allen died on August 25, 1947 at age 66.

# 6. THE ANNOUNCERS

During its nine-year run on radio the *Ellery Queen* series employed a total of five announcers, beginning with Ken Roberts. Born Saul Trochman in New York City on February 22, 1906, Roberts began his radio career in 1928, joined the CBS network three years later, and spent most of his career serving as announcer on so many different series that it would probably take a page to list them all. His stint on *Ellery Queen* lasted for all 36 of the series' 60-minute episodes and for the first nine episodes that ran half an hour. Roberts occasionally had acting parts on radio, for example as Cokey on *Easy Aces* between 1937 and 1941, but usually he was an announcer. Among the countless series in which he performed that function during the 1940s are *Big Town, Crime Doctor* and *The Shadow*. Between 1945 and 1947 he emceed the popular game show *Quick As a Flash*. His son, actor Tony Roberts, has been a regular in Woody Allen movies.

Roberts' replacement on *Ellery Queen* was Bert Parks, who was born in Atlanta, Georgia on December 30, 1914 and began his radio career at 16 when he was hired by a hometown station as a singer and announcer. After two years he moved to CBS, where he found jobs as announcer and vocalist on the Eddie Cantor program and later emceed for Benny Goodman and Xavier Cugat.

Parks took over as announcer on *Ellery Queen* late in April 1940 and stayed until September 22 when the series left the air for a hiatus that lasted almost a year and a half. By that time the U.S. was in World War II and Parks joined the Army. After his discharge he returned to radio and, as emcee of programs like *Break the Bank* and *Stop the Music!*, became the most popular quizmaster in the medium. During the 1950s he hosted as many as twelve radio and TV programs a week but he is best known today as the perennial emcee of the Miss America beauty pageants. In his early sixties he played a suspect in an episode of the 60-minute *Ellery Queen* TV series (1975-76) that starred Jim Hutton. He died in La Jolla, California on February 2, 1992.

Ellery and his entourage returned to radio in January 1942 with both a sponsor and an announcer that would stay with the series until the last week of 1944. The sponsor was Bromo-Seltzer and the announcer Ernest Chappell, who was born in Syracuse, New York on June 10, 1903. After graduating from Syracuse University in 1925, Chappell joined local station WFBL and began a career as station manager, production manager and vice-president for programming. During the 1930s he began moving away from the business side of radio and into a new career as an announcer, initially on programs like *Are You a Genius?* and *Show of the Week*. He served as both announcer and production supervisor for Orson Welles' *Campbell Playhouse*, coached Eleanor Roosevelt for her radio broadcasts, and announced Edward R. Murrow's famous news reports from London during Hitler's Blitzkrieg. At the 1939 New York World's Fair he hosted the first beauty contest ever broadcast on television. After his long stint on *Ellery Queen* he served as announcer on anthology series like *The Big Story* and *Quiet, Please* and did Pall Mall cigarette commercials for 17 years. He died of a stroke in North Palm Beach, Florida on July 4, 1983, less than a month after his eightieth birthday.

For the first three weeks of 1945 *Ellery Queen* went on hiatus, returning on January 24 under the sponsorship of Anacin and with a new announcer who, like Chappell, would last precisely as long as the sponsor did. Don Hancock was born in Anderson, Indiana on October 10, 1910 and began his radio career in 1930 as an account executive and part-time announcer for his hometown radio station. He became a full-time announcer after moving to Chicago a few years later. In 1940 he transferred to New York and soon found himself announcing on countless radio programs including such mystery series as *Famous Jury Trials, Front Page Trials, Perry Mason* and *The Shadow*. His stint on *Ellery Queen* continued until September 1947 when the series lost its sponsorship and once again went on hiatus. Hancock continued in broadcasting for another 30 years and served as announcer of the Indiana Symphony's summer concerts even after retirement. He died on May 6, 1980 at age 69.

*Ellery Queen* returned to radio late in November 1947 but without commercial sponsorship. From then until it left the airwaves for good at the end of May 1948 the announcer was Paul Masterson. Before taking over that function he had served as one of the two announcers on bandleader Sammy Kaye's series *So You Want to Lead a Band*.

# 7. THE PRODUCERS AND DIRECTORS

George Zachary was born on June 1, 1911 and joined CBS Radio in the 1930s. He produced and directed the musical variety series *99 Men and a Girl* but had a burning ambition to create an hour-long detective series whose audience would be invited to match wits with the principal character and perhaps even solve the mystery ahead of him. Once he realized that the Ellery Queen novels with their "Challenge to the Reader" approximated his own concept for a radio series, he arranged with Frederic Dannay and Manfred B. Lee to bring their already world-famous sleuth into the new medium. Zachary produced and directed *Ellery Queen* throughout its first season, which consisted of 36 hour-long episodes and 31 that ran half an hour. He continued to serve as producer when the series returned to the air in January 1942 after a hiatus of almost a year and a half but left after a few months to join the Office of War Information. Later he enlisted in the Navy and, at the end of World War II, resumed his career in radio. While producing the *Ford Theatre* anthology series (1947-48) he revived one of Ellery's early 60-minute radio adventures with the original cast. As radio gave way to television Zachary went with the flow and worked on the production of early TV series like *The Life of Riley*. He died of a heart attack in May of 1964.

Bruce Kamman was born in Cincinnati, Ohio on February 18, 1893 and made his radio debut in Kansas City in 1920. He is best known for creating the Chicago-based comedy series *Kaltenmeyer's Kindergarten*, which debuted in 1932 and starred Kamman himself as Professor August Kaltenmeyer, D.U.N. (Doctor of Utter Nonsense). After the outbreak of World War II the series was de-Germanized and revamped as *Kindergarten Kapers*, with Kamman's character renamed Professor Ulysses S. Applegate, but died not long after it was sanitized. Kamman took over as producer and director of *Ellery Queen* at the beginning of 1943 and continued until just before Thanksgiving of that year. He is not known to have directed on any other radio series. He died in October 1969.

Kamman was replaced by Bob Steel, who was born on January 31, 1917 and began as an office boy at the Ruthrauff & Ryan advertising agency. By late 1943 he was producing and directing both the *Ellery Queen* series and *The Shadow* and also writing or rewriting occasional *Shadow* scripts under the byline of Catherine B. Stemmler. He is remembered for trying to get his players to interact better on the air by using overhead instead of floor microphones and for performing yoga-like exercises during script rehearsals. In 1946 the Mystery Writers of America organization awarded Steel a scroll for his work on *Ellery Queen* but the scroll was delayed in production and Steel didn't receive it until forty years later. Among the other series he either produced or directed are *Big Town, Aunt Jenny's Real-Life Stories*, and *The Brighter Day*. After leaving radio he became a manager at one of New York City's Brooks Brothers clothing stores. He died on October 9, 1994.

Tom Victor took over as producer and director of *Ellery Queen* some time during the years when it was sponsored by Anacin and continued until September 1947 when the series lost its sponsor and left the air for a little more than two months.

Upon its return in November 1947 without commercial sponsorship, the producer and director of the next 22 episodes was Dick Woollen. The only other series Woollen is known to have worked on in the same capacities is *Mr. President*, which began with a dramatic episode based on some historical event and then challenged listeners to guess which of the never-named characters in the episode went on to become president of the United States.

For its last five weeks on network radio *Ellery Queen* was produced and directed by Dwight Hauser, who was born on July 4, 1911 and whose career in the medium encompassed everything from acting – for example, on the thriller series *Dark Venture* – to providing spooky sound effects for the horror anthology *The Hermit's Cave*. Prior to his brief stint on *Ellery Queen* he had directed the *Defense Attorney* series and produced *The Adventures of Bill Lance*. Later he directed such adventure and mystery series as *I Fly Anything* and *The Man from Homicide*. He died in January 1969.

## 8. THE MUSIC MAKERS

The first and by far the best known of the composers and conductors who worked on *Ellery Queen* was Bernard Herrmann. Born in New York City on June 29, 1911, Hermann studied composition at NYU and the Juilliard School of Music. In 1931, around the same time he founded the New York Chamber Orchestra, he began his career in radio as an assistant to bandleader Johnny Green, conducting studio musicians in broadcast programs of popular and light classical music. In 1934 he joined CBS as composer and conductor of the network's symphony orchestra, and over the next twenty years he wrote, arranged and conducted music for more than 1200 programs such as *Invitation to Music, American School of the Air* and Exploring Music. Not long before his stint on *Ellery Queen*, Herrmann wrote the music for Orson Welles' *Mercury Theater of the Air*, including the famous 1938 version of *The War of the Worlds* that panicked countless listeners into thinking that Martians had invaded New Jersey. He continued on *Ellery Queen* for only ten weeks. The following year he went to Hollywood to write the music for Welles' first movie, *Citizen Kane*. But even after he had established himself as one of Hollywood's top composers, his music continued to be heard on CBS radio series like *Suspense*. He is best known for writing the scores for dozens of movies, including the Alfred Hitchcock classics *Vertigo* and *Psycho*, but the music he had written under contract for CBS continued to be heard (although without being credited to him) on that network's TV series of the late 1950s including *Perry Mason, Have Gun-Will Travel* and *Rawhide*. Herrmann died of a heart attack on December 24, 1975, at the age of 64.

Herrmann was replaced as composer and conductor on *Ellery Queen* by Leith Stevens, who was born in Mount Moriah, Missouri on September 13, 1909 and, after completing his education, toured the country as the piano accompanist for Madame Schumann-Heink and other singers. In 1930 he was hired by the CBS network and composed the music for series like *The Columbia Workshop, Molle Merry Minstrels* and *Death Valley Days*.

194

Later he headed two musical programs of his own, *Leith Stevens' Harmonies* and *Saturday Night Swing Club*. His tenure on *Ellery Queen* lasted just two weeks. During World War II he joined the Office of War Information and directed radio programs for U.S. forces in the Pacific. After the war he conducted the music for countless radio series including *Big Town, Escape, Suspense* and *Yours Truly, Johnny Dollar*. He died suddenly of a heart attack on July 23, 1970 after learning that his wife had just been killed in an auto accident.

Stevens' replacement on *Ellery Queen* was Lyn Murray, whose tenure was much longer, running from mid-September of 1939 until the series left the air almost exactly a year later for a hiatus that lasted until the beginning of 1942. Born in London on December 6, 1909, Murray worked as a sailor and newspaperman before entering radio. Between 1932 and 1936 he played the male lead on Bill and Ginger, a Philadelphia-based show that eventually went national and brought Murray to New York and CBS. He founded a choral group, The Lyn Murray Singers, which was heard on *Voice of Firestone, Your Hit Parade* and other music programs. He provided background music for countless radio series and led the CBS network's symphony, dance bands and string ensembles. Hollywood called in the late 1940s and Stevens spent the rest of his career preparing music for movies and TV series. He died in Los Angeles on May 20, 1989.

When *Ellery Queen* returned to the airwaves at the beginning of 1942, it had a new sponsor, Bromo-Seltzer, and a new music policy: for the rest of its time on network radio the music accompanying each episode came from an organ. The first organist to play on the series was Charles Paul, who stayed through the second, third and fourth seasons and left in the middle of season five when Bromo-Seltzer dropped the series. During his career Paul also supplied organ music for countless radio soap operas and some mystery series including *The Shadow*.

Ellery was off the airwaves during the first three weeks of 1945 but returned on January 24, now sponsored by Anacin and with an unidentified musician at the organ. How many people sounded eerie chords on the program over its next two and a half years remains a mystery. The next person known to have served as organist on the series is Chet Kingsbury, who took over during the two weeks the series was on the air in June 1947 and returned to his post after its summer vacation. Like Charles Paul, Kingsbury supplied organ music for any number of daytime serials and for mystery series like *Bulldog Drummond* and *Special Investigator*. His time on *Ellery Queen* ended when the series again left the air in September 1947.

It returned in late November 1947 with a new organist who stayed till the cancellation of the series at the end of May 1948. Rex Koury was born in London on March 18, 1911 and came to the U.S. at an early age. After studying music with private tutors he became an organist for the Keith and Orpheum theater chains, then signed with NBC Radio and served as a studio organist and pianist between 1939 and 1942. Later he became west coast music director for ABC, a position he held between 1947 and 1958. From 1963 to 1970 he worked in the same capacity for the west coast stations of the NBC television network, mainly supervising the music for daytime soap operas. In later years he toured as a concert organist.

195

# APPENDIX D:  BIOGRAPHIES IN BRIEF: THE GUEST ARMCHAIR DETECTIVES

The following capsule biographies are designed to provide curious readers with information about the dozens of personalities who served as guest armchair detectives for one or more *Ellery Queen* episodes.  The paragraph numbers are keyed to the episode numbers as they appear in our week-by-week log of the series.  Much more information about most of these men and women can be accessed on the Web with the help of Google or any other comprehensive search engine.

1.  Peter Arno (1904-1968) began selling cartoons to *The New Yorker* in 1925, shortly after the magazine was launched, and continued to do so until his death more than forty years later.

Author Ruth McKenney (1911-1972) is best known as the author of *My Sister Eileen* (1938), a book that became the basis for the smash-hit Broadway musical *Wonderful Town* (1953).

Frederick Chase Taylor (1897-1950), who used the stage name of Colonel Stoopnagle, was one of radio's earliest true satirists.  He began his career on the air in 1930 and hosted and starred in numerous radio programs including *Stoopnagle's Stooperoos* and *The Minute Men*.  The announcer for one of his quiz programs during the early 1940s was Ken Roberts, the first announcer on the *Ellery Queen* series.

2.  Ed Gardner (1901-1963) started out as a theatrical hustler and promoter, working for small stock companies in every capacity from director to script stylist.  He first became involved with radio while working for the J. Walter Thompson advertising agency and wound up as the director of programs such as *Ripley's Believe It Or Not*, *Good News*, *The Rudy Vallee Show* and *This Is New York*.  From directing he turned to acting on radio and is best known as the star of the popular comedy series *Duffy's Tavern*, "where the elite meet to eat."

Humorist Gelett Burgess (1866-1951) wrote comic essays and verses – the best known of which is probably "The Purple Cow" – and also illustrated his own work.

Princess Alexandra Kropotkin, an exile from the Bolshevik revolution, translated an abridged version of Tolstoy's *War and Peace* and also wrote *The Best of Russian Cooking*, a guide to the cuisine of her native land.

Deems Taylor (1885-1966) was a serious composer whose works were performed at the Metropolitan Opera thirty times but he is best known as a music critic.

4.  Craig Earl (1895-1985) was a law school graduate and worked as a circus tightrope walker and magician before becoming involved with radio.  Known as the King Midas of the medium, Earl hosted the game show *Professor Quiz*, which was on CBS during the same season *Ellery Queen* debuted on the same network.

Betty Garde (1905-1989) made her professional stage debut at age 17.  She made her movie debut in 1929 and began her long radio career in 1935 in the title role of *Mrs. Wiggs of the Cabbage Patch*.  She was a supporting actress on hundreds of programs over a 20-year period and played Aunt Eller in the original Broadway cast of Rodgers and Hammerstein's *Oklahoma!* (1943).

Two years after her appearance on *Ellery Queen*, playwright Lillian Hellman (1905-1984) won the 1941 New York Drama Critics Circle Award for *Watch on the Rhine*. She had a long-term relationship with mystery writer Dashiell Hammett, author of *The Maltese Falcon* and other classic crime novels, and another liaison with director Herman Shumlin, who appeared on *Ellery Queen* with her.

Herman Shumlin (1898-1979) first made his mark on Broadway when he directed the stage version of *Grand Hotel* (1930), which was based on a novel by future guest armchair detective Vicki Baum. A few years later he discovered a new playwright named Lillian Hellman, and directed most of the Broadway plays that made her famous. During World War II he came to Hollywood to direct the film version of Hellman's play *Watch on the Rhine* (1943). During the early 1960s he produced and directed the U.S. version of *The Deputy*, Rolf Hochhuth's controversial play about the Jews, the Nazis and Pope Pius XII.

6. Playwright Dale Eunson (1904-2000) was the author of many movie scripts and stage plays, one of which became the basis of the Broadway musical and later movie *How to Marry a Millionaire*. Decades later he wrote scripts for TV series like *The Waltons* and *Little House on the Prairie*. Katherine Albert (1903-1970) was Eunson's wife and writing partner.

John S. Young (1901?-1976) was a radio pioneer who rose to become NBC's highest paid announcer and foreign news commentator. During the year of his appearance on *Ellery Queen* he served as director of broadcasting at the New York World's Fair, hosting the radio show *Let's Go to the Fair* and introducing the new medium of television.

7. All four guest armchair detectives for this episode about a boy's involvement with murder were New York child welfare officials. Daisy Amoury (1901-1984) was manager of the New York *Herald-Tribune*'s Fresh Air Fund, a charity that enabled urban youths to enjoy summer vacations in the country. Lewis Birdseye (1873-1942) was connected with the St. John's Guild Floating Hospital, a vessel based in NewYork Harbor which took city children on river excursions during the hot summer months. Helen Leighty worked for the Children's Welfare Federation and Dr. Lloyd B. Sharp for Life Camps.

9. All four guest armchair detectives for this episode were musicians. Howard Barlow (1892-1972) was music director of the CBS network, a position he held for many years before his appearance on *Ellery Queen* and for three years afterward. Johnny Green (1908?-1989) was a bandleader, pianist and composer whose songs include "Body and Soul" and "I Cover the Waterfront." Raymond Paige (1900?-1965) composed and conducted music for numerous radio programs including *Chandu, The Magician, Hollywood Hotel* and *The Silver Summer Revue*. Mark Warnow (1900-1949) was an orchestra leader and music director who led the *Lucky Strike Hit Parade* radio orchestra for six years.

197

10.   All four guest armchair detectives for this week's episode were photojournalists.   The best known of the four and the moderator for the group was Margaret Bourke-White (1904-1971).   The others were Henry Casler, James Crayhon (1902?-1976) and Don Doherty.

11.   Estelle Levy, later and better known as Gwen Davies, made her radio debut at the age of five on *Helen and Mary*, a program that later evolved into the long-running *Let's Pretend*.   She literally grew up on the airwaves, beginning with youthful roles and eventually playing more mature characters.   Less than two years after appearing on *Ellery Queen* she changed her name to Gwen Davies and became a staff vocalist for CBS, working with Dick Haymes, Bobby Sherwood and Frank Sinatra.

Arthur Ross (1924-    ) became the youngest master of ceremonies in radio when in 1938, at the tender age of 14, he hosted *March of Games*.

12.   All the guest armchair detectives on this episode were artists in different fields.   Tony Sarg (1880-1947) was both an artist and a puppeteer.   During each holiday season beginning in 1935, he designed a new animated window display for Macy's department store which cost $50,000 to install.   He also designed children's clothes with Mother Goose and Alice in Wonderland motifs and decals for decorating children's nurseries.   Dean Cornwell (1892?-1960) was well known for his work in Cosmopolitan.   After his guest appearance on *Ellery Queen* he became famous for his patriotic war posters and his full-page color advertisements for products like Seagram's Whiskey and Coca-Cola.   Ruth Garth was an industrial designer.   Belgian-born Suzanne Silvercruys (1900?-1973), whose father was the chief justice of his country's highest court, worked for the relief of her homeland during and after World War I and sculpted a bust of President Herbert Hoover in 1928.

15.   For the four artists who were guests this week, see 12 above.

16.   Parks Johnson (1891-1970) had served as a World War I army officer and worked as a cotton broker and as head of his own advertising agency before joining with Jerry Belcher in 1932 to create the radio show *Sidewalk Interviews*.   Eventually the program was retitled *Vox Pop* and went national, with Belcher replaced as co-host by Wally Butterworth (1915-1993).   Guests received prizes for guessing the answers to trick questions and were invited to speak their minds on any subject.   Both Johnson and Butterworth appeared on *Ellery Queen* several times as guest armchair detectives.

18.   Harry Kurnitz (1907-1968), a former reporter, came to Hollywood in 1938 and became a prolific writer of screenplays.   He worked on the scripts of M-G-M's *Shadow of The Thin Man* (1941) and *The Thin Man Goes Home* (1944), and years later wrote the screenplay for Billy Wilder's 1957 film version of Agatha Christie's play *Witness for the Prosecution*.

30.   Russell Markert (1899-1980) is best known as the founder of what became the Rockettes chorus line, which began in 1925 when he selected dancing girls for the Missouri Rockets precision dance team.   Markert and his troupe toured the country and eventually found a permanent home at New York's Radio City Music Hall.

Helen Sioussat was assistant to the treasurer of the Planning & Coordinating Committee for the petroleum industry in 1935. While in Washington she met Phillips H. Lord, producer of radio programs such as *Gang Busters*, *Seth Parker* and *Mr. District Attorney*. In 1936 she started a career in radio as Edward R. Murrow's assistant at CBS. A year after her appearance on *Ellery Queen* she created, produced and hosted *Table Talk with Helen Sioussat*, one of the first round-table discussion programs on television.

32. An all-star cast! A positively colossal line-up! George and Martha Washington, Napoleon Bonaparte, Benjamin Franklin and Robert E. Lee! Not the originals of course, who all died long before radio was even imagined, but everyday New Yorkers whose whimsical parents had named them after those historical personalities.

34. Donald Cook (1901-1961) was known primarily as a stage and screen actor but on radio he played Gertrude Lawrence's husband on *Skylark*, Charlie on the daytime serial *Charlie and Jesse*, and Dr. Allison on *My Son Jeep*. Cook had starred as Ellery Queen in *The Spanish Cape Mystery* (1935), the earliest movie about the character.

49. New York sportswriter Arthur Mann (1901?-1963) was attempting to make an appearance on every major New York quiz show during the early 1940s. Three weeks before this *Ellery Queen* broadcast, CBS premiered *Choose Up Sides*, a quiz program on which one four-man team of athletes and another of sports writers matched wits as to their sports knowledge, with each week's winning team receiving fifty dollars. Sports columnist Henry McLemore was the quizmaster, with Mann and boxing expert Caswell Adams serving as team captains. The show was cancelled after three months on the air.

57. Dr. Henry R. Junemann (1912-1996) was an instructor at Columbia University Dental School.

58. Big Band singer Carol Bruce, best known for her role in the musical comedy *Louisiana Purchase*, made one of her early radio appearances on this *Ellery Queen* episode. Two years later she signed on as a regular singer for *The Al Jolson Program*. During the summer of 1945 she became one of the musical ranch hands on the Andrews Sisters' *Sunday on N-K Ranch*.

59. Benny Baker (1907-1994) played a stooge for Lou Holtz in the early version of radio's *The Chesterfield Program*. He also played supporting roles in numerous movies including *The Crime Nobody Saw* (Paramount, 1937), which was based on *Danger, Men Working*, a short-lived stage play written by Ellery Queen creators Frederic Dannay and Manfred B. Lee in collaboration with Lowell Brentano.

60. Doris Sharp is credited with creating the Radio Registry, an office similar to Central Casting in Hollywood, permitting radio producers and directors to make contacts with actors.

61. Andrew S. Telep was the editor of a small-town newspaper in Mayfield, Pennsylvania.

68. Frank Buck (1884-1950) was an outdoor adventurer and so-called lion tamer, whose slogan regarding the hunt for ferocious beasts was "Bring 'em back alive." Between 1932 and 1934 Buck played himself on a radio program of the same name, recounting his exploits capturing wild animals. RKO Radio Pictures transcribed and distributed the programs to local stations as a promotion for Buck's 1932 movie, also entitled *Bring 'em Back Alive*. Buck played himself on the screen in *Wild Cargo* (1934), *Tiger Fangs* (1943), and Abbott and Costello's *Africa Screams* (1949).

Actress Dorothy McGuire (1916-2001) began her career in regional theater, then came to New York and debuted on Broadway as Martha Scott's understudy in *Our Town* (1938). Soon after her appearance on *Ellery Queen* she made her movie debut starring in *Claudia* (1943) and went on to play the female leads in such films as *A Tree Grows in Brooklyn* (1945), *The Spiral Staircase* (1946) and *Gentleman's Agreement* (1947), her performance in which won her an Oscar nomination.

Artist Neysa McMein (1888-1949) drew front cover illustrations for most of the major American magazines of her time including the *Saturday Evening Post, Woman's Home Companion* and *McCall's*, for which she drew every cover between 1923 and 1937. Her best known work of the 1940s is the image of Betty Crocker that she created for General Mills.

For Frederick Chase Taylor, see 1 above.

69. Charles Herbert was a musician known for his numerous compositions. A little more than a year after his guest shot on *Ellery Queen* he became the producer of *The Electric Hour*, a weekly radio musical program broadcast from the soundstage of the Walt Disney Studios.

For Mark Warnow, see 9 above.

Meyer Davis (1893-1976) was a busy orchestra leader before his guest appearance on *Ellery Queen*. He had many units playing simultaneously on different stations during the 1920s and 1930s.

Ham(mond E.) Fisher (1901-1955) created the famous *Joe Palooka* comic strip. Years later he committed suicide after being expelled from the National Cartoonists Society for falsifying information during a court trial.

70. Aubrey Waller Cook began a series of piano recitals in 1926 on Kansas City, Missouri station KMBC, then went national and continued on the air for 26 years.

Big Band singer Bea Wain (1912-    ), voted the most popular female vocalist of 1938, began her radio career as a youthful performer on *The Children's Hour* and *Coast-to-Coast on a Bus*. She and her husband, Andre Baruch, returned to *Ellery Queen* years later as tandem armchair detectives.

Texas-born Lois January (1913-    ) played the female lead in many B Western films of the late 1930s opposite shoot-em-up stars like Bob Steele, Tim McCoy and Johnny Mack Brown.  She had a tiny part in *The Wizard of Oz* (1939), appearing during the song "The Merry Old Land of Oz." By the time of her appearance on *Ellery Queen* she had left Hollywood for New York and was performing in Broadway musicals.

George Jessel (1898-1981) spent most of his early career touring the vaudeville circuit, where he created his famous "Hello Mama" song/routine.  His popularity as an after-dinner speaker led President Franklin D. Roosevelt to call him "Toastmaster General of the U.S.A." He starred in numerous radio programs and made countless guest appearances on other shows, mainly comedies.

71.  Norman Corwin (1910-    ), said science-fiction writer Ray Bradbury, was "the greatest director, the greatest writer and the greatest producer in the history of radio." He was responsible for such series as *The Columbia Workshop* and *26 by Corwin*.  During World War II he won acclaim for a series of patriotic radio plays ranging from *We Hold These Truths*, on the Bill of Rights, to *On a Note of Triumph*, celebrating the Allied victory over Hitler.  He received the One World award, two Peabody medals, an Oscar nomination, an Emmy, a Golden Globe, and an induction into the Radio Hall of Fame.  In his early nineties he remains alive and active.

Gypsy Rose Lee (1914-1970) was one of the most famous strippers of all time, receiving more free press than anyone else in the business and sometimes called the most publicized woman in the world..  She was billed as the author of two whodunits – *The G-String Murders* (1941) and *Mother Finds a Body* (1942) – but both were actually written by veteran mystery novelist Craig Rice, who herself was a guest on *Ellery Queen* years later.

72.  Baseball legend Mel Ott (1909-1958) played with the New York Giants for 22 seasons.  Using an unorthodox batting style of lifting his right foot prior to impact, he smashed 511 home runs, hitting 30 or more in a season eight times and winning or sharing home run honors on six occasions.

Hank Worden (1901-1992) was raised on a Montana cattle ranch and toured the country in rodeos before settling in Hollywood and becoming a bit-part actor in low-budget movies.  Billed as Heber Snow he appeared in several Tex Ritter B Westerns of the late 1930s.  As Worden he became a regular in the epic Westerns directed by John Ford and is perhaps best known for his role as old Mose in Ford's *The Searchers* (1956), which many consider the greatest Western film ever made.

Tenor Frank Forrest appeared as a regular for a short time on *The Camel Caravan* and as a semi-regular on radio's *Double Or Nothing* quiz show.

Soprano vocalist Lucille Manners had started out as a stenographer in a law office, but after studying voice at night she broke into radio.  In 1936, four years after her radio debut, she replaced Jessica Dragonette on the long-running *Cities Service Concerts* program.  Praised for her performance in *The Desert Song*, she appeared as a guest singer on numerous radio programs that regularly featured operettas.

73. The guest billed as Lady Hardwicke was in all probability Helena Pickard (1900-1959), an English-born actress who between 1928 and 1950 was married to actor Sir Cedric Hardwicke.

Mary Lewis was a soprano who sang with the Metropolitan Opera.

For Parks Johnson, see 16 above.


74. Actress Gilda Gray (1899-1959) is best known for her supporting roles in *The Devil Dancer* (1927), *Rose Marie* (1936), and *The Great Ziegfeld* (1936), in which she played herself.

Joe Howard (1867-1961) was a singer and composer who at the time of his appearance on *Ellery Queen* was co-starring with Beatrice Kay on *The Gay Nineties Program*, another CBS show.

For Parks Johnson, see 16 above.


75. Austrian-born Vicki Baum (1888-1960) was one of the most widely read authors of her time. Her novel *Menschen im Hotel* (1929) was the basis of *Grand Hotel* (1932), the Oscar-winning movie that starred Greta Garbo, Joan Crawford, Wallace Beery and Lionel Barrymore.

Theatrical producer Howard Dietz (1896-1983) brought to life such shows as *Between the Devil, At Home Abroad, Sadie Thompson,* and *That's Entertainment.* Several of his plays were based on his own books.


76. Bandleader Blue Barron organized his popular dance band in 1935 and had his own radio program, *The Music of Yesterday and Today Styled the Blue Barron Way,* which aired coast-to-coast. Years after he appeared on *Ellery Queen* his radio program was scheduled opposite the Queen series on a different network.

Bill Stern (1907-1971) graduated from a Pennsylvania military college and, in 1934, began announcing sports events for NBC Radio. He was an outstanding athlete at school but that part of his life ended in 1935 when he lost a leg in an auto accident. He is best remembered for the bizarre and unbelievable yarns about armless baseball pitchers and blind football heroes that he spun on *Bill Stern's Sports Newsreel.* During the late 1930s and early 1940s he narrated the M-G-M *News of the Day* newsreels and also played himself in several movies. He returned as a guest armchair detective on *Ellery Queen* almost two and a half years after his first appearance (Episode 191), and thirteen days later Ellery himself (or rather Sydney Smith who was playing the part each week at that time) guested on Stern's program.

For Aubrey Waller Cook, see 70 above.


77. For George Jessel, see 70 above.


79. Jim Ameche (1915-1983), actor Don Ameche's younger brother, made his radio debut starring as *Jack Armstrong, The All-American Boy.* In later years he starred in *Attorney-at-Law.* He served as announcer on numerous radio series including *Mr. Keen, Tracer of Lost Persons.* During the 1960s he hosted a morning radio show on New York City's WHN.

Leo G. Carroll (1892-1972) and Judith Evelyn (1913-1967) were starring in Patrick Hamilton's grisly stage melodrama *Angel Street* at the time of their appearance on *Ellery Queen*. In the early 1950s Carroll starred in TV's comedy series *Topper* and in the mid-1960s he played Mr. Waverly on the popular spy series *The Man from U.N.C.L.E.*

80. Lois Wilson (1896-1988) started as a schoolteacher and acted briefly on stage before entering films in 1916. She played Daisy Buchanan in the long-lost 1926 version of *The Great Gatsby* and continued to appear in movies well into the sound era. On television she played Mrs. Alice Aldrich on *The Aldrich Family* and Mrs. Lowery on the daytime serial *The Guiding Light*.

Selena Royle (1904-1983) studied acting at the American Academy of Dramatic Art during the early 1920s and became a staple on radio, television and the motion picture screen. Behind the scenes she was active in The American Theatre Wing, British and French War Relief Funds and was instrumental in organizing the New York Stage Door Canteen for service personnel during the Second World War. She played supporting roles on dozens of radio programs including *The Goldbergs*, *Stella Dallas*, *Grand Central Station* and *Woman of Courage*. She also appeared on numerous radio mysteries including *Crime Doctor* and *Strange As It Seems*.

81. Bandleader Bill Johnson (1872-1972) was one of the first musicians to take the New Orleans jazz style outside its birthplace. Between 1912 and 1918 his Original Creole Orchestra toured the country on the Orpheum circuit. Later he played and led his own band in Chicago, retiring from music and moving to Mexico in the 1950s.

Allen Prescott (1904-1978) was a radio comedian whose program *The Wife Saver* was popular during the late 1920s and early 1930s. At the time of his guest spot on *Ellery Queen* he was starring in his own thrice-a-week radio program *Prescott Presents*.

Singer Marian Anderson (1897-1993) became the center of a civil rights controversy in 1939 when the Daughters of the American Revolution refused to let her perform in Washington, D.C.'s Constitution Hall because she was black. First Lady Eleanor Roosevelt resigned from the DAR in protest and helped arrange for Anderson to give an outdoor concert at the Lincoln Memorial on Easter Sunday.

Arthur Murray (1895-1991), whose name is synonymous with social dancing, was among the first to use advertising techniques considered cutting edge. As early as 1912 he conceived the idea of selling dance lessons by mail, one step at a time. His business acumen and creative use of print advertising attracted national attention. Arthur Murray teachers were a regular part of every first-class steamship cruise prior to World War II. In the movie *The Fleet's In* (1942) Betty Hutton, backed by the Jimmy Dorsey Orchestra, sings "Arthur Murray Taught Me Dancing In A Hurry."

82. Author Octavus Roy Cohen (1891-1959) was a popular humorist of his time. His stories about Florian Slappey and his pals, set in the southern black ghetto and featuring farcical characters and dialect humor, are riddled with political incorrectness by today's standards but remain historically important because they created the blueprint for radio shows like *Amos 'n' Andy*. Cohen also wrote stories about Jim Hanvey, a fat white Southern private eye. His non-series novel *The Crimson Alibi* (1919) was adapted into a popular stage play. Cohen himself was scheduled as guest armchair detective for this *Ellery Queen* episode but, for reasons unknown, he couldn't make the broadcast and was replaced by his wife.

83. Bernardine Flynn was a veteran radio actress whose most famous role was as Sade on *Vic and Sade*. She also had her own radio show, *The Flynn Daily News*, which was billed as "news for women, not a women's news program."

Cartoonist Otto Soglow (1900-1975) is best known for his comic strip "The Little King" but his activities extended beyond the drawing board. He was a central figure in many charitable activities, a founder of the National Cartoonists Society and the recipient of its prestigious Reuben award in 1961. He continued to draw for *The New Yorker*'s "Talk of the Town" until 1972 and kept the Little King strip going until his death.

Ward Greene (1892-1956) was the author of numerous short stories and novels. His grim 1936 novel *Death in the Deep South* was adapted into the movie *They Won't Forget* (1937) and his lighthearted short story "Happy Dan, The Whistling Dog" became the basis of the Disney animated feature *Lady and the Tramp* (1955).

84. Shirley Booth (1907-1992) was co-starring with Ed Gardner in radio's popular comedy series *Duffy's Tavern*. They had married in November 1929 and were still a couple when they made their guest appearance on this *Ellery Queen* episode. A few months later they filed for divorce.

For Ed Gardner, see 2 above.

85. Orchestra leader Shep Fields (1910-1981) led his first band while studying law at St. John's University. He developed the gimmick of blowing bubbles into water with a straw to create a sound he called "rippling rhythm." The phrase was to become his trademark. On radio he and his band performed on *The Fitch Bandwagon, If I Had the Chance* and *The Rippling Rhythm Revue*. In 1955 he became a DJ on his own radio program, *Ripplin' Rhythm Rendezvous*.

Lawrence E. Spivak (1900-1994) was editor of the *American Mercury* magazine. His company was the original publisher of *Ellery Queen's Mystery Magazine*, which was launched in the fall of 1941, less than a year before his appearance on the Queen radio series. In 1945 Spivak and Martha Rountree created *Meet the Press* for NBC radio.

For Bea Wain, see 70 above.

87. Alice Marble (1913-1990) was a champion tennis player who pioneered the women's serve-and-volley style of play. In 1939 she became the first woman in the 20th century to win the Triple Crown at Wimbledon. During World War II she was almost killed while working for U.S. Army Intelligence, investigating a Swiss investment banker with Nazi ties. Her autobiography, *The Road to Wimbledon*, was published in 1946.

88. Actress Joan Caulfield (1922-1991) made her movie debut playing herself in *Duffy's Tavern* (1945), which was based on the radio series of the same name. On TV she played Liz Cooper on *My Favorite Husband*, which was also based on a radio series of the same name.

Budapest-born bandleader Emery Deutsch (1906-1997) was well known for violin stylings in the gypsyesque Fritz Kreisler manner. Many dismissed his music, which was described by one critic as "sounding as though his strings were soaked in chicken fat." Nevertheless he served as the CBS radio network's music director for 11 years.

89. Singer and composer Joan Edwards (1917-1981) made numerous appearances as a guest armchair detective on *Ellery Queen* and also appeared on such radio programs as *The Royal Gelatin Hour, Your Hit Parade* and *The Danny Kaye Show*. She played herself in two movies: *Hit Parade of 1947* and *Screen Snapshots: Holiday in Las Vegas* (1947). She also performed on the Broadway stage, composed songs and scores for shows, toured the nightclub circuit, recorded for several labels and, during the summer of 1950, hosted her own television program.

Warren Hull (1903-1974) starred in three of Columbia Pictures' 15-chapter cliffhanger serials: *The Spider's Web* (1938), *Mandrake the Magician* (1939), and *The Spider Returns* (1941). He is best known during the 1940s as co-host of radio's *Vox Pop* program and during the 1950s as solo host of the TV quiz show *Strike It Rich*.

Joana Leschin (1911-1978) was a concert pianist.

90. Lem Ward (1896-1984) was a woodcarver and painter who overcame severe illness to produce some of the best-loved wildfowl art extant today. Lem and his brother Steve grew up along the marshes of the Chesapeake Bay in Maryland and subsisted as barbers and foragers. They created carved and painted ducks to please themselves, as works of art, while carvers around them were making decoys just good enough for hunting.

Jack McManus was cinema and radio editor of *PM*, a liberal newspaper founded in 1940.

For Lois January, see 70 above.

91. Alphonso d'Artega, known professionally only by his last name, was a conductor, arranger and composer whose rumba and samba music was very popular on radio in the early 1940s. His orchestra was regularly heard on radio's *Believe It Or Not* and *The Saturday Morning Vaudeville Theater*. He played Tchaikovsky in the movie *Carnegie Hall* (1947) and also conducted the soundtrack for the film.

Singer Kay Lorraine, known as the slow-burning blues chanteuse, was heard regularly on *The Chamber Music Society of Lower Basin Street*, a radio program of musical satire that lampooned popular songs of the day.

Baritone Conrad Thibault (1903-1987) began his singing career with the Philadelphia Grand Opera Company. He was a regular on numerous radio programs including *Log Cabin Revue, Manhattan Merry-Go-Round* and *Uncle Charlie's Tent Show*. In later years he taught at the Manhattan School of Music and the Palm Beach Atlantic College.

For Joan Edwards, see 89 above.

92. James Kilgallen (1888-1982) was a well-known New York journalist. In 1943 he went to the Bahamas to report on the WWII era's biggest murder trial, in which Alfred de Marigny was tried in a British court at Nassau for the murder of his wealthy American-born father-in-law Sir Harry Oakes.

James' younger sister Dorothy Kilgallen (1913-1965) quit college to work for *The New York Evening Journal* and had already established herself as a society gossip columnist before she was old enough to take a legal drink. She hosted her own radio program, *The Voice of Broadway*, and was a regular panelist on *Leave It To the Girls, What's My Line?* and other series. On November 8, 1965, she was found dead in her apartment shortly after returning from Dallas, where she had interviewed Jack Ruby and conducted her own investigation of the Kennedy assassination.

93. Benay Venuta (1911-1995) was a singer and actress best remembered for playing Dolly Tate in the film version of *Annie Get Your Gun* (1950).

Baritone Clyde Barrie (1909-1945), apparently the second black performer to serve as a guest armchair detective on *Ellery Queen*, was born in the British West Indies. He sang regularly on the radio series *Musical Americana*, which was devoted to "music of and about the American Negro." His promising career was cut short by his death of bronchial pneumonia at age 36.

Dick Stabile (1909-    ) moved to New York in 1926 to join the orchestra of George Olsen. He moved to Ben Bernie's band, then in 1936 formed his own band, which became popular at New York hotels and ballrooms and remained in business while he served in the armed forces during World War II, his wife taking over in his absence. After the war Stabile adjusted his repertoire to accommodate the radio audience. After moving to the West Coast he became musical director for Dean Martin and Jerry Lewis, appearing regularly with them on television and in some of their films.

94. At age 16 George McManus (1884-1954) became both the fashion editor and a cartoonist for the *St. Louis Republic*, for which he created *Alma & Oliver*, his first comic strip. He is best known for his later strips, particularly *Bringing Up Father,* starring the unflappable Maggie and the ever-mischievous Jiggs, which began in 1913.

For Benay Venuta, see 93 above.

95. Journalist Harriet Van Horne (1919-1998) moved from Syracuse to New York City in 1942 to become radio critic for the *World-Telegram*. By the end of the decade she was writing for newspapers and magazines about the new medium of television and continued to do so for twenty years.

96. Oscar Serlin (1901-1971) was a well-known Broadway theatrical producer whose biggest success was the blockbuster hit play *Life with Father*.

97. English-born playwright John Van Druten (1901-1957) is best known for *Old Acquaintance* (1940), *The Voice of the Turtle* (1943), *I Remember Mama* (1944), *Bell, Book and Candle* (1950), and *I Am a Camera* (1951). Most of his stage plays were later adapted into movies.

Flora Robson (1902-1984) was a distinguished British stage actress and graduate of the Royal Academy of Dramatic Art whose career spanned nearly 60 years, usually in character roles calling for strength and determination. She portrayed Queen Elizabeth I in *Fire Over England* (1937) and, after relocating to Hollywood, played the same role again in Errol Flynn's swashbuckler *The Sea Hawk* (1940). Her performance as Ingrid Bergman's fiercely protective servant in *Saratoga Trunk* (1945) earned her an Oscar nomination.

98. Comedian Jerry Lester (1910-1995) was a semi-regular on radio's Kraft Music Hall. In the early years of TV he hosted *Broadway Open House*, which was the forerunner of *The Tonight Show*.

For Lucille Manners, see 72 above.

99. Actor/singer Lanny Ross (1906-1988) was the star of his own radio show and made numerous guest appearances on *The Magic Key of RCA, Your Hit Parade, The Camel Caravan* and other programs. During World War II he served in the Southwest Pacific area as an Army officer in charge of USO shows for the fighting troops.

Les Brown (1912-2001) conducted his own "Band of Renown" during the Big Band era of orchestra leaders like Glenn Miller and Artie Shaw. He worked with such luminaries as Dean Martin and Bob Hope and had his own late-evening ballroom music program for local New York radio stations.

100. Eva Gabor (1921-1995) was the "good girl" of the three Gabor sisters. She arrived in the U.S. in the 1930s and appeared in films such as *Star Spangled Rhythm* (1942) and *The Mad Magician* (1954). She is best remembered as socialite-turned-farmwife Lisa Douglas on the TV series *Green Acres*.

101. Maverick publisher Bernard J. Geis (1909-2001) began his career in publishing as an editor for *Esquire* and *Coronet* magazines, which led to work with some of the nation's biggest publishing houses. While at Prentice-Hall during the 1950s he served as the editor of TV host Art Linkletter's *Kids Say The Darndest Things*, a book that garnered respectable sales until Linkletter casually mentioned it on his program.

Sales more than doubled after the TV plug and Geis realized there was an untapped potential to media crossover. With financial backing from celebrities who were willing to trust him with their memoirs as well as their money, Geis launched his own publishing house in 1959, making a fortune out of authors like Jacqueline Susann and Helen Gurley Brown.

102. Sally Rand (1903-1979) left home at age 13 to work as a cigarette girl in a Kansas City nightclub. She became an acrobatic dancer in the circus and later performed in nightclubs, becoming famous for the Lady Godiva routine she performed on Mrs. William Randolph Hearst's yacht in 1933. The next day she was hired to perform her fan dance at Chicago's Century of Progress exposition. She starred in several Paramount features, such as *Bolero* (1934) with George Raft, and continued to perform her dance routines in her seventies.

Barry Wood (1907?-1970) was an emcee, producer and singer, appearing as a guest on radio musical shows like *Your Hit Parade* and *Johnny Presents*. He also starred in his own radio program, which lasted from 1937 until the early 1950s. Years after his guest appearance on this *Ellery Queen* episode, Wood's program was scheduled opposite the Queen series on another network.

103. Broadway songwriter Irving Caesar (1895-1996) was the lyricist for more than 1,000 published songs, collaborating with George Gershwin, Vincent Youmans, Rudolf Friml, George M. Cohan and others. He was a charter member of the American Society of Composers, Authors and Publishers and was still on its board in the 1960s.

For Lady Hardwicke, see 73 above.

104. Walter B. Gibson (1897-1985) was a magician and pulp magazine writer who was hired to write novels about "The Shadow," a character who had begun on radio as the narrator of a weekly mystery anthology series. In 1937 Gibson's version of the character became the inspiration for the new radio series *The Shadow*, whose premiere episode Gibson co-authored. During the 1938-39 season eight or more *Shadow* scripts were written anonymously by Fred Dannay and Manny Lee, the creators of Ellery Queen. Gibson also wrote scripts for *The Avenger*, *Nick Carter, Master Detective*, and *The Adventures of Frank Merriwell*. John Nanovic, editor of the pulp magazine *The Shadow*, appeared as an armchair detective on *Ellery Queen* about four months after Gibson.

Choo Choo Johnson was a well-known hobo musician.

For Hank Worden, see 72 above.

105. Ann Corio (19 -1999) was six years old when she saw a traveling vaudeville company perform and became entranced with show business. Largely self-trained as a dancer, at 15 she started in the chorus of a Minsky burlesque show in New York and within a year became a headliner. In 1933 she introduced Lou Costello, who was a comic in her troupe, to his future wife, Anne Battler, who was in the show's chorus. Corio remained good friends with the Costellos throughout their lives. In 1936

she headlined a burlesque show that featured the new team of Abbott and Costello, who eventually migrated into vaudeville and later radio, movies and TV. In the 1940s, with burlesque fading, Corio worked in a few low-budget films and summer stock. Later in life, as headliner of *This Was Burlesque*, she revived the entertainment form that had made her famous.

106. Walter Compton (1912?-1959) began his broadcasting career in 1936 and subsequently served that industry as announcer, commentator, emcee and executive. He was best known as the original emcee of the long-running radio quiz *Double Or Nothing*. Five weeks after his appearance on *Ellery Queen* he left the quiz program which he had hosted from its beginning.

Actress Peggy Wood (1892-1978) played Marta Hansen on the TV series *Mama* during the early 1950s. Among her best known movie roles is that of the Mother Abbess in *The Sound of Music* (1965).

107. Jean Holloway wrote scripts for such radio series as *The Hallmark Playhouse, Mr. President, The Railroad Hour, Theatre of Romance, Hollywood Showcase* and *Mayor of the Town*. In the first decade of television she scripted many episodes of *Wagon Train*.

Frank Luther (1899-1980) was a band singer with The High Hatters and later served as announcer for numerous radio programs including *The Life and Love of Dr. Susan* and *Luncheon at the Waldorf*.

For Ann Corio, see 105 above.

108. John G. Chapman (1900-1972), drama critic of the New York *Daily News* at the time of his appearance on *Ellery Queen*, hosted his own radio program, *Best Plays*, nine years later.

For Joan Edwards, see 89 above.

109. William Fawcett was the owner of Fawcett Publications, Inc., which published numerous comic books and, beginning in 1950, original paperback novels.

110. Harry Conover (1912- ), founder of the Conover Modeling Agency, represented countless beautiful young women who went on to fame and fortune as actresses.

Singer Bob Allen (1913-1989) joined Tommy Dorsey's band in 1944 and was heard on the *All-Time Hit Parade* program. In 1945 he left for military service and never enjoyed much success in show business after returning to civilian life.

111. Candy Jones (1925?-1990), born Jessica Mae Wilcox, was a top model and WWII pin-up girl who was prominently featured in posters encouraging women to enlist in the WACs. In 1960 she was put under hypnosis by the CIA and used as a courier for secret documents. She was married to radio personality Long John Nebel during the last years of Nebel's life.

For Harry Conover, see 110 above.

112.  Bandleader and lead drummer Abe Lyman (1897-1957) headed an ensemble that was best known for tastefully arranged dance music but also on occasion played jazzier arrangements like "Shake That Thing."  He helped launch the career of Dale Evans, who sang with his group before becoming famous as Roy Rogers' silver-screen sidekick and real-world wife.

For Joan Edwards, see 89 above.

113.  Radio actor Bob Bruce was a semi-regular on *Michael Shayne* and *The NBC University Theater.*  He played Operator 63 on the soap opera *The Gallant Heart* and was the announcer on *Glamour Manor.*

Harmonica-playing comic Herb Shriner (1918-1970) was a regular on radio series like *The Camel Caravan, Herb Shriner Time* and *The Philip Morris Follies of 1946.*  When radio was displaced by television he hosted *Two for the Money* and other TV game shows.

115. Nanette Fabray (1920-    ), who began her show business career as a starlet at Warner Bros., eventually became well known as a comedienne-singer-dancer and also as a humanitarian who has often testified before Congressional committees on the problems of handicapped persons.

Actress Luana Walters (1912-1963) was the sexy and fiery female lead in countless B Westerns opposite shoot-em-up stars like Buck Jones, Gene Autry, Charles Starrett and Tim Holt.

Actress Nancy Kelly (1912-1985) was known in radio as a Scream Queen for having played the female lead in countless horror dramas.  Later, after winning a Tony award for her performance on Broadway in *The Bad Seed*, she reprised her performance in the movie of the same name.

Ed Sullivan (1902-1974), known as The Great Stone Face, began as a Broadway columnist and radio announcer. In 1948 the variety series that he hosted moved from radio to television and, as *Toast of the Town*, became a Sunday night favorite of viewers for decades to come.

116.  Helen Twelvetrees (1908-1958) starred in many "weeper" movies of the early 1930s.  In 1935 she played the female lead opposite Donald Cook in *The Spanish Cape Mystery*, the first movie adventure of Ellery Queen.

Actor William Prince (1913-1996) made hundreds of appearances in radio soap operas but is best known for his career in television. In the 60-minute live TV mystery series *The Mask* (1954) he and Gary Merrill co-starred as two brothers who were both lawyers and amateur detectives. Later he had continuing roles in TV daytime dramas including *Another World, The Edge of Night, Search for Tomorrow* and *A World Apart.*

John Shuttleworth was not a real person but the editor of the fictitious *True Detective Magazine* and the host of *True Detective Mysteries*, a radio anthology series that ran from 1929 until 1958.  During the 1930s and 1940s the role of Shuttleworth was played by Richard Keith, who guested on *Ellery Queen* in the guise of his character.

117. For Jerry Lester, see 98 above. For Frank Forrest, see 72 above.

118. F. Beverley Kelley was director of publicity for Ringling Bros. Barnum & Bailey Circus.

For Bob Bruce, see 113 above.

119. For Jerry Lester, see 98 above. For Alphonso d'Artega, see 91 above.

120. Doris McFerrin was managing editor of *Radio Mirror*.

Leonard Sillman was a Broadway producer best known for plays like *Fools Rush In*, *New Faces of 1936*, *Journey's End* and *They Knew What They Wanted*.

For Lois January, see 70 above.

121. Dorothy Arzner (1897-1979) began in Hollywood in 1919 as a typist and script girl and rose to become a film editor, a scriptwriter and ultimately the only woman director in Hollywood. Among the stars she directed are Clara Bow, Claudette Colbert, Joan Crawford, Katharine Hepburn and Rosalind Russell.

Actress Brenda Forbes (1909-1996) is best known for her supporting roles in WWII films like *Mrs. Miniver* (1942) and *The White Cliffs of Dover* (1944).

For Bill Johnson, see 81 above.

122. Actress Virginia Gilmore (1919-1986), the daughter of a retired British army officer, made her stage debut with a San Francisco company at age 15 and appeared in her first movie five years later. After years of supporting roles in relatively unimportant films she left Hollywood in 1952 but continued to appear in stage plays and on TV and eventually became a drama coach.

John Nanovic (1906-2001) was an editor best known for his tenure on the pulp magazine *The Shadow*.

123. Jimmy Jemail (1893-1978) was a columnist with New York's premier tabloid newspaper, the *Daily News*. His feature "The Inquiring Photographer" ran in that paper for more than 20 years.

124. Actress Celeste Holm (1919-   ) debuted on Broadway in her late teens and appeared in many dramas and musicals including *The Women* and *Oklahoma!* before signing a contract with 20th Century-Fox in 1946. She won both a Golden Globe award and an Oscar for her performance in *Gentleman's Agreement* (1947) and received two more Oscar nominations over the next few years.

Actor Richard Widmark (1914-   ) debuted on radio in 1938 on the daytime serial *Aunt Jenny's Real Life Stories*. During the early 1940s he appeared in countless New York-based radio programs such as *Front Page Farrell*, *Inner Sanctum Mysteries* and *The Cavalcade of America*. He made his screen debut in *Kiss of Death* (1947), playing the psychotic killer who throws a wheelchair-bound old woman down a flight of stairs to her death, and is best known for playing assorted tough guys and creeps in movies ever since.

For Joan Caulfield, see 88 above.

125. French-born Bretaigne Windust (1906-1960) moved to the U.S. with his family in 1920, developed an interest in the theater while a student at Princeton, and became an actor, stage manager and finally director on Broadway. When not working on a stage drama he directed movies and, later, episodes of live and filmed TV series.

Actor Alexander Kirkland appeared in many movies of the early 1930s including *Charlie Chan's Chance* (1932) and *Devil's Lottery* (1932). At the time of his appearance on *Ellery Queen* he was married to a previous guest detective on the show, Gypsy Rose Lee.

126. Patricia Peardon (1924-1993) played children and juveniles on many radio programs including *The Aldrich Family*, *Let's Pretend* and *Orphans of Divorce*. About five years after her appearance on *Ellery Queen* she starred on Broadway in *Junior Miss*.

127. Actress Ruth McDevitt (1895-1976) starred in numerous radio programs including *This Life Is Mine* and *Keeping Up With Rosemary*.

Bandleader Guy Lombardo (1902-1977), one of seven children of a musically minded tailor, began playing gigs with his brothers while still in school. In 1934 he signed with Decca, selling more than 100,000,000 records of "the sweetest music this side of heaven" over the next few decades. He and his band traveled 60,000 miles each year to perform in small towns and at colleges but he is best known for his New Year's Eve musical programs which ran on radio and later TV from 1929 until his death.

128. Nellie Revell (1873?-1958) was a newspaperwoman by profession but also worked in radio on occasion. She was the hostess on *Strolling Songsters,* which was heard on the NBC Red Network during the early fall of 1935 and featured songs and old jokes by Harvey Hindermayer and Earl Tuckerman, known to listeners as The Gold Dust Twins. In 1947 she had another radio series called *Neighbor Nell.*

129. Actress Arleen Whelan was signed by 20th Century-Fox in 1938 and a year later played a major role in John Ford's classic *Young Mr. Lincoln* (1939). Most of her roles were in undistinguished films but Ford brought her back for a part in *The Sun Shines Bright* (1953).

Yugoslavian-born Mia Slavenska (1914-    ) began dancing at age 5 and became the Zagreb Opera's prima ballerina. After appearing in Jean Benoit-Levy's dance film *La Mort du Cygne* (1938) she came to the U.S. to promote the film and stayed permanently, working as a dancer and teacher. She founded the Slavenska Ballette Variante and later the Theatre Ballette. In 1954 she became prima ballerina of the Metropolitan Opera Ballet.

For Guy Lombardo, see 127 above.

130. English-born actress Virginia Field (1917-1992) had supporting roles in countless movies including *Charlie Chan in Monte Carlo* (1937) and three of 20th Century-Fox's Mr. Moto series starring Peter Lorre.

212

Norman Tokar (1919-1979) was a child actor both in plays and on radio. As a young man he starred as Henry Aldrich on *The Aldrich Family* for a month before entering the military and serving in World War II. After the war he became a director and spent most of the rest of his life making theatrical and TV movies for the Walt Disney organization. Among the Disney pictures he directed are *The Boatniks* (1970) and *Candleshoe* (1978).

Comic actor Joe Besser (1907-1988) began in vaudeville and broke into movies in the early 1930s, appearing frequently in Abbott & Costello pictures and later as a regular on Bud & Lou's TV series. Between 1956 and 1958 he was one of the Three Stooges.

For Gypsy Rose Lee, see 71 above.

131. Christine Ayers was a showgirl with the Ziegfeld Follies.

For William Fawcett, see 109 above. For Virginia Field, see 130 above. For Norman Tokar, see 131 above.

132. James Montgomery Flagg (1877-1960), a native New Yorker, was a magazine illustrator whose best-known work is the World War I poster of Uncle Sam with the caption "I Want You!"

For Harriet Van Horne, see 95 above.

133. Announcer Harry Von Zell (1906-1981) was heard on radio programs such as *The Fred Allen Show, Bright Star, The Aldrich Family, The Smiths of Hollywood, The March of Time* and *The Dinah Shore Show*. He is best known for his work in television as the announcer on *The George Burns and Gracie Allen Show*.

Orchestra leader and choral director Fred Waring (1900-1984) found his niche in music in the late 1920s when he expanded his small orchestra and chorus, renaming the group Fred Waring and his Pennsylvanians. He and his troupe performed on numerous radio shows including *The Old Gold Program* and *The Chesterfield Supper Club*. He also held the patent on the Waring Blender and served as CEO of the Waring Mixer Corporation, which manufactured his invention.

Phil Baker (1896?-1963) was an accordion-playing vaudeville comic whose own radio program achieved a high rating in the early 1930s despite being heard on only part of a national network. At the time of his appearance on *Ellery Queen* he was hosting his own radio quiz show, *Take It Or Leave It*.

Nebraska-born singer Donna Dae was a regular on radio's musical variety series *The Fred Waring Show*.

134. For Joan Edwards, see 89 above.

135. John Wayne (1907-1979) starred in serials and B Westerns throughout the 1930s and graduated to more prestigious films when director John Ford cast him as the Ringo Kid in the classic *Stagecoach* (1939). At the time of his appearance on *Ellery Queen* he was starring mainly in WWII films. After the war he rose to legendary superstar status.

Former band singer Janet Blair (1921-    ) signed a contract with Columbia Pictures in 1941 and appeared in such movies as *Three Girls About Town* (1941) and *Blondie Goes to College* (1942). She is best known for her role in the film version of *My Sister Eileen* (1942), which was based on a book by previous guest armchair detective Ruth McKenney.

Actress Paula Stone appeared in a number of movies during the 1930s including the first of the 66 Westerns that starred William Boyd as Hopalong Cassidy. Two years after appearing on *Ellery Queen* she became the moderator on *Leave It To The Girls*, a radio show with all-female panelists.

136.   Bandleader and composer Paul Lavalle (1908-1997) began his radio career in 1933 as a staff musician at the NBC network. He conducted orchestras for numerous radio programs including *The Chamber Music Society of Lower Basin Street*, *Fantasy in Melody*, *The Dinah Shore Show*, *Strictly Business* and *The Cities Service Band of America*. Decades after appearing on *Ellery Queen* he conducted music at the 1964 New York World's Fair and served as music director of Radio City Music Hall.

For Ann Corio, see 105 above. For Virginia Gilmore, see 122 above.

137.   Actor Jay C. Flippen (1898-1971) debuted on stage in *Broadway Brevities* (1920). He sang, danced, acted and clowned alongside Jack Benny and other vaudeville luminaries and also did a stint on radio as announcer for New York Yankees games. Between acting jobs on stage and radio and in movies and TV he served as president of the American Guild of Variety Artists.

Vocalist Mary Small took singing lessons from her father and developed her own voice without the use of a voice coach. She first performed on radio at age 11, billed on *The Rudy Vallee Show* as "the little girl with the big voice." Later she played the title role on *Little Miss Bab-O's Surprise Party*. During the 1940s she was married to songwriter Vic Mizzy, who years later composed the theme song for TV's *The Addams Family*.

For Ann Corio, see 105 above.

138.   Actor Jay Jostyn (1901-1976) is best known for starring on radio's *Mr. District Attorney* but also played supporting roles on *Our Gal Sunday, Second Husband, Gang Busters, This Day Is Ours* and *Foreign Assignment*.

Danton Walker (1899-1960) conducted the "Broadway Spotlight" column for the New York *Daily News*, covering Broadway plays and performers' offstage peccadilloes. In the mid-1950s he hosted the public service radio program *Broadway in Review*, which was sponsored by the U.S. Navy and distributed free of charge to stations across the country.

For Paul Lavalle, see 136 above. For Paula Stone, see 135 above.

139.   Polish-born tenor Jan Kiepura (1902-1966) spent most of his career in opera but also starred in a few Hollywood movies including *My Song for You* (1934) and *Give Us This Night* (1936).

Stage magician Rajah Raboid, born Maurice P. Kitchen, is best known as the originator of the illusion that a woman has been sawed in half.

214

Ralph Edwards (1913-    ) became a radio announcer immediately after graduating from UCLA in 1936. He was the creator, producer and host of *This Is Your Life* and *Truth Or Consequences*, both of which began on radio in 1940 and moved to TV in the 1950s.

For Danton Walker, see 138 above.

140. Otto Preminger (1906–1986) was born in Vienna, the son of the Austro-Hungarian Empire's chief prosecutor. He directed plays in Europe and earned a law degree on the side before coming to the U.S. and beginning his career as a movie director, principally at 20th Century-Fox. Among the crime-suspense films he made for that studio are *Laura* (1944), *Fallen Angel* (1946), *Whirlpool* (1950) and *Where the Sidewalk Ends* (1950).

For Rajah Raboid, see 139 above.

141. Ezra MacIntosh produced and directed *The Kraft Music Hall*, a radio variety series that featured Bing Crosby, Bob Burns and Victor Borge.

Spike Jones (1911-1965) put together a musical group called The City Slickers which emphasized comedy, parodying both classical and popular music with equal finesse. He had his own radio program under various titles such as *Spike's at the Troc, Spike Jones' Spotlight Revue* and *The Spike Jones Show*.

For Christine Ayers, see 131 above.

142. Actor Richard Coogan (1914-    ) played supporting roles on many radio mystery series including *Molle Mystery Theater*, *The Mysterious Traveler* and *Hour of Mystery*. At the time of their appearance on *Ellery Queen*, he and fellow guest armchair detective Julie Stevens were co-starring in the radio version of *Abie's Irish Rose*. For a short time in late 1946 and early 1947 Coogan himself played Ellery Queen on the radio series. He moved into television very early in the new medium's history, becoming the first actor to play *Captain Video* and later starring as Marshal Matt Wayne in the Western series *The Californians*.

Actress Julie Stevens (1916-1984) appeared in a number of low-budget mystery-adventure films like *Private Detective* (1939) and *Murder in the Air* (1940) but is best known for starring in radio's long-running daytime serial drama *The Romance of Helen Trent*, in which she lasted from 1944 until the series went off the air in 1960. She was also heard on radio in the title role of *Kitty Foyle*.

For Candy Jones, see 111 above. For Spike Jones, see 141 above.

143. Jack Dolph (1894-1962) began as a race horse trainer and went on to become an actor, producer and network manager in radio. Between 1948 and 1953 he wrote five mystery novels with racetrack backgrounds.

Violinist David Rubinoff (1897-1986) was so well known during the early 1930s that he was often billed simply by his last name. In 1931 he and his violin and orchestra provided the musical entertainment for radio's *Chase and Sanborn Hour*, although when he was called upon to speak his lines were read by actor Lionel Stander. Rubinoff and his orchestra were heard on prime-time radio until 1937, after which he began making guest appearances on other shows including *Ellery Queen*.

215

Don Dunphy (1908-1998) started out as a sportswriter for the New York *World*, then in 1935 landed a radio job with WHOM in New Jersey. In 1941 he was chosen to announce the heavyweight championship fight between Joe Louis and Billy Conn. For the next 24 years he provided blow-by-blow ringside descriptions of the boxing matches broadcast on Gillette's *Cavalcade of Sports*.

For John Wayne, see 135 above.

144. Radio actor Jackie Kelk specialized in playing juvenile roles, appearing as Jimmy Olsen on *The Adventures of Superman*, Junior on *Dick Tracy*, and Terry Lee on *Terry and the Pirates*. He is best known for having played Henry Aldrich's quaking-voiced best friend Homer Brown on both the radio and TV versions of *The Aldrich Family*.

"Senator" Ed Ford was one of the four jokesters who entertained audiences for years on the radio quiz show *Can You Top This?* Two of his colleagues in comedy on that long-running program were Harry Hershfield and Joe Laurie, Jr., who also served as guest armchair detectives on *Ellery Queen* this week.

Cartoonist Harry Hershfield (1885-1974) began selling comic illustrations at age 14 and created strips like *Homeless Hector* and *Desperate Desmond* early in the 20th century. His most famous and long-running strip, *Abie the Agent*, established him as one of the great pioneer comic artists.

Joe Laurie, Jr. (1901?-1964) started out as a vaudeville comedian and went on to write hundreds of skits and collaborate on several screenplays including *Union Depot* (1932). He wrote scripts for radio shows and two books on show business: *From the Honky Tonk to the Palace* and, with Abel Greene, *From Vaude to Video*.

For Mary Small, see 137 above.

145. All of this week's guests had sports connections. Al Schacht (1892-1984) played three seasons with the Washington Senators but retired from big-league baseball in 1921 because of a sore arm and became a coach, developing a comedy routine that he would perform for fans at the ballpark. Art Flynn was a journalist who wrote for *The Sporting News*. Ken Sears (1917-1968) was playing for the New York Yankees. Joe Gordon (1914?-1978) began his major league baseball career with the Yanks and stayed in the big leagues until 1950.

For Don Dunphy, see 143 above.

146. Character actress Hope Emerson (1897-1960) began as a vaudeville and stage comedienne. At six feet two and 230 pounds she found an excellent niche for herself in the post-WWII film noir genre, appearing in *Cry of the City* (1948) and *Caged* (1950) and winning an Oscar nomination for her role as a sadistic prison matron in the latter picture. In her last years she played Mother, the jazz-club owner on TV's private-eye series *Peter Gunn*.

147. Singer Nadine Conner (1907- ) made her debut as a Metropolitan Opera soprano in 1941 but was also heard singing popular melodies on several radio programs including *The New Old Gold Program*, *The Railroad Hour*, *The Song Shop* and *Show Boat*.

148. Earl Carroll (1893-1948) began his stage career in 1914 and went on to produce, direct and write words and music for many Broadways hits including *Earl Carroll's Vanities, Murder at the Vanities, Laff That Off* and *The Rat*.

Beryl Wallace (   -1948) had appeared in a small number of B pictures like the Kermit Maynard shoot-em-up *Rough Riding Rhythm* (1937) but was best known as a showgirl, headlining the extravaganzas produced by her lover and fellow guest Earl Carroll. At the time of her appearance on *Ellery Queen* she was the host of *Furlough Fun*, a West Coast radio program on which servicemen returning from action in the Pacific were entertained and interviewed. She and Carroll died together in a plane crash.

Singer Edythe Wright (   -1965) was one of the original vocalists with Tommy Dorsey's orchestra. Later she sang with the orchestra headed by radio and eventual TV star Ozzie Nelson.

149. English-born Eric Blore (1887-1959) started working as an insurance agent, then toured Australia as a stage actor before appearing in shows and revues in England. He came to the U.S. in 1923 and appeared in several Broadway plays and more than 80 movies including five of RKO's nine musicals starring Fred Astaire and Ginger Rogers. Between 1940 and 1947 he played the butler Jamison in ten Lone Wolf mystery films.

150. Actress Linda Watkins (1909-1976) was under contract to the Fox studio in the early 1930s, appearing in such films as *The Gay Caballero* (1932) with George O'Brien and *Charlie Chan's Chance* (1932) with Warner Oland. During the golden age of radio she played numerous supporting roles on mystery series including *Gang Busters, Mr. and Mrs. North*, and *Under Arrest*.

At the time of his appearance on *Ellery Queen*, Edward Pawley (1903-1988) was starring as crusading newspaper editor Steve Wilson on radio's *Big Town* series.

151. At the time of her appearance on *Ellery Queen*, Fran Carlon (1913-1993) was appearing on radio's *Big Town* series as newspaperwoman Lorelei Kilbourne. Her co-star on *Big Town* and fellow guest on *Ellery Queen* was Edward Pawley.

For Edward Pawley, see 150 above. For Linda Watkins, see 150 above.

152. For Virginia Field, see 130 above. For Ed Sullivan, see 115 above. For Parks Johnson, see 16 above. For Warren Hull, see 89 above.

153. Boxer Jack Dempsey (1895-1983) began his professional ring career at age 17 and became a champion in 1919 when he delivered a brutal beating to former champ Jess Willard. He is considered a pioneer of modern boxing and one of the toughest men ever to enter the ring.

154. For Arthur Murray, see 81 above. Kathryn Murray (1906-1999) was Arthur's wife and dancing partner.

155. Vocalist Ginni Young was the wife of actor Alan Young. When Alan had his own radio series, Ginni led the group known as The Regulaires which, along with singer Diane Courtney and George Wyle's orchestra, provided the music for the program.

For Arthur Murray, see 81 above. For Kathryn Murray, see 154 above.

156. Ted Collins (1901-1964) was a salesman for Columbia Records when he discovered Kate Smith and took over as her manager, director, producer, announcer and friend. He was responsible for introducing Bud Abbott and Lou Costello and the Aldrich Family to the radio audience on Smith's program.

Broadway gossip columnist Earl Wilson (1907-1987) penned the syndicated column "It Happened Last Night" and wrote several books on show business. Almost a year after his appearance on *Ellery Queen* he began hosting his own radio series, *Earl Wilson's Broadway Column*.

158. Singer Joan Brooks, billed as "the girl with the voice you won't forget," was the vocalist on radio's *Lavender and New Lace*. Between the summer of early 1944 and early 1945 she had her own late-night radio program on CBS.

Ben Grauer (1906-1977) served as host, announcer, emcee and newscaster on many radio series including *Ripley's Believe It Or Not*, *Grand Cental Station*, *Information Please*, *Irene Rich Dramas*, *The Magic Key of RCA* and *The Lux Radio Theatre*. He was also the announcer for numerous radio mysteries such as *Behind Prison Bars*, *Mr. Keen, Tracer of Lost Persons*, *Mr. District Attorney*, and *Sleep No More*.

Actress Pamela Kellino (1918-1996) was the daughter of Isidore Ostrer, the head of the family that controlled the Gaumont-British movie studio, and appeared in several English movies such as *I Met a Murderer* (1939). Between 1940 and 1964 she was married to actor James Mason and, during the summer of 1949, co-starred with him on the radio anthology series *Illusion*.

159. Actor John Boles (1895-1969) served as a U.S. spy in Germany, Bulgaria and Turkey during the World War I period, then became an actor and appeared in more than 50 movies beginning in 1924.

Agatha Christie (1890-1976), perhaps the best-known English detective novelist of the 20th century, was the creator of eccentric Belgian detective Hercule Poirot, who became the star of his own radio series in February 1945. Unable to travel abroad during World War II, she appeared on *Ellery Queen* via transatlantic hookup.

For Joan Brooks, see 158 above. For George McManus, see 94 above.

160. Bill O'Connor was a regular performer on *National Barn Dance* and was also one of the announcers on *The Silver Eagle* in 1951.

161. Actress Jeanne Cagney (1919-1984) was the younger sister of James Cagney and appeared with him in *Yankee Doodle Dandy* (1942), *The Time of Your Life* (1948), *A Lion Is in the Streets* (1953) and *Man of a Thousand Faces* (1957).

Gloria Swanson (1899-1983) became a star in 1919 under director Cecil B. DeMille. In the 1920s she became the mistress of business tycoon Joseph Kennedy, the father of JFK and the producer of the last silent film in which she starred, *Queen Kelly* (1929), directed by Erich von Stroheim. It was von Stroheim's copy of this film that Swanson watches when, playing Norma Desmond in *Sunset Boulevard* (1950), she leaps into the projector beam shouting "Have they forgotten what a star looks like? I'll be up there again, so help me!" In later years Swanson was a clothes designer and artist and the founder of Essence of Nature Cosmetics. She appeared on TV through the 1960s and 1970s, doing cameos and pushing health foods.

For Bill O'Connor, see 160 above.

162. Playwright Marc Connelly (1890-1980) is best known for his Pulitzer Prize-winning stage play *The Green Pastures*, a fantasy of Biblical history presented in terms of the religious life of Southern blacks.

Actress Martha Scott (1914-    ) captivated Broadway theatergoers with her portrayal of Emily Webb in the original production of Thornton Wilder's *Our Town*. She reprised her stage performance for the movie version in 1940, earning an Academy Award nomination. During the 1970s she played Bob's mom on *The Bob Newhart Show*.

Howard W. Blakeslee (1880-1952) was science editor for the Associated Press.

163. Character actor Eddie Mayehoff started as a comedy writer for radio programs. He acted on radio in shows like *The Edgar Bergen and Charlie McCarthy Program* and later appeared in Broadway musicals and dramas and on TV.

Hollywood costume designer Edith Head (1898-1981) influenced American fashion for decades by dressing countless female movie stars. During her 44 years at Paramount Pictures she was nominated for 34 Academy Awards and won eight Oscars.

For Bea Wain, see 70 above. For Agatha Christie, see 159 above.

164. For John Shuttleworth, see 116 above. For Ben Grauer, see 158 above.

165. For Brenda Forbes, see 121 above. For Candy Jones, see 111 above.
For Benay Venuta, see 93 above.

166. Paris-born Irene Bordoni (1893?-1953) was best known as a star of the musical stage, where she spiced up many saucy musical revues from the mid-teens through the 1930s. During her brief time on radio she sang a few songs and spoke in broken English.

Al Trace (1900-1993) led a band called Shuffle Rhythm and wrote songs that were sung by Frank Sinatra, the Andrews Sisters and other top performers of the time. He also sang songs written by others including the novelty hit "Mairzy Doats."

Eddie Dowling (1889-1976) worked on the stage, in Hollywood and on radio as an actor, writer, producer, director and singer. He made his Broadway acting debut in 1919 and over the next several decades appeared in countless stage productions, the most memorable being Tennessee Williams' *The Glass Menagerie*.

Dowling made his radio debut in 1932 as emcee of *The Follies of the Air*, going on to host *We, The People* and *The Big Break*. As a director he received a Pulitzer Prize (for William Saroyan's *The Time of Your Life*) and as a playwright he won four Drama Critics Circle awards. On February 27, 1944, the day after his appearance on *Ellery Queen*, he began hosting *Wide Horizons*, a Sunday afternoon radio program that included interviews with servicemen, new stage talent, and a variety of subjects relating to aviation. The program folded after 13 weeks.

Helen Menken (1902-1966), star of the daytime serial *Second Husband*, was also the inspiration behind *Stage Door Canteen*, a radio program recreating the many canteens set up by the American Theater Wing during World War II.

167. Arlene Francis (1907-2001) appeared in several movies of the early sound era such as *Murders in the Rue Morgue* (1932) but is best known for her work in TV, appearing for 25 years as a panelist on *What's My Line?* During the late 1950s she became the first woman to host a network TV newsmagazine show, NBC's *Home*.

Singer Lucy Monroe (1906?-1987) appeared on numerous radio programs including *Manhattan Merry-Go-Round*, *Lavender and Lace*, and *Echoes of New York*. Two months after appearing on *Ellery Queen* she became the host of her own short-lived radio program, *Swing Shift Frolics*. She is best known for having publicly sung the national anthem more than 5,000 times.

Actress Helen Hayes (1900-1993) was known as the First Lady of the American Theater but also won two Oscars during her long career: for her performance in *The Sin of Madelon Claudet* (1931) as a woman who sacrifices everything for her illegitimate son, and for her role as an ingenious stowaway in *Airport* (1970).

Lindsay MacHarrie (1900?-1960) was director of *The Cinnamon Bear*, a syndicated Christmas radio serial that is still heard over various stations during the holidays. He also directed the daytime serial *The Story of Myrt and Marge*.

168. Actress June Vincent (1919-   ) appeared in many mystery movies during the 1940s. She is perhaps best known for playing the title role in the haunting *Black Angel* (1946) opposite Dan Duryea, Broderick Crawford and Peter Lorre.

Stan Lomax (1899-1988) was a sports announcer for WOR Radio in New York.

For Aubrey Waller Cook, see 70 above. For Irene Bordoni, see 166 above.

169. Connee Boswell (1907-1976) lost much of her ability to walk at age four after falling out of a wagon. She spent the rest of her life in a wheelchair but made an impact on music during the 1930s when she performed with her sisters. All the Boswell girls were musically talented and capable of providing their own backup on piano, cello or violin. When her sisters married, Connie (as she was then) went solo, changing the spelling of her name during the 1940s. She sang regularly on Bing Crosby's *Kraft Music Hall*.

Spanish-born bandleader Xavier Cugat (1900-1990) formed his own band specializing in Latin American rhythms and eventually became known as The Rumba King. He was also renowned for his talent as a caricaturist. At the time of his appearance on *Ellery Queen* he had his own radio series on the ABC network.

For Joan Edwards, see 89 above.

170.   For Nanette Fabray, see 115 above. For John G. Chapman, see 109 above.

171.   Canadian-born singer Dick Todd made his radio debut in 1933 and, after coming to the U.S., appeared on *The Magic Key of RCA* and *Your Hit Parade*.

172.   Marc Lawrence (1910-    ) was a character actor who played numerous heavies in crime-suspense movies.   During the Red Menace scare of the early 1950s he was called before the House Un-American Activities Committee and admitted having once belonged to the Communist party.   Blacklisted in Hollywood, he continued acting in English and Italian films.
Milton Cross (1897-1975) enjoyed a long career as a network radio announcer. An opera lover since youth, he is best remembered for his 43 years as host and narrator of *The Metropolitan Opera* broadcasts.

173.   Author and lecturer Dale Carnegie (1888-1955) became world renowned for his book *How to Win Friends and Influence People* and his courses on public speaking.   Two radio programs of the 1930s – *Little Known Facts About Well Known People* and *How to Win Friends and Influence People* – were based on Carnegie's books.
Ted Fio Rito (1900-1971) was a bandleader, pianist, organist and songwriter during his musical career and also owned a nightclub for a while.   He was often heard on radio and had his own show on the Mutual network.   Among the songs he wrote are "Charlie My Boy," "I Never Knew," "Sometime" and "Toot Toot Tootsie."
For F. Beverley Kelley, see 117 above.   For Marc Lawrence, see 172 above.

174.   For George McManus, see 94 above.

175.   Clayton Rawson (1906-1971) was not only an award-winning mystery writer but a professional magician.   His stage name, The Great Merlini, was also the name of the magician-detective in his mystery novels.   In the 1960s he was the managing editor of *Ellery Queen's Mystery Magazine*.

176.   J.C. Lewis was a producer of numerous radio programs including *The Cisco Kid*, *The Jack Kirkwood Show* and *The Johnson Family*.
Actor Martin Kosleck (1907-1994) fled Nazi Germany, resettled in Hollywood and became well known for his icy demeanor and piercing stare as he played countless Nazi officers, concentration camp commandants, enemy spies and domestic psychopaths. Among his film credits are *Nick Carter, Master Detective* (1939), *Calling Philo Vance* (1940), *The Frozen Ghost* (1945), and the Sherlock Holmes movie *Pursuit to Algiers* (1945).

221

177.	Actor Rex Harrison (1908-1990) had a long career in Hollywood, playing the male leads in *Anna and the King of Siam* (1946), *The Ghost and Mrs. Muir* (1947) and many other films. He is best known for his role as Professor Henry Higgins in both the original stage production of *My Fair Lady* and in the 1964 film co-starring Audrey Hepburn.

John J. Anthony was not a real person but the persona under which Lester Kroll (1902-1970) acted as host of radio's *The Goodwill Hour*, a program he created for himself in which, as John J., he claimed to be an expert on all areas of human relationships, giving simple and dogmatic answers to the most difficult financial and matrimonial questions. Throughout its run the show was under constant attack by judges, social organizations and radio critics, many of whom considered "Anthony" a rogue.

Singer Rose Marie Lombardo (1926-	) was the sister of bandleader Guy Lombardo, who appeared twice on *Ellery Queen* as a guest armchair detective. During the 1920s Guy and Rose Marie and their three brothers moved from Canada to the U.S. and began performing on radio.

178.	Actress Marjorie Lord (1918-	) played numerous roles in mystery movies including *Sherlock Holmes in Washington* (1941), *Flesh and Fantasy* (1943) and *The Strange Mrs. Crane* (1948). She is best remembered for playing Danny Thomas' wife on the TV sitcom *Make Room for Daddy*. At the time of her appearance on *Ellery Queen* she was married to actor John Archer, who himself played armchair detective on the show two weeks after her.

179.	Henry Daniell (1894-1963) left England to act on the Broadway stage, where he appeared opposite Ethel Barrymore. He played Nazis in *The Great Dictator* (1940) and *Watch on the Rhine* (1943) but is best known among movie buffs for his performances in several of Universal's Sherlock Holmes films starring Basil Rathbone and Nigel Bruce. He was playing Prince Gregor of Transylvania in the movie version of *My Fair Lady* when he died of a heart attack.

Bandleader and pianist Vincent Lopez (1909-1975) was taught piano at an early age by his father. In 1921, over WJZ in New York, he inaugurated the first dance band remote ever broadcast on radio. As an adult he played countless hotels and ballrooms and for 25 years his dance band was a fixture at the Hotel Taft Grill Room in New York. His theme song "Nola" and his greeting "Lopez speaking" became familiar to millions when his band began playing on radio. He recorded on several labels, performed in movies and Broadway musicals, operated the Casa Lopez nightclub, and appeared on television later in his career.

180.	Actor John Archer (1915-1999), born Ralph Bowman, broke into movies and changed his name after winning a talent search contest on the *Jesse Lasky's Gateway To Hollywood* radio program. Best remembered for playing heroes in B films, Archer also made a significant impact on radio. He appeared on *The FBI in Peace and War*, and for one season he starred as *The Shadow*. He was also heard on *David Harding, Counterspy*, *Gang Busters*, and *Quick As a Flash*. He was married to actress Marjorie Lord, who had appeared on *Ellery Queen* two weeks before him.

Actress Carol Thurston (1923-1969) appeared in numerous Westerns including *The Last Round-Up* (1947), *Apache Chief* (1949) and *Flaming Feather* (1951). On television she played Emma Clanton on *The Life and Legend of Wyatt Earp*.

Rose Marie Curley (1925-    ) took the country by storm when she was first introduced on radio in 1927 as a child singing star. By 1932 Baby Rose Marie had her own weekly 15-minute show, broadcast over the Blue network and sponsored by Tastyeast. Even as a child she was gifted with an adult-sounding singing voice that was a curiosity and a delight to radio audiences. By 1938 she had dropped the Baby from her name but was still belting out songs. In addition to her own show, she also performed with Vincent Lopez, Leo Reisman, Rudy Vallee, and Paul Whiteman. On television she is best known for her long-running role on *The Dick Van Dyke Show*.

181.   Royal Arch Gunnison, a newscaster for the Mutual radio network, became an overnight celebrity with his own 15-minute program, which aired twice a week between December 1943 and September 1944. Two days before his appearance on *Ellery Queen* he was covering the Normandy landings for his radio audience.

For Carol Thurston, see 180 above.

182.   Jane Cowl (1883-1950) began her acting career as a child and went on to become well known on both stage and screen. She also wrote a number of plays including *Smilin' Through* and *The Flaming Sign*. She was instrumental in the operation of the Stage Door Canteen during World War II and played herself in the 1943 movie of the same name. On radio she was heard regularly on the Danny Kaye program and also hosted her own show, *Just Between You and Jane Cowl*.

British-born actor Roland Young (1887-1953) began in mystery films quite early in his career, playing Dr. Watson in the silent *Sherlock Holmes* (1922), which was filmed in London with John Barrymore as Holmes. His book of theatrical caricatures, *Actors and Others*, was published in 1925. After coming to the U.S. he appeared in *The Bishop Murder Case* (1930), which starred Basil Rathbone as Philo Vance. Outside the mystery field he is best known for playing the title role in *Topper* (1937), which earned him an Oscar nomination, and for his part as Katharine Hepburn's uncle in *The Philadelphia Story* (1940). Soon after his appearance on *Ellery Queen* he had a major role in *And Then There Were None* (1945), based on Agatha Christie's play and novel.

184.   Radio actress Claudia Morgan (1911-1974) is best remembered for playing Nora Charles – opposite a variety of Nicks including Les Damon, Bill Smith, Les Tremayne and Joseph Curtin – throughout the entire run of *The Adventures of The Thin Man*. She also had supporting roles on many daytime serials including *David Harum*, *Against the Storm*, *Lone Journey*, *We Love and Learn*, and *The Right to Happiness*.

Hildegarde, born Hildegarde Loretta Sell in Milwaukee, Wisconsin, became famous as a singer after she and her friend and agent Anna Sosenko concocted for her an almost totally fictitious persona of uncertain nationality, designed to give her an international flavor. She starred for many years in her own radio program, *Hildegarde's Raleigh Room*, heard on NBC.

185. Four years before appearing on *Ellery Queen*, actor Michael Whalen (1902-1974) had played the murderer in *Ellery Queen, Master Detective* (1940), first of Columbia's series of EQ movies with Ralph Bellamy in the lead. For years after his EQ encounters he played badguy parts in B movies, cliffhanger serials like *Batman and Robin* (1949), and early TV series like *The Cisco Kid*.

For Royal Arch Gunnison, see 181 above.

186. For Michael Whalen, see 185 above.

187. "A Japanese attack on Pearl Harbor is a strategic impossibility," said Major George Fielding Eliot (1894-1971) some time before it happened. Nevertheless he was hired by CBS as a military and naval correspondent and news analyst after the U.S. entered World War II. In between making strategic assessments he wrote stories for ꝟlp mystery magazines.

Assistant to the Chief of Staff of the Fourth Army Corps during World War I, John Stilwell (1886-1963) rose to the rank of Colonel and was addressed by that title for the rest of his life. His brother, General Joseph "Vinegar Joe" Stilwell, commanded U.S. troops in the China-Burma-India theater during World War II.

188. For Claudia Morgan, see 184 above.

189. Jane Russell (1921-   ) was discovered by Howard Hughes while working as a receptionist for his dentist and offered a 7-year movie contract. Her screen credits include *The Outlaw* (1943) and *Gentlemen Prefer Blondes* (1953).

For Jane Cowl, see 182 above.

190. Actress Dorothy Hart (1923-   ), originally a model, was signed by Universal Pictures and cast in everything from Red Menace melodramas like *I Was a Communist for the F.B.I.* (1951) to jungle adventures like *Tarzan's Savage Fury* (1952). In 1953 she appeared as a regular panelist on TV's *Take a Guess*.

For Major George Fielding Eliot, see 187 above.

191. Actor John Mills (1908-   ) appeared in over 100 movies during his career, first in his native England where he appeared in *Great Expectations* (1946), later in the U.S. During the 1967-68 TV season he starred in the TV series *Dundee and the Culhane*, playing a British barrister in the old West. He won an Oscar for his supporting part as the village idiot in *Ryan's Daughter* (1970). In the TV movie *Sherlock Holmes and the Masks of Death* (1984) he played an aging Dr. Watson.

For Bill Stern, see 76 above.

192. John Conte (1915-   ) began his radio career in 1934 as announcer for a Los Angeles station. Later he performed the same function on radio programs such as *Kay Kyser's Kollege of Musical Knowledge*, *The Screen Guild Theater*, *The Silver Theater*, and mystery series like *The Adventures of Sherlock Holmes* and *Big Town*.

For Joan Edwards, see 89 above.

193. For Fred Waring, see 133 above. For Earl Wilson, see 156 above.

194. Singer Allan Jones (1907-1992) is best remembered by film buffs as the charming but irresponsible cad Gaylord Ravenal in *Show Boat* (1936), where he sang the songs of Jerome Kern and Oscar Hammerstein as though they had been written for him alone, and as the foil for the Marx Brothers in *A Night at the Opera* (1935) and *A Day at the Races* (1937). His son by actress Irene Hervey is singer Jack Jones.

195. Singer Josephine Antoine (1908-1971) performed with the Metropolitan Opera for over ten years and also sang with the Chicago, San Francisco and Cincinnati opera companies. Later she taught music at several universities and professional schools. On radio she was a guest on *The Musical Moments Revue* and *The Ford Sunday Evening Hour*.

196. Cornel Wilde (1915-1989), a champion fencer on the U.S. Olympic team who spoke at least six languages, quit the team just before the 1936 Berlin Olympics in order to take a role an a stage play. He soon migrated to Hollywood and earned an Oscar nomination for his role as the composer Chopin in *A Song to Remember* (1945). The rest of the decade he spent as the leading man in romances and swashbucklers. Perhaps his best movie role was as the tough cop Diamond in Joseph H. Lewis' film noir *The Big Combo* (1955). In 1966 he produced, directed, and starred in *The Naked Prey*, a tour-de-force adventure drama which brought him acclaim as a director.

198. For "Senator" Ed Ford, see 144 above. For Harry Hershfield, see 144 above. For Joe Laurie, Jr., see 144 above.

199. Ken Sobol wrote numerous books including *The Cosmic Christmas* and *The Clock Museum*. He is best known for his biography *Babe Ruth and the American Dream*.
Belgian-born Armand Denis (1896?-1971) was an explorer and documentary film-maker whose passion was African wildlife. His *Savage Splendor* (1949) was the first full-length color film shot in Africa.

200. Singer Vaughn Monroe (1911-1973) led his own orchestra on numerous radio programs including the quiz show *How'm I Doin'?* In 1946 he signed a long-tern contract to appear on *The Camel Caravan* and proved so popular that the show was eventually retitled *The Vaughn Monroe Program*.

201. Leonard Levinson (1904-1974) was the first scriptwriter for radio's *The Great Gildersleeve*. He also wrote scripts for *Fibber McGee and Molly*, *The Jack Carson Show* and *The Stu Erwin Show*.

202. Actress Aline MacMahon (1899-1991) played supporting roles in numerous movies including *Five Star Final* (1931), *Stage Door Canteen* (1943), *The Eddie Cantor Story* (1953) and *Cimarron* (1960).

225

203. Actor, writer, toastmaster, dialect comedian and storyteller Peter Donald (1918-1979) was born into a show business family. He wanted to write for both stage and radio but spent most of his career in front of the microphone. He is best remembered as Ajax Cassidy, the feisty Irishman residing in Allen's Alley on *The Fred Allen Show*, and as one of the quartet of jokesters on *Can You Top This?* His three colleagues in comedy had appeared together on *Ellery Queen* five weeks before him.

Nora Stirling wanted to be a radio actress and played Mary on *Mary and Bob*, one of the first network radio romance shows, but spent most of her career as a scriptwriter. At the time of her appearance on *Ellery Queen* she was writing scripts and polishing dialogue for NBC's *Words at War*.

204. Announcer, emcee, producer and advertising executive Tom Slater was the younger brother of sportscaster Bill Slater. His credits as an announcer include *The Court of Human Relations, The Better Half, Kitty Keene* and *Melody Puzzles*.

Red Barber (1908-1992), known as The Ol' Redhead, was one of America's best known sportscasters during the 1930s and 1940s. He broadcast his first of many World Series games in 1935. Four years later he moved to New York City and became the play-by-play commentator for the Brooklyn Dodger games heard over radio stations WOR and WHN. In 1941 he was hired to narrate Pathe Newsreels' sports films. About a year after his appearance on *Ellery Queen*, Barber took over as sports director for the CBS network, replacing Ted Husing who himself would guest on *Ellery Queen* a few months after the Redhead.

205. Fannie Hurst (1889-1968) was a popular author of romantic novels and magazine stories. During 1942 she had a short-lived radio series on which she would read her own stories and poems to the audience. At the time of her appearance on *Ellery Queen* she was spending her Saturday mornings as host of another program of her own, *Fannie Hurst Presents*.

206. Rouben Mamoulian (1897-1987), born in Russia of Armenian Jewish descent, earned a law degree from the University of Moscow while studying at the Moscow Art Theatre. After coming to the U.S. in the 1920s he taught and directed at New York's Theater Guild. At the peak of his career he alternated between directing Broadway musicals – including *Porgy and Bess* (1935), *Oklahoma!* (1943) and *Carousel* (1945) – and making Hollywood movies, including *Dr. Jekyll and Mr. Hyde* (1932) and *The Mark of Zorro* (1940).

For Jeanne Cagney, see 161 above.

207. Actor Victor Jory (1902-1982) had character parts in countless movies and the title role in the 15-chapter cliffhanger serial *The Shadow* (1940). At the time of his appearance on *Ellery Queen* he was starring on CBS Radio's *Matinee Theater*, an anthology series in which he played a different leading man each week. He also appeared regularly on *Quick As a Flash* and *Suspense*.

Actress and author Ilka Chase (1903-1978) moved in high society but also devoted much of her time to charitable causes, raising funds for hospitals, Actors Equity, Bundles for Britain and wildlife protection. On radio she hosted *Cresta Blanca Carnival* and *Luncheon at the Waldorf* and was a panelist on *Leave It to the Girls*.

208. Actor Barry Sullivan (1912-1994) appeared in countless Hollywood mystery-suspense films and Westerns. Among his credits are *The Woman of the Town* (1943), *Lady in the Dark* (1944), *Suspense* (1946), and *Forty Guns* (1957). On television he played Sheriff Pat Garrett in *The Tall Man*.

Frank Graham (1893-1965) was the announcer for numerous radio programs including *The Judy Canova Show*, *The Electric Hour*, *The Rudy Vallee Show* and *The Purple Heart Program*. At the time of his appearance on *Ellery Queen* he was hosting the CBS series *Theater of Romance*.

209. Actor Neil Hamilton (1899-1984) began his movie career in 1918 and got his big break when he appeared in D.W. Griffith's *The White Rose* (1923). After performing in several more Griffith films he was signed by Paramount in the late 1920s and soon became one of the studio's most popular leading men. Over the decades he worked everywhere from glittering MGM to rock-bottom PRC. Known to old-movie buffs as Dr. Jack Petrie in *The Mysterious Dr. Fu Manchu* (1929) and *The Return of Dr. Fu Manchu* (1930), he is best remembered by younger audiences as Commissioner Gordon in the 1960s TV series *Batman*.

For Harriet Van Horne, see 95 above.

210. Austrian-born actress Luise Rainer (1910-    ) came to the U.S. in the 1930s and won two consecutive Oscars, for playing showgirl Anna Held in *The Great Ziegfeld* (1936) and the patient Chinese woman Olan in *The Good Earth* (1937). She became an American citizen in the early 1940s and married playwright Clifford Odets, a tumultuous marriage that ended in divorce. She is still alive today and was a guest at the 70th Academy Awards show.

211. Former band singer Janet Blair (1921-    ) signed a contract with Columbia Pictures in 1941, appearing in films like *Three Girls About Town* (1942), *Blondie Goes to College* (1942) and the fantasy *Once Upon a Time* (1944). She played the title role in *Burn, Witch, Burn* (1962).

212. George Givot (1903-1984) had small roles in many movies and occasionally a much better part, for example in the Hopalong Cassidy feature *Leather Burners* (1943) where he played a crazed giant living in a cabin inside an abandoned mine and plotting to become dictator of the United States. His proficiency at foreign accents won him many parts as sinister characters in movies of international intrigue. He supplied the voice of Tony the Italian restaurant owner in the Disney animated feature *Lady and the Tramp* (1955).

213. Dean F. Willey was assistant general manager of the New York, New Haven & Hartford Railroad.

214. For Howard W. Blakeslee, see 162 above.

215.  Announcer Ted Husing (1901-1962) was a radio sportscaster and was also heard as the announcer or emcee of many series including *Tonight on Broadway, Saturday Night Swing Club, The Eddie Cantor Show* and *Cheers From the Camps.*  For a short time he narrated the *March of Time* newsreels.  Two years after appearing on *Ellery Queen* he became a disc jockey for New York station WHN, earning an annual salary of $250,000 as host of *Ted Husing's Bandstand.*  He also worked as a sportswriter, appeared in several movies, and wrote an autobiography, *Ten Years Before the Mike.*

216.  Advertising executive H. W. Roden (1895-1963) changed careers in the 1940s, writing crime stories for pulp mystery magazines and also publishing five private-eye novels, beginning with *You Only Hang Once* (1944).

217.  Dick Powell (1904-1963) started his film career as a crooner in Warner Bros. musicals of the 1930s.  During the late Thirties he sang regularly on radio.  But by the time of his appearance on *Ellery Queen* he had reinvented his screen persona, playing Raymond Chandler's private eye Philip Marlowe in *Murder, My Sweet* (1944), and a vengeance-driven war veteran in *Cornered* (1945). On radio he also played hardboiled investigators, starring as Richard Rogue on NBC's *Rogue's Gallery* and later as *Richard Diamond, Private Detective.*  When radio was displaced by television he and three other movie stars formed Four Star Productions and began turning out anthology series like *Four Star Theater* and *Zane Grey Theater*, the latter hosted by Powell himself.

218.  For Earl Wilson, see 156 above.

219.  Milo Boulton came to radio from the Broadway stage and was heard regularly as both actor and emcee during the 1930s and 1940s.  Most of his acting roles were in daytime serials like *The Goldbergs* and *Pepper Young's Family.*  Between 1941 and 1947 he hosted *We, The People.*

220.  Actress Jane Wyatt (1911-    ) migrated from stage to screen in the early 1930s when she was placed under contract by Universal and made her film debut in director James Whale's *One More River* (1934).  A few years later, on loan to Columbia, she co-starred with Ronald Colman in Frank Capra's *Lost Horizon* (1937). In the 1950s she co-starred with Robert Young in the classic TV sitcom *Father Knows Best.*

221.  For F. Beverley Kelley, see 173 above.

222.  Anne Fromer was managing editor of *Magazine Digest.*

223.  Monroe Wheeler (1899-1988) was a well-known book designer who remained modest about his talents in that field and as an art critic.  Between 1941 and 1968 he headed the Department of Exhibitions and Publications at the Museum of Modern Art.

228

224.  Jo-Carroll Dennison (1924-   ) was Miss America of 1942 and thereby earned a few supporting roles in movies including *Winged Victory* (1944) and *The Missing Lady* (1946), one of a series of three films based on radio's *The Shadow*.

225.  Author Jack Gaver edited and co-authored many books on stage drama and radio.  At the time of his appearance on *Ellery Queen* his current book was *There's Laughter in the Air*, a compilation of radio comedy scripts from the 1930s and 1940s including rarities like *The Jack Kirkwood Show* and *Easy Aces*.

226.  Orlo Robertson was General Sports Editor for the Associated Press.

227.  Ted R. Gamble (1905?-1960) was director of the U.S. Treasury Department's War Finance Division during WWII.  After the war he became president of a corporation that owned radio and TV stations in Portland, Oregon.

228.  For James Montgomery Flagg, see 132 above.

229.  Metropolitan Opera singer Annamary Dickey (1911-   ) sang on radio not only in operas but with popular performers and musicians like Frank Sinatra and Benny Goodman.  Later in her career she co-starred on Broadway with Yul Brynner in *The King and I*.  She taught voice for 20 years at the University of South Florida and received an honorary degree from that institution in 1982.

230.  Operatic mezzo-soprano Gladys Swarthout (1904-1969) debuted in 1924 with the Chicago Civic Opera and first performed with the Metropolitan Opera five years later.  During the 1930s she starred in a few movies.  On radio she was heard regularly in the Metropolitan Opera broadcasts and also on less highbrow programs like *The Prudential Family Hour*, *The Railroad Hour*, *The Magic Key of RCA* and *The Ford Sunday Evening Hour*.
For Ted R. Gamble, see 227 above.

231.  Colonel Joseph S. Snyder was executive officer of Camp Kilmer, a WWII army post near New Brunswick, N.J., through which more than twenty divisions passed on their way to the battlefronts of Europe.
Actress Joan Tetzel (1924-1977) appeared on the Broadway and London stage as well as in movies like *A Game of Death* (1945) and Alfred Hitchcock's *The Paradine Case* (1947).  Three years after her appearance on *Ellery Queen* her picture appeared on the cover of *Life Magazine* (February 14, 1948).  Later in her career she played the evil nurse in the stage version of *One Flew Over The Cuckoo's Nest* and had a continuing part in the long-running TV cop series *Police Woman*.

232.  Publisher, editor and raconteur Bennett Cerf (1898-1971), the founder of Random House, helped launch countless authors' careers.  In 1960 he made a $50 bet with Dr. Seuss (Theodore Geisel) that Seuss couldn't write an entire book using only fifty words.  The result was *Green Eggs and Ham*.

With his large balding head, bulbous posterior, short limbs and nervous manner, comic actor Victor Moore (1876-1962) specialized in portraying the ineffectual milquetoast characters he had developed years before in vaudeville and on stage. His film credits include *Gift of Gab* (1934), *This Is the Army* (1943), and *Duffy's Tavern* (1945).

233. Harvard graduate George Frazier (1911-1974) was the entertainment editor of *Life* magazine and a columnist for the Boston *Globe*.

234. George Lait was a war correspondent for the International News Service and one of the technical advisors on the movie *The Story of GI Joe*.

235. Hong Kong-born actress Wendy Barrie (1912-1978) played the female lead in *The Hound of the Baskervilles* (1939), which marked Basil Rathbone's debut as Sherlock Holmes. She appeared regularly, although as a different character each time, in RKO's series about The Saint, and later had a continuing part in the early entries of the same studio's series about a somewhat similar character, The Falcon. At the time of her appearance on *Ellery Queen* she was co-host of the radio quiz show *Detect and Collect*. She hosted many other radio and television programs during her long career.
Radio quizmaster Fred Uttal was Barrie's co-host on *Detect and Collect*.

236. Actress Julie Gibson specialized in playing women with foreign accents in movies like *Hail the Conquering Hero* (1944) and *Chick Carter, Detective* (1946).

237. Vocalist Gertrude Niesen (1902-1983) was in the 1936 Ziegfeld Follies, which featured Fanny Brice in her final Broadway appearance. She appeared in Hollywood musicals like *Top of the Town* (1937), *Rookies on Parade* (1941) and *Start Cheering* (1943), and on Broadway she appeared in *Follow The Girls* where she sang what became one of her biggest hits, "I Want To Get Married."

238. Actress Evelyn Keyes (1919-    ) is best known for playing Suellen O'Hara in *Gone With the Wind* (1939). Later while under contract to Columbia Pictures she co-starred with Robert Montgomery in *Here Comes Mr. Jordan* (1941) and with Larry Parks in *The Jolson Story* (1946). Her private life was notoriously turbulent. She divorced her first husband (who then shot himself), married director Charles Vidor, and left him after two years for director John Huston, to whom she was married for four years. Later she lived with producer Mike Todd and had a cameo in his *Around the World in Eighty Days* (1956). In 1957 she wed bandleader Artie Shaw.

239. Sally Eilers (1908-1978) was a leading lady in numerous silent features during the 1920s. She was married to rodeo champion and screen cowboy hero Hoot Gibson until the early 1930s when she became a bigger star than he was. At the time of her appearance on *Ellery Queen* she was no longer a star but was appearing in cult director Edgar G. Ulmer's low-budget film noir *Strange Illusion* (1945).

240.  Jonah J. Goldstein (1886-1967) was a New York judge who in 1935 and 1936 appeared regularly on radio's *The Goodwill Court*.  At the time of his appearance on *Ellery Queen* he was the Republican candidate for mayor of New York City.

241.  Coloratura soprano Virginia MacWatters was well known during the early 1940s for her Zerbinetta and for her performance on Broadway as Adele in *Rosalina*.  At the time of her appearance in *Ellery Queen* she was starring in the musical comedy *Mr. Strauss Goes to Boston*.

242.  For Shep Fields, see 85 above.

243.  George V. Denny, Jr. (1899-1959), associate director of the New York League for Political Education, was invited in 1935 to serve as host and moderator on *America's Town Meeting of the Air*, a public affairs discussion program that remained on the air until the early 1950s.

244.  Actress Edith Spencer, who had been playing the title role on the long-running radio soap opera *Aunt Jenny* since 1937, appeared on *Ellery Queen* in the persona of her character.  She continued as Aunt Jenny until the early 1950s when she was replaced by Agnes Young.

245.  Carol Stone was a Broadway actress who later moved into TV and had the continuing part of Kate Holliday on *The Life and Legend of Wyatt Earp*.
     For Eddie Dowling, see 166 above.

246.  Jan Clayton (1918-1983) appeared in Westerns and other movies beginning in the late 1930s.  After playing the female lead in the Hopalong Cassidy feature *In Old Mexico* (1938) she married Russell Hayden, who had a continuing role in the Hoppy pictures as William Boyd's feisty protégé Lucky, but the marriage didn't last.  At the time of her appearance on *Ellery Queen* she was starring on Broadway in Rodgers & Hammerstein's *Carousel*.  During the 1950s she played Ellen Miller on the *Lassie* TV series.
     For Danton Walker, see 138 above.

247.  Commander Henry H. Hale was skipper of the aircraft carrier Franklin, which was under his command when it was crippled in the Pacific and managed to make it back to the Brooklyn Navy Yard for repairs.

248.  Comic actor Edward Everett Horton (1886-1970) appeared in over 100 movies.  He played the title role in the silent *Ruggles of Red Gap* (1923), the Mad Hatter in *Alice in Wonderland* (1933) and a doctor in Alfred Hitchcock's *Spellbound* (1945).  At the time of his appearance on *Ellery Queen* he was host and star of his own radio series, *The Kraft Music Hall*.  In old age he remained active doing voice-overs for animated shorts and narrating *Fractured Fairy Tales* during the early 1960s.

231

249. For Victor Jory, see 207 above.

250. Joseph Curtin and Alice Frost appeared on *Ellery Queen* in the guise of their characters from another whodunit series, NBC's *Mr. and Mrs. North.* Curtin was a regular on many detective and mystery series including *Mr. Keen, Tracer of Lost Persons, Cabin B-13,* and *Mr. District Attorney.* He played Max Chandler on *The Whisper Men* and was the third of the four actors who portrayed Nick Charles on *The Adventures of the Thin Man.* He also narrated the Metropolitan Opera broadcasts. Alice Frost originated the role of big sister Ruth Wayne on the serial drama *Big Sister* and also appeared on *The F.B.I. in Peace and War, Colgate Mysteries, Mr. District Attorney, The Big Story, Famous Jury Trials* and *The Shadow.*

252. Vera Zorina (1917-   ), born in Norway as Birgitta Hartwig, was a star dancer in the mid-1930s, performing all over Europe and often touring in the United States, where she came to stay in 1937 at the invitation of producer Samuel Goldwyn. She became a regular on Broadway in a succession of hits and appeared in such films as *The Goldwyn Follies* (1938), *Star Spangled Rhythm* (1942) and *Follow the Boys* (1944).

253. For Helen Hayes, see 167 above.

254. Major General Emmanuel E. Lombard was a French army officer who served as liaison between General Eisenhower and General Charles de Gaulle during World War II. He retired at the end of the war.
For Vera Zorina, see 252 above.

255. Actress Virginia Vale (1920-   ) appeared in movies from the late 1930s until the end of WWII, frequently opposite George O'Brien in his Western series for RKO and in the same studio's Western musical shorts starring Ray Whitley. After retiring from the screen she worked at Lockheed for more than thirty years.
Actor Ralph Morgan (1883-1956) appeared in a huge number of mystery and detective films including *Charlie Chan's Chance* (1932), *The Kennel Murder Case* (1933), *The Lone Wolf Spy Hunt* (1939), *Dick Tracy vs. Crime, Inc.* (1941), *Gang Busters* (1942), *Song of the Thin Man* (1947) and *Mr. District Attorney* (1947). Three years before his appearance on the *Ellery Queen* radio program he had appeared in *A Close Call for Ellery Queen* (1942), an entry in Columbia's short-lived series about the master detective.

256. Baritone and composer Jean Sablon (1906-1994), known as the French Troubadour, was an international entertainer who performed in nightclubs, on the musical stage and over the airwaves. On radio he was heard on *Hollywood Hotel, The Magic Key of RCA, Shell Chateau* and *The Royal Gelatin Hour.* At the time of his appearance on *Ellery Queen* his own musical variety series, *The Jean Sablon Show,* was airing on CBS.

257. Saul Pett (1918-1993) wrote a daily column on radio for the International News Service but is best known for what he accomplished long after his appearance on *Ellery Queen*. In 1963 he wrote "The Torch Is Passed," describing America's sorrow upon learning of the Kennedy assassination. In the early 1980s he won a Pulitzer Prize for his story on the federal bureaucracy.

258. Radio personality Arthur Godfrey (1903-1983), known as the bad boy of the airwaves, is perhaps best remembered for attacking his sponsors' products while on the air, which caused controversy but also helped the products vanish from store shelves in huge quantities. His low-key rambling style and habit of discussing his personal likes and dislikes made him one of network radio's best known personalities. He hosted his own program, sang, played the ukulele and produced several hit records. In the first decade of TV he hosted *Arthur Godfrey's Talent Scouts*.

259. Actor Morgan Conway (1900-1981) had supporting roles in many detective movies including *Charlie Chan in Reno* (1939), *The Saint Takes Over* (1940) and, by a curious coincidence, *A Desperate Chance for Ellery Queen* (1942). At the time of his appearance on the Queen radio series he was playing Chester Gould's comic-strip cop in RKO's *Dick Tracy* (1945) and *Dick Tracy vs. Cueball* (1946).

260. James L. Cox was a young inventor who, at the time of his appearance on *Ellery Queen*, was best known for the Safreen fluorescent lamp, which at the time was considered the brightest practical light known to man.

262. Actress Marjorie Rambeau (1889-1970) was an extra in countless films and a character actress in many. In 1940 she played the title role in *Tugboat Annie Sails Again* and a sweet little old lady who led an outlaw gang in the Hopalong Cassidy feature *Santa Fe Marshal*. At the time of her appearance on *Ellery Queen* her most recent movie was *Salome, Where She Danced* (1945).

263. Belita was a professional ice skater and dancer who appeared in a few films like *Suspense* (1946), *The Gangster* (1947), and *The Hunted* (1948), usually playing a skater or ballerina.
For James L. Cox, see 260 above.

264. The name Willie Mosconi (1913-1993) is synonymous with pocket billiards. He was a prodigy with the pool cue by the time he was seven, and at age 20 he went on a hectic cross-country exhibition tour with his idol, then world champion Ralph Greenleaf. Mosconi gave numerous exhibitions, helped popularize his sport, and won its World Title fifteen times between 1940 and 1957. His book *Willie Mosconi on Pocket Billiards* was published in 1954.
In 1934, while still in his teens, classical pianist Eugene List (1918-1985) performed Shostakovich's First Piano Concerto in its U.S. premiere, under the direction of Leopold Stokowski. He was a personal favorite of Harry Truman, who was president of the United States at the time of List's appearance on *Ellery Queen*.

265.  Craig Rice (1909-1957), who was born Georgiana Ann Randolph but preferred male bylines for her novels and stories, was one of the most famous and prolific mystery writers of the WWII years, so much so that a caricature of her appeared in 1944 on the cover of *Time*.  Several of her novels – including *The G-String Murders* which she ghosted for stripper Gypsy Rose Lee, a previous guest armchair detective on *Ellery Queen* – were turned into movies, and others were adapted for radio's *Molle Mystery Theater*.  Her short stories were often published in *Ellery Queen's Mystery Magazine*.

Radio announcer Dick Joy started out as a newscaster during his early tenure on radio but soon found himself the emcee and announcer for numerous radio programs including *Dr. Kildare, I Want a Divorce, Kay Kyser's Kollege of Musical Knowledge, The Saint, The Adventures of Sam Spade* and *Vox Pop*.

266.  Alfred Eichler (1908-    ) was an advertising executive who also wrote a number of mystery novels, most of them dealing with the advertising business.

267.  Austrian-born Sam Spiegel (1901-1985) is best known for the classic movies he produced  in the 1950s and later, such as  *The African Queen* (1951), *On the Waterfront* (1954), *The Bridge on the River Kwai* (1957), *Lawrence of Arabia* (1962) and *Nicholas and Alexandra* (1971).  At the time of his appearance on *Ellery Queen* he was producing *The Stranger* (1946), directed by and starring Orson Welles who guested on the same program the following week.

Betty Forsling was radio editor of *Newsweek*.

268.  Orson Welles (1915-1985) first made his mark in his very early twenties, directing prestigious Broadway plays and working simultaneously in radio.  When *The Shadow* as star of his own series debuted over the airwaves in 1937 it was Welles who played the character.  His 1938 radio adaptation of H.G. Wells' *The War of the Worlds* caused countless listeners to believe that Martians had actually invaded New Jersey.  Welles himself invaded Hollywood in 1941 and directed his first movie, *Citizen Kane*, which is often named the finest American film of all time.  He was a frequent guest star on radio programs like *This Is My Best, The March of Time, The Columbia Workshop, The Cavalcade of America* and *Hello Americans*.  At the time of his appearance on *Ellery Queen* his current movie was *The Stranger* (1946), which he both directed and starred in.

269.  Private Pat Berkeley, a veteran of the Army Medical Corps, was recovering from war wounds at New York's Halloran Hospital when he appeared on *Ellery Queen*.

270.   Australian circus performer Con Colleano (1899-1973) became an international star during the 1920s and 1930s.  His skill and daring on the high wire earned him star billing for eleven years with the Ringling Brothers Barnum and Bailey circus.  He was the first man in the world to perform a forward somersault on the wire, a feat previously thought impossible because the performer loses sight of the wire while somersaulting.

At the time six of the Goldwyn Girls appeared on *Ellery Queen*, producer Samuel Goldwyn's current film was *The Kid From Brooklyn* (1946), starring Danny Kaye. Research fails to identify exactly which of the Girls played armchair detective. But if we list all the Girls who appeared in *The Kid From Brooklyn* – Betty Alexander, Shirley Ballard, Virginia Belmont, Jan Bryant, Betty Cargyle, Jean Cronin, Karen X. Gaylord, Donna Hamilton, Helen Kimball, Vonne Lester, Joyce Mackenzie, Martha Montgomery, Diana Mumby, Mary Simpson, Kismi Stefan, Virginia Thorpe and Ruth Valmy – we have inevitably included the half dozen who appeared on this episode of *Ellery Queen*.

271. Carolyn Rolland was associate editor of *Seventeen* magazine.

272. For the Goldwyn Girls, see 270 above.

274. For Joan Edwards, see 89 above. For Saul Pett, see 257 above.

275. For Red Barber, see 204 above.

276. Vernon Pope was editor of *Pageant* magazine.
Singer Margaret Whiting (1924-   ) was the daughter of songwriter Richard A. Whiting and the older sister of actress Barbara Whiting. Both Whiting girls were heard on radio with Johnny Mercer on *Your Hit Parade*. Margaret performed in nightclubs and in movies including *Home Sweet Homicide* (1945), which was based on a novel by previous *Ellery Queen* guest Craig Rice. In 1948 CBS aired *The Margaret Whiting Show* as the summer substitute for the Spike Jones program. Margaret guested on many radio shows including *Club Fifteen*, *The Barry Wood Show*, *The Railroad Hour* and *The Eddie Cantor Show*. In 1955 she and Barbara starred in their own TV series, *Those Whiting Girls*.

277. Puerto Rico-born vocalist Elsa Miranda is best known for impersonating a banana as she sang the "Chiquita Banana" novelty song.
Actress and comedienne Lucille Ball (1911-1989) began her movie career in the late 1930s and was heard on radio at the same period, appearing with Jack Haley on his variety show sponsored by Wonder Bread. She was a regular panelist on *Leave It to the Girls* and, during the early 1940s, made frequent appearances on *Orson Welles' Almanac*. In 1948 she co-starred with Richard Denning on the sitcom *My Favorite Husband*. She is most fondly remembered of course as the star of *I Love Lucy* and other classic TV comedy series.

278. Francis Lederer (1906-   ) was a European matinee idol who came to the United States but failed to duplicate his overseas success. He starred as the debonair jewel thief Michael Lanyard in *The Lone Wolf in Paris* (1938) but his accent made him unconvincing as an American and he was quickly relegated to playing foreigners, notably as the infamous Count in *The Return of Dracula* (1958).

Announcer and emcee John Reed King (1914-1979) was the host or quizmaster for numerous radio programs including *Break the Bank, Double or Nothing, Give and Take*, and *What's My Name?* He announced for *The Victor Borge Show, The Heinz Magazine of the Air, So You Think You Know Music*, and *The Treasure Adventures of Jack Masters*, and spent his later years as director of the First Federal Savings Association in Fresno, California.

279. Dorothy Dunn was a young woman from Cincinnati, Ohio who was invited by *Charm* magazine to visit New York and serve as guest editor for one of the magazine's issues.

280. Archie Mayo (1891-1968) was a versatile movie director whose credits include *Svengali* (1931) with John Barrymore, *The Case of the Lucky Legs* (1935) with Warren William as Perry Mason, and *The Petrified Forest* (1936) with Bette Davis and Humphrey Bogart.
For John Reed King, see 278 above.

281. For Elsa Miranda, see 277 above. For Francis Lederer, see 278 above.

282. For Joseph Curtin and Alice Frost, see 250 above.

283. Actress Dolores Moran (1924-    ) is best known for her supporting roles in films like *Yankee Doodle Dandy* (1942), *To Have and Have Not* (1944), *Hollywood Canteen* (1944) and *The Horn Blows at Midnight* (1945). She was also a talented singer and violinist.
Actor Richard Long   (1927-1974), fresh out of high school and already in major movies, played Loretta Young's brother in *The Stranger* (1946) and appeared on *Ellery Queen*, as the film's producer Sam Spiegel and director-star Orson Welles had done not long before, in order to publicize the film. Among the TV generation Long is best known as Jarrod Barkley in the Western series *The Big Valley*.

284. Composer/lyricist Sunny Skylar's career in music comprises hundreds of recordings. Skylar started as a band singer with Abe Lyman, Paul Whiteman and others and later sang solo. He wrote band material for actress Betty Hutton and even released an album of Christmas music. Perhaps the best known song he wrote is "Besame Mucho."

285. Actor Alan Baxter (1908-1976) played supporting roles in such films as *The Lone Wolf Strikes* (1940), *Shadow of the Thin Man* (1941) and Alfred Hitchcock's *Saboteur* (1942). At the time of his appearance on *Ellery Queen* he was starring in the Broadway play *Voice of the Turtle*.

286. Author Ben Hecht (1894-1964) was one of Hollywood's most prolific and successful screenwriters but claimed to hate the movie industry and all it stood for. *The Front Page*, a stage play he wrote with Charles MacArthur, not only became a huge

236

hit on Broadway but was adapted into no less than three movies. He and MacArthur co-authored and co-directed *Crime Without Passion* (1934) and *The Scoundrel* (1935), which were filmed not in Hollywood but New York. He worked without credit on the scripts of some of the most famous American movies including *Gone with the Wind* and with credit on many more including Alfred Hitchcock's *Spellbound* (1945) and *Notorious* (1946).

287. Dancer Ray Bolger (1904-1987) began in vaudeville, signed a movie contract with M-G-M, and debuted on the screen playing himself in *The Great Ziegfeld* (1936). Among his many dancing and singing performances he is best remembered for playing the scarecrow in *The Wizard of Oz* (1939). On radio he appeared regularly on Rudy Vallee's program and, during the summer of 1945, starred in his own musical variety program, *The Ray Bolger Show*.

288. Comedian Milton Berle (1908-2002) began his show business career at age 5 and went on to perform on Broadway and in vaudeville, night clubs, movies, radio and television. On radio he was heard with Vincent Lopez on *Plough's Musical Cruiser* in 1934, on *The Ziegfeld Follies of the Air* the same year, and in 1940 on *The Show of the Week*. He co-starred with Charles Laughton on *Three Ring Time* and appeared often on Rudy Vallee's radio program. He became truly famous, however, only on television. Beginning in 1948 when the medium was in its infancy, his visual comedy routines on the tube paid off with phenomenal success and earned him the nicknames of "Uncle Miltie" and "Mr. Television." He died on March 27, 2002, as these capsule biographies were being finalized.
For Joan Edwards, see 89 above.

289. For Paula Stone, see 135 above. For Benny Baker, see 59 above.

290. For Warren Hull, see 89 above. For Parks Johnson, see 73 above.

291. Former Powers model Marsha Hunt (1913-  ) was signed by Paramount Pictures and made an effective film debut in *The Virginia Judge* (1935). She co-starred with Gilbert Roland in *Thunder Trail* (1937), one of the best Westerns based at least nominally on a novel by Zane Grey, and had the female lead in *Ellery Queen, Master Detective* (1940), first and perhaps best of Columbia's short-lived series about the sleuth. She moved to M-G-M and played lesser parts in films like *The Human Comedy* (1943). Three years after her appearance on *Ellery Queen* she starred in *Mary Ryan, Detective* (1949).

292. For Jean Sablon, see 256 above.

293. John Carradine (1906-1988) was a gaunt, deep-voiced Shakespearean actor who played shadowy character parts in numerous Westerns and horror pictures. His early screen credits include *Daniel Boone* (1936), *The Hound of the Baskervilles* (1939) and *Mr. Moto's Last Warning* (1939). Two years before appearing on *Ellery Queen* he had starred in cult director Edgar G. Ulmer's low-budget classic *Bluebeard* (1944).

294. Rear Admiral H.B. Miller was a recently retired career officer who had served as the Navy's Director of Public Information during World War II.

295. Paul Douglas (1907–1959) was at home on Broadway, in movies, and on radio and later television. On radio he hosted *The Horn and Hardart Children's Hour* for eight seasons. He did sports commentary for Fred Waring's *Pleasure Time Show* and *Paul Whiteman Presents* and served as announcer on *Buck Rogers*, *Jack Armstrong, The All-American Boy*, *The Jack Benny Program* and *The Big Show*. At the time of his appearance on *Ellery Queen* he was starring in the hit Broadway comedy *Born Yesterday*.

296. Carmina Freeman was the editorial director of *Baffling Detective* magazine.

308. For Victor Jory, see 207 above.

309. Puerto Rico-born Jose Ferrer (1909-1992) played S.S. Van Dine's private investigator Philo Vance on radio, in a summer replacement series broadcast in 1945. Months after his appearance on *Ellery Queen* he became host of *The Prudential Family Hour of Stars*. But he is best known as a movie actor, winning an Academy Award for *Cyrano de Bergerac* (1950).

310. Actress Jean Parker (1916-      ) was discovered by Louis B. Mayer's personal assistant after winning a poster contest for her painting of Father Time. She appeared in dozens of movies, playing the female leads in *Bluebeard* (1944) and *Dead Man's Eyes* (1944), both top-notch mystery/horror pictures. She had her own extremely short-lived detective series, starring in *The Adventures of Kitty O'Day* (1945) and *Detective Kitty O'Day* (1945). After World War II she left Hollywood for Broadway where she starred in *Loco* and *Born Yesterday*. On radio she was in the supporting cast of *The Hardy Family*, a syndicated series of the early 1950s.

311. Movie actress June Knight appeared in *Gift of Gab* (1934), *Broadway Melody of 1936* (1936) and *The House Across the Bay* (1940). Her last film was released six years before her appearance on *Ellery Queen*.

312. Baritone Alfred Drake (1914-1992) appeared in the original Broadway productions of *Oklahoma!*, *Kismet* and *Kiss Me Kate*. On radio he hosted the musical variety series *Broadway Matinee* in late 1943 and early 1944. During the summer of 1946 he sang regularly on radio's *Festival of American Music*.

313. For Parks Johnson and Wally Butterworth, see 16 above. For Warren Hull, see 313 above.

314. Actor Bela Lugosi (1888-1956), a matinee idol in his native Hungary before he came to the U.S., is best known for his starring role in *Dracula* (1931). He appeared on radio only about two dozen times, one of them being this guest spot on *Ellery Queen*.

315. Ted Malone began his radio career in 1929 with his program *Between the Bookends*, a poetry series that became successful almost overnight. He was also an announcer, an emcee and a foreign correspondent during World War II.

316. Andre Baruch (1908-1991), married to band singer Bea Wain since 1938, was a photographer, illustrator and pianist, with a long career in broadcasting as an announcer. In 1946 the couple co-hosted the chatter and disc jockey show *Mr. and Mrs. Music*. Between 1947 and 1949 Baruch was the announcer on *The Shadow*.
   For Bea Wain, see 70 above.

318. For Arthur Godfrey, see 258 above.

319. Tall blonde actress Nina Foch (1924-   ) was under contract to Columbia and starred in many of that studio's crime, suspense and horror films including *The Return of the Vampire* (1943), *Cry of the Werewolf* (1944) and *My Name Is Julia Ross* (1945).
   Pioneer broadcaster Dorothy Gordon (1889-1970) began broadcasting children's programs in 1924 with *Dorothy Gordon's Children's Corner* and later *Yesterday's Children*, offering songs and fairy tales for young listeners. Gordon's biggest claim to fame was her service between 1931 and 1938 as musical director for *The American School of the Air*, perhaps the most outstanding show in educational radio. During World War II she was director of children's radio programs for the Office of War Information. She received the George Foster Peabody Award, which is radio's equivalent to an Oscar.

320. Vocalist Marion Bell (1919-1997) was a regular on *The Gordon MacRae Show* from 1945 to 1946 and a member of the original Broadway cast of *Brigadoon* (1947). During the early 1950s she sang frequently on *The Railroad Hour*.
   Cy Steinhauser was radio editor of the Pittsburgh *Press*.

321. Fay McKenzie (1917-   ) appeared in dozens of movies, playing the female lead in several Gene Autry Westerns during the early 1940s but usually having such small parts that she didn't receive screen credit. If you look carefully, you'll see her in *Gunga Din* (1939) and *Breakfast at Tiffany's* (1961).
   For Eddie Dowling, see 166 above.

322. For Eddie Dowling, see 166 above. For Marion Bell, see 320 above.

323. Movie actor Jeffrey Lynn (1909-   ) joined the U.S. Air Force soon after Pearl Harbor and earned a Bronze Star. He appeared on *Ellery Queen* soon after his discharge from the service, then resumed his career in Hollywood after six years' absence.
   Metropolitan opera soprano Patrice Munsel (1925-   ) debuted on radio's *Metropolitan Opera Program* on Christmas of 1943, playing Philine in *Mignon*. Later she guested on numerous radio musicals and appeared in many stage productions and television dramas of the 1950s.

325. Actor John Emery (1905-1964) starred in the radio pilot for the *Philo Vance* detective series in the summer of 1945 but is best known for his roles in suspense, science-fiction and horror films including Alfred Hitchcock's *Spellbound* (1945), *Rocketship X-M* (1950), *The Mad Magician* (1954), and *Kronos* (1957).

Pam Camp was Miss Arkansas during the Annual Miss America competition of 1947, losing out to Barbara Walker from Memphis, Tennessee.

326. Actor Kent Smith (1908-1985) made his Hollywood debut in a Philo Vance detective film, *The Garden Murder Case* (1936). He is best remembered for his roles in Val Lewton's *Cat People* (1942) and *The Curse of the Cat People* (1944) but went on to play doctors, military officers and other authority figures in dozens of movies and TV series episodes.

Sonya Stein was radio editor of the Washington *Post*.

327. For Danton Walker, see 138 above. For Jean Sablon, see 256 above.

328. For Warren Hull, see 89 above. For Parks Johnson, see 16 above. For George Frazier, see 233 above.

331. Zuma Palmer (1897-1991) was gossip columnist for the Hollywood *Citizen-News*. She had less power than her rivals Hedda Hopper and Louella Parsons but often used her clout to get minor movie parts for young hopefuls who went on to become important stars.

332. Dick Williams (1915-1987) was west coast editor of *Pic*, a movie magazine. Later he became the editor of *Theater Arts*.

333. Fabius Friedman was west coast editor of *Radio Best* magazine.

336. Jerry Devine (1908-    ) played young Billy in the silent film *Sherlock Holmes* (1922). He left movies in the 1930s and became involved with radio, first as an actor, then as a writer of comedy material for Kate Smith and Tommy Riggs. He is best known as a scriptwriter for mystery series like *The Shadow, Mr. District Attorney* and *This Is Your F.B.I.*

337. Radio comedian and quiz show panelist Henry Morgan (1915-1994) (not to be confused with actor Harry Morgan) possessed an excruciatingly sarcastic wit. During the late 1930s and early 1940s he was the announcer for radio's *The Morey Amsterdam Show* and *Dorothy Gordon's Children's Corner*. (Gordon had guested on *Ellery Queen* a few months earlier.) His own program, *Story from the Stars*, began in May of 1947 but was canceled after two broadcasts.

338. Hollywood columnist Erskine Johnson began in journalism as an office boy with the Los Angeles *Record* and rose to the position of city editor. During the late 1930s he started a column that was later syndicated in several hundred newspapers nationwide.

On radio he hosted *Erskine Johnson's Hollywood News*, a syndicated series that lasted seven seasons, and also appeared regularly on *Let's Talk Hollywood.* In later years Johnson and his wife ran a restaurant in California.

339. Actor/producer Charles "Buddy" Rogers (1904-1999) was also a musician and orchestra leader, playing in ballrooms and hotels and on radio. In Hollywood he had a running part in three of RKO's Mexican Spitfire films starring Lupe Velez. During War II he served in the U.S. Navy as a flight training instructor. He was married to silent screen star Mary Pickford for more than 40 years.

340. Hollywood columnist Edith Gwynn was also a panelist on radio's *Leave It to the Girls*. Six months after appearing on *Ellery Queen* she became a regular panelist on *Let's Talk Hollywood*, answering questions about moviemaking submitted by the audience.

341. Virginia MacPherson was a journalist for the United Press Syndicate.

342. Seymour Nebenzal (1898?-1961) was born in New York City but is best known as the producer of some of the finest German silent and early talking films including *Pandora's Box* (1929) and *M* (1931). At the time of his appearance on *Ellery Queen* his current film project was *Siren of Atlantis* (1948) starring Maria Montez.

343. Actress Joan Barton (1925-1977) appeared in a few movies of the late 1940s, the best known being *Angel and the Badman* (1947), which starred former guest armchair detective John Wayne.

Radio announcer John Nelson was the emcee for *Live Like a Millionaire, Add a Line, Breakfast in Hollywood*, and *Bride and Groom*, on which each week he would question, joke with and bestow a shower of gifts on a couple just before their marriage in the chapel of the Chapman Park Hotel. Months after appearing on *Ellery Queen* he became the announcer and one of the producers for Eleanor Roosevelt's post-war talk programs over the ABC network.

344. Kirk Douglas (1916- ) was born into immigrant poverty, won an acting scholarship and had some small parts on Broadway before entering the Navy in World War II. After his discharge he resumed his stage career until, at the urging of his acting school classmate Lauren Bacall, movie producer Hal Wallis first tested Douglas and then cast him as the male lead in *The Strange Love of Martha Ivers* (1946). That was the beginning of a stellar acting career which Douglas continues to carry on in his mid-eighties.

345. London-born Sheilah Graham (1904-1988) was a Hollywood salesgirl in the late 1930s when she met and fell in love with novelist F. Scott Fitzgerald, who was under contract to M-G-M as a scriptwriter. After Fitzgerald's death she became a well-known Hollywood columnist. Her book about her relationship with Fitzgerald became the basis of the movie *Beloved Infidel*, starring Gregory Peck and Deborah Kerr.

346.  Actress Agnes Moorehead (1906-1974), a highly educated woman who taught speech and drama for several years, started working in radio during the 1930s, often impersonating Eleanor Roosevelt on *The March of Time*.  Orson Welles recruited her for his Mercury Theater radio productions and later invited her to join him in Hollywood and play his mother in the classic *Citizen Kane* (1941).  On radio she is best remembered as the helpless invalid in the *Suspense* broadcast "Sorry, Wrong Number" – a role she reprised seven more times before *Suspense* went off the air in 1962.

347.  Arlene Rogers appeared on *Ellery Queen* by virtue of having won a contest for the title of America's Champion Movie Fan.

348.  Jimmy Starr (1904-1990) was motion picture editor for the Los Angeles Herald-Express and the author of three mystery novels.  One of these was filmed as *The Corpse Came C.O.D.* (1947).

349.  Gene Handsaker (1909-1985) was a Hollywood columnist for the Associated Press.  In 1961 he helped singer Peggy Lee, who guested on *Ellery Queen* a few weeks after him, with the nationwide promotion of her "Meals for Millions" project.

350.  Voice caricaturist Mel Blanc (1908-1989) created the voices for Warner Bros. cartoon characters from Elmer Fudd to Bugs Bunny and also wrote the "Woody Woodpecker Song."  On radio he played comic characters on *The Jack Benny Program*, *The George Burns and Gracie Allen Show*, *The Judy Canova Show*, and *The Abbott and Costello Show*.  During the 1946-47 season he had his own radio program, *Mel Blanc's Fix-It Shop*, which aired over CBS.

351.  Journalist Florabel Muir (1889?-1970) covered Hollywood celebrities and New York gangsters for the *Daily News*.

352.  Singer and actress Peggy Lee (1920-2002) sang with Benny Goodman and Will Osborne's swing bands during the 1930s.  The radio audience heard her voice on *The Kraft Music Hall*, *The Jimmy Durante Show*, *The Andy Russell Show* and other programs.  Beginning in 1951 she starred in her own radio program, *The Peggy Lee Show*.  In the Disney animated feature *Lady and the Tramp* (1955) she was the voice of Lady and also sang "The Siamese Cat Song." She died as these biographical notes were being completed.

353.  Harve Fischman (1930-    ) was a former member of radio's *Quiz Kids* program. In later years he changed his name to Harve Bennett and became a well-known TV producer.

354.  Comic actor Cliff Arquette (1905-1974) is best remembered by radio fans as the original Gildersleeve character on *The Fibber McGee and Molly Show* but also worked on *The Dick Haymes Show, Point Sublime, Lum and Abner* and *Hollywood Spotlight*.  In the 1950s he moved into TV, creating the memorable Charlie Weaver character for *The Dennis Day Show*.

# INDEX

## TITLES OF EPISODES

# ABOUT THE AUTHORS

**Francis M. Nevins** is a professor at St. Louis University School of Law, where he has taught since 1971. In addition to his writings on legal subjects he is the author of six mystery novels: PUBLISH AND PERISH (1975), CORRUPT AND ENSNARE (1978), THE 120-HOUR CLOCK (1986), THE NINETY MILLION DOLLAR MOUSE (1987), INTO THE SAME RIVER TWICE (1996) and BENEFICIARIES' REQUIEM (2000). He has also written about forty short stories which have appeared in ELLERY QUEEN, ALFRED HITCHCOCK and other national magazines and many of which have been reprinted in leading mystery anthologies. A collection of his shorter fiction, NIGHT OF SILKEN SNOW AND OTHER STORIES, was published in 2001, and a second collection, LEAP DAY AND OTHER STORIES, is scheduled for early 2003. He has edited more than 15 mystery anthologies and collections and has written several nonfiction books on the genre. Two of these nonfiction titles – ROYAL BLOODLINE: ELLERY QUEEN, AUTHOR AND DETECTIVE (1974) and CORNELL WOOLRICH: FIRST YOU DREAM, THEN YOU DIE (1988) – have won him Edgar awards from Mystery Writers of America. He has written articles, book reviews and similar short pieces on mystery fiction for newspapers, magazines and reference works. He has also published many articles dealing with movies and four books on the same subject: THE FILMS OF HOPALONG CASSIDY (1988), THE FILMS OF THE CISCO KID (1998), JOSEPH H. LEWIS: OVERVIEW, INTERVIEW AND FILMOGRAPHY (1998) and PAUL LANDRES: A DIRECTOR'S STORIES (2000).

**Martin Grams, Jr.** is the author and co-author of numerous books and magazine articles, including SUSPENSE: TWENTY YEARS OF THRILLS AND CHILLS (1998), THE HISTORY OF THE CAVALCADE OF AMERICA (1998), THE CBS RADIO MYSTERY THEATER: AN EPISODE GUIDE AND HANDBOOK TO NINE YEARS OF BROADCASTING (1999), RADIO DRAMA: AN AMERICAN CHRONICLE (1999), THE HAVE GUN-WILL TRAVEL COMPANION (2000), THE ALFRED HITCHCOCK PRESENTS COMPANION (2001) and INVITATION TO LEARNING (2002). He has also written numerous magazine articles for SPERDVAC, FILMFAX, SCARLET STREET, OTR DIGEST and RETURN WITH US NOW. He has contributed various chapters for VINCENT PRICE: MIDNIGHT MARQUEE ACTOR SERIES (1998) and THE ALFRED HITCHCOCK STORY (1999). Martin is the recipient of the 1999 Ray Stanich Award. He is presently completing INNER SANCTUM MYSTERIES: BEHIND THE CREEKING DOOR.

# THE SOUND OF DETECTION:
## Ellery Queen's Adventures in Radio

**Francis M. Nevins and Martin Grams, Jr.**

- Did you borrow this book from your local library?
- Has your friend been looking for a copy of this book?
- Looking for the perfect Ellery Queen gift to give this Christmas?
- Did you borrow this book from your friend and won't give it back?

Now you can order a copy for yourself or your friends!

## ORDERING INFORMATION:

Please provide the following information:

1. Your name, mailing address, city, state, zip code, and phone number (in case we have a question, we can contact you.)
2. Enclose a check for $24.95 per book. Postage is $4.00 for the first copy, and $2.00 per additional.
3. For credit card orders, please list what kind of card you are using (Visa / Mastercard) , the card number, expiration date, and the name as it appears on the card.
4. Mail to: OTR Publishing, Po Box 252, Churchville, MD 21028.

Please allow 2 – 3 weeks for delivery. Wholesale prices are welcome, dealer inquiries are welcome.

## ALSO CHECK OUT OTR PUBLISHING'S OTHER BOOKS!

The Alfred Hitchcock Presents Companion – by Martin Grams, Jr. and Patrik Wikstrom.

The Have Gun-Will Travel Companion – by Les Rayburn and Martin Grams, Jr.

Invitation to Learning – by Martin Grams, Jr. (limited to a 500 printing!)

# THE SOUND OF DETECTION:
## Ellery Queen's Adventures in Radio

**Francis M. Nevins and Martin Grams, Jr.**

- Did you borrow this book from your local library?
- Has your friend been looking for a copy of this book?
- Looking for the perfect Ellery Queen gift to give this Christmas?
- Did you borrow this book from your friend and won't give it back?

Now you can order a copy for yourself or your friends!

## ORDERING INFORMATION:

Please provide the following information:

1. Your name, mailing address, city, state, zip code, and phone number (in case we have a question, we can contact you.)
2. Enclose a check for $24.95 per book. Postage is $4.00 for the first copy, and $2.00 per additional.
3. For credit card orders, please list what kind of card you are using (Visa / Mastercard) , the card number, expiration date, and the name as it appears on the card.
4. Mail to: OTR Publishing, Po Box 252, Churchville, MD 21028.

Please allow 2 – 3 weeks for delivery. Wholesale prices are welcome, dealer inquiries are welcome.

## ALSO CHECK OUT OTR PUBLISHING'S OTHER BOOKS!

The Alfred Hitchcock Presents Companion – by Martin Grams, Jr. and Patrik Wikstrom.

The Have Gun-Will Travel Companion – by Les Rayburn and Martin Grams, Jr.

Invitation to Learning – by Martin Grams, Jr. (limited to a 500 printing!)

# THE SOUND OF DETECTION:
## Ellery Queen's Adventures in Radio

**Francis M. Nevins and Martin Grams, Jr.**

- Did you borrow this book from your local library?
- Has your friend been looking for a copy of this book?
- Looking for the perfect Ellery Queen gift to give this Christmas?
- Did you borrow this book from your friend and won't give it back?

Now you can order a copy for yourself or your friends!

### ORDERING INFORMATION:

Please provide the following information:

1. Your name, mailing address, city, state, zip code, and phone number (in case we have a question, we can contact you.)
2. Enclose a check for $24.95 per book. Postage is $4.00 for the first copy, and $2.00 per additional.
3. For credit card orders, please list what kind of card you are using (Visa / Mastercard) , the card number, expiration date, and the name as it appears on the card.
4. Mail to: OTR Publishing, Po Box 252, Churchville, MD 21028.

Please allow 2 – 3 weeks for delivery. Wholesale prices are welcome, dealer inquiries are welcome.

### ALSO CHECK OUT OTR PUBLISHING'S OTHER BOOKS!

The Alfred Hitchcock Presents Companion – by Martin Grams, Jr. and Patrik Wikstrom.

The Have Gun-Will Travel Companion – by Les Rayburn and Martin Grams, Jr.

Invitation to Learning – by Martin Grams, Jr. (limited to a 500 printing!)